The Dynastic Imagination

The Dynastic Imagination

Family and Modernity in Nineteenth-Century Germany

ADRIAN DAUB

The University of Chicago Press
Chicago and London

The University of Chicago Press, Chicago 60637
The University of Chicago Press, Ltd., London
© 2021 by The University of Chicago
All rights reserved. No part of this book may be used or reproduced in any manner whatsoever without written permission, except in the case of brief quotations in critical articles and reviews. For more information, contact the University of Chicago Press, 1427 East 60th Street, Chicago, IL 60637.
Published 2021

30 29 28 27 26 25 24 23 22 21   1 2 3 4 5

ISBN-13: 978-0-226-73773-7 (cloth)
ISBN-13: 978-0-226-73787-4 (paper)
ISBN-13: 978-0-226-73790-4 (e-book)
DOI: https://doi.org/10.7208/chicago/9780226737904.001.0001

The University of Chicago Press gratefully acknowledges the generous support of Stanford University toward the publication of this book.

Names: Daub, Adrian, author.
Title: The dynastic imagination : family and modernity in nineteenth-century Germany / Adrian Daub.
Description: Chicago ; London : The University of Chicago Press, 2021. | Includes bibliographical references and index.
Identifiers: LCCN 2020027475 | ISBN 9780226737737 (cloth) | ISBN 9780226737874 (paperback) | ISBN 9780226737904 (ebook)
Subjects: LCSH: Families—Germany—Philosophy—History—19th century. | Germany—Civilization—19th century. | Germany—Intellectual life—19th century.
Classification: LCC DD66 .D38 2020 | DDC 306.850943/09034—dc23
LC record available at https://lccn.loc.gov/2020027475

Contents

Introduction: An Essay on Mediate Family 1
1 Into the Family Gallery 24
2 Nuclearity and Its Discontents 46
3 Abortive Romanticism 65
4 Feminism, or The Hegelian Dynasty 91
5 Wagner, or The Bourgeois Dynasty 114
6 Naturalism, or The Dynastic Romance 134
7 Freud, or The Reluctant Patriarch 155
8 George, or The Queer Dynasty 176
Epilogue: Black Sheep 207

Acknowledgments 217
Notes 221
Index 249

INTRODUCTION

An Essay on Mediate Family

> We may worry about our children and perhaps our grandchildren; but beyond what we can hope to stroke with these hands of ours we have no obligation.
> GIUSEPPE DI LAMPEDUSA, *The Leopard*[1]

In "Vom Nutzen und Nachteil der Historie für das Leben" ("On the Advantage and Disadvantage of History for Life"), the second of his 1874 *Untimely Meditations*, Friedrich Nietzsche distinguishes three modes of looking at the past: the monumental, the antiquarian, and the critical. The last one is perhaps the most complicated from Nietzsche's point of view, since its logic of retrieval and self-reflection seems to put the lie to the essay's central thesis: that there can be such a thing as too much past, or learning too much from the past. And so Nietzsche is careful to introduce this critical approach as another way in which history can be pressed into "the service of life." The critical approach to history, he says, must be inquisitorial, antagonistic. "It isn't justice who sits in judgment here, let alone clemency who renders the verdict: it is life alone, this dark, driving, insatiable, self-desiring power."[2] Any verdict it renders is by necessity unkind, merciless, unjust.

Nevertheless, even this kind of unfair judgment requires a productive myopia. "It requires much force [*Kraft*] to live and at the same time to forget to what extent living and being unjust are one and the same."[3] Nietzsche frames the kind of critical remembrance in which he is interested as the destruction of memory: nothing is being preserved in it; healthy, prophylactic amnesia is itself momentarily destroyed. "At times the same life that requires forgetfulness requires the temporary destruction of that forgetfulness: when we are trying to show how unjust the existence of a certain thing, a certain privilege or a certain dynasty, how much that thing deserves its destruction."[4] Not for nothing does Nietzsche here echo a line from Johann Wolfgang von Goethe's *Faust*, spoken by Mephistopheles:

> For all that which is wrought
> Deserves that I should come to naught.[5]

This sadistic return to the past is a process "dangerous to life itself": as freeing as it is fraught. Historical moments and people who turn to the past in this way are at once "dangerous and endangered." In articulating the risks of this forgetting, Nietzsche turns to the family—or rather, to a specific kind of family. "For since we are after all the results of earlier families [*Geschlechter*], we are also fully the results of their delusions, passions and errors, yes even crimes. It is impossible to fully disentangle oneself from that chain."[6] Clearly, Nietzsche is thinking not of an earlier family that we ourselves have encountered during our lifetime but of one whose influence reaches into our very lives. This more distant, more alien family does double work in passages like this one: it's an index of a tradition from which critique should aim to sever the present, and it's a reminder of the extent to which that present moment is nevertheless determined by "earlier families," their "delusions, passions and errors." Nietzsche is as sympathetic to breaking this seemingly endless familial "chain" as he is skeptical of the success of ever doing so.

Most important, however, this study takes seriously the suggestion that underpins Nietzsche's invocation of the extended family: that its categories frame an approach to life. Nietzsche doesn't seem to regard the dynasty as primarily historical factum. He seems interested in the dynasty as a way of imposing meaning on family structures, on history, on temporality—one that has great advantages and disadvantages for life. In the preface to *Der Untergang des Abendlandes* (*The Decline of the West*, 1918), one of Nietzsche's great admirers, Oswald Spengler, seems to suggest that it isn't so much the dynasty that disappears but the sense of continuity required in order to look for it in the first place. In the great "world city" of modernity, Spengler says, we find "not a people [*Volk*], but a mass. Its incomprehension for anything traditioned [*Überlieferte*], by which it fights culture [*die Kultur*]—the nobility, the privileges, the dynasty, the conventions in the arts, God-given limits in the sciences— . . . all that signifies . . . an opposition to the province, a totally new, late, futureless yet inevitable form of human existence."[7]

When the dynasty appears in Spengler's list, it's essentially as a stand-in for a whole sense of existential embeddedness—"anything traditioned." Neither Nietzsche nor Spengler seems primarily interested in whether there are dynasties in modernity. They wonder how moderns think about them. And they suggest that how moderns think about them has consequences for everyday life. This book likewise deals with ideas about the family, not the shape actual families take. Those appear, at least when it comes to the dynasty, strangely independent of actual lived practice. *The Dynastic Imagination* is not a book about different ways of organizing families, even though some of the texts considered here will be about that. It is a book about different ways of making sense of family structures, and about how these ways inform our broader sense of history.

Nietzsche calls this larger familial "chain" a *Geschlecht*. Throughout the nineteenth century, there were in fact several terms in circulation that designated an expanded sense of family—*Dynastie*, though not unheard of, was among the rarer ones and inconsistently applied. The *Damen-Conversations Lexikon* of 1835, for instance, defines *Dynastie* as a "row of rulers from one and the same family," but then glosses the Wasas as a "dynasty" and the surely equally dynastic Bourbons as a "family."[8] *Stamm*, *Geschlecht*, *Haus*, and *Sippe* all designate something between a tribe and a family. The *Ahnenreihe* or the *Väter* imply a more patrilinear (and simply more linear) construal of ancestry. Most of the dictionaries and encyclopedias around the turn of the nineteenth century define these terms by reference to one another. Whenever these works attempt to subsume one under the other (e.g., saying that *Stamm* could designate a branch of a *Geschlecht*, as several do),[9] they almost immediately relativize this subsumption. Together, these terms tell of a keenly felt desire to make distinctions, to give shape to broader structures of kinship, but also tell of serious trouble in agreeing how to do so.

Perhaps the most philosophically ambitious reflections on these different familial monikers are provided by Johann Christoph Adelung's *Grammatisch-kritisches Wörterbuch der Hochdeutschen Mundart* (Grammatical-critical dictionary of high German speech, 1796). For *family*, Adelung provides two definitions: on the one hand, "persons making up a domestic society [*eine häusliche Gesellschaft*], marital partners and their children"—in other words, what we would today call the nuclear family. On the other, "in a second meaning, an entire *Geschlecht* with all in-laws and side-relatives" (2:201). *Family* was thus both what we would today call the nuclear family and something more far-reaching, which I will call the "dynastic family" for the simple reason that it is the designation least native to the nineteenth century.

But more far-reaching in what way? Here, too, the encyclopedias and dictionaries written in Germany roughly around the year 1800 register several ambiguities: does a *Geschlecht*, *Haus*, or *Sippe* expand the scope of the family synchronically or diachronically? Implied in that question is a related ambiguity in how a family was formed: there were designations suggesting it was constituted genetically, set by one's ancestry. And there were others suggesting it was constituted by a process of accretion and selection—individuals married, hired help, allowed relatives to move in. The latter could also be designated a *Haus*, but here, too, the usage was inconsistent. As Adelung points out, "Only those persons demonstrably descended from a common founder of the family [*Stammvater*] are authentically part of the *Geschlecht*, even though relatives from the female side are frequently counted also" (2:201). The definitions in Adelung and elsewhere thus suggest a tension that contemporaries were well aware of but didn't work particularly hard to resolve.

The *Geschlecht*, Adelung notes, has to do with similarity—usually "the similarity in terms of origin [*Gleichheit des Herkommens*]," and thus could designate either humanity (insofar as it was the offspring of Adam) or a particular family line traceable back to a particular ancestor ("like an aristocratic *Geschlecht*"). Significantly, Adelung doesn't yet mention the word *nation* here, but his omission designates a space that the nineteenth century would labor hard to fill with biologized concepts of race and nationality. Adelung also notes that to be a *Geschlecht* is not a purely biological fact, that to look at a family as a *Geschlecht* confers on it a certain status—"in a narrower sense in some free cities of the *Reich* a *Geschlecht* only designates a family capable of being voted into the *Bürgerrat* [*rathsfähiges Geschlecht*], and thus patricians" (2:202). This is another reason I am calling what I trace the "dynastic" family: because it wasn't altogether clear that everyone got to have a *Geschlecht* or a *Haus*—these designations hovered somewhere between a universal biological fact (the way everyone in the nineteenth century was said to belong to a "race") and something tied up with position, class, and esteem.

One place where the word *Geschlecht* was less frequently used was in the emerging conceptual arsenal concerning race. While there were some attempts to describe Jews as a *Geschlecht*, biblical translation tended to follow Luther in rendering the biblical Greek ἔθνος, or the Vulgate's gens, without recourse to the semantic field of lineages. But, as we shall see in the pages that follow, the question of Jewishness was never far from the discourse about heredity, albeit not always explicitly.

One reason the dictionaries of the age gave time and again when confronted with these terminological insufficiencies was that most of the terms for the expansive forms of family were antiquated. And this explanation addresses not so much the words used to describe the dynastic family as the dynastic family itself. If dynasties exist in modernity, then they do so with trouble attaching themselves to everyday experience. In your life you will, if all goes well, encounter four generations of your family other than your own. You may still remember your great-grandmother's hands and look at old Polaroids of her with some glimmer of recognition; but by the time you became conscious of what a family was, there was you, there were your parents, and there were your grandparents. And by the time you die, maybe you will have seen your great-grandchild's face, but you won't know much about that child. You will die having left impressions only on your children and grandchildren.

AN ESSAY ON MEDIATE FAMILY

Dynastic thinking concerns the territory that lies beyond this known universe of hands and faces: people you call Auntie or Uncle because you have no clue how they're related to you—a mad thicket of repeating names, of echoing biographies. They form the outer tendrils of the nuclear family, people that, if you asked your mother or father, or if you had asked your grandfather or grandmother before they died, might yet be assigned location in the little domestic nucleus. They constitute, or represent, that part of our familial past that not only is inaccessible to us but also makes us realize how inaccessible even our immediate familial environs can be. It pulls apart our domestic universe, renders strange the familiar hands that have cradled us, pulls them off into worlds unimaginable. As David Warren Sabean has pointed out, the conceptual foreshortening described here seems to have had little analogue in how German families actually lived.[10] Economically, the family remained expansive and varied; and insofar as there was a concentration of sentiment, as Niklas Luhman proposed it, it happened over and against the economic base.[11] Kinship networks remained extensive, and as Stefani Engelstein has recently demonstrated, relations of siblinghood remained compelling to nineteenth-century imaginaries.[12]

But there was also a pronounced conceptual change. The dynasty concerns the stories, the heraldry, and the fixed points we imagine in order to make sense of those reaches in our family tree that we haven't encountered or never will. More frequently, this concerns our family's distant past (e.g., when White Americans claim some mathematically impossible percentage of Cherokee extraction), but it could just as well concern the distant future. "We may worry about our children and perhaps our grandchildren," Giuseppe di Lampedusa has his aristocratic protagonist Don Fabrizio say in *Il Gattopardo* (*The Leopard*, published in 1958 but set in the mid-nineteenth century), "but beyond what we can hope to stroke with these hands of ours we have no obligation."

The dynastic imagination is founded on a sense that we do. Don Fabrizio contrasts the limited reach of familial obligation with the immortality of the church. So long as we experience the nuclearity of the family as to some extent an effort at creative amnesia, the idea of a family in which the obligations backward and forward do not diminish with time almost naturally suggests itself as its opposite. Think of how original sin, according to Roman Catholic dogma, is passed on cleanly from generation to generation. When the divine right of kings was supposed to tether certain ruling families to certain lands in Europe, this fiction was founded on the idea that somehow, even before they ever set foot on the land, the land had been divinely deeded to their bloodline. Implicit in this figure of thought was that landholders wouldn't simply pass that land on to their children or their children's children. It implied the idea that they must pass it on to unborn generations in perpetuity.

The dynasty functions for both Nietzsche and Spengler, and for modernity more broadly, as a fantasy of perpetuity. It is one that may not always be good for an individual's health, and one that both misses and expresses some essential, if unwelcome, truths about us. And if that fantasy always runs up against natural limits, Nietzsche and Spengler think that awareness of those limits intensifies in modernity. Modernity for them is the point at which the reflexive amnesia of the nuclear family allies itself with the constitutive amnesia of the modern. What makes us moderns is that we lack the sort of dynastic imagination that allowed the great aristocratic lines to imagine an endless series of successors going down through the millennia.

Modernity is supposed to have bred that dynastic imagination out of us, to some extent. In Western societies we are, or are supposed to be, deeply suspicious of people who derive their sense of self from their ancestry, and we venerate the "self-made" among us—the ones who were given nothing and fashioned something, or who were given one thing and fashioned something entirely different. Our leaders do not derive their legitimacy from who their parents were; they must assert that legitimacy anew every few years. But as Western societies more generally become more stratified, more unequal, isn't our claim to be nondynastic a delusion? And isn't it quite possible it was never more than that?

Nietzsche's description of a critical faculty that severs a dynastic "chain," only to discover that "we are after all the results of earlier families" will furnish one of the guiding intuitions of this book: that in a way, modern wants to imagine itself as antidynastic, yet lives in secret horror that it might in fact be dynastic. As Auguste Comte put it in his *Positive Philosophy* (1856): what if, after the revolution, we find ourselves with "just another dynasty"? At stake is modernity's very claim to genuine newness, to a genuine break with the past. The dynasty is the index of our own incapability to break with our ancestors. "When, by internal revolution military chiefs have triumphed over the priests," Comte wrote, "they soon involuntarily acquire the theocratic character, and all that has happened has been a change of persons or of dynasties."[13]

Therefore, the bulk of this book is devoted to the nineteenth century. It was the era in which the bourgeoisie turned its modes of existence into the standard of what was desirable, proper, moral, part of which was that one relied on one's own labor to gain recognition in the world. But it was also the era that, between the discovery of natural selection and the discovery of the unconscious, was obsessed with the possibility that our seeming self-directedness might be a sham, that in truth the species, evolution, a collective unconscious, or the like might be pulling our strings from some dark place millennia ago.

The Dynastic Imagination

The dynasty represents a *caput mortuum* of modernity, and it does so across Europe. But my argument in this book is that this terminal moraine came to matter more and matter differently in Germany than it did elsewhere. In France and in England, the dynasty was a foundling, a venerated, perhaps curious, object stranded from an earlier age. In Germany, the range of fundamental questions about modernity, autonomy, and nation that it could be used to raise was far broader. And those questions were about the present. That is because the dynastic question co-emerged with problems of German nationhood in the first decades of the nineteenth century.

Goethe premiered his musical allegory *Des Epimenides Erwachen* (Epimenides' awakening) in 1815, at the conclusion of what would come to be known in Germany as the Wars of Liberation. In this *Festspiel* (stage play written for a celebratory occasion), Goethe adapts the story of Diogenes Laertius, according to which Epimenides allowed himself to be submerged in a decades-long sleep by the gods in exchange for the gift of foresight. It was a potent story for a region (or was it a nation, a people, perhaps a country?) seemingly coming to itself after decades of chaotic and confusing disruptions. On the surface, *Epimenides' Awakening* is a patriotic fantasia about the end of war and the coming of peace, but just below that surface it's about the struggle to make sense with what just happened.

Goethe wrote *Epimenides' Awakening* at a time when, by all appearances, the clock within the erstwhile Holy Roman Empire had been turned back to before the history-disjointing shocks of the twenty-five years between the storming of the Bastille and the Battle of Waterloo. In Germany, that meant the reestablishment and in fact the retrenchment of the dynastic houses. Their number had decreased, but since the *Reichsdeputationshauptschluss* of 1803 had secularized the last ecclesiastical principalities of the Old Reich, Germany after 1815 had only temporal rulers, and that meant it almost exclusively had rulers legitimated by dynastic means.

This age would become known by the term *Restaurationszeit*, based on the multivolume work *Restauration der Staatswissenschaft* (The restoration of the science of the state, 1816–34) by the monarchist Swiss thinker Karl Ludwig von Haller. The work, according to the subtitle of its third volume, is a "macrobiotic of the patrimonial state," intended to restore the natural understanding of community over and against the "chimera of the artificial bourgeois [*bürgerlich*]" understanding. Part of the naturalness Haller sought to safeguard was the titular "patrimonial" portion of the state: how it was perpetuated and legitimated through mechanisms of inheritance shared by the individual family and the state. Using the great "dynasties" of England, Austria, and Russia as his examples, Haller tried to show in immense detail that electing a king is always a symptom of a disordered polity—the dynasty is the ultimate guarantor of political stability.[14] The French Revolution, Haller thought, had destroyed the bourgeois family of father, mother, and children and thereby the patrimonial aspects of the state. The anarchy that descended on Europe was a direct consequence.

Turning back the clock was not an easy thing to do, and the dynasties stayed in power largely through repression. In Austria, chancellor Klemens Wenzel Lothar von Metternich sought to ensure continuity by preventing any and all constitutional disruption of dynastic legitimation. After 1815, the people of the German *Bund* had a right to a "landständische Verfassung," but what exactly this tortuous phrase meant was subject to some debate. The conservative jurist Friedrich von Gentz wrote a justification of Metternich's policies, "Über den Unterschied zwischen den landständischen und den Repräsentativ-verfassungen" ("On the Difference between Landständische and Representative Constitutions," 1819), in which he argued that it meant only that every German state must have a mechanism by which certain corporations (e.g., the aristocracy) could send representatives to parliament to have their voices heard—no representative or any body of representatives assumed the role of the entire body politic. Metternich even tried to pressure German states with representative constitutions, such as Baden and Bavaria, to abandon them.

In the hands of Gentz and similarly minded conservatives, the dynastic became a repository of all that was divine and providential in human politics, while the constitutional sought to subsume everything under the legitimacy of the popular will. Gentz simply denied that such a legitimacy existed: "Render to the crowns what belongs to the crowns, and to the people what belongs to the people," he wrote. And while he conceded that the people could demand any number of rights from their sovereign, he insisted that "not every right, no matter how sacred and highly esteemed, also constitutes legitimacy."[15] German nationalists of all stripes dismissed the dynastic family as an organizing and legitimating principle, preferring the national family, that is to say, one defined by a close relation in custom, faith, or language. Gentz dismissed this as well: the family that mattered was the one that had made the state what it was—the dynasty. "The laws according to which states form in the real world have little to nothing to do with relatedness with respect to language, custom or faith."[16]

But as the conservative economist Adam Heinrich Müller wrote to Gentz in 1819, the dynastic question was broader yet: basically, it posed the question of modernity. "The maintenance of the ruling dynasties, and the order tied to their continued existence," were safeguards against the destabilizing influence of modish "concepts of popular sovereignty" and "natural law."[17] In other words: for many reform-minded thinkers, the persistence of nearly a hundred princely dynasties with bizarrely shaped and heavily hyphenated demesnes to their name made very little sense, which they interpreted as a sign that these dynasties were no longer really meant to be. But for thinkers like Müller and Gentz, the very fact that these dynasties didn't make sense rendered them deeply worthy of defense: they served as reminders that not everything in politics must make sense, that divine dictate and the vagaries of tradition must be borne and accepted.

But as Müller, Gentz, and Haller mounted a last attempt to justify the dynastic family in Europe on philosophical grounds, the policies founded on their thinking gave rise to a very different ideology of the family. After the assassination of the antinationalist poet August von Kotzebue in 1819, the German princes enacted the Carlsbad Decrees, which restricted most arenas of public life: the press and publishing, the universities, and even public sports. As a result, historians agree, German culture and politics largely retreated into the domestic sphere, into the deliberately bounded, reduced, and intimate setting of the family, usually the nuclear family. After 1815, then, German politics and culture unfolded along two contradictory familial axes: the dynasties that ruled by the force of history and habit, or simply by force, anachronistic but powerful; and the nuclear family that ruled by the force of its authenticity, by the transparency and purity of its affects, clearly the future but in retreat from history.

Much of the literature of the early nineteenth century played these two axes off against each other: it increasingly framed the sentimental and the traditional as antipodes and therefore often positioned the intimate, the plausible, the natural-feeling as the opposite of the foreordained. In the second act of *Epimenides' Awakening*, Goethe gives his main character a vision of family. After his long dream, Epimenides comes back into his world through the nuclear family, through the timelessness of the domestic sphere:

> The father rests on his broad sofa,
> Wife on a chaise, children around
> Of every age; servants bring things,
> Even the horse neighs at the door;
> The table is set, joy- and restful.
>
> Der Vater ruht auf seinem breiten Polster,
> Die Frau im Sessel, Kinder stehn umher

> Von jedem Alter; Knechte tragen zu,
> Das Pferd sogar es wiehert an der Pforte;
> Die Tafel ist besetzt, man schwelgt und ruht.[18]

But the chorus forces Epimenides to see more, to see beyond the domestic scene, beyond father, mother, children, couches, and the set table—toward the founding of "a house." He resists them ("Go further? No, oh dear ones, no!"),[19] and as they urge him onward he senses something demonic in them. And unlike the calm and silent rest of the immediate family, the perspective the "house" forces on Epimenides is a source of anxiety:

> If you have founded a house,
> Beseech the gods,
> That until you're carried from it
> It won't sink into dust
> And that for many years hence
> Serve the children of your children
> And around it a fresh arbor
> Renew verdantly time and again.
>
> Hast du ein gegründet Haus,
> Fleh' die Götter alle,
> Daß es, bis man dich trägt hinaus,
> Nicht zu Schutt zerfalle
> Und noch lange hinterdrein
> Kindeskindern diene,
> Und umher ein frischer Hain.
> Immer neu ergrüne.[20]

If the nuclear and the dynastic simply persisted side by side without much traffic, their story in Germany in the nineteenth century wouldn't be particularly interesting. Instead, in the early decades of the century the uncanny, threatening, and enervating persistence of the dynastic urged many to adopt the optic that the chorus forces upon Epimenides: to see the dynastic in the nuclear. Around the same time, jurists debated the virtues of different modalities of inheritance law. Did laws permitting a dead person to project a no longer existent will into a far future conform to natural law? Were the wish and the ability to project one's will past the expiration date of one's body an important part of human nature, or was the dynastic wish ultimately a bit of aristocratic hubris?

In these first decades of the nineteenth century, then, the dynasty, the house, the *Geschlecht*, emerged as far more than a monarchic concept. It functioned as an epistemic order—a way of conceptualizing temporality and historical causality.[21] And it was one that writers and thinkers seemed unable to shed, however much they may have wanted to be done with it. Goethe wrote his *Festspiel* with its uncanny dynasty while employed by one of the German dynasties. His stance toward the dynasty, a devotion tinged with a profound sense for the uncanniness of the dynastic, was fairly typical for his age. Georg Wilhelm Friedrich Hegel, for instance, in his *Elements of the Philosophy of Right* (1821), claimed that only marriage can effect the "complete creation [*Stiftung*] of a particular [*eigentümlichen*] and real [*wirklichen*] family," while "family" in a more expansive, dynastic sense (Hegel is thinking of Roman concepts like stirps, and gens) is "nothing but an abstractum slowly slipping into the distance and becoming less real with each generation."[22] But at the same time, he was a vociferous defender of hereditary monarchy as a safeguard of the subjective, embodied moment in the logic of the state.

In the course of the nineteenth century, the word *dynasty* largely disappeared from German political discourse. Other words—*Geschlecht, Haus, Familie*—were more common to begin with, but they became suffused so broadly throughout a variety of discourses as to make speaking of a specific discourse lose any meaning. Nevertheless, the problematic that the dynasty had named around 1815 survived—partly because it seemed to name an aspect in which Germany remained an out-of-step nation politically ("below the level of history," as Marx wrote),[23] but more important because both progressive and conservative thinkers had made the dynastic a central bellwether for modernity. In so doing, they retained what we might term the dynastic imagination—the gaze at the uncanny flickering shadow cast by the very closeness of the nuclear family.

The dynastic imagination geologizes the family, turns our ancestors into something altogether different from ourselves. It extrapolates from distant, more seemingly fixed stars in our familial firmament: we imagine our past or our future more like the stark miracles of grandparental existence, not like the bumbling of the parental kind. When we moderns look to our distant forebears or our distant offspring, we tend to see them as monoliths: strapping masters or downcast slaves, noble or barbaric, Eloi or Morlocks, immiserated or decadent, not as the decidedly discordant gaggle of diverse individuals they quite likely were or will be.

The dynasty is about continuities, about smoothness, where the nuclear family is all about jagged edges, all-too-visible scars. In his late poem "The Family Face," Thomas Hardy posits a "years-heired feature" that leaps across the "human span / Of durance." In fact, he says the feature can "despise" that span. When Arthur Schopenhauer made the family a matter of will instead of a matter of love, he similarly framed the family in much longer terms than the Romantics would have. And he similarly suggested that the overwhelming "will of the species" has little but disdain for the immediate human passions through which it works. It makes use of them and then discards them.

But if the "family face" floats coldly above the pulsations of the nuclear family, its despising points to the very different emotions connecting it to the dynastic family: pride, yes, fear, shame; but never love. As the emotional structure of the Romantic family became compulsory, as love, affection, and support became obligatory, the chilly remove of the dynasty became a refuge of sorts. For those who felt contempt for the regulation of affect that seized thinking about the family in the wake of Romanticism. For those who didn't feel about family or within family the way they were supposed to:

> I am the family face;
> Flesh perishes, I live on,
> Projecting trait and trace
> Through time to times anon,
> And leaping from place to place
> Over oblivion.
>
> The years-heired feature that can
> In curve and voice and eye
> Despise the human span
> Of durance—that is I;
> The eternal thing in man,
> That heeds no call to die.[24]

"Projecting trait and trace"—at a time when family was supposed to be a matter of love, the dynasty remained a stark protuberance of sheer will. And of fate: we look at the receding hairlines of our immediate family with affection and caring concern; we look at those outside the immediate family with an anguished, and deeply cold, calculation of whether we might have inherited that.

The Survival of the Dynasty

The *Encyclopédie* (1751–66) of Diderot and d'Alembert followed Aristotle and Thucydides in consigning the dynasty to the distant past and to foreign lands. Its entry on the dynasty discussed the keyword only in terms of ancient history, and preclassical ancient history at that. Dynasty was something the ancient Egyptians practiced, or the Persians; there's no mention made of the Capetians, the Valois, or the Bourbons. Even Frederick the Great, discussing his own House of Hohenzollern, called it a dynasty only when discussing its origins in the days of the Great Elector.[25] Although many Germans still called such houses dynasties, the linguistic trick remained the same: by 1800, saying "dynasty" meant describing a thing of the past.

Dynasticity was for the Greeks something outsiders practiced—let the tyrants of Asia Minor rule by heredity, Greek democracy was renewed with every generation. Both Thucydides and Aristotle opposed *dunasteia* to *isonomia* or *politeia*,[26] which suggested that true politics was self-rule (of the state by its citizens). *Dunasteia* meant precisely the absence of such self-rule and self-reliance, or it named those features within democracy that were on their face undemocratic. Aristotle designated by the term the tendency for political clout to accrue to certain families or power players, and other Greek thinkers followed him in using the word for something like an oligarchy. But Michel Foucault suggests that *dunasteia* meant more than that: "The problems of *politeia* are problems of the constitution," whereas "the problems of *dunasteia* are problems of the political game, that is to say, problems of the formation, exercise, limitation, and also guarantee given to ascendancy exercised by some citizens over others."[27]

Dynasty thus had to do with a force imposed on our actions, usually from the past. It is the friction that besets the operation of rules, the inertial quality that attends the application of all rules. It is a habitual force distending and limiting what we can hope to accomplish. Unlike the political constraints of a state constitution, which are in some sense self-imposed—even if we weren't the ones who passed constitutional provisions, we renew their passage with our loyalty to it—dynasticity refers to those constraints that are unwritten, that have grown up over time.

Did the *Encyclopédie*, and discourses of the Enlightenment more broadly, seek to consign such friction to the past by locating dynasties only in ancient Thebes and Beijing and not, say, at Versailles? Probably not, but it's possible they meant to consign to the past certain sources of such friction. As Jean-Jacques Rousseau put it in his 1782 book *The Government of Poland*, "a hereditary throne and a free nation are incompatible."[28] This ideological shift away from the dynasty mapped onto actual practice, but only to a certain extent. Those entities that operated dynastically—the great aristocratic lines of Europe, the tradesmen and farmers who had passed down the same parcel of land for generations, and on a more metaphorical level the clergy—found that passing down land, sovereignty, and title dynastically was getting tougher. Those newer entities that sought to create new dynasties—the great industrial families, for one—found their efforts persistently thwarted. Something in the new century seemed inimical to dynasties.

And yet it's no accident that dynastic heredity declined in importance around the same time that the idea of genetic inheritance took hold of the bourgeoisie. The same dimensions of the far future and the distant past held open by the dynastic concept became in the nineteenth century an anxious concern with one's own heredity and what one might bequeath to offspring one never met. What had been a symbolic relationship structured through heredity now became a symbolic relationship structured through sex. As Foucault has put it, the bourgeoisie "placed its hopes for the future in sex by imagining it to have ineluctable effects on generations to come."[29]

Foucault speaks of a "transposition into different forms of the methods employed by the nobility for marking and maintaining its caste distinction." Rather than "antiquity of its ancestry" and "the value of its alliances," the bourgeois family "looked to its progeny and the health of its organism."[30] It's important, however, not to overstate the cleanliness of this transposition. The bourgeoisie did, at least in this regard, not simply ape aristocratic forms of legitimation. Rather, its emphasis on inherited health was intended as a critique of the aristocracy: the bourgeois, having married for love, had a fresher gene pool than the inbred aristocrat. But of course, any such critique of the dynastic was shot through with an imagination very much like the one it claimed to condemn.

Early evolutionary theorists such as Prosper Lucas implicitly offered a biological critique of the aristocratic way of life: inbreeding and intermarriage could now be shown scientifically to produce terrible offspring, making aristocratic rule an inherently self-defeating enterprise.[31] The events of 1789 weren't accidents of history or a result of Enlightenment—they were the result of calamitous moral and reproductive choices. In a strange way, then, accounts like Lucas's replaced the divine right of kings with the evolutionary right of bourgeois families. Those that were on top were on top for biological reasons. Those who had fallen from grace (such as the great aristocratic families) had likewise fallen for biological reasons. And those who had never risen in the first place were too indolent, cretinous, atavistic, or whatever other biological moniker one wanted to affix to render their subjection a scientific necessity rather than a historical accident.[32]

At the same time, of course, it was hard not to read a book like Lucas's and think it provided a blueprint for how to do dynasty better: what should a bourgeois pater familias do to keep the bloodline fresh, to avoid the fate of the Bourbons? How, in other words, could the bourgeoisie avoid the systemic problems of aristocratic heredity, yet project its will dynastically forward through the generations? The nineteenth century wound up reading Charles Darwin in much the same way: what, after all, was social Darwinism other than the attempt to biologically shape the direction of the future? Darwin, as Devin Griffiths has pointed out, rejected designer theories, partially because the "Darwinian imagination" imbued organisms with much autonomy and self-direction.[33] But autonomy's liberal politics also always committed the individual to control, to planning, to optimization.

This ambivalence in Lucas points to another strange fact about the antidynastic impulse in modernity. Autonomy, at a certain point, becomes itself dynastic. "Heredity, like gravity, has its laws,"[34] Émile Zola wrote, and when one sought to wrest oneself free from heredity's dictates, or else sought to bend them in one's favor, one did so in order to establish something equally binding for one's descendants. In other words, at some point our autonomy entails wanting to project our will into the future well beyond the part of it we'll actually witness. We provide for our offspring, even those we have never met and never will, not out of love for them but out of love for ourselves. What is at work in such a moment of projection is the kind of imagination we encounter in racism: not even the most psychotic racists think that the West will be overrun by, say, Muslims within their own lifetime, and they aren't usually even thinking about their own children or grandchildren. What upsets them is the very idea that it might one day be so; the notion is intolerable no matter how distant the day.

All of this seems to suggest that severed from the newly triumphant nuclear family, the dynastic vestiges lay prostrate but nevertheless crawled with uncanny life. Writers and philosophers harnessed aesthetically and politically what power these vestiges emitted in their crumbling—whether they presented the dynasty as a terrifying bugaboo, a secret engine of world history, the Archimedean point from which the world could be vaulted from its hinges, or a countermodel to the vicissitudes of modernity, the dynasty remained surprisingly potent in the German imagination.

More than a decade ago, Lee Edelman proposed that queer theory take seriously the link right-wing ideologues usually made between queerness and a culture of the death drive. Rather than embrace "reproductive futurism," he argued, queer theory ought to tarry with those practices that stake or certify no claim to the future.[35] In light of Edelman's critique of "reproductive futurism," the figure of the dynasty is a strangely ambivalent one. On the one hand, few figures would seem to be as future obsessed as the dynasty: if parental willing, such as wanting one's children to "have it better," is already intemperate, dynastic willing is intrinsically megalomaniacal. It wants to regulate not just the child's life—it helicopter-parents future centuries.

It will be an argument of this book that this stridency, this outrageousness, has made the dynasty one figure for queerness in modernity. There's something inappropriate, something louche, something rather demented about wanting to project one's will so far into the future. Edelman wanted to know what happens when we take seriously the libidinal charge of the death drive. *The Dynastic Imagination* is about what happens when the death drive takes the shape of a family. The reason behind this occurrence may well be that nuclear fixation on the figure of "the Child," as Edelman apostrophizes the figure we're constantly exhorted to think of, has managed to hide its phantasmic dimensions in modernity. It seems *natural* to think of children, of their needs and their desires, in a certain way; it doesn't feel natural to think of one's great-great-great grandchildren with the same sense of certainty. But in truth, the latter is no more delusional than the former. This book explores the allure of this chilly dynasticism, which shadowed the sentimentalization of the family as its sociopathic twin.

Before long, the perversity of the dynasty made it a welcome resource for the critique of the ideology Edelman describes. Before long, the dynastic aspects of the family relinquished their one-sided political connotations, though they by no means relinquished their power to unsettle. In the 1820s and 1830s, those who waxed wistfully over dynastic structures tended to regard this as a rejection of the French Revolution, the Enlightenment, or what they perceived as their aftereffects. By the 1850s, attention to the dynasty meant no such thing—the dynasty had emerged as a mobile irritant that could be deployed from various corners to various purposes.

This book thus charts a strange reversal in German philosophical and literary thinking about the family. The dynasty gradually turned from a vestige of the old order into a possible tool for critiquing the new one. The bracketing of these elements initially had been part of a progressive political project: a rejection of the kind of familial hierarchy that had, since Hobbes and Locke, legitimated monarchical power. By insisting on marriage, siblinghood, and other more horizontal forms of family as models for politics, the German Romantics sought to celebrate communal life without endowing certain elements of that community with natural authority. If the Romantics rejected the dynasty as a vestige of aristocratic authoritarianism, by the early twentieth century writers turned to the dynasty itself as a tool for critique. These discontents understood the nuclear family as a mode of conformity and political conservatism. They availed themselves of its dynastic features to critique what they understood as the limitations of the nuclear family and the bourgeois lifeworld it anchored.

Plan of the Book

Chapter 1, "Into the Family Gallery," traces a prime trope through which German literature after 1815 staged the confrontations between the dynastic and the nuclear family: individual, often forlorn characters entering their family gallery. This portrait-filled space is a fascinating location, insofar as historians tell us that both nobles and burghers maintained one, that some galleries told of long dynastic lines and others simply commemorated recently deceased loved ones. Nevertheless, literature tended to charge the gallery with a very particular form of contradiction: in poems, plays, and novels of post-Romantic literature, it was imagined as a place where the nuclear family of the present came to be judged by the dynastic line, a place of self-justification or self-castigation before the ancestors.

Bourgeois writers turned the family gallery into a staging ground where they could lampoon the heraldic pretensions of the bourgeoisie—but where they could also subtly mark the dynastic obsessions of the aristocracy as outdated and ultimately tragic. It furnished them an arena for marking out the nuclear family as more groundbreaking, disruptive, and novel than it really was, and for marking out the dynastic one as more superannuated, more neatly tied to the world of the aristocracy than it really was. At the same time, the very clarity of these juxtapositions created the possibility for a recuperation and reevaluation of the dynasty: as the nineteenth century ventured into the family gallery, the dynasty in modernity had a rhetorical force it wouldn't have otherwise had.

Chapter 2, "Nuclearity and Its Discontents," deals with a strand of critique of modernity that regarded the truncation of the family as a symptom of a general loss of sense for natural hierarchies. It charts the development of this topos in Germany from a straightforward defense of actual existing dynasties (proffered by critics of the French Revolution in Switzerland and Germany, and largely imported from the French counterrevolutionaries) to a more general critique of bourgeois modernity. When Karl Ludwig von Haller, Franz von Baader, and others wrote about the dynasty, they were still very much thinking of the prerevolutionary order, but they were also critiquing the legacies of Enlightenment philosophy. Before long, the latter detached from the former: by the 1850s and 1860s, the novelist Adalbert Stifter and the anthropologist Wilhelm Heinrich Riehl could critique bourgeois conceptions of the nuclear family from a dynastic standpoint without having a specific dynasty in mind that they wanted to retain, restore, or defend. The dynasty had become available as a plausible base for critique of bourgeois sentimentality, philistinism, and presentism.

If love begins a *vita nuova*, dynasty begins with death. Dynasty is about transmission of things we fear may not in fact get to transmit, about exerting force when we're no longer around to exert it ourselves. Chapter 3, "Abortive Romanticism," is the first of these chapters about moments of organic life cut short, when the great blooming profusion of people and ideas around us seems to come to a stop, and when a point of anxiety becomes how ideas, texts, and lives will transmit themselves into our future.

The concept of organic life held promises for the nineteenth century, promises of regularity in difference, of progress in inconstance. And yet organic life often failed to live up to its end of the bargain. When Percy Bysshe Shelley left Lerici for Livorno in the *Don Juan*, he did so as part of the future of English literature and politics. He, like Ozymandias, could say, "Look on my Works." That future was cut short and it was left to his widow to reflect on what happens when the umbilical connection to the zeitgeist turns in an instant into a "colossal wreck." The three texts from Germany and England discussed here reflect on Romanticism in the process of passing, and on what, if anything, its children and grandchildren will look like. This chapter thus looks at postmortems of Romanticism—from its own protagonists, from its bemused fellow travelers, and from the "Young Germans" looking to bury it.

The first of these is Friedrich Wilhelm Joseph Schelling's novelistic dialogue *Clara, or On Spirit's Connection to the Spirit World* (1811); the second is Mary Shelley's novel *The Last Man* (1826); the third is Goethe's posthumously published *Faust II* (1832). All three reflect a sense that Romanticism had failed in its generational, its generative force: it had failed to behave how an organism is supposed to behave—it had failed to pass on a legacy, failed to externalize before dying away.

In the traditional framing of intellectual history, Romanticism's decline left open an interregnum experienced as troubling and disorienting by many of its protagonists. But of course the posthumous fate of Hegel's philosophy inspired an efflorescence of critical thought, as self-declared Hegelians and self-declared Hegel apostates alike came to grapple with the implications of his system and what it would take to make good on its insights. Among them, a new group of thinkers could leverage the philosophical vocabulary inherited from Hegel to altogether new ends: the first generation of German feminist philosophers. Chapter 4, "Feminism, or The Hegelian Dynasty," explores how in the decade and a half that elapsed between Hegel's death and the revolutions of 1848, writers like Bettina von Arnim (née Brentano), Louise Dittmar, and Louise Aston sought to insert themselves into the Hegelian interregnum. And they did so largely as guardians of Hegel's legacy, intent on maintaining a commitment to Idealism as his more radical students were itching to dispose of it. In so doing, these writers turned to dynastic questions (around legitimacy, around political sovereignty) in highly creative ways.

After the failure of the 1848 revolutions, German women writers largely abandoned this interest in the dynastic, either in critical terms or as guardians of older legacies. Instead, they deliberately avoided speaking in dynastic terms—nowhere more strikingly than when it came to the thought of Johann Jakob Bachofen. When Bachofen's 1861 book *Das Mutterrecht* (*The Mother Right*) proposed that much of human history and culture constituted an inheritance of a violent suppression of a matriarchate by men, many radicals of the day seized on the thesis. From Friedrich Engels to the founders of German social democracy, from Nietzsche to the American feminist Mathilda Joslyn Gage, they found in Bachofen's thought a welcome opportunity to critique sexism and capitalism in one breath. The only group that largely ignored the idea of an original matriarchate were the German feminists.

Chapter 5, "Wagner, or The Bourgeois Dynasty," moves from the Hegelians to one of their most eclectic readers. Richard Wagner combined their distrust of the dynasty (and the unquestionably given authority the dynasty depends on) with modish ideas of descent as a kind of racial family (which he culled from Schopenhauer and Arthur de Gobineau). This central contradiction animates above all Wagner's great opera cycle *Der Ring des Nibelungen* (*The Ring of the Nibelung*, 1870–76), which on the one hand valorizes characters that resist the demands placed on them by decisions made and plans hatched well before their own births, but on the other seems to distinguish between a good and a bad kind of dynasticity.

In many ways, the *Ring* tells the story of two dynasties, or rather two types of dynasties, both of which precipitate and shape the tragic events of the cycle. There is, for one, the god-father Wotan, who relentlessly fathers children, who tries to influence his children and use them to safeguard his power, sometimes successfully, sometimes not. In Wotan, Wagner presents in many respects a mythicized version of the bourgeois pater familias. However, from the very beginning his dynastic project is shadowed and threatened by exponents of a completely different sort of dynasty: its members do not transcend themselves in procreation but instead refashion themselves, maintaining their essence but altering their outward appearance to suit their ends. These include the giants Fasolt and Fafner (the latter of which transforms himself into a dragon, the better to guard his hoard), and the brothers Mime and Alberich, who either try to adopt children and fashion them in their image or father children simply as tools of revenge.

Wagner casts Wotan's dynastic project as a risk-taking endeavor—often enough, his offspring develop ideas of their own, turn against his designs, or simply misbehave. Conversely, the pseudodynasties set up by Wotan's antagonists depend on control and command—each iteration must be identical to the one that preceded it; any autonomy in the procreative chain becomes the occasion for vitriol and anxiety. Wagner's narrative scheme thus displaces the politically regressive aspects of the dynasty onto his dynastic outliers, while reimagining dynastic relations among Wotan's brood as characterized by autonomy and free transmission—both ideas very much opposed to the picture of the dynastic found both in Hegelianism and among early nineteenth-century reactionaries like Joseph de Maistre or Karl Ludwig von Haller.

This chapter traces the origins and ramifications of Wagner's peculiar opposition by locating him in a "dynasty" of his own; it shows how his operas assimilated conceptions of family and dynasty culled from Ludwig Feuerbach and the Young Hegelians, from Arthur Schopenhauer and Wilhelm Tieck. It then moves to Wagner's own increasingly dynastic household, showing how his chosen successor, son Siegfried Wagner, addressed the dynasty in his operas, how the Bayreuth project was itself increasingly understood in dynastic terms by devoted Wagnerians and critics alike.

Lynn Hunt once proposed a "family romance" operative in discourses around the French Revolution. Chapter 6, "Naturalism, or The Dynastic Romance," investigates a writer whose novels suggest that the Second Empire of Louis Napoleon is essentially structured around a dynastic romance. Émile Zola's Rougon-Macquart cycle, twenty novels that collectively aspire to tell the story of that empire, map its fortunes via two families—the titular Rougon-Macquarts, descended from the same Provençal woman but split into three branches that fare quite differently in the years between the revolution in 1848 and the disaster at Sédan in 1871; and the Bonapartes themselves, who rarely appear in the novels but whose fortunes become entwined with those of the Rougon-Macquarts again and again.

Zola proposes to understand both fortunes in terms of heredity and descent; he famously begins his novel cycle by outlining the Rougon-Macquart family tree, and he obsessively provides hereditary background for his characters. By the time we meet them, they have two or three generations of distributed responses to a certain milieu behind them. This chapter opens, however, with a consideration of the Austrian monk Gregor Mendel, an early researcher in what would become the field of genetics. Mendel's insight, central to the dynastic imaginary of modern genetics, was that if transmission from generation to generation was a matter of disposition, the transmission to the generation after the next was largely a matter of statistics. Likewise, Zola (who drew from Prosper Lucas rather than Mendel but came to a similar realization) focuses on the second filial generation and turns to probability rather than morals to trace the rise and decline of a family.

The chapter closes with a different vision of descent, and a different sort of "race." From Mendel's garden and Zola's hothouse we move to the garden of Mme. de Villeparaisis in Proust's *Sodome et Gomorrhe* (1921–22) Proust stages a dynastic chain across an immense gulf of improbability—the coming together of two homosexual men, the Baron de Charlus and the tailor Jupien. The chapter shows that Proust's *race des tantes* operates by rules diametrically opposed to those seemingly governing the dynasty of the Rougon-Macquarts—a dynasty of improbability, a dynasty without nucleus, a dynasty without heredity.

Although Richard Wagner had been deeply troubled by the possibility that dynastic outliers could form a pseudodynasty of their own, late nineteenth-century "decadent" thought, from Wilde to Lautréamont to Huysmans, began conceiving of such a mode of transmission as a positive. Whether it was Baudelaire's appeal to his *semblable*, or what Eve Kosofsky Sedgwick has identified as the "avunculate" of Wilde's comedies, they relied on family structures, and familial modes of transmission, that sidestepped the straightforwardness of either nuclear family or ratified dynastic descent. In Germany, the most sustained effort to create a dynasty without nucleus was undertaken by the poet Stefan George, who grouped around himself a gaggle of talented young men and insisted he could impart to them mysterious teachings—a social formation at various times referred to as a "confederacy" (*Bund*), a "circle" (*Kreis*), and, most ominously, a *Reich*. The mysteries of his cult had, in the tradition of decadence, a pronounced erotic edge, but unlike in Wilde they weren't simply or straightforwardly erotic.

On first glance, psychoanalysis seems predisposed to emphasize the nuclear family over the extended, let alone the dynastic. The Freudian universe, the one in which concepts like the primal scene, the Oedipus complex, latency, and so on make sense, is that of the bourgeois nuclear family, with children raised by two parents who function as arbiters or potential objects of infantile desire. And even though several of Freud's patients hailed from the aristocracy, the schema applied in their treatment was usually that of the bourgeois household.

But as chapter 7, "Freud, or The Reluctant Patriarch," shows, while the early Freud seems to have operated largely with a familial unconscious that constituted and reconstituted itself with each passing generation, his later writings begin to allow for types of unconsciousness that seem far more ancient in origin. When he suggests that the ancient Israelites' murder of Moses forms something of an ethnic unconscious, when he suggests in *Totem and Taboo* (1913) and *Civilization and Its Discontents* (1930) that a primal horde's parricide continues to make itself felt in our social pathologies, he is expanding the possible sources and modes of transmission of the unconscious.

When psychoanalysis turned to the idea of a dynastic transmission of unconscious drives, it did so at a time when its own transmission was very much in question. Between Freud's insistence on an unconscious inheritance traveling from Moses to his day, and Carl Gustav Jung's strange insistence on certain "Germanic" archetypes that outsiders (and especially Jews) couldn't understand, there loomed behind the debates over the transmissibility of the unconscious a question about whose discourse psychoanalysis was, and whom it should or could speak to. Was psychoanalysis and its picture of the unconscious universal, or was it either a "Jewish" or a "Teutonic" science?

Even when it came to the analysis of the individual, Freud had suggested that certain dreams seemed to come from neither an analysand's childhood nor the analysand's adult experience but rather emerged from "the experience of one's forebears." Here, several of Freud's students would pick up. Independently of Freud's remarks (which were published posthumously), the Hungarian analyst Léopold Szondi developed his theory of the "familial unconscious," which he thought drove an individual's biography and could be unearthed in a so-called *Schicksalsanalyse*.

Whereas Freud's "hereditary traces in the id" asserted themselves mostly in dreams, Szondi suggested that the familial unconscious had a hand in shaping the individual's biography, down to important life events, partner choice, and even death. Jung, much like Freud, mostly sought out his "archetypes" in dreams, myths, and cultural products, and he usually posited them as universal. At other times, however, he suggested that they consisted of information inherited almost biologically within a family, a tribe, and, most troubling, a race.

As chapter 8, "George, or The Queer Dynasty," shows, what exactly the relationship was between the erotic and the *Bund* or *Reich* Stefan George claimed to be setting up was left to his many disciples to puzzle out. George bequeathed them with an impossible conception of homoerotic community. In his early work, he gave the word *Bund* a melancholic, decadent temporality: it has an erotic tinge, but precisely because it's temporary. He regarded it as holy precisely because it's doomed not to last. Two encounters seem to have combined to change George's conception of *Bund*: he became a reluctant interlocutor to the so-called Cosmic Circle of Neoplatonist mystics in Munich's bohemian Schwabing district, and he encountered a young man named Maximilian Kronberger, who would become the George Circle's founding myth under the moniker Maximin. From the Cosmic Circle, George seems to have learned that homoeroticism need not be momentary and doomed but could instead be sustained and institutionalized. Maximin helped him do just that.

When the boy passed away shortly after turning sixteen, George turned him into the centerpiece of an ersatz religion and in the process reconceived of the *Bund* as one that not only could endure but was centrally concerned with transmission—a homosocial (and latently homoerotic) dynasty. The remainder of the chapter deals with George's complicated legacy as the all-male dynasty he had inaugurated began to grapple with what had been entrusted to them and how it was to be transmitted.

1

Into the Family Gallery

It's late at night, but the old nobleman can't sleep. He tosses and turns while his thoughts fixate on the long ancestral line whose crests limn the galleries of his castle, and on the one son or daughter who's left of that line. He gets up, studies the resemblance between his child's face and those of the child's great ancestors. In some cases, he's scanning for difference, for evidence of decline; in others he's scanning for sameness, for his family's inability to evolve. Either way, the gaze he casts is diagnostic and not fully his own. In this moment, he stands in for another group of people, usually not nobles, or at least not owners of castles. These are the people who in that very moment in history have started to examine their own family in the way he examines his, but who also insist that their family is nothing like his. He is their fiction.

The worried old paterfamilias and his nightly vigil by the visual depictions of his ancestral line constitute a frequent trope in German literature in the nineteenth century. The trope cuts across narrative literature, poetry, drama, and even philosophy. And it's more historically specific than we might at first suppose. It stages for a bourgeois readership a transition: like the Native American overlooking a valley he'll soon lose to the railroad, the image crystallizes an optic of momentary and ultimately somewhat sadistic pity, pity that implies obsolescence. Aristocratic families had maintained ancestral galleries for centuries, even if many of the most spectacular ones in Germany, such as the Wittelsbach gallery in the Residenz in Munich, were eighteenth-century designs. But these galleries came to be viewed differently, came to matter differently, at the turn of the nineteenth century. If ancestral galleries had been staging centuries-long chains of legitimation, they entered literature at a time when that mode of legitimation had itself lost legitimacy.

In the wake of the French Revolution, the family line had emerged as potentially uncanny. In a famous notice on the execution of Louis XVI with which Lynn Hunt opens her study *The Family Romance of the French Revolution*, the newspaper *Révolutions de Paris* suggested that the shedding of the blood of Louis XVI "cleanses us of a stigma of 1300 years." After all, the note argues, generation upon generation of his subjects have "consecrated slavery by our example," but now, the polemic continues, it is time to atone.[1] The paper calls the king "Louis Capet," thus taking the integrity of the French dynastic tree more seriously, if anything, than the Bourbons themselves did. It turns an old fantasy of the dynasty against the dynasty: the same fictional seamlessness that once ensured its rightness now certifies the rightness of its violent destruction.

This realignment in political imagination about the dynasty in the wake of the revolution also animates the scene of the aristocratic pater familias in his family gallery. The very features that had once made the family line unquestionable now made it questionable. The features that had made it legitimate now threatened to render it illegitimate. Those features that had made it reassuring now made it unsettling. And the old aristocrat dwarfed by the images of his ancestors is the spectator before whom the dynasty unfolds its demonic side. The person who stands before the glowering representations of long-dead ancestors is, typically, the last of his line. The dead in this scene vastly outnumber the living, and their ancestral seat is possessed of a gothic isolation rather than lively industriousness. The motif is deeply efficient: the old nobleman, usually a widower, sometimes living with a single, sickly child, with no mention of any servants.

The chapters that follow will move chronologically, from the heyday of Romanticism to the onset of modernism, from the Wars of Liberation to the aftermath of World War I. This chapter, however, isn't really part of that sequence. That's because the motif it traces persists throughout the period in question, never varying by much. It persists so long as aristocratic life is still socially present, but present within a social order increasingly experienced as bourgeois. We find it in works written during the Restoration period (1815–30), but we also find it in works by the young Thomas Mann and by Rainer Maria Rilke. In real life, the opposition of the nuclear and the dynastic family from which this motif drew its power had little bearing on how families actually lived in the interim. What did change was what novelists, poets, philosophers, and composers thought they could and should do with that opposition.

Ad Penates

In an 1815 poem, the Romantic poet Ludwig Uhland describes a final descent into the family crypt, where the protagonist comes face to face with his ancestors.

"Die Vätergruft" ("The Crypt of the Fathers") has an old man in an older suit of armor enter the crypt, where one final unoccupied coffin remains. Rather than his ancestors' faces, he is confronted with their voices, a spectral chorus. Rather than fear them, he reacts to them eagerly and self-confidently—and in fact joins them both in their chorus and in the grave. He contemplates his vaunted predecessors with something approaching awe, but he seems to feel no shame or anxiety before them:

> I have heard your call,
> You heroic spirits!
> Your row I am to complete
> Hail me, for I am worthy.
>
> Wohl hab' ich euer Grüßen
> Ihr Heldengeister gehört.
> Eure Reihe sol lich schließen
> Heil mir! Ich bin es werth.[2]

In Uhland's ballad, ending an ancestral line means fulfilling it: the poet stages the encounter with the dynasty as an affirmation of both the ancestral line and the individual at the end of it. The last spawn of the family and the family line are on speaking terms, and they can enter a dialogue as equals. Neither sits in judgment of the other. And the fact that the old knight meets other knights without the ballast of a nuclear family (or its vestiges, at any rate) seems to be part of why he can face them on their terms: there's no question of continuing the line.

In poems like Uhland's, the juxtaposition of the reduced family of forlorn final descendants to the imposing sublimity of the dynastic line could still be resolved to the individual's satisfaction. In the drama *Iphigenie auf Tauris* (*Iphigenia in Tauris*, 1786), Johann Wolfgang von Goethe gives Orestes, "of your tribe the last man,"[3] a vision of his gens. Generation by warring generation, the fractious Tantalids walk in Hades, reconciled and hand in hand. Addressing his dead mother, Clytemnestra, Orestes says, "See your son," only to correct himself and address his family line collectively: "What you have sown, he has reaped."[4] The central question for Orestes, as for Uhland's knight, is whether the individual is the redemption of his line or simply a continuation of it.

In the early nineteenth century, this motif underwent a profound transformation—rather than the final spawn joining or even redeeming the ancestral line, that individual simply canceled it out. For instance, Franz Grillparzer's first play, *Die Ahnfrau* (*The Ancestress*, 1817), premiered two years after the Napoleonic Wars ended and the Vienna Conference reordered Europe—primarily by returning it to its dynastic *status quo ante*. The play confronts the destructive results that come from challenges to traditional structures and the failures of those challenges. It returns to the questions already posed in the works I just touched on—questions about the continuity of the dynastic line that became more acute as revolution failed and counterrevolution prevailed. But above all, it signals that certain kinds of continuity and certain kinds of continuation had become impossible. To the diplomats in Vienna, Friedrich Engels would later write, "The smallest dynasty counted more than the largest people."[5] Grillparzer's tragedy reflects on the question of familial continuity in an age where that continuity becomes visible as second rather than first nature. All of Europe had seen that it could be otherwise. Only it was not otherwise.

Many plays, poems, and stories of the era took up the idea of a family line coming to an end precisely by reaching back into its beginning. Narratives of this kind asked about the origins of the aristocratic order and whether something of so problematic an extraction could ever be repurposed as a force for good. And these works seemed drawn to the fantasy that the dynastic past just might fully consume itself, might come to an organic completion and of its own accord make room for something new. Most of the works I discuss below come from the ambit of midcentury realism and reflect a nostalgic look at the dynastic line, but one suffused with a sense that its passing is a historical inevitability. But a few will come from an earlier period, roughly the age of the French Revolution, suggesting that what emerged as a full-on trope in midcentury had its origins in foreshocks around 1800.

Grillparzer's drama tells the story of Count Borotin and his daughter Bertha, the last of a line haunted by the ghost of its furthest ancestress. Married off against her will and slain by her husband, it is said that she will find peace only after the misbegotten line has gone extinct. Bertha is involved with Jaromir, a neighborhood boy who turns out to be the leader of a group of robbers that have been terrorizing the count's estates. Snatched from his family at an early age by the brigands, the young man pleads that the way he has been raised left him with no choice:

> Raised among highwaymen,
> Grown up among highwaymen,
> Witness to their deeds at early age,
> Unacquainted with milder examples,
>
> Unter Räubern aufgewachsen,
> Groß gezogen unter Räubern,
> Früh schon Zeuge ihrer Taten,
> Unbekannt mit milderm Beispiel,[6]

At the end of the play, it is revealed that the home this young man had been abducted from was Count Borotin's castle. At this moment, Jaromir has just mortally wounded the man who turns out to be his father with the same dagger by which the ancestress had been slain. Bertha, after realizing that the object of her desires is in fact her brother, has taken her life. Coming face to face with the ancestress, Jaromir recognizes Bertha in her face, her cheeks, and rushes toward her. Even when she tells him that she is not his beloved but his "mother," he seeks her embrace:

> Nevertheless it is Bertha's visage
> And my place is at its side!
>
> Das ist Berthas Angesicht
> Und bei dem ist meine Stelle!⁷

This final tragic recognition depends specifically on family resemblance, on the oneness and continuity of the family face. At the same time, it forces itself on a young man who thought himself outside and opposed to the system he is ultimately fated to bring to completion. Young Jaromir attempts to break from a history that he turns out to be continuing. But in embracing that continuity, he actually breaks from it, ends it altogether.

This coiled relationship between familial continuity and its disruption reflects the upheavals that had constituted European history for much of Grillparzer's life up until 1817 (he was born in 1791). *The Ancestress* is about a challenge to traditional structures, and about the destruction wrought by both those structures and the challenges to them. It is also, in its oblique way, about the temporality of revolution, albeit a revolution that comes to naught. The disruption of the family line by emancipated individuals reveals itself as an effect of a different kind of heredity: young Jaromir terrorizes the estates of the Borotin family, not because he wants to liberate the present from the past, but because he is himself overburdened by the past. He robs because those who raised him have always robbed, a family line born of bad decisions and poverty but just as firm as the ancestral line of the Borotins. More important, however, young Jaromir turns out to be a member of the Borotin family tree after all: he's been part of the very thing he's gone to war with. The promise of disruption turns out to be simply the fulfillment of patrimony. In an extended monologue in the fourth act, Count Borotin recognizes that logic:

> Here, where the spirits of my ancestors
> Float round me in tranquil levitation,
> Here, where from high walls
> A long-esteemed line,

Which raises even now its fame,
Looks down on its heir,
Where once the fathers lived,
Shall now the final grandson die!

Hier, wo meiner Ahnen Geister
Mich mit leisem Flug umschweben,
Hier, wo von den hohen Wänden
Eine lange, würd'ge Reihe,
Die noch jetzt der Ruhm erhebt,
Niederschaut auf ihren Erben,
Wo die Väter einst gelebt,
Soll der letzte Enkel sterben![8]

The Ancestress tells the story of a family whose line is at its logical end point, whose mode of enduring in time has lost its legitimacy. The origins of this line, the lovelessness and violence that helped launch and sustain it, will now bring it to an end. It wouldn't have been particularly hard for audiences in 1817 to hear in the fate of the Borotins the faint echoes of largely aristocratic families pouring into central Europe from revolutionary France and French-controlled German areas in the 1790s. German literature had long registered revolutionary energy, precisely insofar as it affected aristocratic family trees: it was an easy way to make rather overwhelming historical changes palpable and comprehensible, and it was an easy way to sentimentalize them.

In 1795, Goethe had written his *Unterhaltungen deutscher Ausgewanderten* (*Conversations of German Refugees*), a cycle of short novellas modeled on Boccaccio's *Decameron* but substituting the French Revolution for the bubonic plague. In the framing story, the narrator introduces his cast of storytellers as members of an aristocratic family forced to leave their landholdings and flee across the Rhine "in order to escape from the vicissitudes threatening all high-ranking persons, whose only crime was remembering their fathers with joy and honor, and had some advantages that any right-thinking father would want to procure for his children and descendants."[9] As Peter Fritzsche has noted, one of the great legacies of the French Revolution was that "people began to visualize history as a process that affected their lives in knowable, comprehensible ways."[10] One way in which it did so was by inscribing itself into the lives of families—as a disturbance, as a reordering of historical time within the domestic sphere.

This experience of the French Revolution as a wanton disruption of genealogical structures is one that Goethe shared with not just conservatives like Edmund Burke or Joseph de Maistre but also confirmed radicals like Pétion de

Villeneuve and Maximilien Robespierre, though the latter two men naturally thought that breaking the hold of dynastic families on the present was an altogether good thing.[11] In modernity, Peter Sloterdijk has argued, "heredity itself emerges as a defect, against which the true moderns have to put up resistance."[12]

In Germany, both the fact of restoration and the manner by which it was accomplished created a sense of an inherent contradiction. At least to the minds of many German intellectuals, Napoleon had been pushed out by popular uprising, by a nascent spirit of nationalism, by individual generals contravening rather than following the orders of the nation's monarchs. Thinkers like Johann Gottlieb Fichte had cast Germany's reawakening as a matter of autonomy: "Should such a sunken nation nevertheless be able to save itself," he had proclaimed in his *Reden an die Deutsche Nation* (*Addresses to the German Nation*) in 1807, "then this would have to occur by . . . the creation of an entirely new order of things."[13] But after 1815 that reawakening was instead hushed by what Heinrich Heine in 1842 would call the "heavenly eiapopeia."[14] And the shape this renewed surrender of autonomy took was the continuation of dynastic lines past the point at which they should have given way—organically, dynastically—to something else.

This was the basic contradiction in which German thinking about family politics found itself in the early nineteenth century: as it refused a certain inheritance, it could think of nothing but inheritance. As a later text of Goethe's, part 1 of the *Faust* tragedy (1808), has it, laws and customs transmit themselves "from family to family [*Geschlecht*]," "like an inherited disease":

> I scarcely blame your sentiment,
> I know about the state of this endeavor,
> We drag prerogatives and laws
> From place to place by slow degrees;
> Age handing age ancestral flaws
> Like an inherited disease.
> Sense turns to nonsense, boon to plague,
> Woe to the grandson that you are![15]
>
> Ich kann es Euch so sehr nicht übel nehmen,
> Ich weiß, wie es um diese Lehre steht.
> Es erben sich Gesetz', und Rechte
> Wie eine ew'ge Krankheit fort;
> Sie schleppen von Geschlecht sich zum Geschlechte,
> Und rücken sacht von Ort zu Ort.
> Vernunft wird Unsinn, Wohltat Plage;
> Weh dir, daß du ein Enkel bist!

The horror of being a descendant (*Enkel*) arises from the fact that the parameters by which we live our lives are themselves hand-me-downs: "The right that's born alongside us," as Mephistopheles says, "unfortunately never is the question."[16] Those rights may have emerged from a living, breathing context, but they have atrophied in the passage. To be an heir is to live with a will that's not your own, with laws and rights that have come to you secondhand, that may have long outlived their usefulness but have stuck around anyway. In a play obsessed with origins and what newness can be made of them, the descendant is the epigone (ἐπίγονος), the one cursed by late birth, the one doomed to fight his father's war.

But Mephistopheles pities mankind for being a gaggle not of children but of grandchildren, for having not one parental generation but two. He speaks the line to a student (*Schüler*), and he speaks it wearing Faust's robes. The young man, he implies, is a student's student. Goethe would frequently express his sense that each generation rejects the world inhabited by the previous one, but by that token comes around to the position of its grandfathers. He makes claims like this one as early as the period of his novel *Wilhelm Meisters Lehrjahre* (*Wilhelm Meister's Apprenticeship*, 1795) and his discovery by and of the Romantics; by the 1820s, this idea had become a reassurance with respect to his own legacy. "I have the luck," he wrote to the economist and historian Georg Sartorius, "that the most recent generation is more in harmony [*Einklang*] with me than the middle one."[17]

While Goethe thought this was a good thing for him, he didn't always seem so sure it was quite so wonderful for that second filial generation. In 1818, when his own first grandchild, Walther Wolfgang, was born, he wrote him a "Wiegenlied dem jungen Mineralogen" ("Lullaby for a Young Mineralogist")—an object lesson in gradual transformation in geologic time, from a grandfather to his infant grandson.[18] To be an *Enkel* is to resonate with the sounds of the long-ago, to be someone else's immortality, like it or not. Mephistopheles thus gives voice to what Oswald Spengler would later call the "Faustian" spirit of modernity: that "the right that's born alongside us" is the only one that legitimately applies to an individual. It's the sense that inheritance can't be accepted uncritically, that even simply maintaining the old needs to be understood as a reauthorization rather than a continuation.

The last scion of the dynasty coming face to face with the overwhelming past feels a peculiarly modern form of loneliness; the nuclearity of his own family is cut off from other forms of kinship. In 1811, the philosopher Friedrich Wilhelm Joseph Schelling wrote a dialogue titled *Clara, oder Über den Zusammenhang der Natur- mit der Geisterwelt* (*Clara, or On Nature's Connection to the Spirit World*), a connection that the narrative explores largely through the medium of the family. Clara, the childless last descendant of a long family line, has retreated from the world after the death of her beloved. Two old friends, a physician and a priest, await her arrival at an old monastery long supported by her family, even though Clara, a Catholic who married a Protestant, has previously been unwelcome there. As the men wait for her in a hall, they examine the long line of portraits there—some of them are of Clara's forebears, others are of long-dead brothers in Christ:

> Some of the portraits that were hanging in the hall, he explained, were those very forebears; even the brother of one of them was portrayed in his monastic habit.... Had we doubted the clergyman in the slightest, the striking resemblance between the picture and our friend would have been enough to have persuaded us of the truth of what he was saying. We couldn't express enough amazement about this resemblance coming back two centuries later, and the clergyman opined that such a sight could well provoke belief in the transmigration of souls.[19]

The hall of portraits opens up a sudden panorama onto two decidedly nonnuclear families interlaced in mysterious ways: a dynasty and a long line of monastic "brothers." Long-ago blood ancestors who look exactly like their distant scion mix here with predecessors bonded to their modern-day brethren in spiritual brotherhood. The spiritual families offered by these premodern structures, aristocratic and monastic, put to shame the motley assortment of mortals that gather before them. The ever-disrupted, ever-dissolving, ever-rearranging sentimental family finds its looming, mysterious Other in the endless "transmigration of souls."

In Annette von Droste-Hülshoff's 1840/41 ballad "Vorgeschichte (Second Sight)," an aging baron lies awake at night, worried about his sickly little son. "Like Ahasuerus," the old man's thoughts wander the heath, the castle, the moonlit night, settling again on the last spawn of his illustrious line. Each night, he puts the boy to bed before an immense family tree:

> He's had the small one's family tree
> Placed at the foot of his bed,
> So that after the goodnight kiss and evening prayer
> He can lovingly fold his hand over it;

> Hat er des Kleinen Stammbaum doch
> Gestellt an des Lagers Ende,
> Nach dem Abendkusse und Segen noch
> Drüber brünstig zu falten die Hände;[20]

The giant tree is an overwhelming sight:

> The parchment flicker in moon's glow
> Showing crest upon crest in nigh endless row
>
> Im Monde flimmernd das Pergament
> Zeigt Schild an Schilder, schier ohne End (1:211)

a mad proliferation of heraldic roses and arrows. Eventually, the baron has a vision of a massive funeral, only to realize he is seeing his own. Here, Droste-Hülshoff describes a long parade of the recently dead and the long dead, her verses lavishing on them the attention they pointedly withhold from the weak child asleep in his bed. In "Vorgeschichte (Second Sight)," the dead greatly outnumber the living:

> All of them lined up at the wall,
> The baron knows them all.
>
> Und alle gereihet am Mauerrand,
> Der Freiherr kennet sie alle. (1:211)

The "second sight" of the title shows the baron how powerless he is before his family's ultimate demise: before this gaze, the family reveals an endlessness that, strangely enough, brings about the end, continuity that speaks of the impossibility of further continuity:

> So the baron sets his lamp alight,
> And writes his testament that very night.
>
> Dann hat er die Lampe still entfacht,
> Und schreibt sein Testament in der Nacht). (1:213)

"Vorgeschichte (Second Sight)" isn't a celebration of genealogy: if anything, the baron and the sickly young boy he frets over suffer from an overabundance of past. The ancestors overwhelm the tattered vestiges of this nuclear family. In scenes such as these, the nuclear family at its puniest cowers before the mathematical sublimity of the dynasty. Here, the gesture by which the sentimental family severed itself from blood, tradition, and lineage turns into one of huddling retreat before the silently towering ancestors almost without count. The *mores maiorum* become a source of self-recrimination, a source of powerlessness.

It is also telling how scenes in which the nuclear family comes face to face with its dead ancestors typically play with gender. Often, the mother is missing. She has already crossed over, has become an escutcheon of the family tree, beckons from among the multiplying dead, with only her widower and their child to feebly resist her siren call. In a strange way, then, however patrilinear dynasty may be when it is deployed affirmatively, when it comes back to haunt the nuclear family it does so in a feminized form.

Droste-Hülshoff's poem describes the complexities of the family tree in some detail. Of the baron's ancestral line, she writes,

> In rightward direction a branch of his blood,
> The old baronial escutcheons"

> Rechtsab des eigenen Blutes Gezweig,
> Die alten freiherrlichen Wappen (1:213)

She contrasts the stern row of crests with the moderating influence of the mother's line:

> And to the left the mild mother's dynasty,
> The pious one resting in a grave cell

> Und links der milden Mutter Geschlecht,
> Der frommen in Grabeszellen. (1:213)

Apart from received sentimental notions of gender complementarity, this distinction may point to what leads to the peculiar gendering of the dynastic line in such scenes. For what overshadows the nuclear family isn't ultimately anything foreign, invasive, menacing. It is the family itself, looking to lure its final offspring into its bosom.

The strange way in which the missing mother genders the dynasty—a feminized siren call from a line of masculinized ancestors—finds its complement in the uncertain gender of the fussed-over last scion:

> He thinks of his lovely, only child,
> His gentle, weak little boy,
> Over whose life his father's prayer
> Stands like a quivering flame.

> Denkt an sein liebes einziges Kind,
> Seinen zarten, schwächlichen Knaben,
> Ob dessen Leben des Vaters Gebet
> Wie eine zitternde Flamme steht. (1:213)

The only child takes a line to become a boy, and when he does, he is gentle, weak, and little. His androgyny may arise from fears of degeneration, from famous androgyne figures like Goethe's Mignon—but above all, they seem to indicate one thing: like young Bertha, who picks, of all the young men in the world, her brother for her mate, these last scions won't have offspring. They constitute the *petitio principii* of the familial line: they unite so many branches, traits, and genders that to the logic of the nineteenth century, they must constitute living end points.

Tourists in the Ancestral Gallery

For all their stark imbalances when it comes to power, dignity, and vigor, these encounters in the family gallery can feel rather intimate. But in fact, a third person is of course present: the storyteller who observes and frames the scene, who gives it meaning. And by his or her very gaze, that third person is distinguished from the person being observed by the storyteller. The aristocratic pater familias standing by his child's bed represented a mode of looking that the reader was meant not to inhabit but rather to experience as exotic, as an index of obsolescence, as perhaps a moment worthy of pity. What made this gaze a sentimental one, in other words, was that in some sense the baron was a tragic victim of an inevitable, and perhaps ultimately positive, historical process. Modernization, bourgeoisification, and democratization hover over the scene as inevitable, ultimately affirmed outcomes.

The nineteenth century brought into increasingly sharper focus just what this interloper saw in the family gallery. Far more prosaically, it also gave the interloper access to the spaces in which to see or imagine these encounters. Theodor Fontane opens a section in the first volume of his *Wanderungen durch die Mark Brandenburg* (Rambles through the March of Brandenburg, 1862–89) with the final lines of Uhland's "The Crypt of the Fathers." He leaves the quote unattributed, and both the identity of the old man hailing his ancestors and the identity of these ancestors themselves are thus left open. Fontane's hike in the section that follows, across the Ruppin Plateau via Gottberg to Gransee, is one through a tangle of interwoven aristocratic family lines. But—and this seems to be why he opens with Uhland's poem—most of those dynastic lines are no more. "From that point on," he remarks at one point, "the Zieten family of Wustrau and the Jürgaß family of Ganzer walked together in suffering and joy, only to finally, like an old couple, also go to their graves together."[21] The great aristocratic lines give shape to Fontane's hikes through the Mark Brandenburg, and their deaths make his hikes possible in the first place.

Adalbert Stifter's novella *Der Hochwald* (*High Forest*, 1842) tells of the end of an old dynastic family through the lens of its now-ruined ancestral seat. Its narrator offers up the story of the decline of a family as a tourist would see it—and being a tourist seems to mean being an altogether different kind of person from the people on display. *High Forest* opens with a lengthy description of a landscape in southern Bohemia, focalized through the travels of a hypothetical wanderer who traverses this land in the third person: "when a wanderer turns west from the old city and castle Krumau, that grey widow of the long-faded Rosenberger line," before long he will come across "a ruined knightly castle."[22] The castle turns out to be the seat of the Vítkovci dynasty, whose origins Stifter would trace in his novel *Witiko*. But far more interesting is just who the wanderer turns out to be.

The ancestral lines of the Vítkovci family, their ruined castles, and the tales of their ruins form part of the landscape, but one that presents itself to a peculiar gaze. Throughout the story's opening, the wanderer's identity is itself mobile. At first, the wanderer seems to be a hypothetical everyman. Then he's identified as the narrator, who introduces the reader to Castle Wittigstein, where "I enjoyed spending my days even before I knew the fate of those who last lived in this melancholy place."[23] Soon thereafter, the narrator imagines his reader as a wanderer in the same locale, "your stunned and confused gaze going out over the many green peaks," and offers an invitation to "you, dear wanderer": "once you've taken it all in, come back with me two centuries."[24] In the hands of Stifter's narrators, the family histories of the aristocracy become another destination to hike to.

To whom is this opening of *High Forest* addressed? It's easy to assume that how Stifter shifts between calling the solitary walker "I," "you," and "he" is meant to indicate that just about anyone could be that walker. But this discounts the pervasive sense that the interloper into ruined aristocratic space is a very different kind of person from the people whose lives he will be describing: he comes to the space as both a tourist and a nostalgist. Stifter's narrators often take on both roles. In the preface to *Witiko* (1864), Stifter himself returns to Castle Wittigstein, saying that "as a young man . . . I spent many a day in the ruins of the ancestral castle of this family [*Geschlecht*]."[25] And in other texts of his, such as *Die Narrenburg* (The castle of fools) *Nachkommenschaften* (Descendants), a tourist discovers that the family whose castle he visits is in fact his own—and finds that discovery more troubling than exciting.

Fictional aristocratic protagonists and actual bourgeois readers may have had opposite reasons for heading into the ancestral gallery. But they would have agreed on the meanings of the space itself. The physical space that Droste-Hülshoff's baron occupies is aristocratic and ancestral; its very organization testifies to its inhabitants' dependence on storied forebears, forebears that press down on them with an almost architectural weight. Aristocrats dwell in their past; members of the bourgeoisie get to reconfigure theirs. They can tear down houses and rebuild them. For them, domestic architecture has the force of fiction—it can insist on some fantasy until it becomes reality.

Off the printed page, having an ancestral gallery was one of those forms of visual self-staging that the bourgeoisie learned from the aristocracy and imitated clumsily, never quite making it its own. At the same time, the literature of the period frequently framed that clumsiness as secretly a sign of vigor. Members of the bourgeoisie frequently appear as inveterate fakers of family trees and are mocked for it, but at least, the authors imply, they have the energy and creativity to fake something. For the nineteenth century, the decline of the ancestral gallery traces the decline of aristocratic life-forms and the increasing imaginative power of bourgeois self-invention. Or, perhaps to put it more accurately, realist writers like Theodor Fontane, Gottfried Keller, and Theodor Storm tended to cast everything that smacked of self-making in an emphatically bourgeois light, projecting the self-destructive, decadent aspects of the family onto aristocratic lines. For all the sympathy Fontane felt for the Junkers, this may have been his optic in visiting their ancestral seats as well.

Fontane's fiction is rich in the architecture of heredity. He visited many of the manor houses and small chateaux dotting the landscape of the Mark Brandenburg, those of well-off families and those that possessed mostly a famous name and some soil. The *Wanderungen durch die Mark Brandenburg* were in their very form predicated on an access and mobility that would have been all but impossible to someone of his station a generation before. "Without a care I collected them," Fontane wrote in his preface, but adds: "not like one who goes out with a sickle to harvest, but like a hiker pulling a select few grains from a rich field."[26] He arrived at these ancestral seats with genuine reverence, but also as the exemplar of a decidedly modern form: he visited as a tourist, ready to assess and to compare, ready to contrast the astonishing history of these ancient homes with their unprepossessing present.

Both this fixation on the architecture of heredity and the tourist's semi-reverent approach carry through into many of Fontane's novels. In his first, *Vor dem Sturm* (*Before the Storm*, 1878), which draws heavily from the *Wanderungen*, the touristic gaze he had practiced there becomes a formal principle. In this novel, and in many others that would follow, he investigates an age "at whose border we ourselves once stood, or of which our parents told us."[27] Even though Fontane's realism positions the historic novel explicitly within the compass of perceptions gathered in the nuclear family (e.g., there's no invocation of distant ancestors, as in works by his great inspiration, Walter Scott), ancestral galleries, real or metaphoric, abound in his works—sometimes to mock those of late birth, at others to sustain them; sometimes to suggest mysteries and complications, at others to resolve them. The family gallery provides a horizon against which the dissolution of the gentry can be charted. But that horizon never means just one thing, and there are many ways to relate to it.

Before the Storm paints a picture of the Prussian aristocracy at the tail end of the French occupation. The action is set in a number of castles and manor houses along the River Oder in the winter of 1812. And the narrative tells the story of the old families of the Mark in a moment of disruption. As one character, General Bamme, himself the last scion of an old noble house and representing a hope for renewal, puts it, "I abhor all this cousin and auntie-principle [*Vettern- und Muhmenprinzip*], especially when it comes to marrying and procreating."[28] The German words *Vetter* and *Muhme* are carefully chosen: both designate familial relationships that are particularly numinous and imprecise—they describe an atmosphere of relatedness rather than a definitive relationship. Again and again in Fontane's fictions, the intricate dynasties of the Junker aristocracy provide a background for the action—but they no longer exert enough pull to provide anything more than that background.

In one scene in *Before the Storm*, a number of characters retreat into the gallery of Castle Drosselstein, "which ran the length of the left wing of the palace, consisting of three halls of which the first contained the family pictures." The count has placed ethanol lamps in the space to warm it, and the lamps cast blue flames across the ancient visages. Behind the windowpanes clatters a sudden wind. "It's the right tone for ghost stories," General Bamme remarks. One picture especially attracts the visitors' attention, "a beautiful head, but uncanny"; the blue flames give her likeness "ghostly life" (2:304). The woman in question, they are informed, is Wangeline von Burgsdorff, a tragic plotter and a great-aunt of the current Count Drosselstein.

But several characters push back on any uncanniness attaching to Wangeline. They seem reluctant to grant any singularity to her, and largely attribute her scary tale to family pretension. While the others marvel at how real yet uncanny her portrait seems, Berndt von Vitzewitz remarks that "in every old gallery you find such pictures," and that it's strangely always the pretty young girls to whom the tragic story attaches (2:304). Importantly, the narrator seems to agree that the uncanniness is essentially a pretense: again and again he mentions the blue flame. What the reader is supposed to notice is that this bit of spiritualism is brought about by ethanol—*spiritus* in German. In effect, the spell cast by the ancient gallery comes about via the less-than-magical innovations of modern chemistry.

At the same time, the narrator seems dismissive of any attempts to ignore that spell outright. When General Bamme chimes in to critique the story, the narrator ironically describes him "shak[ing] his head historically-critically" (2:305). There is something ridiculous about standing in awe before the pictures of your forebears to imagine a fanciful ghost story about an old painting, but there's something equally ridiculous about waving away such awe and stories altogether.

General Bamme considers the story of Wangeline von Burgsdorff a dynastic trick. He claims that the Burgsdorffs "simply created their own ghost woman [*weiße Frau*]," having pilfered the story of an *actual* ghost—namely, the story of the "Orlamünderin" (a real-life myth, which Fontane reports in the *Wanderungen*) and embellished their ancestral line with it. The Burgsdorffs are thus pretend-haunted as part of a more general dynastic pretense and out of sheer jealousy. Thus, "by creating this pretender the Burgsdorffs sought to avenge themselves and sought to keep up with the old established hauntings" (2:306). Part of competing with the old established families, Fontane suggests, is pretending to match the sheer number of old established skeletons in their closet. The count is not amused by this suggestion, and Bamme realizes he has insulted the man. So he seeks to temper the accusation that the Wangeline story is nothing but the decidedly ghost-free Burgsdorff family putting on ancestral airs. She may be a copy of a fiction, he asserts, but if he can help the spectral Madame Wangeline, he's happy to spread her fame, precisely because he has great love "for all toppling and removing from the throne." "Besides," he adds with yet another antidynastic flourish, "my old friend, the Orlamünderin," has become a bit tyrannical and "deserves dethroning." In other words, he seeks to foment rebellion in the realm of local legend. After all, "she won't stick to the law and lawlessness destroys any dynasty, even in the spirit realm" (2:306).

Despite all the time he spends in the ancestral galleries of the aristocracy, Fontane shares General Bamme's reverence for those factors that disrupt succession, that force successors to get creative. His novels reserve for dynastic succession a touristic attachment: the very fact that the tourist can view the dynastic chain in this way tells him that the dynasty has ceased to function traditionally. "Whatever . . . pushes aside tradition with a laugh piques my interest,"[29] Fontane wrote in a letter. In *Ellernklipp* (1881), Hilde, a young orphan rumored to be the bastard daughter of the young count who has died in the Seven Years' War, is adopted into a small family and causes its destruction through no fault of her own. It is her beauty alone that "disorders the order of things." Through this "adopted child [*angenommenes Kind*]," *Ellernklipp* investigates, as Fontane puts it in another letter, "the demonic-irresistible power of that which is illegitimate."[30] The power that comes with illegitimacy reveals itself to a gaze aware of its own illegitimacy.

The titular family of *Die Poggenpuhls* (*The Poggenpuhl Family*, 1896) hails from the impoverished lower nobility; its pater familias has "left [it] nothing but a name and three commemorative coins [*Krönungstaler*]." These coins, minted for Wilhelm I's accession to the royal throne in 1862, link the family inheritance to dynastic succession. But where the Hohenzollerns transition from one generation to the other, the Poggenpuhl family experiences generational change as a break rather than continuity. It has in its salon a collection of daguerreotypes and photographs, which it calls "the ancestral gallery of House Poggenpuhl."[31] The designation is meant in jest, the narrator informs us, since the pictures depict only living people. But there's a double irony, of course, to living surrounded by pictures of the living: granted, it means you don't have a lot of past to be proud of, but it also means you have a lot of present. Realist fiction often treats with some ambivalence those threadbare gestures by which upstarts seek to conjure up a lineage for themselves. However ridiculous the attempt, it betrays a creativity that the aristocratic figures in texts like Droste-Hülshoff's "Vorgeschichte (Second Sight)," cowering before their overwhelming family trees, can no longer afford.

Most important, novelists frequently regarded the attempt at imitating aristocracy as akin to their own work as storytellers. Recognizing a family's great past can immobilize the individual member of that family. But inventing such a past empowers the individual—indeed, it may even become a self-fulfilling prophecy. Gottfried Keller's cycle *Die Leute von Seldwyla* (*The People of Seldwyla*, 1865) comprises frequently humorous novellas centered on a collection of townsfolk who have more ambition than dedication, and whose schemes frequently read as poorly executed social climbing. In one novella, *Der Schmied Seines Glückes* (*The Smith of His Own Fate*), old Adam Litumlei invites his nephew Hans Kabis (who has renamed himself John Kabys to give himself a "nimbus of Anglo-Saxon entrepreneurship") into his hall of ancestors—his *Rittersaal* (knight's hall). He declares, "I am the first of my own line, which means as much as: I have decided to found a great and famous family [*Geschlecht*], as you see on the walls of this hall! For these are not my ancestors, but members of an extinct patrician family of this city. . . . For I had a great fortune, but no name, no ancestry, and I do not even know the baptismal name of my grandfather."[32] However great the ridicule many nineteenth-century authors heap on figures who invent their own genealogy, they can't but respect the storytelling prowess that goes along with such invention. Adam Litumlei's ability to spawn the fiction of a great dynasty indicates, at least to his mind, his ability to spawn one in real life. And to some extent, *The People of Seldwyla* agrees. Better to control the story of your family than to be controlled by it. And in the nineteenth century, there seems to be a pervasive sense that bereft of fictional lightness, too much family is indeed a deeply terrifying thing. In an essay on Thomas Mann's *Royal Highness*, Ida Boy-Ed makes the following point: Mann's comedic novel imagines that "healthy bourgeois blood unites with the blood of an ancient dynasty, promising new flowering."[33] This turn at the end of the narrative, Boy-Ed notes, moves this novel decisively out of the sphere of the social critique—it becomes more of a fairy tale.

But if members of the bourgeoisie could recognize themselves in the inventive familial fantasists, they of course also recognized themselves in the ancient nobleman, though perhaps not in terms of social status. Yet the nobleman's anguished look was one deeply familiar to nineteenth-century audiences, above all bourgeois ones. While their individual ancestry was supposed to matter little for their current status, bourgeois Germans were instructed on how to scan their families for more global heredity: for signs of physiological inheritance, for inherited pathologies, and later for the hereditary features of the species as such, for justifications of their ascent and for harbingers of their decline.[34] In some way, the insouciant gesture of familial self-invention was a way to overstate their newness, to wash their hands of a past they secretly worried resolutely clung to them.

Thus, the ancestral line ceases to be about legitimation and becomes instead about knowledge—a gesture that is, on the one hand, democratizing and, on the other, deeply concerned with preserving inequality within democratization.[35] In *Menschliches, Allzu Menschliches* (*Human, All Too Human*, 1878), Friedrich Nietzsche notes that "one has a right to be proud of a line of *good* ancestors up to one's father—but not of a line as such, for everyone has this."[36] The line itself is beside the point, since "everyone" has one—it's transformed from a form of legitimation into a simple fact of life.

At the same time, Nietzsche's idea of a "genuine nobility of birth" (den echten Geburtsadel) seems to double down on the importance of familial extraction—at first a few characteristics mattered (nobility, character), but suddenly they all matter. If genealogy reappears as biology, it by the same token appears in a panoptic form. Nietzsche is clearly being facetious in suggesting that "a single break in the chain, *one* evil ancestor, cancels out all nobility of birth."[37] His point is ultimately the uselessness of the concept of nobility. But the unremitting logic of "one single break" is deeply symptomatic of the one-drop logic of his age. Among the German popularizers of Darwin, above all Ernst Haeckel in his influential *Anthropogenie* (1874), humanity itself became a *Geschlecht* and its ancestors *Ahnen*. Was this a democratization of the dynasty? Or a betrayal of liberalism by means of vestigial dynasticism?

Condemned to Familiarity

If the dynastic line could preserve the important role of fiction, fantasy, or make-believe in politics and in life, to those continuing to live among dynasties it also increasingly seemed to be the outdated stuff of stories, even a form of madness. Consider Adalbert Stifter's *Die Narrenburg* (The castle of fools, 1841/42), where Heinrich, a young, ostensibly bourgeois scientist, gains access to an all-but-abandoned castle in some Austrian province, only to encounter himself in the ancestral gallery.

Before long, Heinrich is recognized as the new owner of the Castle of Fools. "Recognized," in this case, neither by dint of a legal claim nor through genealogical proof (though both exist) but rather because the Scharnast family's factotum, who has remained in the castle since the last count died (and has gone slightly mad there), confuses him for Count Sixtus II, whose image in the family gallery indeed looks exactly like Heinrich: "feature by feature, to the point of indistinguishability [*bis zum Ununterscheidlichen*], it was Heinrich on that canvas, albeit in adventurous, foreign garb."[38] What certifies Heinrich's claim to the old castle, then, is some strange mixture of derangement and logic. The aged factotum senses a truth that Heinrich will have to expend much research to establish as fact; yet the old man essentially gets it wrong, confusing one member of the line for another and making an overall botch of the passage of time. Perhaps no better image for the dynastic sense exists than its standing astride the family line and yelling "Stop."

In the end, Stifter's protagonist accepts the servant's perspicacious foolishness and makes it his own. He decides to continue the Scharnasts' family line, as the deranged castellan puts it, to "bring servants and people onto the mountain so that it may live and throng again, that a posterity [*Nachkommenschaft*] take shape, which will fill out the entire gallery and the entire future until the End of Days."[39] How posterity in Stifter quickly steers the nuclear family toward an apocalyptically distant future will occupy us in chapter 2. But in *Die Narrenburg*, the family gallery has a more immediately disordered effect.

Joining the family line comes with one condition: a family trust inaugurated by the first Scharnast patriarch, Hanns. Castle Rothenstein has a massive archive in which every lord must set down his life chronicle and read those of his ancestors. Given that over the centuries, the Scharnasts have left in this repository not so much great and edifying records of lives well lived as tales of escalating eccentricity, the archive has become the means by which the family, in an endless feedback loop, has driven itself insane.

Die Narrenburg is a tale of the respect with which individuals ought to treat their inheritance, and with which they need to consider what they pass on to their descendants. The ancestor to one of the minor characters, a proprietor of a simple country inn, resurfaces in Stifter's novella *Prokopus* (1847) as a counterpoint to the irresponsible and dissolute Scharnasts. It turns out that existing alongside the escalating and self-consuming dynasty up on the mountain has been a long line of innkeepers who "arrange things in order and look towards the future with care."[40] Of course, the differences between the two families revolve around class—but class difference asserts itself in various degrees of self-consciousness through which these families constitute their dynastic line. The economy with which this other family tells its own story is of a piece with the even keel on which that story runs. The eye the family casts on itself can occasion the very chaos it anxiously looks out for.

Not too far below the moralistic surface, *Die Narrenburg* is about the abject horror of having to know exactly where one came from. The ancestral line immortalized in Castle Rothenstein's gallery is full of grotesques, and owing to the family's congenital archival mania, none of their grotesqueries can ever be forgotten.[41] As Peter Sloterdijk puts it, in modernity human beings are "emancipated from original sin, but increasingly understand themselves as entangled in other stories of heredity."[42] Heredity was a thing to be banished and yet a thing obsessively pursued, not least of all in literature. It's no accident, after all, that at the end of the nineteenth century Sigmund Freud would call the fantasy that one's family is not one's family—an emancipatory gesture so radical that only a neurotic could dare it—a "family novel."

At the very end of one such novel, the thirteen-hundred-page, centuries-spanning *Ahnen* (Ancestors, 1874–80), Gustav Freytag has one character remark on the importance, the luxury, the freedom, of not knowing one's ancestors and, by the same token, being surprised by what one passes along to future generations. The one thing the aristocratic pater familias can't feel in his family gallery, the feeling neither the eugenicist nor the physiognomist is liable to be seized by, is simply surprise: "I will leave you, you great admirer of family memories, with something else and something greater. Perhaps the deeds and sufferings of our ancestors influence our thoughts and works in ways that transcend what we living can really comprehend. But it is a wise arrangement of our world that we do not know to what extent we continue the life of past humans, and that we notice only occasionally, and only with some surprise, how we live on in our children."[43]

Having to invent what others simply received is the curse and the privilege of the modern. The final gesture of Droste-Hülshoff's baron—writing his will—is in a way profoundly modern. Granted, written wills had been part of aristocratic life for a long time. Yet Droste-Hülshoff positions the baron's writing of the will as a substitute for a lived succession: something needs to be secured that in the old days, the days of "crest upon crest in nigh endless row," went without saying, went without writing down. This is the perspective with which the last scions of nineteenth-century literature looked at their forebears: the unthinking automatism of succession and inheritance had given way to an active effort.

As Ulrike Vedder writes, "Vorgeschichte (Second Sight)" strongly links "the gift of vision and genealogy,"[44] and more generally in Droste-Hülshoff we could speak of a connection between genealogy and visibility. Which stories are recorded, passed on, or even tellable in the first place has to do with genealogical and familial structures. But what Vedder doesn't specifically thematize is the poem's form: the ballad, which manages to combine the family tree with the premonition that inspires the writing of a will. The poem is about an ambient sense (a hallucinatory vision) that inspires a very precise genre of written transmission.

Both forms of inheritance and their regulation had become codified and standardized in the German-speaking world only in the waning days of the eighteenth century, in a way that at once strengthened the nuclear family and turned it into a site for the application of state power: the state got to decide what within the family was transmissible from generation to generation, what it had to pass on (and later wouldn't be allowed to) in order to benefit society. As Max Weber once put it, one of the arenas in which the modernization of the family made itself felt most clearly in Germany was in the question of how broadly testamentary freedom (*Testierfreiheit*) ought to be construed, and what exceptions ought to be imposed. The Preußische Landrecht of 1794, the Code Civil in revolutionary France, and the common-law tradition in the United States all dealt with this problem, and each offered different solutions.[45]

Writing a testament thus allows Droste-Hülshoff's baron to make explicit what his family tree and his row of crests had once taken care of implicitly. Yet it gives him a final recourse only in the moment he is faced with his own death. Before he has his ghostly vision, there is another reason why the old man needn't make his testament: he simply doesn't need a piece of paper to regulate his relationship with his son. The will thus becomes an intermediary in a double sense, in each case interloping into relationships that once functioned immediately. As Georg Wilhelm Friedrich Hegel would suggest in his account of the nuclear family in the *Grundlinien der Philosophie des Rechts* (*Foundations for the Philosophy of Right*, 1821), the nuclear family was a central source of affective legitimacy within civil society—its members became one person before the law precisely because the bonds of civil law could not account for what they meant and owed to one another. But at the same time, the family's very embeddedness within civil society revealed that that oneness was always at risk of being undone. Yes, the members of the family weren't parties to a contract so long as they were a family; but they were always *potential* parties: the moment they ceased to be a family (because the parents divorced, because the children grew up).

It is surely significant that Droste-Hülshoff's poem presents as modern a practice as old as the Salic law. When it comes to the family, its organization and its place in society, it is fair to say that not much changed in practice over the revolutionary period—but that the modes of understanding that practice underwent a marked transformation. Whether it be the attempts at family reform during the French Revolution or the sexual experiments of the early Romantics, they largely left the lived reality of everyday people untouched. But by the mid-nineteenth century, it turned out that the same thing could be viewed very differently.

Whether transmitting one's individual will to future generations through a testament was a practice to be encouraged was hotly debated at the time. Broadly speaking, proponents of positive law (e.g., Friedrich Carl von Savigny) emphasized the importance of inheritance and inherited will, while natural law theorists tended to regard it as problematic and hubristic to want to project one's own will past one's own death—Annette von Droste-Hülshoff's favorite cousin, Clemens August, numbered among the latter camp. In his *Lehrbuch des Naturrechts oder der Rechtsphilosophie* (Textbook of natural law or philosophy of right, 1831), he wrote that "the will of a deceased person is a ground that . . . no one needs to respect."[46] "Vorgeschichte (Second Sight)" raises pointed questions in that regard: How and by what right do we impose our wills into the distant future? And how do we deal with the will of the past reaching out into our own present?

2

Nuclearity and Its Discontents

The idea that family and state are somehow analogous dates to at least Aristotle. Having recourse to familial relationships as a model for the organization of a state was a central facet of philosophical justifications of absolutism. But by the turn of the nineteenth century, the straightforward patriarchalism or Adamism of Sir Robert Filmer's *Patriarcha* (1680), which had likened the relationship between king and subject to that between a father and his offspring, was no longer viable. In both France and Germany, critics of the French Revolution sought to revive it. But in Germany they had to revive it in a new guise.

French counterrevolutionary thinkers like Joseph de Maistre and Louis de Bonald posited that the common error of thinkers during eras of the Enlightenment and the French Revolution had lain in the fact that the likes of Diderot and Rousseau and their political followers dissolved familial bonds and, by extension, social bonds. This criticism was an odd fit to begin with, but in Germany it simply did not apply—whether they were late Enlightenment *Popularphilosophen* or dissident Romantics, German philosophers and popular writers were anything but hostile to the family. So when they imported the writings of the French reactionaries, German conservatives made a small but significant change to their indictment: the Enlightenment, the revolution, and the moderns had not destroyed the family, they had truncated it.

In the 1850s, the conservative sociologist Wilhelm Heinrich Riehl would claim, "Especially during that time span when one could justifiably claim that our nation's existence was above all a literary one, German literature ignored nothing more fastidiously than the family and its interests."[1] This will strike today's reader as strange, given that the Romantic generation (which Riehl is referring to here) was fascinated with love, with intersubjectivity, and with the bonds by which marriage was more than a contract. It would be strange to say that its thinking dissolved bonds; if anything, it overemphasized them. But Riehl's charge is founded on an altogether different conception of what made a family—namely, it was more than a couple. And it is founded in a sense that something other than affection holds the family together. In this respect, Riehl had a point.

For the Romantics indeed tended to reduce the family to its nucleus, or at least assigned particular political import to the feelings that structured its nucleus.[2] The Romantic generation spoke in terms of coupledom and brotherhood, often explicitly juxtaposed to intergenerational family structures. In 1798, for instance, the poet Novalis (Friedrich von Hardenberg, 1772–1801) wrote *Glaube und Liebe* (*Faith and Love*), subtitled *The King and the Queen*, which set the tone for the Romantic politicization of the family. Traditional comparisons of the family to the state had emphasized the vertical axes of the family—they regarded the monarch's authority as analogous to that of the pater familias over his brood, or else they thought it flowed directly by dynastic succession from Adam's authority over his progeny. In contrast, Novalis insisted that what could and should make the state like a family was the feelings within the royal family, which would radiate outward into the broader polity.

Even though Novalis speaks generically of "the king" and "the queen" throughout, he clearly wanted his readers to associate these figures with a specific royal couple. When Friedrich Wilhelm III became king in November of 1797, his ascension to the throne seemed to promise a new style of kingship. This was partly due to Friedrich Wilhelm's more bourgeois values and affect, at least when measured against his father, a hard-living carouser. More than the personality of the king himself, however, it was his choice in queen that seemed to signal a break with the dynastic past. The young royal couple appeared to be united in genuine affection, their union as much one of sympathy and inclination as of dynastic necessities.

Some connections did exist between the Romantics around Novalis and the French reactionaries. One was the figure of Madame de Staël, who had hosted both Maistre during his flight from the French Revolution and Bonald later in life, and who would meet brothers Friedrich and August Wilhelm Schlegel during her German travels. But it is not clear how aware the French reactionaries and the German Romantics were of one another's thinking. For Maistre, Bonald, and German thinkers like Karl Ludwig von Haller, Friedrich von Gentz, Adam Müller, Franz von Baader, and Johann August Freiherr von

Starck, the correspondence between family and state flowed from the premise that patriarchal power was like state power. This was a notion, born of the upheavals experienced during the revolutionary period, that in the 1790s Friedrich Schlegel and Novalis sought to avoid. As they got older, however, the surviving members of the Romantic circles largely came to agree with it.

However Jacobin they were in their sympathies, even the young Romantics would not have disagreed that many of the Enlightenment's thinkers were overly reductive and abstract in their treatment of family cohesion, and that this extended to their understanding of social cohesion as well. German Romantic theories of family, love, and marriage took aim at pictures of sociability that to them seemed to be based on atomized units that only in a second step entered into relation with other such units. Thinkers like Novalis seemed to agree with the basic impulse of the French reactionaries: that one could use the sense of instinctual community and embeddedness within a family to critique atomistic premises of certain social theories of the Enlightenment. But if they thought there was critical purchase to analogizing family and society, they pointedly refused the additional step of positing an analogy between child and royal subject. Novalis attempted, in other words, to critique the social effects of Enlightenment without slipping into counterrevolutionary language.

By the 1820s, this was no longer the Romantic project: Schlegel's later "philosophy of life" as well as Friedrich Wilhelm Joseph Schelling's "positive" philosophy were invested in tradition and inheritance. And as far as monarchists such as Gentz, Müller, and Starck were concerned, the family mattered for the state largely because of how it channeled sovereign authority, which is to say it mattered to them as a vertical rather than a horizontal arrangement. They increasingly understood the encomia that Romantic texts of the 1790s and early 1800s had delivered to the family, the couple, friendship, and brotherhood as undue truncations and distortions of what made a genuine family.

Antimodern positions in Germany were frequently cast in a dynastic mode. And since the debate of the early nineteenth century had been primarily academic and aesthetic, revolving largely around the redescription of existing aristocratic families as horizontally rather than vertically structured, the dynastic position retained an aesthetic validity well beyond the increasingly narrow slice of the German intelligentsia that was straightforwardly monarchist. These thinkers may not have been proud partisans of, say, the Hohenzollerns, but they saw the appeal of Müller's description of Friedrich Wilhelm III's accession to the throne: "the will, the manner of dominion, the family physiognomy of the ancestors step out, reawakened and youthful, into the bright present day."[3]

The King and the Queen

Luise, soon to be crown princess of Prussia, first entered Berlin on December 22, 1793. Witnesses described something close to a triumphal march. Huge crowds came to witness her arrival, and "so many bouquets [were] thrown that we were swimming in flowers."[4] The princesses, Luise and her younger sister Friederike, drove down Unter den Linden, stopping first to greet children from the French "colony," then making another stop for girls "of the German nation." Luise crossed the Lange Brücke under the towering equestrian statue of the Great Elector, Friedrich Wilhelm (1620–1688), and arrived at the southern gate of the Hohenzollern castle. Her wedding to Friedrich Wilhelm III took place there on Christmas Eve, in the White Hall of the royal palace. Luise later reflected on the event, but less in terms of her joining the Hohenzollern dynasty (though the sitting king and queen, as well as the widow of Frederick the Great, were in attendance). Instead, she highlighted "the sacred hour at which I became an inhabitant of Berlin."[5]

In the end, what made the wedding important was what the king's subjects, and indeed admirers across Europe, read into it. The union was neither as modern as that of Luise's sister, who married into the Thurn and Taxis clan, the wealthy but slightly lower-status family in charge of Germany's mail service; nor was it as traditional as the wedding between Friedrich Wilhelm's younger brother Louis and Luise's younger sister Friederike two days later. (Louis already had a mistress, but she wasn't marriageable, and so the young prince was married off as part of a package deal.) But Luise herself was modern and natural: her directness and openness with her emotions soon led to misunderstandings at court and a growing legend among the populace. When the neoclassical sculptor Johann Gottfried Schadow created a dual statue of Luise and Friederike, he put the two women in decidedly uncourtly drapery. He was allowed to take live measurements of the two princesses, ensuring a degree of realism unusual in a ruler portrait.

Schadow's sculpture is emphatically unforced, its figures unguarded. The artist seemed intent on bracketing the dynastic context and focusing on two flesh-and-blood women.[6] At the same time, the two figures do not and cannot leave the dynastic behind entirely. For one thing, there are two of them—Friedrich Wilhelm and Luise may have found each other not exclusively by dynastic contrivance, but the same could not be said of her sister's marriage. For another, Schadow respected the spatial arrangements directed by heraldic tradition: since Luise is a future queen, she stands to her sister's right and slightly in front of her sister.

This is how Luise came to function in the legend that grew up around her during her lifetime, and one that only intensified after she succumbed to a sudden illness in 1810. She combined the unprecedented in traditional garb or the traditional in unprecedented garb, and the fact that she could be understood both ways made her a potent symbol. The beautiful, tragic queen and her love for her husband and king seemed to map onto the fortunes of their kingdom. She had embodied hope in dark times, she could embody a hope for change as much as one for continuity, she had given Prussians something to love about their royals at a time when the House of Hohenzollern seemed hopelessly adrift in the vagaries of the European war. And her death was interpreted as a call to fully throw off the French yoke, as a banner for the coming war. The poet Theodor Körner (1791–1813) wrote in 1813:

> You were chained to the undignified age,
> Your extinguished eyes exhorted us to revenge.
>
> An die unwürd'ge Zeit warst du gekettet,
> Zur Rache mahnte dein gebroch'ner Blick.[7]

While this sort of cult was not at all unprecedented, the specific kind of attachment Queen Luise inspired was certainly new. Christopher Clark is probably overstating the case when he reduces her legend to "sex appeal,"[8] but there was a strange kind of intimacy to her subjects' fixations. She was an icon, but she was more than that. The writer Heinrich von Kleist produced three drafts for a poem on her thirty-fourth (and final) birthday in early 1810—the final one was a sonnet, addressed from her subjects to their queen.

When King Friedrich Wilhelm came back to Berlin from his eastern exile in 1809, the conservative Romantic Adam Müller wrote that his return signaled that "what belongs together will stay together, monarch and people and capital and the provincial tribe of the old Reich and the graves of the kings."[9] The victories against the French, in other words, certified the connection between Prussia and the Hohenzollern dynasty. Yet when Luise died in 1810, Müller wrote that while "it would mean to intrude upon the sacred grief of our king if one were to speculate what he lost as a husband,"[10] her death was also her people's loss: "the morals [Sitte], which God imbued with the power to transfigure [verklären] the laws, but also to destroy them, no longer have a representative, a guardian in this kingdom."[11] Müller frames her loss in terms of conjugal love (for the king) and in terms of a Romantic ideology of gender complementarity (for the populace). Once Luise entered the picture, it was not the long family tree that sustained the kingdom but the dyad of king and queen.

In this, Müller picked up on an interpretation of the young couple pioneered by the poet Novalis. One of the central strands running through Novalis's diverse oeuvre is an abiding fascination with the interrelation and interaction between the intimate and the political. The collection *Glaube und Liebe* (*Faith and Love*) was written in early 1798 and published in July of the same year. It attempts to describe a polity based not on the constraint of the selfish individual (as theories in the natural law tradition would) but rather on the outward ripples of voluntary self-limitation.

Novalis insisted on the organic nature of the ideal state, postulated a desire for a reconciliation of particular and universal, and rejected social atomism and eudaemonism. At a moment when Friedrich Wilhelm III's accession seemed to herald a rejuvenation of the old Prussian monarchy, Novalis's fragments sought to point to a way out of the "machine-like administration" of traditional statecraft.[12] Given the level of theoretical abstraction, however, and given also Novalis's highly poetic language, it was perhaps inevitable that the text did not actually manage to intervene directly into its historic moment. Nevertheless, it was to prove influential down the line.

Novalis's text deploys what appears to be a straightforwardly monarchist model for ends that are actually deeply opposed to those that monarchist thinkers were developing simultaneously. Although the subtitle of *Faith and Love* is *The King and the Queen*, Novalis uses the duality (and indeed coupledom) of the two monarchs to forestall certain conclusions the French reactionaries drew from similar intuitions about the royal family and its relation to the state. Patriarchalists from the seventeenth-century political theorist Robert Filmer to Maistre and Bonald at the turn of the nineteenth argued that there was a mystery at the heart of the family, something that can't be penetrated by the reason of Enlightenment social theory. The very ground of the analogy of state and family (sovereignty) was providential and inaccessible to reason. Novalis agreed, but he attempted to identify the kind of faculty that could claim access to this ground. He turned to the concept of love as (1) the factor making state and family resemble each other and (2) the faculty by which the parallel between state and family becomes visible in the first place.

While emphasizing the inherent relationality that underpinned political cohesion, Novalis was careful to sidestep the hierarchical implications of these relations. He eliminated children from the picture (as Bonald would charge Jean-Jacques Rousseau with doing), and he substituted a semiotic relationship for the filial relationship. The bond between parents and children became that between signifier and signified. "A true royal couple is for the whole human being what a constitution is for the mere understanding," he noted.[13] A constitution, in other words, allows individual citizens to locate themselves in a system of rules and formulas. This is its great advantage and its great defect. For the individual's self-localization is always necessarily abstract, it is always mechanistic, and among the human faculties it speaks only to understanding. By contrast, the royal couple could symbolize, could make sensual, yes, could embody, the relation between the individual and the body politic for a far broader range of human faculties.

It is almost as though the French reactionaries and the early Romantics were looking at a reversible figure when envisioning the family: Novalis and his fellow Jena Romantics insisted on emphasizing the equitable aspect of the family (the couple) over the inherently inequitable one (paternity). Joseph de Maistre and Louis Bonald ignored the relation of husband to wife or attributed full dominion over his wife to the husband, acting as though families consisted only of fathers and their children. The Romantics gave the children short shrift, reducing the family to the couple constituted naturally—not through authority but through attraction.

Clearly, the straightforward paternalistic conclusions that Maistre and Bonald drew from the analogy between state and family lost all usefulness when confronted with such an elusive structure. And more important, the very analogy Novalis posits between (nuclear) family and state depends on the fact that the two are indeed noncontiguous. King and queen are separated by a wide gulf from the polity and only for that reason can they function as its symbol. It is apparent where the extension of the family, its branching, its dynastic side, even just children would become problematic in such an undertaking: their fecundity always suggested that a family could swell to the size of a state, that the family could plainly be the origin of the state. This is something Novalis clearly did not want to conclude—Friedrich Wilhelm and Luise gave him an opportunity to turn into symbol what otherwise threatened to become essence.

In the decades following Novalis's death, however, his friend and ally Friedrich Schlegel, who had initially turned to similarly complex methods to forestall an oversimplified analogy between state and family, gradually came to endorse the version of the analogy preferred by Maistre and Bonald. Even in Novalis's *Die Christenheit oder Europa* (Christianity or Europe), a text that attained a certain infamy as supposed evidence of his reactionary turn toward the end of his life, the indivisible Christian church he envisions is entirely divested of the paternal and the patrimonial: it is a lateral, all-enveloping community radically separated from the dynastic, from tradition, from received authority. German Romanticism's rightward turn, which Novalis did not live to witness, largely consisted in the breakdown of this radical separation.

Missing Children

While much of his work is preoccupied with the topic, Maistre's unfinished essay "De la souveraineté du peuple" ("On the Sovereignty of the People," written 1794–96) most decisively returned to the parallelism of family and state and adapted it for an age of revolution: "To say that sovereignty does not come from God because he uses men to establish it, is to say that he is not man's creator because we all have a father and a mother."[14] Fatherhood and royalty were not the same thing, but they structurally resembled each other with respect to Divine Providence. An individual father produces offspring, but the final cause of that offspring is Divine Providence operating through the father; likewise, an earthly authority makes laws and constitutions, but that authority derives from Divine Providence as mediated through the earthly sovereign.

Where patriarchalism in Filmer's mode had considered the parallelism between family and state literally, Maistre offered the parallel provenance of man-made legislation and biological offspring simply as a convenient metaphor. Others, however, made that link much more explicit. In 1801, Bonald, alongside Maistre the most important theorist of the French reaction, wrote *Du divorce* (*On Divorce*). His book critiques what he regarded as the deleterious effects of Enlightenment atomism and rationalism on human sociability, singling out Rousseau's philosophy of sexuality. Unlike Maistre's broadsides against Rousseau, which tended to focus on the idea of a social contract, Bonald was particularly concerned with the relationship that furnishes Maistre's metaphor—that between parents and their offspring.

Bonald took as his point of departure the claim that children are somehow missing from Rousseau's account of the sexual relationship. Given that Rousseau devoted an entire book, *Émile*, to the education of children, this charge may seem absurd. But Bonald's charge was not that Rousseau neglected children and their role in the family; instead, he claimed that in posing the very question of the sexual relationship between man and woman, Rousseau missed the point of family life ("domestic society," as Bonald called it) altogether: "Fathers and mothers [are] considered by philosophy as males and females."[15] Bonald thought that Rousseau treated human beings as sexed independent of, or prior to, the relationships to which their status within the family committed them. This threatened to reduce to mere biology the spiritual relationships that constituted social life. Only the family made men and women, and it made them men and women as fathers and mothers, sons and daughters. No one "enters" the "domestic society" of the family, just as no one enters society at large through a "social contract"—being human means being always already embedded in both kinds of society.

For Maistre and Bonald, the family constituted the hinge between the providential sphere of human essence and the political sphere. But it was also the primary form in which human common life is ordered and hierarchized: "The first man was king of his children; each isolated family was governed in the same way."[16] The family represented the irreducible hold of sovereignty over human beings, a sovereignty ultimately underwritten by God. And for Maistre and Bonald's German confederates, the dynastic family in particular became an emblem for the contiguity and multiplicity of our dependencies. In attempting to get rid of the dynasty, they thought, the French Revolution had ultimately sought to reject the idea of a society of mutually dependent individuals, the idea of a body politic.

For Rousseau, education in accordance with nature leads to ethical education, whereas for Bonald ethical education consists in canceling out the barbarizing effects of nature. Part of this civilizing mission of good parenting was an insistence on hierarchies. The family that raised its children according to the precepts of Rousseau's philosophical anthropology essentially would regress into something like an egalitarian pack of animals. Bonald's critique of Rousseau's theory of sexuality was intended as a critique of the French Revolution: once the bonds of the family were severed by the cold, abstracting materialism of the Enlightenment, Bonald argued, "political society was shaken to its very foundations."[17]

It seems to have been among the articles of faith of the anti-Rousseauist reaction in both France and Germany that a perverted theory of the family automatically entailed a mistreatment of the family in pragmatic terms. Not only did the Enlightenment think of the family as a disaggregated unit of particulars, but it also necessarily lived according to this idea. One of Maistre and Bonald's German confederates, Johann August Freiherr von Starck (1741–1816), made explicit that for the European reactionaries the demise of the family was causally connected to the French Revolution. In his book *Der Triumph der Philosophie im achtzehnten Jahrhunderte* (The triumph of philosophy in the eighteenth century, 1804), a gossipy, cantankerous, scattershot, and frequently ad hominem stocktaking of what the author considered the disastrous influence of Enlightenment philosophy on the eighteenth century, Starck presents the spread of revolutionary ideas as identical to the end of the family.

For Starck, revolution and the family's demise went hand in hand—had the European aristocracy cohabited in accordance with bourgeois morality, the catastrophe of revolution might have been averted. At certain moments in his giant tomes, Starck came close to being a conspiracy theorist, wildly speculating as to what might have possessed the crowned heads of Europe to bring to their courts the philosophes and propagandists of the Enlightenment, "who, as the worst enemies of the state and [the king's] own person, should have been banished far away." He identified women of high birth as among the main culprits: "Voltaire's conspiratorial project" was "pushed above all on women," who soon began "to fornicate intellectually with philosophism" (mit dem Philosophismus Geistesunzucht zu treiben).[18]

It was precisely the lack of family cohesion, Starck argues, that allowed the philosophers to infiltrate the royal courts: he remarks that "the lack of faith and the convenient moral theory preached by the philosophers were all too well suited to the tendency to complete independence so prevalent among our higher classes."[19] To hear him tell it, social cohesion was a bourgeois experience; the aristocrats of the eighteenth century lived atomized lives, which made them accept atomistic social theories that would have struck the other estates as absurd. Since the philosophers "knew the character of the nation, in which the so-called fair sex could accomplish much," they tried to reach the great men "through their mistresses."[20]

Maistre and Bonald's theory of the familial polity found its definitive echo in the German-speaking world in the work of the Swiss jurist and political theorist Karl Ludwig von Haller (1768–1854). Haller was a militant enemy of the French Revolution to the point of being forced to leave his homeland when France invaded Switzerland, and he was a staunch defender of sovereign royal power, from the Hapsburg emperor to the Bourbon monarchy. Haller's program is encapsulated in the title of his chef d'oeuvre: *Restauration der Staats-Wissenschaft; oder, Theorie des natürlich-geselligen Zustandes, der Chimäre des künstlich-bürgerlichen Entgegengesetzt* (The restoration of the science of the state, or The theory of the natural social state as opposed to the chimera of the artificial-bourgeois one), which he wrote over an eighteen-year period, from 1816 to 1834.[21]

As ponderous as the work's title is, its five volumes in essence sought to vindicate the claim contained within it: "artificial-bourgeois theories," by which Haller means largely the Enlightenment's natural law and Rousseauist social theories, had degraded the traditional social fabric and brought about the French Revolution. Such theories, he argues, were invariably founded on a distinction between a state of nature and a state of culture and on a transition from one to the other by means of a social contract or other implicit conventional subscription. Like Maistre and Bonald, Haller insists instead that human beings continued to live in the state of nature even when they lived in larger communities or states, that society grew naturally out of social instincts present among the savages untouched by culture.[22] From this reappraisal, an organic, rather than "artificial," theory of the state could be generated, by which the traditional state could be "restored" from its twin debasements by Enlightenment and revolution.

Haller followed Maistre and Bonald in rejecting the social contract and in claiming that the Enlightenment's theories of the state of nature depended on atomized individuals and the disruption of organically grown social structures. For him, the individual's a priori insertion into a family indicated that relations of domination were inevitably part of any human polity. Rousseau, and the Enlightenment generally, he charges, assumed "against all natural observation an impossible independence of *all* human beings."[23] He instead insists on an a priori dependence of human beings, ties that bind any human being no matter how savage and ties that necessarily structure social life hierarchically. As one pushed universal dependence back in time toward that elusive point "before" the social contract, that interdependence assumed increasingly familial features. Haller's examples come overwhelmingly from the sphere of family and reproduction. "Every human being is from childhood a subject," he claims. "Even before birth every child is imprisoned in its mother's womb for nine months." Once it successfully escapes, "it has two overlords already, neither of which it has made or endowed, and many subaltern commanders" (339).

Even once an individual outgrows the interdependence of the household, that person is likely to be drafted into new corporations, associations, and communities—to say nothing of that renewed interdependence entailed by starting a new family: "Should love lead him to marriage, he will be forced to relent often; a thousand new snares bind him" (340n). Family was thus the name for the universal servitude of human beings, for the fact that they are never as free as Rousseau's natural man. All that human beings manage to do as they age is to precipitate regime changes, shifting from one sort of servitude to another: "In short, man is born into utter dependency, becomes freer with time, changes the nature of his bondage [*wechselt die Bande*], runs through all manner of social situations, patriarchal, military, ecclesiastical authorities, societies or republics, with or without representation" (340n). Even the sovereign, who at first appears beholden to no one, is dependent on the grace of the divine Father above.

Indeed, Haller proposes that our inherited political language encodes the fact that state and family constitute one complex of variously rearranged dependency—and it was here that the question of dynasty explicitly entered the conversation among the German reactionaries. The Greeks, he notes, "used the term *basileus*," which he renders as "the foundation or the source of a people";

"*dynast* from *dynaeis*, productive power," and "even the word despot, much-maligned today, meant to them nothing other than the pater familias, the head of a family" (443). Haller's interest in the dynasty was only secondarily about the Bourbons, or about the restoration of dynasties—by the time he wrote, Germany's dynasties were, after all, restored. But he thought that the spirit that had sought to distinguish the sort of dependency characteristic of a state from the dependency of a child before its parents was still very much alive.

Franz von Baader, an eclectic philosopher from Munich and friend of Friedrich Wilhelm Joseph Schelling's, drew explicitly from Louis de Bonald's theory of the family in his work. He gave the thought of the reactionaries an explicitly German cast, deemphasizing the question of sovereignty and instead centering on the concept of love, as Novalis had. And where Joseph de Maistre and Bonald had, for all their misgivings about theories of natural law, treated territory as essentially brute matter that became important only as the reflection of a sovereign will, Baader sought to show that the same love connected a certain group to its land. In one of his fragments, he proposes that "just as God's love descends to Man," that love also "spreads itself horizontally as love of the same (brotherly love or love of humanity). Then it descends further and raises that which is below it—unintelligent nature and creature—to its level."[24]

Baader gives Bonald's patriarchalism a characteristically pantheistic and mystic cast—but when it comes to the effects of the French Revolution on the system he describes, we are back with the ideas of the French reaction. Modern atomism and "mobility," Baader claims, weaken the link between divine love and love of the land, dissolving the "marriages" that bind the human being to each. "It has come to a point," he remarks, "that people walk away from their ancestral inheritance [*Stamm-Erbe*], or find it leaving them behind, with the same carelessness with which during the Age of Revolution they left behind their dynasties."[25] A lack of sensitivity to the diachronic commitments entailed in family had brought about the French Revolution, and continued to dominate the age even after Napoleon had been defeated. For Starck, Haller, and Baader, then, the dangerous ideology was not one that severed children from their parents but one that severed the nuclear family from its dynasty.

The Dynasty in a Nuclear Age

Both Wilhelm Heinrich Riehl (1823–1897) and Adalbert Stifter (1805–1868) came from bourgeois families that were thrown into disorder by early tragedy. When he was twelve, Stifter lost his father to a carriage accident. The boy was then raised by his grandfather. Riehl was born into a bourgeois family and the old order. His father, Friedrich August, who had worked as a civil servant for the Dukes of Nassau, killed himself when Wilhelm was sixteen, throwing the family into disarray. Both men, the *völkisch* sociologist and the novelist, would write some of the most hymnic accounts of the family in nineteenth-century Germany. Both men's view of the family was deeply entwined with conservative, anticosmopolitan positions. And curiously, both men seemed to recoil from the nuclear family, seeing the family's larger social implications, its salvific potential, in the filigree of its branches.

Riehl argues, for instance, that "the family is the ground [*Urgrund*] of all organic formations in the personality of a *Volk*."[26] For him, concepts like morals (*Sitte*), culture, and indeed the very idea of an organic "personality" of a people make sense only as family concepts scaled up into a broader society. Riehl picked up on an idea that had animated Bonald and Haller: where civil society is premised on the idea of universal equality, the family remains the vital guardian of natural inequality among all society's members. When in *Der Nachsommer* (*Indian Summer*, 1857) Stifter has an adopted father figure say that "the family is what our age has need of, more need than for art and science, than commerce, progress and whatever else we might think desirable," then this almost certainly reflects something of Stifter's view. "Art, science, human progress, the State, rest on the family," he says, in a distant echo of the reaction from Maistre to Baader.[27]

In the 1850s, Riehl began his pioneering work in what he termed a "science of the *Volk*" that used the physical and social structures of landscape, home, and family to arrive at a sketch of a German national character. Riehl found the data for his studies by traveling through Germany, mixing general observations about, say, its forestland or the homes of its peasantry with detailed studies of particular milieus. In his preface to the first edition of *Die Familie* (1855), Riehl suggests that though he regards his work as scholarship, he wants a nonscholarly audience for it as well. "Call it something of an idyll of the German home," he says, and expresses hope that it will find its way into many a home, and particularly into the hands of female readers.[28]

For good reason: the book had a rather explicit message. Riehl regarded the prominence of the nuclear family as a symptom of social decline: the family that consisted of parents and two children crammed into one apartment building with dozens of others and ready to move if a nicer one opened up signified everything that had gone wrong in Germany. *Die Familie* was part of an antihumanist and anticosmopolitan politics. "It is in the nature of the thing," Riehl wrote, "that cosmopolitanism, ignoring of social forces, and underestimating the family always go together."[29]

Stifter was not nearly as dismissive of the nuclear family, but by some strange gravity his view of the nuclear always seemed pulled toward whatever the opposite of the nuclear was. In his stories, novellas, and novels, parents are constantly lost and substitutes found. Aunts and uncles proliferate, including those that seem to be simply called aunts and uncles. And many of Stifter's plots concern a young man and a grandparent (in *Granit* [*Granite*, 1853]) or even a great-grandparent (in *Die Mappe meines Urgroßvaters* [*My Great-Grandfather's Briefcase*, 1864]).[30] Knowledge, care, and sense of kinship rarely if ever accrue to or flow from the nuclear family: the further out into the branches they travel, the more self-knowledge they grant the individual. For Stifter, finding out how one fits into society—that great obsession of the nineteenth-century novel—is quite literally finding out how one is related to it.

But perhaps more important, whenever the nuclear family appears it quickly opens a terrifyingly wide window on both the distant past and the faraway future. Stifter is often understood to be the consummate writer of the Biedermeier ideology of interiority and privacy.[31] But for all his fixation on the family, his families are as nurturing as they are terrifying—and become more so as his oeuvre matures.[32] They persist uncannily somewhere between the picturesque and the sublime. For instance, Stifter's 1848 novella *Der Hagestolz* (*The Bachelors*, 1845) tells of Heinrich Drendorf, a young man who, having lost his father and mother at an early age, determines not to marry, despite being close to his adoptive mother and sister: "Who wants to marry, [and] carry the ridiculous fetters of a wife and sit like a bird on the bars of a cage?"[33] Before he leaves town to take up a position in the civil service, his uncle summons him to a lonely island in a nearby lake.

The old man, who himself has remained unmarried, impresses on him the importance of joining a family and thereby joining the human family. In the end, the young man marries, but his uncle doesn't come to the wedding—"everything is too late" for him. In closing the story, Stifter broadens the nuptials into a downright terrifying wide shot, taking in, it seems, all human history and the nullity of any individual within it:

> Then the sun rises again and again, the blue sky smiles from one millennium into the next, the earth wears its renewed green and the families [*Geschlechter*] descend by a long chain down to the youngest child: but he is removed [*ausgetilgt*] from all that, because his existence [*Dasein*] has not minted an image, because his sprouts [*Sprossen*] do not drift down the river of time. Even though he left other traces, they will expire as everything earthly expires. And when at last everything finally submerges in the ocean of days, even the greatest and the most joyful, then he goes under earlier, for in him everything is already in the process of submersion, even as he breathes, even as he lives.[34]

This passage encapsulates Stifter's thinking about the family: although profoundly fatalistic, his works are animated with a sense that the family alone may provide some respite, some minor transcendence. In *The Bachelors*, Stifter frames this transcendence in terms of a distant, almost cosmic future.[35] But in other works, such as *Indian Summer*, he links the vision of the family as a locus of permanence in an impermanent world, as a small immortality in an ocean of unremitting transience, to the nuclear family as well.

Indian Summer closes with another adoption, as Gustav von Risach presides over Heinrich's wedding and calls him his son. But again the marriage plot doesn't so much close the loop as throw it wide open. Besides Heinrich and his bride Natalie, the day turns out to be about a spectral line of descendants, one at risk of decline and degeneracy. "If marriages do not lead to a joyful family life, you can bring forth the highest in science and culture and it will have been in vain. [For] you are handing it to a house [*Geschlecht*], which degenerates with respect to morals [*sittlich*], for which ultimately your gift can do no good, which eventually will stop producing such goods in the first place."[36]

Stifter's families are characterized by two factors. The first is that they are defined by relationships outside paternity, filiality, or fraternity—parents either do not appear or appear in negative contexts. Children tend to be only children, or they reveal they have siblings only in asides. And whether it is knowledge, inspiration, or affection, it travels by more distant paths, from grandfathers, great-grandfathers, or even more far-flung relatives. By the same token, the families tend to reach across generations—*Bunte Steine* (*Many-Colored Stones*, 1853) has a few brother-sister pairs, but couples of the same generation, be they lovers or siblings, are rare. When Stifter has Risach in *Indian Summer* say that "the family is what our age has need of,"[37] then his fiction would suggest that by *family* we are to understand a broad, knotty, intergenerational formation, not the loving couple in which, say, Novalis had sought the foundation of political practice.

Riehl's *Die Familie* (1855) clearly draws from a similar line of critique, but both his target and his specific criticisms are no longer those of Haller and Baader. He has stopped being critical of the Enlightenment, let alone individual philosophers like Jean-Jacques Rousseau, but instead offers a critique of modernity in general. And he no longer suggests that modernity has lost the sense of *the* family as such, but rather that modernity has lost its sense for certain *aspects* of the family. For him, modernity's great deformation of the family consists in what he regards as its focus on the nuclear family and its home at the expense of the extended family, the family line, and the ancestral house.

Like the reactionaries of the Restoration era, Riehl was concerned that his age was witness to "a dissolution of family consciousness."[38] Specifically, he meant by this that the "individual companions of the 'house' particularize into separate groups: man and wife, the children, the servants, the hired help, etc." (142).[39] Unlike Haller and Starck, however, Riehl identifies this problem as primarily that of the bourgeoisie: aristocracy and peasantry hold on to a premodern conception of a "whole house." The "house as encapsulation of a common social personality . . . has had to make way for the atomization [*Vereinzelung*] of the family" (184).[40]

Riehl positions his critique of atomization explicitly as one of the bourgeoisie and of urban life more generally. His description of the family quivers with distaste for an age in which the home becomes an apartment, in which families move rather than expand homes as they evolve, or in which a family's social position frequently depends more on denying its forefathers than to carry forward their legacy. He excepts farmers and aristocrats from many of his points of criticism, lauding them for maintaining what he considers authentic German ways. All others, however, have truncated the house into a mere home and have truncated the clan into a nuclear family.

Riehl sees the vestiges of this disturbed and disordered sense of family all around him. He points out that the German word *Namensvetter* (cousin in name) suggests that surnames have a totemic power: names create potential relations rather than reflect them; in fact, such potential is "a moral idea" (eine sittliche Idee). The "name-cousin" is "a potential cousin, whose revelation patiently awaits the later research of the genealogist" (178).[41] The same goes for another practice common within both aristocratic and large rural families, Riehl argues: the recycling of first names. "Among the educated middle class," he writes, "there is absolute arbitrariness when it comes to choosing the first name; it is a matter of personal enthusiasm [*Liebhaberei*], not the family itself." Whereas in traditional families a single name may sustain the dynastic line for centuries, in many bourgeois families "it does not even last for a single individual throughout their life" (179).[42] Nicknames, rechristening, reinvention, noms de guerre, and noms de plume abound.

Stifter investigates the question of the extended family in his 1864 novella *Nachkommenschaften* (Descendants). The secret theme of the text may be what it means to be the descendant (*Nachkomme*) of one's forebears (*Vorfahren*). Like the apocalyptic ending of *The Bachelors*, the text is obsessed with the question of before (*vor*) and after (*nach*), even as the main character seeks to make his life and his art independent of his predecessors and successors. The reader meets a young man named Friedrich Roderer, who soon meets another man named Roderer—a cousin in name. As the story goes on, young Mr. Roderer becomes convinced—uneasily, at first—that this man, Peter Roderer, is a cousin in more than just name.

Nachkommenschaften frames family, art, and money as being characterized by a peculiar surfeit. The young Mr. Roderer is a landscape painter, even though he can't quite say why: "So I suddenly became a landscape painter," he begins, and immediately adds, "It is awful." The problem with landscape painting, we soon learn, is that there is too much of it, and the fate of the landscape painter is to add to that excess. Roderer, it turns out, is exacting in his creations, but by dint of the very type of aesthetic object he has chosen to create, he contributes to a deadening sameness. The terror of aesthetic overproduction is shadowed closely by another one: an overproduction, an overabundance of life that characterizes the family line. Young Roderer wants to calculate the number of oil-painted landscapes that will likely fit into what time is left of his life, and realizes to his despair that the number is altogether too large: "I am now twenty-six, my father is fifty-six, my grandfather eighty-eight and both are hale and hearty enough to live to a hundred. My great-grandfather, my great-great-grandfather and their grandfathers and great-great-grandfathers, according to my grandmother, lived to be ninety: If I were to live to be that old and keep painting landscapes, and if I don't destroy them and if I decide to display them in their frames, then I should require fifteen carriages with two good horses [to get them out of the house]."[43]

Roderer experiences art, family, and even money as caught up in a process of constant inflation. He has inherited wealth that, if he does nothing, will nonetheless keep growing; he has a talent that will easily fill his home with rather good paintings; he will live to a ripe old age and may even accidentally have some offspring. Just as his family's long history of longevity threatens to overwhelm him with the fruits of his own artistic productivity, so the Roderer line's incredible fertility seems to inspire something akin to claustrophobia, as he calculates that "I have a sister who has children, my uncles have children, which children will one day have children, such that upon reaching old age I shall have nieces, nephews, sibling-children, great-nieces, great-nephews, great-sibling children, great-great-nephews, great-great-sibling children."[44] The Malthusian sublimity with which the facts of the *oikos* tower over him strand him in a quintessentially modern position: precisely because he has too much family, he no longer belongs to it.

As passages like the one just cited make clear, when the family enters the story its very syntax and style become overloaded. Friedrich Roderer encumbers his narration with relations of all kinds; his sentences proliferate uncontrollably, buckling under the sheer lexical weight of so many words for consanguinity. In German, this kind of prolixity is often called a *Suada*, a word derived from the name of a minor Roman goddess of persuasion, but in fact Roderer's exhaustive family lists end up being less than persuasive. Against the nearly sublime horizon of distant relations, the narrator's language crumbles into repetitive, denatured verbiage: when the protagonist endeavors to "compare my Roderers with Mr. Peter Roderer's Roderers,"[45] the exponential procreation of Roderers becomes a syntactical problem, colonizing and overrunning the sentences like rabbits afield.

Whereas Wilhelm Riehl understood the totemic value of the family name in terms of premodern social forms, passages such as this one suggest that Adalbert Stifter regarded the inflation of Roderers as a peculiarly modern phenomenon. There is, for one, the curious way in which the Roderers, by dint of their very omnipresence, precipitate crises of meaning and reference. There is, for another, the aesthetic problem of the commodification of art and the multiplication of needs and offerings, which Georg Wilhelm Friedrich Hegel had already suggested was characteristic of bourgeois civil society.[46] And there is, lastly, the cousins in name, the source of Friedrich Roderer's persistent consternation. When he tells his landlady at a country inn about the coincident names, she fails to see the relevance: "We have lots of Meiers, Bauers and Schmids."[47] The repetition of names in a rural setting is normal and unremarkable.

Meeting another Roderer provokes anxiety in Friedrich, however. This is at least in part because the Roderers are a strange dynasty: the meanings of the three names the landlady mentions (Meier, Bauer, Schmid) can be traced back to a profession (dairy farmer, farmer, and smith, respectively). They are local and fairly generic, but they also assign the individual a place in society, something the Roderers have trouble with. When we first learn of them as a family, that is, about the fact that the identical name may signify a common ancestor, we learn about the strange family curse. Roderers, Peter Roderer claims, all seek to push themselves to excel in one area, only to fail and find unexpected success in an altogether different one. Individual will is superseded almost entirely by the fate of the family—and the family's spawn are consequently spread out across the world by their strange combination of failure and wealth.

In the end, young Friedrich Roderer finds his salvation not in art but among the Roderers. For all the claustrophobia that familial proliferation occasions throughout the narrative, in the end our narrator decides to stop worrying and love a Roderer. He marries Peter Roderer's daughter Susanna and burns his paintings and sketches. The only way to stop the runaway inflation and expansion of his world is to choose the family: yet not the nuclear family with Susanna but rather the absurdly extended one. As his new father-in-law declares in his wedding toast, "The Friedrich Roderer present here, the youngest of this name, has shown in recent times that he is an absolute Roderer. My daughter Susanna has also proved herself a Roderer woman [*Rodererin*]; today we bring these two together by marriage, and we expect that something even more Rodereresque will emerge from them than from all the other Roderers."[48]

With this characteristically ironized ending, *Nachkommenschaften* registers a certain discomfort with the dynastic line—certainly more discomfort than Riehl, Haller, or the French counterrevolutionaries would have evinced. Nevertheless, Stifter ended up typifying a certain strain of conservatism throughout the nineteenth century, at least in the German-speaking world: one that understood the rise of the nuclear family as a coefficient of modernization, of atomization, of democratization, and criticized it as such. As in the case of *Nachkommenschaften*, it isn't always clear whether the dynastic family is being held up as an explicit countermodel or simply as an Archimedean point from which to dislodge the increasingly entrenched ideology of the nuclear family. But in some way, the fact that it became a nonentity helped the dynasty become a tool of critique. It haunted the nuclear family as its distant ancestor, as a phantom pain.

3

Abortive Romanticism

Romanticism has had trouble growing old. Until today, studies of German Romanticism have gravitated toward whatever is early, pre-, or proto- about it. German Romanticism's later years, when the dizzy raptures of the revolutionary 1790s had given way to nationalism, clericalism, and political conservatism, are something of an embarrassment in scholarship, are avoided like an artist's inferior late output. When it comes to defending Romanticism, it's the forward-looking aspects of it that scholars fetishize, not the many arenas in which Romantics seemed ceaselessly born into the past.

In the *Athenäum*, the first of many Romantic periodicals Friedrich Schlegel conceived with various collaborators, there's a famous fragment that speaks of three "great tendencies" of the age. One of them was Johann Gottlieb Fichte's philosophy, another the French Revolution, and the final one Johann Wolfgang von Goethe's *Wilhelm Meisters Lehrjahre* (*Wilhelm Meister's Apprenticeship*, 1795).[1] But while the Romantics' diagnosis of their own age was susceptible to shifting loyalties, they had perhaps the greatest fealty to the idea of tendency itself: their age wanted—no, needed—to go somewhere.[2] "Everything today is only tendency," Schlegel wrote elsewhere. "The age is an age of tendencies."[3] However, it hadn't yet gotten there: "But whether I am of the opinion that all these tendencies are to be brought to fulfilment by my own person, or whether by my brother or by [Wilhelm] Tieck, or by someone else of our faction, or only by a son of ours, our grandson, our great-grandson, our descendant in the twenty-seventh generation or at the Day of Last Judgment, or never, that I will leave to the wisdom of the reader."[4]

The great tendencies, then, tended toward fulfillment. Perhaps not yet, not in one lifetime, but whether as problem or solution they would constitute Romanticism's inheritance, its family project. But the enormous space of fulfillment Schlegel maps out in this passage, his ironic deferral *ad kalendas Graecas*, emerged as a problem for the Romantics in practice. These writers were animated by a peculiar urgency that knitted together their lofty political projects and the indeed unprecedented ways in which they conducted their personal life, be it within erotic relationships, collaborative ones, or the "circles" in which German Romantics tended to organize. These were revolutions that would grow old well before they arrived at their great-grandson, let alone the twenty-seventh generation.

For early German Romantics, youth, immaturity, and impudence had important theoretical heft. The mere fact of growing older represented a kind of failure. It was a failure their contemporaries, from Goethe to Heinrich Heine, were only too happy to chronicle. And they preferred to chronicle failures in the terms and categories popularized by the Romantics themselves. German Romanticism and Idealism alike had derived historic self-evidence from an organicism suggesting metaphors of maturation and refinement, of internal logic and lawful progression. But the development of German Romanticism itself pointed to experiences of maturation cut short; of the regular course of life disrupted; of faces aged before their time; or of faces having aged somehow inorganically. In this chapter, I argue that this dual experience, one that held sway both among the Romantics themselves and among outside observers, came to define nineteenth-century thinking about the dynastic family, about sexuality, about procreation in Germany.

On July 8, 1822, Percy Bysshe Shelley set out from Livorno in a sailboat he had christened the *Don Juan*. Sometime that night, Mary Shelley was made a widow and for the rest of her career was left to grapple with the question of tendencies cut short. "At the age of twenty-six," Barbara Johnson writes, "she considered herself the last relic of an extinct race,"[5] a feeling to which she gave artistic shape in *The Last Man*, published in 1826. The novel is a symbolic restaging of Shelley's death as well as Lord Byron's and those of her children Clara (in September 1818) and William (in June 1819).[6] It represents a stocktaking of the thought, the aspirations, and the failures of the circle around the Shelleys and Byron.

But the story the novel tells isn't of failures brought on by intrinsic features of Romanticism—it is, rather, a record of promise and aspiration unfairly undone. In *Frankenstein* (1818), as Denise Gigante has noted, Mary Shelley allegorizes "the Romantic obsession with discovering the power or the principle of life,"[7] to understand why living things existed and were contoured as they were. In *The Last Man*, she sets out to think through a world where all normal organic development, all *Bildung* (education) and generational succession in human life, are disrupted.

In 1825, Goethe decided to revisit the notes on the Faust legend that had lain largely dormant since the publication of the first part of the tragedy *Faust* in 1808. In his play, he returns to debates that had raged twenty, sometimes thirty years before, and as witty and playful as his references to these debates are, one gets a sense of mourning. His onetime sparring partners are missing, but he isn't finished sparring with them. There had once been somewhere these debates needed to go, there had been somewhere Spirit wanted to move, but it never went there. Scholars have sometimes wondered whether Goethe's misgivings about the Romantics softened in his old age. But perhaps the better question is whether he simply wanted to return to a conversation with young men and women who drew from his work and seemed to him to misrepresent it in central respects.

Goethe had encountered members of this generation at the cusp of middle age and, as Nicholas Boyle has put it, regarded them as the "ambassadors of youth" itself.[8] He had encountered them when they had gathered at the University of Jena, where the spirit of the age had chosen to concentrate in hitherto unprecedented clarity, a place that Goethe in a letter to Friedrich Schiller called "the uterus of the *alma mater*."[9] And though he hardly agreed with them on most things, he had high hopes for their potential: in 1795 he expressed excitement that Friedrich Schlegel would be reviewing Schiller's periodical, *Die Horen*, simply because Schlegel was "a man of the new generation, for it looks like we'll never agree with the old one."[10] This generation—including Fichte, whom Goethe brought to the University of Jena in 1794, along with August Wilhelm Schlegel and Friedrich Wilhelm Joseph Schelling, for whom Goethe secured academic positions there in 1798—reappears in those moments of *Faust II* most concerned with generation and generations. And it appears in the form of ghosts of the 1790s.

In mapping out the realm of frustrated or disappointed tendency, Romantic melancholy constructed the spectral space beyond the nuclear family. When it came to the dynasty, Romanticism thus bequeathed a dual legacy to the rest of the nineteenth century. Early Romanticism had generally celebrated the revolutionary potential of the freely chosen bond between two people. But there was an equal—and as time wore on, more pronounced—preoccupation with the far more mysterious and multifarious claims that those beyond the immediate family had on the individual.

The Spiritual Dynasty: Schelling

The Monastery of Maulbronn lies in the Kraichgau north of the Black Forest. Founded in the twelfth century by Cistercian monks, it was secularized in 1556 and turned into a Protestant seminary. Behind the monastery chapel lies a small, walled-in lawn, where a single memorial marker stands. Until recently, the six-foot obelisk had been hidden by a rambling hedge of ivy, but today it dominates the space, flanked by a forlorn-looking birch tree and a mossy wall. It bears an inscription: "Rest in peace, you pious soul, until our reunion in eternity."

The woman memorialized by the obelisk (though she is interred outside the monastery walls) seems an odd fit for such austere, traditional environs. Caroline Böhmer-Schlegel-Schelling was as restless a troublemaker, as resolute a free spirit as a woman could afford to be in provincial Germany at the turn of the nineteenth century. She was born into an academic family, her father teaching theology and "oriental studies" at the University of Göttingen. As such, she grew up with an unusual amount of education and training by the standards of her age. She married early, was a mother at twenty-two, and a widow by twenty-four. In 1791 she moved to Mainz, where she hid a friend and follow literary translator from an abusive husband and entered a close relationship with the noted world traveler and noted Jacobin Georg Forster and his wife, Therese.

In October of 1792, Mainz fell to the troops of revolutionary France, and Caroline Böhmer, along with the Forsters, began the work of erecting the first republic on German soil. Once the Mainz Republic fell to the combined forces of the German principalities, accompanied in the field by Goethe, Caroline spent some time in Prussian jails or under house arrest. Largely persona non grata upon her release, she eventually married August Wilhelm Schlegel, the brilliant literary critic who may or may not have been homosexual, and carried on a possibly nonplatonic infatuation with his brother Friedrich. Together Caroline and August Wilhelm contemplated immigration to the United States, but instead settled in Jena, where they became the center of one of the legendary circles of early German Romanticism. Among the "Republic of Free Spirits," the "spirit families" established there, Caroline was perhaps the freest.[11]

In Jena, Caroline met Friedrich Wilhelm Joseph Schelling, the youngest and wildest among the philosophers building on the thought of Immanuel Kant and Johann Gottlieb Fichte. The two fell in love. By 1803, Caroline had divorced Schlegel, earning the sobriquet "Lady Lucifer" in the bargain, and moved with Schelling to Würzburg, where he accepted a professorship. Later, the couple relocated to Munich. And then, amid all these new beginnings, Caroline died. In late August 1809, Friedrich and Caroline had left Munich to visit Maulbronn, where Friedrich's father was head of the monastery school. "She was happy, serene, as always when we traveled," Schelling would recall.

During the trip, "she was quiet and seemed in a miraculous way reflective, even though her outward expression was always one of complete inner serenity. A hundred times I felt like asking her why she was so quiet, and each time I was prevented by our ample company from doing so."[12]

In 1800, Caroline's daughter Auguste had died of dysentery at fifteen, her only child to have lived that long. Her letters describe her and Friedrich's herculean efforts at finding something productive that would assist in processing their grief, in transfiguring suffering into joy. Then in 1809, Caroline herself suffered Auguste's fate. That September, she fell ill and declined rapidly. In the morning hours of September 7, she succumbed. She was buried in the old graveyard of the monks—the only woman in a brotherhood of men, and hers the only marker remaining today in what is otherwise just a lawn. Moreover, she was buried by herself: none of the children who had preceded her in death and neither of her husbands who followed her to the grave, nor the one who had died before her—none of her vast ghostly family were to keep her company.

Schelling was devastated by Caroline's death. Although he had regarded life in a biological sense, "only the bridge towards death," as he put it in the *Erster Entwurf eines Systems der Naturphilosophie* (*First Outline of a System of the Philosophy of Nature*, 1799),[13] he now experienced the loss of his wife as a philosophical as well as a personal crisis. On September 24, he wrote a four-page letter to Caroline's good friend Luise Gotter, and the way he informs her of Caroline's death is heartbreaking in how novelistic it seems—as though falling back on sentimental conventions were the only way he could make sense of what had happened, could inform Caroline's many friends. Conversely, his wife's death made itself actively felt in Schelling's philosophical work. As David Farrell Krell has pointed out, from early on Schelling had proposed a deeply fatalistic philosophy of nature as "monistic even as it kills the monad"[14]—but now the question of what justified this killing naturally attained greater urgency in his work. The seminars he gave in nearby Stuttgart in 1810 reverberate with the enormity of his loss, as do the drafts for *Die Weltalter* (*The Ages of the World*, 1811). But perhaps the most direct echo comes in a fragment that is either a dialogue or a novel, and certainly the philosopher's most literary work: *Clara, oder Über den Zusammenhang der Natur- mit der Geisterwelt* (*Clara, or On Nature's Connection to the Spirit World*), written in the immediate aftermath of Caroline's death, but published only posthumously in 1862.[15] *Clara* was a departure from Schelling's previous style. Unlike his earlier *Bruno, oder Über das göttliche und natürliche Prinzip der Dinge* (*Bruno, or The Natural and Divine Principle of Things*, 1802), it has an ambitious narrative structure. Even though the fragmentary nature of the dialogue leaves the overall story obscure, the work's mixture of plot and philosophical debate is reminiscent of the great philosophical novels of the turn of the nineteenth century—Friedrich Schlegel's *Lucinde*, Friedrich Hölderlin's *Hyperion*.

Clara is full of narrative detours, of romantic locales like churchyards and monasteries. Except that nothing happens in what Schelling actually wrote of *Clara*: what makes the text narratively intricate is that the relationships between its discussants have a complicated backstory. Where *Lucinde* and *Hyperion* are stories of development, even if not actual *Bildungsromane*, *Clara* is mostly a story of a development that comes to nothing, a past that lies stiflingly and hauntingly over the text's debates about the immortality of the soul.

Clara takes place across three seasons: fall, winter, and spring, each realigning the three concepts Schelling wants to trace: nature, the spirit, and the soul. Thematically, the first portion of the dialogue, set on All Souls' Day, a day of remembrance, a day of the dead, is the most pessimistic. It's also the most novella-like, in terms of both how much scene-setting Schelling engages in and how much incidental detail he provides. A priest and a physician (identified only by their professions) arrive in a small town to meet Clara at a monastery, where she has found refuge after the loss of her husband. She's drawn to the spirit realm; in her grief, there's very little that holds her in this life. There are suggestions in the text that the finished book would have concluded with her death.

The first conversation, involving Clara, the priest, the physician, and a clergyman, takes place in a large hall, where the characters begin imagining two very different families merging into one: the living and the dead, the nuclear and the far-flung dynastic. The hall's portraits, they observe, position long-dead ancestors as virtual brothers and sisters of Clara's. And the room itself—located in an institution that recognizes brotherhood and sisterhood across the chasm of centuries and is dedicated to rendering eternal the bond between the living scions of Clara's line and its long-defunct branches—suggests the great theme of the dialogue: that the divide between the living and the dead may not be sustainable or worth sustaining, that mortal life "would only be complete" if "those whom we call the deceased were not to cease living with us, but rather came to constitute another part of the great family." In the text's second dialogue, Clara and the physician agree that while Kant may have located the source of human autonomy among the noumena, true human freedom dwells in the spirit world. Only insofar as we are part of this broader spiritual family are we truly free (28).

Everyone senses that these two families are one *sub specie aeternitatis*, just as the brothers of the abbey are one brotherhood across time. But the question Clara raises is a quietly heartbreaking one: Why, then, can they not be together? Or, as the physician will put it in another dialogue, "Philosophers may well say: there is no death, in itself nothing fades away. . . . However, what we others call [death] still remains, nevertheless, and words can no more explain this than they can explain it away" (22). Throughout the text, Clara seeks to probe why this metaphysical truth, once recognized, cannot make itself felt in life. Although Schelling likely didn't mean for it to have this effect, her questioning remains the dialogue's final word: even if she grants the priest the suggestion that in death human nature, spirit, and soul are simply reorganized, and reorganized in a better, less iniquitous way, then this may be well and good for our animal nature and our spirit. But where does the soul find succor?

Ultimately, the cleric, the physician, and the priest each seek to defend the need for a separation between a dwindling physical family and an ever-growing spectral one, even if humanity's goal must be to transcend that separation. The cleric argues in a Kantian mode: to remove the boundary between the eternal world and our own would be to destroy what makes us human. But he also rehearses certain arguments that the proponents of natural law would marshal against the rationality of inheritance: we owe our moral duties to the living, precisely because they are mortal. Morally speaking, a debt owed to someone who is no longer among the living is self-defeating. *Clara* plays off living with one's dead ancestors against the necessity of cutting oneself off from them in order to recommit to immediate, living relations—and ultimately comes down on the side of the dead.

For the cleric is quickly sidelined in the dialogue, and the three remaining discussants—the physician, the priest, and Clara—assume the titular connection between natural world and spirit world. Each assumes that the kind of Kantian cleavage as performed by the cleric is not only infeasible but ultimately detrimental to one's humanity. After all, they agree, human beings have a natural and a spiritual side, and their spiritual dimension is by necessity connected to the soul, to the immaterial, to the memory, and indeed to the world of the dead. The dialogue's second section consists largely of a dialogue between Clara and the physician. The physician insists that nature itself is not sinful, that its creativity is not to blame for the destruction of all permanence. Clara suggests that in recognizing "the limitations of this world, the holier we will find each appearance of something higher and better within it" (29).

While Clara's grief thus passively opens her to a sense for what is permanent and true within the impermanence of the physical world, the dialogue also explores the active seeking of the spiritual. In the fourth dialogue, she proposes death as a transition to the spirit realm, but her interlocutors add magnetism (the physician) and clairvoyance (the priest). Given that the text gets even more fragmentary toward the end, it is somewhat unclear whether the reader is supposed to credit the visionary practices of the physician and the priest. We know that Schelling was fascinated with them; and before long, Friedrich Schlegel would become independently interested in such phenomena, conducting research about parapsychology with a set of wealthy religious women whom he regarded as his "soul sisters." But given that the dialogue was to conclude with Clara's crossing over into the spirit world by dying, it is possible that Schelling intends to position other means of reaching across the divide as ultimately naïve.

As Denise Gigante has pointed out, while many Romantic thinkers were drawn to vitalistic accounts of an all-pervading life force, many important figures of the age, like Schelling, Hegel, and Goethe, were opposed to such an idea.[16] Schelling's *Clara* points to why: an epigenetic vital force would mean that the transitoriness of all matter constitutes the last word—that it can't be blamed for the sufferings it occasions, that it can't offer hope that those sufferings may be transcended.

Schelling's *Clara* is an organicist text, but it extends that organicism past the boundary of organic life: death is not the end of *Bildung* but rather a transcendence toward a new, better arrangement of nature, spirit, and soul in the human. And it is the dead, the long line of ancestors and their traces within our world, that allow us to sense the foreshocks of the great rearrangement. Schelling offers being part of a spiritual dynasty, part of a family that combines the nuclear family of the living and the wider family of those who are deceased, as a way of coming to terms with how nature falls well short of its own supposed regularity and equipoise.

The "Universal Wreck": Shelley's *The Last Man*

About halfway through Mary Shelley's *The Last Man* (1826), the protagonist, Lionel Verney, sees his son off to Eton College. Rumors of a plague abroad in Greece and Turkey have begun to creep into the narrative, but in the England of the year 2090, life continues to go on much as it had in Shelley's day, and indeed in our own. Fathers drop off their sons at boarding school, reflecting on how these young people will one day take their place. "It was not long since I was like one of these beardless aspirants; when my boy shall have obtained the place I now hold, I shall have tottered into a grey-headed, wrinkled old man. Strange system! riddle of the Sphynx, most awe-striking! that thus man remains, while we the individuals pass away." Verney calls this, quoting Edmund Burke, "the mode of existence decreed to a permanent body composed of transitory parts." He adds, "Willingly do I give place to thee, dear Alfred! advance, offspring of tender love, child of our hopes; advance a soldier on the road to which I have been the pioneer! I will make way for thee. I have already put off the carelessness of childhood, the unlined brow, and springy gait of early years, that they may adorn thee."[17]

The reader knows, of course, that Verney will outlive Alfred, will indeed outlive every one of these children being groomed to take the place of Verney and those of his generation. The passage's Burkean fascination with succession, tradition, and repetition, a position Shelley herself was never fully comfortable with, exists only against the backdrop of a looming, catastrophic rupture of succession, against the backdrop of the "universal wreck"[18] of the human race. We know how this story is supposed to go, Shelley's novel emphasizes. There's meaning, order, and reassurance in it; and when Verney, "the last of the race of Englishmen,"[19] "the offspring of man,"[20] finally makes his abode in the Eternal City of Rome among its palaces, museums, and ruins—storehouses of a legacy he won't get to bequeath to anyone in turn—he finds himself deprived of all these things. "More terrible, and far more obscure, was the unveiled course of my lone futurity."[21]

Verney's existence at the end of *The Last Man* picks up on an insight that animates a chapter in Georg Wilhelm Friedrich Hegel's *Wissenschaft der Logik* (*Science of Logic*, 1812–16): life is not simply an object of contemplation. Rather, organic life and its understanding are braided together into the "Idea," a unity that undoes the opposition between subject and object.[22] Verney is alone, not just because there are no others like him (he contrasts himself to Robinson Crusoe in this regard), but also because his way of making sense of organic life is no longer adequate to his new world. His sense of his world is constituted by the concepts of life animating his relationship to young Alfred and his Eton playmates.

This is a problem Clara raises in Friedrich Wilhelm Joseph Schelling's novella: "Yonder... lies my everything in Its grave" (Dort... liegt mein Alles begraben).[23] If the beloved object is a microcosm of the *hen kai pan*, the organic nexus of all existence—yes, almost a precondition of one's stake in the world, in objecthood in general—then what happens when that object dies? When Shelley's Verney reminisces about his beloved wife, Idris, he exclaims, "Yes, divinity of the world, I read your characters in her looks and gesture."[24] "On every leaf, every small division of the universe," he reflects, "was imprinted the talisman of my existence—She lives! She is!"[25] But what happens to this divinity once every other human subjectivity is no more? The idea that love makes the totality of the world accessible as totality was one the German Romantics and their English counterparts shared. And for both groups, it was an idea soon confronted with the problem of how death, loss, and grief could undo not just this world but this very way of seeing the world.

For Immanuel Kant, the notion of an organism was bound up with teleological judgment: the rules of the organism, the relationship between part and whole, individual and totality could not be deduced according to mechanical laws. Instead, they must be intuited by supposing a purpose, even if, of course, empirical observation could never furnish such a thing as a purpose. Organicism thus dwelled both on the side of the object to be understood and on the side of the subject that could understand the object in this way. Jean Paul's "Rede des Toten Jesus vom Weltgebäude herab" ("Speech of the Dead Christ," 1796–97), Lord Byron's "Darkness," and John Martin's "last man" paintings all deal with the destruction of mankind as a challenge to thought.[26]

Therefore, *The Last Man* oscillates constantly between private loss and the loss of a totality, all humanity, all future. It is no accident that many of the passages reflecting on frustrated teleology vibrate with the echoes of the writings of Mary Shelley's own beloved dead.[27] *The Last Man* creates a fiction in which the loss of futurity entailed in the death of a child is at the same time a loss of the futurity of the species. But the point is that while the plague may be fictional, the connection between the loss of one child and the loss of the future of the species is decidedly not. The sense that a young person ought to have a future as an older person, and the sense that there ought to be a world after us that can ignore or seek to understand us, are one and the same. The plague makes this clear by destroying both.[28]

The novel's language busily shores up the organicism that the plague eventually destroys. Early in the novel, Adrian, Idris's brother, is sick, but Verney has "a presentiment that Adrian will not die; perhaps this illness is a crisis, and he may recover."[29] Indeed, the account of his recovery unspools a quick narrative of organic development, in a language redolent of human sexual reproduction—it's almost as though Lionel were birthing Adrian anew by bringing him back from his catatonia: "What a brimful cup of joyful agony it was, when his face first gleamed with the glance of recognition—when he pressed my hand, now more fevered than his own, and when he pronounced my name!"[30] The passage rehearses a kind of reverse rigor mortis, where becoming "pale and weak"[31] counts as an improvement rather than a worsening of the patient's condition. And at the same time, it entwines this language of undeath, of softened rigidity and "unclosing" eyes, with the language of childbirth, of infancy. Verney's description brims with processes that we recognize as rule-bound and teleological even when they are presented in reverse.

By contrast, the process by which Lionel Verney becomes the Last Man has no such logic to it. As Barbara Johnson puts it, "The Plague itself seems neither entirely unavoidable nor entirely avoidable."[32] The idea that changes in the world are effects of a progressive refinement of our understanding of that world had been the master trope in Romantic assessments of the French Revolution. The transformations brought on by that revolution represent delayed, refracted reflections or, as Hegel would put it, "realizations" of absolute self-consciousness. *The Last Man* describes a world in which all human self-realization remains unrealized, remains somehow shut off from having any effect in the real world. The novel, as Steven Goldsmith has argued, is antiapocalyptic in that it denies "the mind's power to dictate its own transcendence."[33]

The disaster that envelops Verney's world doesn't unfold organically. Yet while the "last man" trope around the turn of the nineteenth century clearly harks back to eighteenth-century fascinations with the sublime, the disease is in many ways exceedingly private: for a story of global destruction, *The Last Man* is extremely reticent when it comes to spectacular, overwhelming set pieces in the mold of Byron's "Darkness." The story of the plague's spread is entwined with the small set of interpersonal relations that the novel's main plot traces using the political questions raised by characters like Lord Raymond and the reformer Ryland, but it never arises causally from any plot development. And a reader familiar with Shelley's biography can detect, in the "strange story"[34] of the foreign sailor who arrives in England carrying disease and whose body must be burned on the beach according to custom, the real-life fate of the body of Percy Bysshe Shelley on the beach at Viareggio. The progression of the disease haunts not only the biography of Lionel Verney but that of Mary Shelley as a confused, indistinct echo.

The turn of the nineteenth century was rich in narratives of negative development, of degeneration, of slow, inexorable decline, of excessive growth leading to catastrophe. In its descriptions of global decline, *The Last Man* conspicuously sidesteps all of them. The novel Mary Shelley had drafted during her Roman stay in 1820, *Valerius, the Reanimated Roman*, would have trafficked extensively in stories of managed, organized decline and how to resist it. Yet the organic, the teleological, the purposive, haunt *The Last Man* throughout, even as the novel increasingly describes events that no observer, certainly not Lionel Verney himself, can understand in these terms.

Again and again, Verney has presentiments that turn out to be correct—all of them concern his fellow human beings, and none concern the plague. Again and again, the early sections of the novel fall back on a sense of how lives are supposed to unfold organically. Merrival the astronomer, for instance, "far too long sighted in his view of humanity to heed the casualties of the day,"[35] talks about humanity as though the disease currently ending it were merely a blip along a preordained trajectory. "While each one, having thrown away his sword with opposing shield alone, awaited the plague,

Merrival talked of the state of mankind six thousand years hence. He might with equal interest to us, have added a commentary, to describe the unknown and unimaginable lineaments of the creatures, who would then occupy the vacated dwelling of mankind."[36]

Consequently, *The Last Man* wavers with regard to how it plays off the nuclear family against the broader family of humankind. The early parts of the novel—Lord Raymond's wooing of Perdita and Lionel's own courtship of Adrian's sister Idris—rehearse the old Romantic defense of the romantic dyad over the larger family. Adrian's mother, the Countess of Windsor, daughter of the Emperor of Austria, represents a dynastic principle built on blood and obedience. Idris and Adrian clearly reject this idea in the name of a higher power, the natural laws of eros and inclination. Love necessitates a break with the past, with filial piety.

When it comes to the nuclear family, as Anne K. Mellor has pointed out, "Shelley's ideological commitments come into conflict with her historical experience of the bourgeois family."[37] In other words, Shelley understood as profoundly problematic the very sentimental formation to which *The Last Man* turns as a refuge. In her most famous novel, published in 1818, the monster asks Viktor Frankenstein to create for him a mate, unleashing in the scientist a fear that such a female monster may be "ten thousand times more malignant than her mate."[38] In other words, Viktor is already scheming how to bring femininity under control in a sort of monster marriage. But noticeably, his fear of her malignancy, while leading him to something like the nuclear family, ultimately has to do with his worries over the consequences of this union.

What Dr. Frankenstein had hoped would be a self-sufficient, paradynastic being demands a mate, and the nature of that mate and the nature of their bond are among his concerns.[39] But the concern Frankenstein reflects on in most detail is a racial apocalypse—the monster may well spawn its own dynasty: "Even if they were to leave Europe and inhabit the deserts of the new world, yet one of the first results of those sympathies for which the demon thirsted would be children, and a race of devils would be propagated upon the earth who might make the very existence of the species of man a condition precarious and full of terror." These monsters, he worries, would be like a disease: "I shuddered to think that future ages might curse me as their pest," who had threatened "the existence of the whole human race."[40]

By the end of *The Last Man*, the species has reclaimed its right. Verney's persistent efforts to insulate those he loves from the misery of the wider world, his repeated gestures of retreat and isolation, have come to naught. Whether it's his return to his family estate upon coming home from the campaign to Constantinople, seeking "happiness, love and peace"; the flight of the four final survivors to the villa in Switzerland; or his final escape with his best friend and his last remaining daughter, Verney's flight takes the shape of a constant attempt at reasserting the nuclear family, the private, the (Romantic) circle, only to have every panicked reconstitution invaded by the fate of humanity as a whole.

In the end, the "last man" finds a measure of purpose only in accepting his role as last of the species. He has mourned his loves, his family, his friends. Once he sets himself up in Rome, and before he decides to set out in a boat to see whether there are any other last men, he mourns what Burke would have called "all we possess as an inheritance from our forefathers"[41]: "I tried to lose the sense of present misery and present desertion, by recalling to the haunted cell of my brain vivid memories of times gone by. I rejoiced at my success, as I figured Camillas, the Gracchi, Cato, and last the heroes of Tacitus."[42]

Yet even in this moment when the long human dynasty remains the focus of Verney's hopes, when the past for him becomes one long patrimony, he envisions the future in terms of the nuclear family. He hopes that "this world be re-peopled" by "the children of a saved pair of lovers, in some to me unknown and unattainable seclusion."[43] A new start, in other words, in a new, thoroughly bourgeois and domestic Garden of Eden. He imagines the descendants spreading across the globe, a hopeful, redemptive version of the race Viktor Frankenstein imagines, then, after many generations, making their way back to the Eternal City, to wonder "how beings so wondrous in their achievements, with imaginations infinite, and powers godlike, had departed from their home to an unknown country."

Revisiting a Tendency: Goethe's *Faust II*

The address *ad spectatores* is one of the hoariest tropes at the dramatist's disposal. Johann Wolfgang von Goethe's *Faust II* contains one of its stranger instances. For as the first scene of act 2 comes to a close, Mephistopheles addresses the audience, and then a subsection of the audience—young people. He has just informed the assembly that a young man's project—one sounding a bit like German Idealism—is really just a rehash of old ideas, however revolutionary the young man may think it. But, he allows, "a few years hence this will have passed," and the ferment of youth will yield "some sort of wine at last." Then he addresses, per Goethe's stage directions, "the younger public in the stalls who fail to applaud":

> I see my discourse leaves you cold;
> Dear kids, I do not take offense;

> Recall: the Devil, he is old,
> Grow old yourselves, and he'll make sense![44]

> Ihr bleibt bei meinem Worte kalt;
> Euch guten Kindern laß ich's gehen;
> Bedenkt: der Teufel, der ist alt,
> So werdet alt, ihn zu verstehen![45]

Mephistopheles is issuing a command: grow older so that you may understand me. This is the old Goethe speaking posthumously and addressing two audiences separately—two audiences that are generationally distinct. Frequently, he thought in terms of generations; always, in terms of how he might get into dialogue with them. Goethe wrote of himself in the preface to *Die Propyläen*, the periodical on fine art he edited from 1798 to 1800, that he wished "to connect to oldest friends . . . and to win new ones among the most recent generation for the rest of his time on earth. He wishe[d] to save the young from such detours as he himself got lost in, and, by taking note and making use of the advantages of the present moment, to preserve the memory of meritorious [*verdienstlich*] earlier efforts."[46]

When Goethe returned to Romanticism in the last years of his life, he if anything intensified these premises. He had been a far less enthusiastic, far less convinced participant in the Romantic heyday than Mary Shelley. And much like his grudging acceptance of individual Romantics (and of their professed adulation for him) around 1800, his melancholic look back around 1825 was shot through with irony. The aging Goethe was no more convinced the Romantics were right than he had been in his prime, but that didn't change the fact that he seemed to miss them. To be sure, many of the young men he had interacted with were still very much alive by the 1820s. But their vibrant circles, their energetic interventions were largely gone.[47] *The Last Man* is to some extent a novel about ideas once full of life in the absence of such life. As Goethe neared the end of his life, he seems to have looked back at Romanticism's heyday in much the same spirit.

In "Markarie's Archive" at the end of his novel *Wilhelm Meisters Wanderjahre* (*Wilhelm Meister's Journeyman Years*, 1821), Goethe includes a note on the "Idealists of older and later ages." Its tone is surprisingly gentle, though its critique is rather forceful. Markarie sketches out an appraisal of German Idealism (and probably also Romanticism) before declaring it "of important concern" (von wichtigem Belang) but too taxing on listeners' patience. She leaves it at the following brief intimations: "A spiritual form is not in the least truncated when it steps out into open appearance, provided that this stepping-out be a true begetting, a true procreation. The begotten is not the lesser of the begetter, yes it is the advantage of organic begetting [*lebendiger Zeugung*], that the begotten may be more perfect that that which begat it."[48] This passage finds Makarie exploring the relationship between the ideal and its concrete instantiation as a *Zeugung*, a form of sexual begetting. But it also finds the author Goethe engaging with his own legacy, with things he created, sometimes even without meaning to. But his generosity is tinged with melancholia. The "Idealists of older and later ages" are no longer with him, "that which begat" has outlived "the begotten."

Goethe's texts of the same era show that the Romantics and the Idealists resurfaced as preoccupations in his thought in the 1810s and 1820s, and they resurfaced as their earlier selves, as past rather than current interlocutors. In 1817, Goethe and the French eclectic philosopher Victor Cousin discussed "Reinhold, Fichte, Schelling, Hegel, Herder, Schiller, Wieland"—Wieland had died in 1813, Fichte had died the year after, and Herder and Schiller over a decade ago. Hegel and Schelling were alive and well, but the way Goethe arrayed them makes it clear that he considered all of them equally historic.[49]

When he reengaged with Idealism and Romanticism in his late work, Goethe was fencing with the shadows of the 1790s. In a conversation in April 1823 with his friend Friedrich von Müller, he refers to the thought of Fichte, Schelling, and Reinhold, German Idealism's great vanishing act.[50] Carl Leonhard Reinhold had died ten days earlier, but it's clear from the context that Goethe did not yet know it. And it's further clear he wasn't thinking of Reinhold's years in Kiel or the linguistic turn in his mature philosophy; he was referring to the Reinhold he had hired for the University of Jena, and who left the post to Fichte in 1794. In an 1827 conversation with the philologist and art historian Gustav Parthey, Goethe runs through Kant, Hegel, Schelling, and Fichte, identifying each according to his position in the debates of the 1790s and early 1800s (by necessity in the case of Kant and Fichte).[51]

Goethe, fascinated by the mechanisms of intergenerational transmission and rejection, had always understood his relationship to the Romantics in terms of his legacy. (We have already quoted his remark to Georg Sartorius, "that the most recent generation is more in harmony [*Einklang*] with me than the middle one,"[52] which gives a sense of his understanding of this mechanism.) At the same time, Goethe was keenly aware of the fact that this orderly transmission represents a form of "progressive metamorphosis," and that a more "regressive" kind also exists and may well constitute the norm. In *Faust II*, very few things progress or metamorphize in an orderly manner. As Wendy Nielsen has pointed out, "Conception, birth and rebirth in *Faust I* and *II* happen by artificial means and follow their own fantastical logic."[53]

With some exceptions, then, Romantic and Idealist positions appear in Goethe's works of the 1820s as part of exactly that logic. His remarks about

Romanticism return again and again to Romanticism's and Idealism's supposed unhealthiness, their lack of life force. For him, this doesn't appear to have been a verdict but rather a source of concern. When August von Goethe died in Rome in 1830, the gravestone erected for him read: "Goethe the son died preceding the father" (Goethe Filius Patri Antevertens obit). Perhaps certain parts of *Faust II* must be read as the literary equivalent to this monument: reflections on an oedipal struggle in which the father comes out on top. To be sure, there is a tinge of literary survivor's guilt to some of Goethe's late work, but one transcended by a concern with the correct passing on of the efforts and achievements of earlier generations—a passing on he doesn't always seem to think worked as it should have. And in this respect, Mephistopheles seems to be among the faithful:

> Young must, for all its most outlandish antics,
> Still make some sort of wine at last.[54]
>
> Wenn sich der Most auch ganz absurd gebärdet
> Es gibt zuletz doch noch e' Wein.[55]

So he assures us in *Faust II*. The possibility Goethe seems to be contemplating is far darker: what if the reassurance carried by the Satanic metaphor of maturation were an illusion?

The question of legacies and the role of the organic in the organization of life and its residue come to the fore in a strange, beguiling figure that emerges as the secret star (and possible protagonist) of Goethe's great late work, *Faust: The Second Part of the Tragedy*. In act 2 of the play, Faust's erstwhile assistant Wagner creates in a beaker a creature named Homunculus. Homunculus quickly abandons its creator, choosing to accompany Faust and Mephistopheles on their sojourn through ancient Greece. Ultimately this creature, made to transcend physical nature, decides that true personhood can be gained only by congress with the physical: it shatters its beaker, begins a biological *Bildungsroman* in the waters of the Aegean, and departs the play. Homunculus enters existence as a being of deeply uncertain parentage: the play leaves it unclear whether Wagner is its true maker, even though Homunculus calls him Father, or whether the creature is brought about only by Mephistopheles' intervention, even though it calls Mephistopheles its cousin. But Homunculus leaves the stage as a paragon of gradual biological development: it's not content to simply leapfrog the Great Chain of Being; it wishes to go through that chain.

What or whom Homunculus might represent, pay homage to, or parody has been the subject of much debate. Clearly, it parodies a philosophical vitalism and its metaphors—as Jane K. Brown has suggested, metaphors that seem to animate Faust's own vitalism, especially in part 1 of the tragedy.[56] But the creature almost certainly also plays with what Denise Gigante has called Romanticism's "vitalist poetics," in which the spontaneous rule-making of poetic form mirrors how epigenesis rather than preformation explains organic phenomena.[57] In either case, Homunculus points up the futility of the hopes placed in spontaneous generation of rules. It's supposed to be a more refined form of life, more autonomous, a more thorough break with the past, yet it turns out to be exactly none of those things. This doesn't make it particularly anomalous within the context of either of the *Faust* plays. As interested as the late Goethe was in reproduction, transmission, and generation, and as much as his theories of morphologies committed him to some regulative ideals by which they ought to be governed, *Faust* rarely if ever relies on these ideals. If anything, the play partakes, as Gail Hart has put it, of "Goethe's poetic convention of discrediting heterosexual procreation."[58] As Wendy Nielsen has pointed out, "*Faust*'s female figures remain vehicles for procreation but never quite inhabit their roles as mothers."[59] Homunculus's creation fits directly into this pattern. But its eventual rejection of its own motherless creation and its search for "normal" development mark it as something of an outlier.

There's always been a temptation to think Homunculus is intended, like so many of the allegories in the two Walpurgisnacht sections in *Faust I* and *II*, as a reference to a specific thinker or group of thinkers. By the mid-nineteenth century, it had become a commonly held view that Wagner's project of alchemical reproduction represented (and perhaps parodied) German Idealism. Wagner's glance away from the natural world and toward higher, more abstract reaches recapitulated for many German Idealism's move away from the a posteriori, the world of experience. Just as Fichte, Schelling, and Hegel wrested the phenomenal world from the merely given and declared it at base a result of human autonomy, so Wagner seeks to wrest from nature its procreative and sexual power and re-create it under the aegis of the absolute subject.[60]

By the time *Faust II* was published in 1832, such literary echoes almost necessarily meant that readers understood Homunculus in terms of then-regnant Hegelianism. Søren Kierkegaard's early satiric play *The Battle between the Old and the New Soap-Cellars* (1837) presents a Faust surrogate named Willibald, who at one point seeks to create "a freak of nature under a glass bell."[61] The play's cast of characters includes a fly that sat on Georg Wilhelm Friedrich Hegel's nose as he was writing *Phenomenology of Spirit*.[62] When Ludwig Feuerbach's friend the philosopher and politician Karl Theodor Grün proposed that Goethe had discovered a "new human," Karl Marx and Friedrich

Engels sneered that this new human was in fact "but Wagner's homunculus." In a note on German literature of the midcentury, Friedrich Nietzsche dismisses the output of Karl Gutzkow and others as "the Goethean Homunculus" (der Goethesche Homunculus), a misbegotten creature that is a "fruit of Hegelism" (frucht der Hegelei).[63]

And indeed, the one group that seemed to find nothing wrong with the creature was the Hegelians—left or right, religious or atheist, they understood Homunculus as very much the moral center of the *Faust* story. As Karl Rosenkranz, one of the earliest philosophical interpreters of *Faust* and one explicitly indebted to Hegel, interpreted the plot of *Faust II* in the 1830s: the mysterious group of "Mothers" to whose abode Mephistopheles and Faust descend represent "probably nothing other than the world of pure thought"; Mephistopheles, on the other hand, represents the antidote to their abstract emptiness—namely, "the understanding, negative determining," which is necessary "in order to not founder in the infinite universality of thought."[64] For Rosenkranz, Homunculus precisely recapitulates their relationship: he basically puts Hegel's *Science of Logic* on the stage.

But if immediately after the publication of *Faust II* most readers tended to wield Wagner's misbegotten in vitro creation as a battering ram against Hegelianism, this was owed more to their own historical moment than to Goethe's intentions. Hegel had died the same year, and as the fight over his stature and legacy began to envelop German universities, it was almost inevitable that the little creature in the beaker would get drafted into the fray. The basic logic of Homunculus's appearance in the play sounded enough like Hegel's *Science of Logic* to incense Kierkegaard; but Wagner's ambitions for his creation, along with his creation's sardonic couplets, didn't really sound like the mature Berlin professor. They sounded like the early Idealists, like the Jena Romantics, back when those two groups were hard to distinguish. So perhaps it is a question not of whom the figure of Homunculus may represent, but rather of what the process bringing it into existence may be referencing—what sort of begetting is it to make a homunculus, and what would it mean to live on in that creature?

Just before Homunculus enters the scene, we meet young Baccalaureus, a broad parody of self-absorbed youth but one who couches his insouciance, his disrespect for what has come before, in a rather specific philosophical language. He declares "creatures of experience" to be "in no way equal [*ebenbürtig*] to the spirit,"[65] claims that "the world was not before I made it be,"[66] and declares of the devil that "he can't exist without my will."[67] Similarly, Wagner's vision of a brain that should "soon by thinkers be designed"[68] seems to combine the German Idealist conception of self-consciousness, Johann Gottlieb

Fichte's formulation of the action (*Thathandlung*) of self-positing, and a simple description of what being young is like. And when Wagner claims for his Homunculus the "dignity" (Würde)[69] that used to fall to natural procreation, he recapitulates Fichte's early lecture "Über die Würde des Menschen" ("On the Dignity of Man," 1794), given when Goethe brought the young philosopher to the University of Jena. Note that these references are largely to the *dernier cri* of German philosophy twenty years before *Faust II*—a "new" philosophy that, by the time Goethe wrote the scenes in the *Gotisches Zimmer* (Gothic room), was in fact well on its way to becoming old hat.

Goethe recasts the medieval phantasm of the homunculus for the Romantic age. He analogizes the self-positing "I" of Fichtean epistemology to an organic entity that can generate itself spontaneously and autonomously—that is, without recourse to external resources. The homunculus is an attempt at reproduction, but it's also an attempt to transcend any number of dualisms in the direction of a broader totality. This is why Goethe has Wagner rehearse a number of relevant unification topoi peculiar to the turn of the nineteenth century in explaining his homunculus project; Wagner insists on *Mischung* ("for on mixture things depend" [Denn auf Mischung kommt es an]),[70] a likely reference to Friedrich Schlegel's famous definition of "universal poetry" in *Athenäum* fragment 116. And he deploys the vocabulary of the organic and the crystalline ("and what she did organically at random, / We crystallize in proper season" [Und was sie sonst organisieren ließ, / Das lassen wir kristallisieren])[71] so frequently invoked by Schlegel's brother August Wilhelm and Novalis.

Wagner's main reason for undertaking this project of crystalline procreation is what he regards as the outmodedness of sexual reproduction:

> Begetting in the former fashion
> We laugh to scorn beside the new.[72]

> Wie sonst das Zeugen Mode war
> Erklären wir zu eitel Possen.[73]

He declares the sexual dualism and "begetting" to be "mere buffoonery" (eitel Possen), associating them with man's animal character:

> If brutes delight still in the former way,
> Then man with his superior resource
> Must henceforth have a higher, higher source.[74]

> Wenn sich das Thier noch weiter dran ergetzt,
> So muß der Mensch mit seinen großen Gaben
> Doch künftig höhern, höhern Ursprung haben.[75]

The idea that a new or true kind of eroticism should have a different kind of product, one "higher" than a biological one, was fairly seriously discussed in the erotic metaphysics of the time—most seriously by Franz von Baader, whose eclectic and far-ranging oeuvre Goethe was well acquainted with.[76]

In a fragment he entitled "Love Is Itself the Child of Those United in Love,"[77] Baader proposes two kinds of product that result from erotic union. The first is the biological one, reproduction—their love leaves the parents and assumes a life of its own. The second, Baader asserts, is love itself that is nurtured in the parents but cannot be externalized. What he adds to Plato's *Symposium* is the Romantic understanding of alienation: spiritual begetting is superior, because it doesn't create some external thing; its creation never faces the creators as an Other, but rather is always and inalienably a part of them.[78] For Baader, an "absolute" love union lies beyond the temporality of the production of a physical child—its ramifications are antibiological and antidynastic. The parents' product does not leave them and therefore is not itself sexually determined, capable of reproducing.

Although Wagner's talk of brains begetting brains obscures this point, the monumental scene titled "Klassische Walpurgisnacht" reveals that the "hermaphroditic" Homunculus transcends sexuality and cannot itself procreate—at least not until it decides "to begin creation anew" (von vorn die Schöpfung anzufangen).[79] For Baader, influenced by the seventeenth-century Protestant mystic Jakob Böhme, sexual reproduction is an index of mankind's fall from pre-Adamic androgyny. Wagner's project seems aimed at a similar kind of apocalyptic androgyny, while Mephistopheles constantly insists on seeing men and women (in the beaker, in Homunculus's wisdom). As Astrida Tantillo has pointed out, Wagner's impulse corresponded to Goethe's own, at least when it came to his works on botany: to understand gendered individuals, as Tantillo puts it, "we must begin by studying the androgynous qualities of plants."[80] The way Mephistopheles insistently essentializes gender dimorphism, wanting to see a "loving couple" in the beaker, thus seems to mock Goethe's own theoretical approaches as well.

In his *Erster Entwurf eines Systems der Naturphilosophie* (*First Outline of a System of the Philosophy of Nature*, 1799), Friedrich Wilhelm Joseph Schelling suggests that in sexuality, nature seeks to transcend the particularity of sexedness—the "product" of the erotic union is nothing other than the species in its androgynous and absolute totality. In bringing together sexed beings into an all-encompassing unity of the species, "nature demands the absolute and strives continuously to present it."[81] But nature fails continuously in its attempt at an "absolute" product; what it produces in its stead is particular, partial, that is sexed, products.[82] For Schelling, the cessation of sexual difference and the production of androgyny are brief, and immediately produce new determinations, sexed individuals that set out anew to cancel out their sexuality and produce an androgyne. "Since this infinite activity has to present itself in finite products, it has to return into itself into an eternal cycle."[83]

As far as Goethe's Wagner is concerned, he wants his Homunculus to function precisely as a stable and noncyclical elision of sexuality: the sexes are dissolved in its "hermaphroditism," without the undignified backslide into the particularity Schelling describes. Wagner's homunculus project aims at the exact same kind of unalienated reproduction, but of course that aim, once realized, is just as unstable as Schelling had feared. If biology and dynasticity are successfully sidelined in Homunculus's creation, they nonetheless begin to undo Wagner's creation well before it shatters its beaker on Galatea's chariot. Homunculus almost immediately rejects its "papa" (Väterchen)—a late and significant change in the text of act 2. Only a few pages after insisting that he's doing away with old-fashioned parenting with all its pratfalls in favor of something "higher, higher," the alchemical father Wagner is left in the position of a fussy parent:

> Farewell! My heart is sore, alack!
> I fear I may not ever see you back.[84]
>
> Leb wohl! Das drückt das Herz mir nieder!
> Ich fürchte schon, ich seh dich niemals wieder.[85]

Homunculus is playing out an oedipal scene without sex, rejoining the eternal line of the Verneys dropping their children off at Eton, in effect rejecting the very project of asexual reproduction.

No Newness May Betide

The process by which *Faust II* brings its homunculus into existence seems designed to lampoon a hope for overcoming the family, (the) generation, sexual business as usual. But it's a process that, as Mephistopheles and Goethe seem to agree, is always already doomed to failure: the endless erotic dynasty will win out. Wagner suggests that "begetting" (Zeugen) is a mere passing "fashion" (Mode), even "buffoonery" (Possen). There is something deeply comical about his consigning millennia of human sexuality to a fashion, but the word has a strange way of rebounding on him. Given that his creation depends on an assist from Mephistopheles, given that his creation Homunculus almost immediately rejects its creator and eventually chooses the laborious path of sexual evolution by shattering its beaker on Galatea's chariot, *Faust II* seems to treat *Wagner*'s ambition as a fashion, a passing fancy without much substance or staying power—especially because Mephistopheles declares Wagner's project "nothing new."[86]

The question of newness and continuity was a central one in natural science at the turn of the nineteenth century.[87] Biological theories based on the idea of preformation postulated that the gap between generations was always already bridged, that whatever was going to emerge through reproduction was predetermined before conception—in a way, as the biologist Johann Friedrich Blumenbach remarked in 1781, preformation "dispenses with all procreation in the world."[88] Goethe's Wagner frames his ambitions regarding Homunculus in precisely those terms: he wants to dispense with procreation but frames this dispensation as unprecedented newness. Joseph O'Neill has pointed to the political baggage that such self-creations had in the age of Goethe—Wagner's dream is to do away with birth as a mediation, a middle, a medium.[89] Mephistopheles reverses these terms: he treats Wagner's ambition as profoundly silly and of no consequence, yet nevertheless indicates that his attempted break with the past stands in a long tradition. Wagner's project, according to Mephistopheles at least, seems to distribute newness and continuity incorrectly.

It is seemingly no accident that the disputation about the status of sex and procreation, about their relationship to historical change, occurs right before and in fact motivates the trip to the scene in *Faust II* titled "Classical Walpurgis Night": a phantasmagoric journey across various ancient Greek locales thronging with figures from mythology, but which for all their overpopulation appear to have been carefully selected by Goethe. As Angela Borchert has pointed out, Goethe's understanding of the grotesque seems to have been positioned between two views. There were those who, like Descartes, regarded the grotesque as a mere grafting of two ideas into a simple chimera. And there were figures like Diderot, who regarded it as a play that generated genuinely new forms.[90] Borchert contends that the Classical Walpurgis Night stages a tug-of-war between the two views. The scenes in which Goethe appears to dredge up philosophemes of yesteryear are thus as rife with the promise of genuine newness, with what Hannah Arendt would later call "natality,"[91] as they are fraught with the fear that, as Nereus puts it in the Classical Walpurgis Night, humans may strive to reach the gods but are yet condemned to self-sameness.[92]

It also seems deliberate that the ideas with which Goethe engages in this parodistic, but surprisingly detailed, look at asexual reproduction are those of writers who frequently styled themselves as his heirs—writers who sought to build on what he had done, but whom he often suspected of having contributed little that was new or had staying power. In thinking about, and having fun with, the idea of creating one's heirs in a lab, Goethe comes face to face with his own ambitions to do something similar. This may answer an objection Katharina Mommsen once raised about the many candidates offered as models for the allegory of Homunculus. Apropos the Austrian scholar Otto Höfler's attempt to link that creature to August Wilhelm Schlegel, she raised a very commonsense question: Why would Goethe bother to comment on a position nearly thirty years old at the time he conceived of Homunculus—a position, moreover, toward which he seems to have harbored no particular animosity in the first place?

But if there is a certain *esprit d'escalier* in most identifications of Homunculus, that belatedness corresponds to the scenes in which the homunculus project is first introduced. After all, the scenes leading up to the creation of that creature are concerned not just with generativity but with generations— culminating in Mephistopheles' assertion that

> At last we after all depend
> Upon dependents we created.[93]
>
> Am Ende hängen wir doch ab
> Von Kreaturen, die wir machten.[94]

Mephistopheles' exchanges with the baccalaureus and with Wagner play off the promise of newness, on the one hand, and the devil's insistence that all this is mere repetition and old hat:

> Who can think anything, obtuse or wise,
> That ages back was not an ancient story?[95]
>
> Wer kann was Dummes, wer was Kluges denken,
> Das nicht die Vorwelt schon gedacht?[96]

Consequently, the scenes leading up to Homunculus's debut raise the question whether simply being newborn can ensure genuine newness.

Within the Classical Walpurgis Night, there is clearly a pronounced reversal of emphasis between what Wagner thinks he has created and what he ends up creating. The homunculus project of Wagner and Baccalaureus is to cleanse reproduction of vestiges of sexuality in favor of an all-encompassing mixture. Homunculus itself, however, feels it has been "wondrously just half-born into this world" (gar wundersam nur halb zur Welt gekommen)[97] and seeks to complete its own creation—not by transcending its own particularity but by becoming more determined. Here once again, German Idealist philosophies of sex emerge as an important interlocutor.[98] Homunculus's exchange with the *Kabiren* and *Tritonen* near the end of the Classical Walpurgis Night partakes of a debate over pre-Olympian Greek cults in the early nineteenth century—according to a line Goethe did not end up using in the final version,

> Gods who give birth to themselves
> and yet know not who they are
>
> Götter die sich selbst erzeugen
> Und nicht wissen was sie sind[99]

Schelling had contributed to this debate with his lecture "Die Gottheiten von Samothrace" (The divinities of Samothrace), which he delivered at the Baierische Akademie der Wissenschaften in October 1815, but which had widely circulated as a supplement to his book *Die Weltalter* (*The Ages of the World*, 1811). In his lecture, Schelling reverses his earlier picture of sexuality in much the same way Homunculus controverts its "project." Whereas the 1799 *Entwurf* had understood the sex drive as an attempt to transcend individuals in the direction of the undetermined and polymorphous species, from which they then tragically lapse into sexual determinedness, "Die Gottheiten von Samothrace" instead presents undetermined beings pining for determinate existence.

Indefiniteness, tendency without a concrete existence: this is how Romanticism often appeared to Goethe. The grotesques of *Faust II* to some extent warn that "the imagination is reproductive," that it invents by "only combining existing elements."[100] They have something virtual, precisely because they are themselves unable to produce newness. This is the sense in which Romanticism passed on a dynastic horizon into literary modernity: as a next step not taken, as a charge unfulfilled. Homunculus is born as a spark of the unprecedented that everyone involved seems to think is far more novel than it turns out to be. Wagner aims to consign certain rules of inheritance to the dustheap of history, only to find them hard to shake. And in the end, the lesson the clever little upstart in a beaker must learn is that going through the successive steps of *Bildung* (formation or education) can't be quite so easily foreshortened. Goethe imbues Homunculus's creation with a whiff of youth, immaturity, and faddishness; moreover, he steeps the process in allusions to the young people who would be his successors in the 1790s, but who failed to be anything of the sort. In other words, as in Schelling and Shelley, he describes eccentric organicism against the background of how such organic succession should by rights have unfolded.

Some such notion of succession stands behind Goethe's remarks of failed transmission as well—but as a telos, one that Romanticism fell short of. Consider a point he makes in his early morphological study *Versuch, die Metamorphose der Pflanzen zu erklären* (*The Metamorphosis of Plants*, 1790). Here, he distinguishes between "regelmäßige" and "unregelmäßige" or even "rückschreitende" "Metamorphose," or progressive and retrograde metamorphosis.[101] Progressive metamorphosis transitions from one shape (*Gestalt*) to the other, "as though on a spiritual ladder" up to the great "summit of nature, procreation through two sexes."[102] Albert Dietrich's *Botanik für Gärtner und Gartenfreunde* (*Botany for Gardeners and Friends of Gardens*, 1837) would cast this botanical process as follows: "how an organ prepared for a higher calling metamorphoses into a lower one," equating it with a "malformation" (Mißbildung).[103] In *Grundzüge der wissenschaftlichen Pflanzenkunde* (*Foundations of Scientific Botany*, 1820), Augustin Candolle and Kurt Sprengel point to environmental factors. To them, regressive metamorphosis means that under certain circumstances—for instance, if the plant is exposed to too little sunlight or is partly underwater—plant parts destined for a "higher" (i.e., sexual) calling (flowers, in almost all of Candolle and Sprengel's examples) actually turn out to be just boring old leaves.[104] This means that strictly speaking, "retrogressive" metamorphosis doesn't regress, except with reference to a teleological conception of ideal development (the "spiritual ladder" of which Goethe speaks). No petal backslides into being a leaf, in other words; instead, what *should* have been a petal turns into a leaf.

Goethe's relationship to the Romantic generation rests on a similar model of regression as a falling-behind in a morphological norm. In discussing generational politics, he frequently falls back on morphological categories of how intergenerational transmission is *supposed* to function. Owing to his interest in morphology, Goethe seems to have preferred contemplating *the* generation to thinking about generation as such—he was interested in steps and progressions, mutable but momentarily stable. Whether we look at Wilhelm's reflections in the *Apprenticeship*, Goethe's multigenerational mission statement in the "Einleitung in die Propyläen," or his letters with Friedrich von Schiller, Goethe seems to have had a very stable sense of how generations organically interact, how one grows out of the other. The grotesques of the Classical Walpurgis Night, of which Homunculus is a first precursor, are all indices of disrupted morphology. While Homunculus will undergo a *Bildungsroman* along the banks of the Peneios, the creatures it encounters there are precisely not subject to the normal, natural course of *Bildung*.

But even those members of the Romantic generation who didn't die young, or who were even to outlive Goethe, appear in such conversations imbued with a sense of potential extinguished before its time, of a progression that should have naturally occurred but failed to. A conversation at Johanna Schopenhauer's house in 1808, on suitable candidates for a Napoleon-like "emperor" of the "deutsche Gelehrtenrepublik," is drenched in a (heavily ironized) regret and nostalgia. Goethe suggests that he himself will be removed from the throne, and the pretender Friedrich Schlegel is already anointed—wrongly so, we gather. Christoph Martin Wieland and Schiller are dead and stripped of their titles by those who survive them. Novalis "could have been [an emperor] in time," but he died too soon. For his part, Goethe claims he hasn't grown attached to "empire and scepter," and that he'll "bear his dethronement with patience."[105]

Goethe's concern with the belatedness, with the out-of-jointness of succession in the age matters to us not just because the age is named for him. It matters because the age largely shared his sense of that time. His admirer Karl Leberecht Immermann, a novelist and dramatist, found perhaps the best formula for the problem. His 1836 novel *Die Epigonen* (The Epigones) is probably the last strictly Romantic work that sought to respond to the third of Schlegel's "great tendencies" of the age, namely Goethe's *Wilhelm Meister's Apprenticeship*. But as the title indicates, it's a novel about coming late to history, about being a grandson to greatness. The age, one character observes toward the end of the novel, "won't allow for slow maturation bearing immediate fruit. Instead, wild, useless saplings are pushed forward by the hothouse atmosphere that predominates, and they have to wilt in order to make room for a second, healthier generation of descendants."[106] The image of a wild profusion of "useless saplings" would dominate German thought in the 1830s and 1840s, in the wake of another great mind's death—as young Hegelians tried to figure out what being a Hegelian meant in the absence of Hegel. But, as one group among them found, an interregnum also constituted an opportunity.

4

Feminism, or The Hegelian Dynasty

What does a revolution do to the dynastic line? It would be easy to say that it simply severs it. The Romanovs in their basement and the Bourbon line on the Place de la Concorde would argue that revolution as event interrupts the flow of dynastic time. And yet in her discussion of the French Revolution of 1789, writing in that other revolutionary year of 1848, the German writer Louise Dittmar regarded the first fall of the Bourbon dynasty as an outcome of another dynastic process, entwined with the one enshrined in history books: "Avenging Nemesis follows the criminal through the centuries, before she catches him; yet she catches him not in person, but in [his] idea. Guiltless Louis XVI paid penance on the gallows for what his predecessors had thrown onto the compost to ferment."[1] As Dittmar saw it, the Capetian dynasty had been shadowed for centuries by another one, a dynasty of victims, avengers: the people, the common folk, the *sans-culottes* who would eventually feed their rulers to the guillotine. She's clearly being somewhat hyperbolic in treating both these dynasties as families, in likening accumulated injustice to the royal blood. But she does propose that the two, the dynasties and its victims, are alike at least in terms of historical transmission.

Although Dittmar pointedly uses the metaphor of putrefaction rather than reproduction, this, too, is an organic process, and like reproduction exerts a pressure lending the kind of force to an action that the weight of a royal line might. In the moment of revenge, she suggests, the revolutionary inherits this accumulated injustice in a way that resembles a family heirloom. Just as royal dynasties reproduce legitimacy and carry it forward, so do those who would punish them. Dittmar and many of her contemporaries were keen on providing a dynastic legitimation for the revolutionary break with the dynasty.

Feminist thought in Germany in the middle of the nineteenth century was forced to contend with a unique bind concerning the nature of the family, one it inherited from philosophy at that century's turn. The sexual politics of German Romanticism had largely understood romantic love as a break with the past, whether such continuity be embodied in the nation, the extended family, tradition, or religion. But socialist accounts of the family largely critiqued it in terms of its etiology, that is to say precisely by reference to national "spirit," to tradition, to religion, and to inheritance—often in the language of the dynasty. Early feminist thought in the German-speaking world took shape by negotiating and exploiting the thorny questions of history, agency, and family that arose from this ambivalence.

It was in this context that the question of dynastic legitimation became a topos of German feminist thought. Like most of the thinkers considered here, most early German feminists did not use the word *dynasty*, instead speaking variously of *Geschlecht* or *Haus*. But many of the more revolutionary among them made a strong analogy between intrafamilial patriarchy and the ancien régime. Both for them were forms of domination legitimated only by a long tradition of domination.

After the failure of the 1848 revolutions, there was a marked turn away from such lines of ancestry. Instead, most explicitly feminist writers in the nascent women's rights movement critiqued the family on emphatically presentist terms, refusing to speculate on the origins of patriarchy and emphasizing the noncontiguity of their own historical moment with the prior history of womankind. At the same time, however, those thinkers (usually men) who sought to link the "woman question" to the question of bourgeois rule more generally retained the earlier model, insisting that only by understanding the dynastic heredity of patriarchy could patriarchy be undone.

German philosophers in the first decades of the nineteenth century saw their role as reflecting on the ramification of the historical moment. Let the French act, let the realities on the ground in France change. In Germany, the old continuities would retain their hold, but the nation's thinkers could comprehend what was happening elsewhere. As Georg Wilhelm Friedrich Hegel put it in his *Phenomenologie des Geistes* (*Phenomenology of Spirit*, 1807), philosophies like his were fed by "the vague foreboding of something unknown" and aimed to understand "the heralds of approaching change."[2] By the 1840s, this sense had calcified as the "revolution in the Spirit," as Johann Gottlieb Fichte had called it, stalled out as much as its real-world analogue had.[3] Not only was German society failing to come around to the "approaching change" Hegel had spoken of, German philosophy was failing to critique it into existence. Dittmar called the 1840s "this half-liberated time" (diese halbentfesselte Zeit).[4]

Before and during the 1848 revolution, women writers in Germany frequently sought to entwine the dynastic question with that of women's emancipation. German feminism may well have been born in a double crisis of dynastic succession: the wholesale destabilization of monarchical rule in the 1848 revolutions and the move away from Hegelian philosophy. And the shape that early German feminist thought would take in the decades after 1848 to some extent grappled with that entwinement. The "woman question" implied an emancipatory break with the past, as Holly Case has recently shown.[5] Yet before 1848, women writers found it useful to insert their efforts into lineages, to construct for themselves an ancestral line. After 1848, they sought their legitimacy largely by breaking with such lines.

"A Change in Dynasty"

The historical moment when the question of inheritance raised itself for women seeking a new place for themselves in society coincided with a succession crisis in Hegelianism. Women participated in this crisis, and many early feminist texts in Germany came about in the turbulent post-Hegelian interregnum. But strangely enough, many women were on the side of orthodoxy, of continuing rather than disrupting a philosophical dynasty. The critic and philologist August Wilhelm Schlegel accompanied the rise of Hegelianism in the 1820s with a smattering of largely satirical poems. In one of them, he casts the new philosophical fashion as "Wechsel der Dynastie in den Philosophen-Schulen" (A change in dynasty in schools of philosophy):

> First had the I the pride of place
> Could stand no Thou nor He besides,
> And it deemed every Not-I nothing;
> The I makes all things right.
>
> Erst stand im höchsten Rang das Ich,
> Litt Du und Er kaum neben sich,
> Und jedes Nicht-Ich schien ihm nichtig;
> Das Ich macht' alle Dinge richtig.[6]

Schlegel is playing here with some of the characteristic theoretical moves of early German Idealist philosophy. He had known many of the protagonists of that heady period of German philosophy personally, and he manages to poke savage fun at them simply by rehearsing their ideas in rapid succession. It's the fact that one follows the other, the fact that they're "dynastic," as in Schlegel's title, that pronounces a judgment about these philosophies. His poem ends with the current ruler of the Idealist roost, Hegel:

> He teaches: what's actual is rational;
> The philistines love him for it.
> Who can say which new trick
> Can push the Concept off its throne?
>
> Der lehrt: was wirklich, sei vernünftig;
> Das macht ihn bei Philistern zünftig.
> Wer sagt uns, welcher neue Kniff
> Vom Thron wird stoßen den Begriff?⁷

For Schlegel, then, German philosophy's drift toward and inevitable drift away from Hegelianism constitute a change in dynasties. Just as Hegel's philosophy replaced Fichte's, and Fichte's Kant's, so something else will replace his. Which also seems to mean: whatever will replace Hegel's philosophy will be more of the same, another "trick." When Schlegel insists on the circularity of this process of dynastic replacement, he is refusing two competing interpretations of the mechanisms by which schools of philosophy may be thought to succeed each other. The more obvious one is the Hegelian interpretation, whereby succession vouches for a process of gradual refinement and clarification. The more covert one has to do with the fate that had, by the time Schlegel wrote his poem, already started to befall the dynasties of Europe: revolution. Schlegel even suggests that the ascent of Hegelianism is a kind of revolution: "For after it long talked about itself," he notes, the concept of the "I" "found its neck wrung."⁸ But in the end, of course, the revolution ends with another dynasty on the throne, with more of the same.

By 1845, when the shift away from Hegel anticipated by Schlegel's poem was well under way, Karl Marx chose to cast that shift not in terms of successive dynasties but in terms of a revolutionary break from dynastic succession. "The philosophers have only interpreted the world in various ways," he concluded his "Thesen über Feuerbach" ("Theses on Feuerbach," published by Engels in 1888). "The point is to change it."⁹ The meaning was clear: Ludwig Feuerbach had sought to play by the succession rules laid out by Schlegel; Marx would seek to dismantle those rules. Marx's "Theses" did not see publication until decades later, but their sentiment was widespread in the 1840s. Whatever followed in Hegel's footsteps would have to differ from him in ways different from how Hegel had differed from his predecessors. Succeeding Hegel would be no ordinary succession.

One of the most striking features of Hegel's account of the family in the *Grundlinien der Philosophie des Rechts* (*Elements of the Philosophy of Right*, 1820) is what he terms "the dissolution of the family." The family appears on the scene as the "substantial unity" of spirit, creates a household, produces children, and then seems to just vanish into what Hegel terms "civil society" without a remainder.[10] Elsewhere in this work, Hegel insists on the importance of primogeniture and inheritance, even of hereditary monarchy. But in the realm of the Spirit, it seemed, their role was a lot more troubled. Hegel died in 1831, and the question of his legacy began to be debated almost immediately. Eduard Gans, one of his more orthodox students, framed the question of succession, very much like Schlegel's satire, in dynastic terms: "Kant lived to see Fichte in his dotage, Fichte still encountered the youthful sharpness of Schelling, Schelling found Hegel growing up beside him and now survives him. . . . Hegel leaves behind a lot of spirited [*geistreiche*] students, but no successor."[11]

Behind the crisis stood more than just a sense that no obvious successor had been anointed. Rather, there was fundamental disagreement as to what exactly Hegel had bequeathed his followers, and what needed to be done to correctly inherit it. Followers of Friedrich Wilhelm Joseph Schelling who excoriated Hegel's philosophy as atheistic and politically subversive thought that in fact he and his heirs should be disowned altogether.[12] Partly in order to defend their late master in these and other controversies, some students of Hegel's assembled under the moniker Verein der Freunde des Verewigten (Society of Friends of the Departed One, the so-called Freundesverein) and undertook the first full edition of Hegel's works. It was the first time in the history of German philosophy that a group of editors sought to present the complete works of a thinker.

This effort was complicated by the fact that much of the Hegelian corpus existed only in synoptic lecture notes, from which Hegel had laboriously extemporized. As a result, upon his death members of the Freundesverein took the unprecedented step of "filling in" the texts with their own notes and recollections of his lectures. At the same time, the group's sense of completeness, as Walter Jaeschke and Christoph Bauer remark, was biased in favor of the mature Hegel, whom they had encountered in lectures—works that would have undercut or complicated individual aspects of Hegel's system of philosophy were systematically excluded from the edition. In the end, then, large swaths of Hegel's writings weren't included in his collected works; conversely, large swaths of his collected works had not, strictly speaking, been written by him.[13]

The Hegelian Left, as John Toews has pointed out, recruited itself from among "younger, academically insecure, and non-Prussian" thinkers.[14] Relatedly, the so-called Young Hegelians generally did not accept that Hegelianism ought to consist of a bringing-to-consciousness of something that had already been accomplished in reality. For them, "Hegel's conceptual structures were transformed from a history comprehended into a program for future action."[15] Rather than a terminus, they aimed to be a conduit toward a new time: their mode of inheriting Hegel took stock of a past in order to engender a different future. This, of course, made their thinking particularly attractive for reformers and revolutionaries.

Even though women were still very much excluded from the established university philosophy of the nineteenth century, the breaking up of the Hegel school allowed their voices to intervene more and more. One such voice belonged to Bettina von Arnim (1785–1859), scion of one of Germany's great intellectual families, respected writer and editor, and personal friend of King Friedrich Wilhelm IV. Von Arnim exchanged letters throughout the 1840s with various figures in the Young Hegelian orbit, and while her reflections on their theories will occupy us in the next section, it's worth paying attention also to the rhetoric by which she framed and accompanied the fraught acts of transmission and contestation of those years. Most instructive in this respect are letters she exchanged with a young thinker in Heidelberg, Heinrich Bernhard Oppenheim (1819–1880).

Throughout her exchange with Oppenheim, von Arnim casts her main concern as being for "the health of the Hegel school."[16] Her own thinking owed a lot to the Young Hegelians, above all Feuerbach and Bruno Bauer, but she framed her defense against critics such as Oppenheim as a concern with preserving the memory of the deceased philosopher. At one point, Oppenheim suggested that Bauer had "jumped away from Hegel, but ended up sticking to him like tar pitch."[17] It was a standard rhetorical gambit of the era, a criticism everyone even vaguely in Hegel's erstwhile orbit seemed to level at everyone else; and von Arnim's response doesn't so much deny that Bauer stuck to Hegel as deny the implicit and related charge that, even if that were so, it would be a bad thing. She would remain impervious to attempts to move too decisively beyond Hegel throughout the 1840s.

That also meant she was unwilling to move too decisively beyond the critique of religion. When the Young Hegelians sought to radicalize the political critique they sensed lay latent in Hegel's philosophy, they did so at first through a critique of religion. But as the 1840s wore on, that critique itself came under fire for ultimately aiming at the wrong target. When Oppenheim echoes that sentiment, von Arnim puts him in his place. The critique of religion remains a central aspect of radical philosophy, she argues, because "the Christian religion has become the Bastille of human common sense."[18] Of course, this critique, unlike the materialist version that sought to replace it, itself had a theory of family transmission—meaning von Arnim's positions on sticking with Hegel and sticking with the critique of religion were really one position.

The family romance of the Young Hegelians had a second familial aspect: it was through the critique of religion that they sought to cut the umbilical cord that connected them to the man who gave their group its name. The question was how thorough that separation ought to be. All the Hegelian Left agreed that through conceptions of the family, theological precepts had survived into supposedly secularized philosophy. The family thus emerged as a point where politics and religion most clearly coincided. Some Hegelians thought that their critiques of religion were simply gutsier, more thought-out versions of their Hegelian ancestor. Then there were those Hegelians who charged Hegelian Idealism with unthinkingly carrying theological legacies into a post-theological age, and who undertook to cleanse Hegel's thought of its religious vestiges.

Both sets of thinkers turned to the family as a place where the step beyond Hegel was most fruitful. Unlike the more conservative Hegelians of the Freundesverein, these thinkers recoiled from thinking of this step as one of descent and inheritance. The combatants of the 1830s and 1840s constantly charged that their respective target had attempted to move past Hegel but was secretly (and often unconsciously) repeating or extending doctrinal Hegelianism. Having inherited Hegel sounded like a threat to them: standing him on his head was many things, but it wasn't a metaphor for inheritance. Therefore, Marx could call his critique of "Bruno Bauer & Consorten" *Die Heilige Familie* (*The Holy Family*, 1845): in the 1840s, the sacralization of the family was both a problem for philosophy in general and a way to attack a particular philosophy.

The squeamishness of both the more conservative and the more radical camps went beyond the mere anxiety of influence: although only Marx's famous final thesis on Feuerbach makes the move explicit, the idea that it was now incumbent on philosophy to transition to something that was not philosophy was a common one among the Young Hegelians. It was a hard process to find a metaphor for, and whatever metaphor was settled on, it wasn't likely to be one of family. Von Arnim herself struggled with this question, but in the years leading up to the 1848 revolution she remained steadfast in defending philosophy that remained philosophy. Critique of religion remained for her the royal road to political reform: "A true revolution can only exist where truth fights against lies,"[19] and a critic of religion like Bruno Bauer is the "concentrated power of this generation, which has become flesh in him in order to destroy mendacity" and hypocrisy.[20]

Or, as Louise Aston, a younger woman writer in league with the Young Hegelians, would put it in 1846, "I know what kind of loss of dignity woman incurs under the holy protection of law and custom." That very holiness easily "turns into the amanuensis of brutal violence."[21] In her attack, Aston not only harked back to a recognizably Young Hegelian critique of society but also inserted herself into a lineage. Defending herself against charges of atheism, she claimed that her faith was founded not on the "authority of a religious figure [*Religionsstifter*]"[22] but rather on the "authority of all philosophers from Spinoza to Hegel, in whose company I'm content to be either damned or saved."[23] Rather than revolutionary, her faith was traditional—just not in the tradition the Prussian state would have preferred. And if that faith were to push her beyond tradition, who could blame her?

Inheriting Hegel

The nineteenth century was characterized by a general move away from blood as a carrier of inheritance and legitimacy, and toward nature as that carrier. Especially in Germany, where the pull of organicist thinking was particularly strong, the French Revolution was understood as the severing of a dynasty of the blood but often regarded as a continuation of a dynastic line carried forward—one defined by nature rather than blood. In many ways, revolution was understood to cut short an organic process of growth, development, and transmission, but in another way it was understood as itself part of such a process.

Just how this discourse played two kinds of legacies off against each other is made clear in Feuerbach's writings on the family and love. Feuerbach felt that society by and large shunned "genuine" marriages, that is to say marriages that exist because the partners united in them will them to exist. Society instead privileges marriages into which parties enter "even against their will, only as a consequence of a physical, moral or pecuniary bankruptcy,"[24] thereby "multiplying the number of unfortunate cripples in body and spirit into infinity."[25] No wonder, he wrote, that society privileges these pliantly dutiful offspring of pliant dutifulness over "natural children," that is, children born out of wedlock: "The children of Love," he claimed, draw their blood "not from the tepid water of a merely dutiful marital office, but directly from the well of Nature."[26]

In passages such as this one, several early German feminists seem to have taken Feuerbach to be making a dual point about legacies. They understood him to be saying that natural children disrupt society's mode of reproduction, whether that reproduction be a matter of religion, morality, tradition, or money. But in rejecting one inheritance, free love reactivates an older one: it connects humanity to its natural origins, be they classical Greece or the German fatherland. The orthodox Hegelian Eduard Gans, for instance, devoted a monumental multivolume work to the role of the concept of inheritance in world history. Gans suggested that the history of inheritance law constituted a gradual reconciliation of the principle of the individual will with the "naturalness of the family." In contrast, Feuerbach linked the naturalness of a love that interrupted the dynastic chain to the demands and values of a new age. In this view, to be a bastard was to be guided by a different kind of extraction—by one's human, classical, and national ancestry rather than by one's literal forebears.

By the 1840s, the last of the male von Arnim children had left the household, and the remaining four women—Bettina, Gisela, Maximiliane, and Armgart)—maintained a lively salon called the Kaffeterkreis (Coffee Circle). Fairy tales formed a large part of this circle's endeavors[27] and an important part of its politics. In the repressive political climate of the early 1840s, the fairy tale genre offered a ready camouflage for unwelcome political ideas, covering public speech in the veneer of genteel domesticity. The von Arnim women barely hid the fact that their fairy tales were intended as public interventions into the politics of the day. In 1843, Bettina wrote a book-length address to King Friedrich Wilhelm IV of Prussia, *Dies Buch Gehört dem König* (This book belongs to the king). It concluded with an in-depth report on the immiseration of the working poor outside Berlin's city gates—but it opened with a fairy tale.

A few years earlier, Bettina had undertaken *Das Leben der Hochgräfin Gritta von Rattenzuhausbeiuns* (The life of High Countess Gritta von Ratsinourhouse, 1840), an ambitious mix of fairy tale and epic elements, in collaboration with her then sixteen-year-old daughter, Gisela. It was discovered only in the early twentieth century, in the form of a typeset-ready manuscript. *Gritta* was not a closet drama, nor was it an amusement between mother and daughter: it was intended for publication, but either didn't get past the censor or was withdrawn in anticipation of that. Given that Bettina would, on one occasion in 1847, only narrowly evade imprisonment on account of publicly taking such positions, it's not hard to guess why the resulting text was not immediately published.[28]

The tale opens in a decrepit old castle. Its wood is worm-eaten, its drawbridge has been gnawed up by various pests, and its walls seem to consist mostly of rat warrens. Meals are served on the backs of rusty shields. The tottering edifice has already claimed the life of Gritta's mother, while her father spends his days working on a mysterious "salvation machine" (Rettungsmaschine), ransacking the house further in search of parts. And yet, what seems like decay, another nineteenth-century ruin as a figure of mourning, another story of the decline of an aristocratic family, turns out to be more complicated. The castle's ruin is inherent in its name: Ratsinourhouse (Rattenzuhausbeiuns) has been its name all along. Though a site of putrefaction, the castle remains a homey space throughout the fairy tale, its outlandish dilapidation a frequent source of comedy.

The Rattenzuhausbeiuns family is an old dynastic line at the end of its last branch. Its family tree is no longer organic, and the father's obsessive tinkering is a mechanical, linguistic extension of something biological reproduction once took care of. In a characteristically ironic passage, the German word for "great" in *great-grandfather* (*ur-*) transforms into the German word for "clock" (*Uhr*): "For he had a great-great-great-great grandfather, who, since he was great four times over, understood the craft of clock- and machine-making from the ground up; [this great-great-great-great grandfather] was made Count of Rattenweg thanks to a machine with which he healed [King] Peter the Pre-First of an injury."[29] All Gritta's castle and line have to recommend them are origins—all royal, paternal, and social authority brought to bear on the girl in the course of the story derives from absurdly removed origins, origins so original they themselves are *vorerst*, meaning literally "before the first" or "provisional." Things in *Gritta* can recede so far toward the origin that they're hardly there at all. Their legacy and legitimacy perpetuate themselves only by force. When Gritta won't do as she is told, her father remarks that "there should still be enough reeds growing off the high comital family switch tree to drive a cowardly girl's blood a bit faster."[30] The family tree functions as a mere source of rote discipline, of force, of wanton violence.

Castle Rattenzuhausbeiuns, as its name indicates, is overrun with vermin: rats, worms, spiders, and dust. But as Gritta learns toward the beginning of the story, generation after generation of these creatures have helped raise her in the face of paternal neglect. As an infant, the young countess got her milk from a rat's tail; she was guided around the crumbling home by rodents. In other words: Gritta has a second ancestry, one that, the story implies, has left traces in her physiognomy and her mind (her father, for instance, speaks of her "hare's heart"). But this ancestry is not organized as a tree; it legitimates itself through living spirit rather than dead letter, and it nourishes rather than demands.

When the rats take infant Gritta under their care, they make a solemn promise to her dying mother "in mine and in my brothers' names."[31] Given the life cycle of the common rat, by committing their "brothers" to Gritta's care, the rats commit future generations to this project. A brotherhood across time that is conceived nondynastically and that can make and reauthorize commitments even without being identical to itself: in the 1840s Germany this description would have sounded almost automatically like "the people." The

Middle Ages had known this as the *populus qui non moritur*;[32] the French Revolution, as the general will.[33]

The ancestral tree, the transmission of the castle from father to child, depends on a brotherhood of faceless rats; and yet those rats increasingly take over and indeed become the castle. In *The Royal Remains*, Eric Santner suggests that the doctrine of the "king's two bodies" survived the end of absolutism in Europe but in the shape of a second body of the people: the "surplus of immanence that oscillates between the sublime and the abject," as Santner writes, moves from the mystical sovereign body of the king to the equally mystical body of "the people."[34] The titular royal remains became transmuted into a series of abjections that European personhood had to wash its hands of again and again—grotesque, diseased, and putrefied. But the king's other body, the transcendent guarantor of divine law in a contingent world, became what Georges Bataille called "personal sovereignty," the self-possession of the individual.

Gritta was written at a time when the shifts Santner describes were still under way. Nevertheless, when it comes to the young countess Gritta, the people's first body nurtures the second: her personal emancipation not only depends on the crumbling of the aristocratic order around her—it's nurtured, in fact, by the forces of decomposition. That these forces take the guise of a family as well is surely no accident: *Gritta* is not a straightforward celebration of individualism. Self-empowerment comes from choosing to inherit, from picking one lineage over the other. The past, the fairy tale seems to say, is what you make of it.

The Dissolution of the Family

In 1835, Ludwig Feuerbach published his eviscerating critique of Carl Friedrich Bachmann's "Anti-Hegel." Bachmann, Professor of Moral Philosophy and Politics at the University of Jena, had attempted to juxtapose Hegel's concept of the family to the reality of actual families. In his response, Feuerbach scoffed that an agglomeration of defects and shortcomings hardly sufficed for the deduction of a concept. He asked, "Should crippled bastards be the philosopher's models, or rather the genuine creations [*die genuinen Erzeugungen*]?"[35] Offspring begotten by anything but genuine love are the true illegitimate children. Legitimacy rested on a *cutting* of dynastic lines, not their continuation. Feuerbach's broader point in his philippic against Bachmann was that the family was something created ex nihilo through logic rather than deduced from actual practice, either past or present. But he was, of course, also defending a legacy.

German reimaginings of the family at midcentury were antihistorical gestures: what mattered was the logic of the form, not its provenance or past practice. And it was an antihistorical gesture that wasn't confined to philosophy. In 1849, Malwida von Meysenbug (1816–1903), black sheep of her monarchist family, decided to cope with the end of the revolution by reading Hegel's *Vorlesungen über die Philosophie der Weltgeschichte* (*Lectures on the Philosophy of World History*, edited by Gans and published in 1837) with a neighborhood friend, one of the few women she was allowed to leave the house to see. She had read Feuerbach before the revolution. But it was the act of reading Hegel afterward that made her draw personal consequences: "For the first time," Meysenbug wrote in her memoirs, "I told myself clearly that one has to free oneself from the authority of one's family."[36] Domesticity was not a defense against an oppressive state—it was its extension. She decided on a path that would eventually bring her to the first women's university on German soil, later into exile in London and into the house of Alexander Herzen, to whom she became a confidante as well as a substitute mother to his children—a "family of free choice," as she calls it in her memoirs.[37]

The more conservative Hegelians had been worried about the correct way of inheriting Hegel and, within their editing of his and their own philosophies, cast the dissolution of the family as a risky moment in which proper transmission became most important. The Young Hegelians had taken the opposite tack, increasingly understanding that *Auflösung* (dissolution) to be a theoretical/methodological desideratum. For them, the family as a mode of transmission became thoroughly suspect. In fact, in *Die Zukunft des Christenthums* (The future of Christianity, 1847), Meysenbug's friend Theodor Althaus had seemed to suggest that all inherited rules ultimately alienated those they regulated, that in some way transmission inescapably produced illegitimacy: "When the fathers have freely elected themselves a hereditary monarch, then they are free under a lord of their choosing. But their sons, over whom the born monarch rules, are no longer free."[38] As his title indicates, Althaus meant this as a critique of "positive" religion, but he also applied it to human politics in general: "All Law originates as free action, but all free action of a community becomes necessarily Law."[39]

In *Das Wesen des Christentums* (*The Essence of Christianity*, 1841), Feuerbach proposed that what made the family "sacred" was its spontaneity, not its resemblance to some kind of divine plan.[40] For him, the Holy Family was family cleansed of animal aspects that early Christians regarded as fallen. As Albrecht Koschorke has pointed out, the nineteenth century was indeed animated by an increasing difficulty in balancing the spiritual aspects of the family (i.e., the ascetic energies of the early Christian church) and the increasingly emphasized idealization of lived familial cohabitation.⁴¹ Feuerbach attacked this neuralgic point: just as "God emerges from a feeling of lack," so does the Holy Family come from a sense of how biological family falls short.⁴² Most centrally, the divine father and son pair of Christian doctrine has one advantage over its terrestrial cognates. On earth, "one is the creator, the other His creation,"⁴³ which is not true in heaven. The family was a vestige of inequality, and always risked reinforcing inequality along generational lines. In contrast, the Holy Family is a critique of the family. Max Stirner gave this idea an existential hue: the Holy Family was a fantasy that kept the individual in an artificial state of unfreedom. The holiness of the family is now an indictment. As an ideal, it confronts the *Einzigen* (the ego) in much the same way that religious stricture once had: "a thing above Me . . . an Above-Me."⁴⁴ Love was nothing but submission and heteronomy in their seemingly most pleasurable guise.

Independent from one another, Malwida von Meysenbug's, Louise Dittmar's, and Bettina von Arnim's position in this confrontation was closer to Feuerbach than to Stirner. They felt that the Hegelian inheritance was worth maintaining, and they had much impatience with the widespread drive to be done with Hegel. And they ultimately seem to have suspected that to move beyond the critique of religion into materialism risked sacralizing history: maintaining a link with Hegel ultimately enabled them to more effectively break with the past. In a letter to von Arnim in late 1841, Heinrich Bernhard Oppenheim charged that the relentless unmasking of religious tradition among the Young Hegelians amounted to "affront [*Hohn*] vis-à-vis any historic sacrality."⁴⁵ Von Arnim, however, resisted: to her, the point of Hegel's philosophy was that history was the least sacred thing of all.

The Turning Point: 1848

The revolutions of 1848 brought women intellectuals and poets out of the domestic sphere and into the public sphere as never before. They put pressure on a culture of domesticity that previously had been unproblematically identified with the feminine. At the same time, when the German writer Fanny Lewald recalled the revolutionary year, she claimed that "no matter how much one recognized the intellectual legitimacy of women, seeing them appear personally in the mass of the people lay outside of the German national character."⁴⁶ Feminism in 1848 consisted not in the radical notion that women were people but in the even more complex one that women could be *the* people.

The most prominent women's voices, however, clearly endeavored to cast their political intervention in what the era considered "feminine" trappings:

Lewald herself was essentially a war reporter at the time, but she camouflaged her reports as personal letters and her politics in tropes of sentimentality. Bettina von Arnim turned to fairy tales and to personal letters she exchanged with Friedrich Wilhelm IV, but within these domestic genres was blunt to the point of recklessness. Few men would have dared claim that the king's advisors were turning him against his people, or that the claim of royal absolutism was essentially a deal with the devil. Yet she did just that and addressed her interventions directly to the king.[47]

But other women intervened in the debates of the revolutionary year by refusing the traditional genres thought proper for their gender. Louise Dittmar (1807–1884) was another reader of Bruno Bauer and Max Stirner, and was a friend to Ludwig Feuerbach. Feuerbach in fact had pressured his publisher Wigand into publishing the journal *Soziale Reform* (*Social Reform*), which Dittmar edited and which was the first German periodical to explicitly address itself to both men *and* women.[48] Dittmar's essay collection, *Das Wesen der Ehe: Nebst einigen Aufsätzen über soziale Reform* (The essence of marriage: In addition to some essays on social reform, 1849), combined social critique and revolutionary agitprop, and it made no bones about either fact. By making a philosophical intervention and a revolutionary one in her writings, she was poaching two traditionally male preserves at once.

At the same time, it was precisely her investment in post-Hegelian philosophy, and in staking out a place in it, that led Dittmar to connect a critique of the monarchy to a critique of the family. "Her feminism," as Peter Caldwell has argued, "was wrapped up in an attempt to lay the groundwork for a new Feuerbachian 'religion' of revolution."[49] But conversely, her revolution was one that also needed to destroy the familial basis of the old order. As she put it in a poem published during the revolutionary year,

> Trading in an older godhead for one that suits today:
> Yesterday it was "police state" then the "nation" thereupon
> Everything stays in the family, father dies and son rules on;
> Cousin quiet, uncle's daughter, it's about the dynasty.
>
> Nur den alten Gott vertauschen gegen den der heute paßt:
> Gestern war's der 'Polizeistaat,' heute ist es die 'Nation,'
> Immer bleibt's in der Verwandtschaft, stirbt der Vater, herrscht der Sohn;
> Schweigt der Vetter, schwatzt die Base, allzeit gilt's der Dynastie.[50]

Dittmar's *Das Wesen der Ehe* was notable for how explicitly it defended both the 1848 revolutions and women's emancipation as twin descendants of the French Revolution. "The Man is the Prince of the Woman," she wrote, "her absolute monarch."[51] This point is an old one, but whereas political theorists like Robert Filmer and Jean Bodin had proposed that the king was like a pater familias to justify absolute monarchical rule, Dittmar turns this idea on its head.[52] Like the philosophical defenders of patriarchalism, she proposes that monarchical rule and patriarchy within the family are cut from the same cloth, but she suggests that they are both therefore equally illegitimate.

As Stirner had put it in 1844, "The state ... is the extended *family* ('Father of the State,' 'Mother of the State,' 'Children of the State')."[53] As such, the family cannot furnish an Archimedean point from which to critique the state. Rather, any criticism made of the state is likely to apply to the family as well. Dittmar argues similarly, attacking monarchists and antifeminists in one fell swoop. To defenders of constitutional monarchy, she points out that "laws can only be made in the spirit of those for whom they are intended, so long as those are involved in making them." If this is not the case, "then the representative is a warden and not an organ."[54] Both the paternalistic state and the paternalistic family are inorganic. "In absolute monarchy everything is absolute: the state, the law, order, God, religion, Christianity, the cleric, the monarch of the school, the parents, the husband, servitude" (3).[55] A democratic republic, on the other hand, "makes all connection dependent only from the freedom of inclination" (3).[56]

At the same time, Dittmar suggests, those among the revolutionaries who called for republican government but were unwilling to empower women were undercutting their own demand for political emancipation. For what if nature or Providence *had* appointed men to make decisions for women? "Then," Dittmar suggests mischievously, it's just as possible that "the Prince would be the safest guarantor and representative of his people, and [said people] should place itself trustingly and without care into his paternal arms" (15).[57] In other words: so long as men insist that in the family woman ought to place her trust in her husband, men have no reason not to place their trust in their monarch.

While the rhetoric of the family and the state as immanentist and always reauthorized by the consent of those within them seemed to marshal the effects of the nuclear family against the forces of tradition, religion, and law, those aspects of Dittmar's essays of 1848–49 that would prove most controversial actually dealt with the dynastic family.[58] For on the one hand, she insisted that the French Revolution entailed a break in familial modes of transmitting legitimacy. But on the other, as we saw, she posited the revolution and its own descendants, the pan-European uprisings of 1848, as a crossing of two sets of dynastic lines. The revolutionary violence in both 1789 and 1848, she suggests, constitutes the dividends of centuries of oppression from the Capetians onward.

But if in Louis XVI a dynastic system of oppression finally met its end, the "avenging Nemesis," too, had a dynastic structure. In her biographical portrait of Charlotte Corday, the "angel of assassination" who went to the guillotine in 1793 for her assassination by stabbing of the revolutionary leader Jean-Paul Marat, Dittmar explicitly seeks to situate Corday in a quasi lineage of her own: "Just as Jeanne d'Arc, under her magic tree, received Mother Mary's call, so Charlotte may well have had, in her seclusion, her celestial forerunners."[59] Where writers like von Arnim cannily camouflaged their political points by confining and containing them in particular genres structured by emotions they pretended were apolitical, and spoke of the family when they were really making points about the state, Dittmar made no such effort. Her biographical sketch has a single point, and it's unmistakably resonant with the one made by von Arnim's *Gritta*: Corday did what she did not from a private, contained upwelling of passion but by drawing a conclusion from millennia of oppression.

For Dittmar, as embedded as Charlotte Corday was in the spirit of her day (she mentions Corday's readings of Rousseau, Voltaire, and Montesquieu), her rebellion had a prehistory not unlike that of King Louis's undoing. Young Charlotte, Dittmar says, constructed for herself an ancestry of "historic heroes" (geschichtlicher Heldencharaktere) through reading: Brutus, Judith, Mucius Scaevola. These were heroes of control rather than inspirations of passion. "Such images had the effect of steeling her spirit and giving her the calmness of soul that allowed her, in the midst of unleashed passions, to follow a sharply drawn path."[60]

Dittmar emphasizes the importance of this long-distant ancestry over any attachments in Corday's own life precisely because she sees her relationship to those ancestors as characterized by intellect and "soul" rather than by "passion." She explicitly resists any attempt at sentimentalization, the lure of suggesting that it may have been her love for a Girondist that motivated Corday, since this "habit" of understanding women "smuggles the drives of the quotidian into heroism."[61] As we might put it today: it domesticates and dehistoricizes political action. "Only by totally misunderstanding her person and her object can her actions be connected to a feeling" of love.[62] By responding to a dynastic prehistory, even if self-constructed, Dittmar thought, Charlotte Corday entered world history as a self-determining subject.

After 1848

In 1848, the dynastic question and the question of patriarchy posed themselves in tandem. In the wake of the failure of the revolutions, the retrenchment of the established order, and Germany's slow unification "from above," the connection the 1848 revolutionaries had made between freedom from dynastic rule and women's liberation came apart. Or rather, it largely disappeared from the writings of women concerned with women's liberation. It remained important for those whose true focus was on the "social question," and who considered the "woman question" an important subcategory of it. But as the first wave of German feminism took shape after 1848, it pulled away from the inheritance of Georg Wilhelm Friedrich Hegel. In fact, its proponents were largely allergic to the element of inheritance in general, the insertion into a dynastic line that had been part of emancipatory politics for Bettina von Arnim, Louise Dittmar, Louise Aston, and others.

This shift in rhetoric emerges most clearly in the strange career of the idea of the matriarchate in feminist politics. In the wake of 1848, the notion that Western culture (and Western capitalism) had grown up around the gradual repression of an original matriarchate became a mainstay of radical thinking—except, ironically enough, radical feminist thinking.

Karl Marx and Friedrich Engels had thematized the idea that capitalism and patriarchy were intertwined in *Die Deutsche Ideologie* (*The German Ideology*) in 1846, but that book had found no publisher. Thus, the most consequential argument in favor of this link came from the Swiss historian Johann Jakob Bachofen, who published *Das Mutterrecht* (*The Mother Right*) in 1861. Bachofen proposed that primitive society had been defined by "hetaerism," a kind of sexual anarchy without any laws concerning marriage or inheritance.[63] When such laws emerged, they transmitted honor, property, and descent matrilineally.[64] However, the civilizing process consisted in the gradual repression and indeed erasure of matriarchy. Bachofen described this process in approving tones, but most readers, perhaps influenced by his friend Friedrich Nietzsche, read what Bachofen saw as a story of progress as one of decline.[65]

Bachofen was ostentatiously uninterested in philosophy, but while his studies of the laws of inheritance never invoked either Hegel's philosophy of history or the philosophy of inheritance law promulgated by Eduard Gans, certain premises of *The Mother Right* are clearly Hegelian: history for him was constituted in and through the progressive elaboration of a particular concept, in this case one of masculine rule-based dominance. And the movement he proposes by which collective forms of right dissolve into highly individualistic Roman law likewise owed a clear debt to the Hegelian account of legal systems over time.

The notion that civilization originated in matriarchy left its imprint on Nietzsche's early writings—the programmatic 1870 text "Die Dionysische

Weltanschauung" ("The Dionysiac Worldview") dwells on the question of "hetaerism," but the term is nowhere to be found in *Die Geburt der Tragödie* (*The Birth of Tragedy*, 1872). This idea also shaped Engels's *Der Ursprung der Familie, des Privateigenthums und des Staats* (*The Origins of the Family, Private Property and the State*, 1884), the Marxist theorist Karl Kautsky's essay series "Die Entstehung der Ehe und Familie" ("The Origin of Marriage and Family," 1882), and many other classics of socialist literature. August Bebel, founder of the Social Democratic Party, drew from Bachofen's book in his *Die Frau und der Sozialismus* (*Woman Under Socialism*, 1879), while the French socialist Paul Lafargue's *La Proprieté: Origines et evolution* (translated as *The Evolution of Property from Savagery to Civilization*, 1895) drew from Bachofen in France. But in the wake of Nietzsche, more right-leaning thinkers took note as well: Bachofen's ideas influenced the German psychologist and philosopher Ludwig Klages, the thinkers and literary men gathered around the poet Stefan George, and the noted misogynist crackpot Otto Weininger. Bachofen had an impact on early ethnography and anthropology in the German Empire, on classical studies and psychology. And the American journalist and suffragist Matilda Joslyn Gage opens her book *Woman, Church and State* (1893) with a chapter on prehistoric matriarchy.

The case of Bachofen points to a broader development: there was a sharp divergence within the arguments offered for women's liberation in Germany in the second half of the nineteenth century. One emphasized the two terms of Lafargue's subtitle, *origins* and *evolution*, and the other fastidiously steered clear of those. From across the Atlantic, American feminists like Gage, Eliza Burt Gamble, and Elizabeth Cady Stanton could invoke the ideas and Charlotte Perkins Gilman could insert them into her 1915 novel *Herland*, but her German analogues largely chose not to. Whether it was the more bourgeois wing of the women's movement, the more radical movement around Minna Cauer and Anita Augspurg, or the socialist feminists, the lack of interest ran the whole gamut. There are a few exceptions—Clara Zetkin was criticized by Lenin for introducing socialist women's groups to Bachofen's ideas—but these are of a distinctly later date than the American appropriations.

The question is, Why were German feminists, particularly German *women* feminists, so reticent to link origin and descent to the question of women's rights? Where Dittmar had been only too happy to do so, the protagonists of first-wave feminism in Germany had a palpable aversion to historical explanation. In a passage in her 1873 pamphlet *Der Jesuitismus im Hausstande: Ein Beitrag zur Frauenfrage* (Jesuitism in the home: A contribution to the woman question), the feminist writer Hedwig Dohm frames the feminist struggle in Germany in the following terms: "We need a crusade against Jesuitism (not against Jesuits). Not to conquer a holy sepulcher, much to the contrary, to rid the soul of a demon. . . . To participate in this battle knight against the modern dragon 'hypocrisy,' as the most modern squire or shield bearer, is the entirety of my ambition."[66]

This passage points to an interesting duality in Dohm's argument: she overindulges in historical analogues, but she retreats from them almost immediately. Crusades, Jesuits, dragons, all these signifiers are briefly picked up, only to then be relativized: "Jesuitism," but not Jesuits! A "crusade," but not one her readers recognize. Dragon slaying, but "without a St. George."[67] History suffuses these passages but is waved away as quickly as it's invoked. This banishing move emerged as a central rhetorical strategy of feminist politics during the period of German unification. Dohm acknowledges that it's possible to try to understand the demands of feminists in terms handed down generation by generation. But at the same time, she relativizes the claim such terms can have on the present problem.

As Cynthia Eller has shown, "most first-wave feminists—both leadership and rank and file—never took an interest in the status of women in prehistoric times."[68] This is all the more remarkable because in the wake of Darwin, the issue of prehistory and origins was a far more dominant feature of the zeitgeist during feminism's first wave than its second, when matriarchy and matriarchal religion did make a decisive entrance into feminist thought. What the Marxist philosopher Ernst Bloch might refer to as the *Ungleichzeitigkeit* (nonsimultaneity) of the currency of maternal myths within feminist thought—the fact that it was avoided when its stock was highest and invoked once its fortunes had waned—requires some explanation.

In her book *Myth of Matriarchal Prehistory*, Eller has pointed to reasons why the idea of matriarchy may be a treacherous ally to modern-day feminists. We can speculate that these reasons to some extent guided early German feminists in steering clear of Bachofen's early adopters—yet this does nothing to explain why US feminists like Gage and Gilman evinced no such leeriness. Moreover, those who adapted matriarchal myths to feminist ends usually made some important modifications: (1) they turned the myth of progress into one of regress; (2) they tended to reduce the family to motherhood; (3) they amplified the role of religion in the transition to patriarchy; and finally (4) they downplayed the intimations of a promiscuity or "heterism" in prehistoric matriarchal societies. In their totality, such changes served to reduce the soupçon of sexual libertinage and allied the critique of patriarchy with the critique of religion.

It seems that this reticence to link origin and descent to the question of women's rights was peculiar to the German context and turned on the distinction between nuclear and dynastic family. While mostly male philosophers and political thinkers reached into the distant heredity to explain the sexual relationship in nineteenth-century bourgeois culture, German feminists just as fastidiously stuck to their immediate surroundings. In a speech given in Leipzig in July 1868, Henriette Goldschmidt similarly framed the distinction between synchronic and diachronic explanations for woman's situation, advocating that synchronic explanations are self-evidently more plausible than those that reach into some savannah-bound ancestry: "If those of us of late birth are still connected with those peoples who are separated from us not just by centuries, but through an infinite mass of unnamable differences, how much closer is the bond that ties each of us to the people and the time to which they belong."[69]

Viewing the individual determined by the world she inhabits rather than by unguessable ancestry was a cornerstone of humanism in the late nineteenth century. In Germany during that time, dynastic thinking was frequently tethered to a conceptual disempowerment of the individual, an antibourgeois animus, and an antihumanist project. Fields like anthropology, linguistics, Völkerpsychologie (essentially population psychology), and "race science" were often explicit in making this link. This antihumanism located etiology of most features of the present in the distant past, results of unimaginably long accretionary or hereditary processes, with present-day humans as the ignorant and largely powerless end point.

The idea that individual autonomy and the nuclear family's autonomy from the larger line of descent were similar in structure had been an important legacy of German Romanticism. The emancipation of the nuclear family from the dynastic family line liberated individual will, feeling, and knowledge; dynastic structures made these same faculties subject to long-dead wills, feelings, and knowledge. In much the same way, a conceptual focus on the nuclear family, on those relationships most unproblematically governed by feeling, by choice, and by reason, overcame the alienation entailed by acceptance of parameters blindly handed down from previous generations, and aided the individual in the self-realization of this autonomy.

A familiar ancestor can be discerned behind this emphasis on self-realization: the philosophy of Hegel, albeit a very different aspect of that philosophy. Hegel's influence had waned since the 1840s but remained influential in the more public-facing arenas of philosophy (i.e., legal theory and jurisdiction) and in political debate and popular history. In an 1868 lecture celebrating her fellow feminist Louise Otto-Peters, Goldschmidt invoked Hegel in much the same way Dohm used history in my earlier example. She failed to mention him with a single word, but then proceeded to give what, in 1868, could have been recognized only as an interpretation of his claim in the *Elements of the Philosophy of Right* that "the rational is actual and the actual is rational": "In the audacious hope that what has been recognized as rational will become real, she moves forward and pays little mind to current conditions, much less respects them."[70]

Hegel had held that at least considered in its "spiritual" aspect, each marriage begins a new family, and dissolves a previous one—a family must generate its formal laws from the individuals freely joined in it. If it were simply to respond to the formal laws and reasons imposed by prior generations, it wouldn't be able to function as a realization of human freedom. Only marriage can effect the "complete creation [*Stiftung*] of a particular [*eigentümlichen*] and real [*wirklichen*] family," while that "family" in a more expansive, dynastic sense (Hegel is thinking of Roman concepts like stirps and gens) is "nothing but an abstractum slowly slipping into the distance and becoming less real with each generation."[71]

The "antihumanist" position of the latter half of the nineteenth century was also always an anti-Hegelian or anti-Romantic position: not only did the meaning of the family not lie within its own confines, but its truth was to be located in that very distant horizon Hegel had consigned to abstraction and unreality. The meaning of the nuclear family rested in the dynastic family, in the heredity of the family concept itself. In fact, the very concept of heredity proved a central line of attack: Hegel had had difficulty with the notion of inheritance. He argued that the fact that a dead person's will ruled over the living, and that that will must be enforced by legal safeguards rather than the feelings and duties that structured life in the nuclear family, meant that "with increasing self-sufficiency of persons and families as a result of the dispersal of civil society," the acquisition of goods through inheritance "becomes more indeterminate as the disposition of unity declines."[72]

For popularizers of Darwin, for naturalistic dramatists and novelists, and for followers of Arthur Schopenhauer, quite the opposite was the case: descent and inheritance *were* the essence of the family. Both the male socialists invoking Bachofen and the female reformers studiously avoiding Bachofen saw themselves as resisting a kind of determinism. And it was precisely the question of inheritance and determination on which they diverged.

One of Bachofen's most central pieces of evidence in *The Mother Right* is the case of the Lycians of Asia Minor, who, as the historian Nicolaus of Damascus (first century BC) claimed, "name[d] themselves after the mother, and [left] their inheritance to their daughters, not their sons."[73] The question of how and why the Lycians did so, and more important, why they stopped, is of course the overriding question of Bachofen's book. But in the wake of

Hegel and the materialist critique of his thought, this question intersected with a more basic one—namely, the essence of inheritance.

In one of his characteristically caustic notes in *Der Ursprung der Familie, des Privateigenthums und des Staats* (*The Origin of the Family, Private Property, and the State*, 1884), Friedrich Engels attacks the German social democratic leader Ferdinand Lassalle's *System der Erworbenen Rechte* (System of acquired rights, 1861), because "as a faithful Old Hegelian, he derives Roman law not from the social relations of the Romans, but from the 'speculative concept' of will."[74] In other words, Lassalle thought that the law of inheritance was primarily about the individual's wish to preserve the contents of his will even beyond death; the property being passed on was secondary to the "logical" content of the testament. But more troublingly for Engels, Lassalle risked substituting an intellectual teleology for a biological one—one in which the individual received problems and ideas rather than markers and attributes.

In other words, it was clear women's lot was determined—but did the factors that determined it hail from distant prehistory, or did they come from the more recent past? And were they by this token quickly reversible? As Goldschmidt puts it in her speech on Peters, the idea is "that Woman is an expression of the Spirit of a People [*Volksgeist*]"; her status is created and recreated at each historical moment, and as the spirit undergoes a process of education (*Bildung*), so her status is transformed.[75] Some pop Hegelianism of this type was a standard feature of German intellectual life outside the university at midcentury. However, I would suggest that Goldschmidt is rather careful in her borrowing. For Hegel does three things for her, as the following passage makes clear: "The Fatherland, into which each person is born as they are into their family, this first condition of our being, which you come to in the way you come to father and mother: we Germans had to give birth to and create it in ourselves."[76]

First, Hegel helps her deny that precedent and heredity carry any weight other than dead objectivity to be worked away by the national subject. Second, he helps her keep the focus on the world passed on by one's parents and the ways in which one can then transform that world. Rather than an inheritance from ancient ancestors, the mandates by which we live and against which we rebel are recent inventions. Just as a family resets its fortunes with each nuclear iteration, so can a national spirit cast the dice anew. But finally, she argues, in the specific case of Germany, the immediate family is not something found but rather something "we had to give birth to and create . . . in ourselves." That German spirit of which Goldschmidt takes herself to be a descendant she claims to have given birth to in the first place. National genesis is still a work in progress, so why should women's roles in the new nation be set in stone?

Especially after 1871, this is a strong undercurrent in the rhetoric of nuclearity in feminist thought: as the national project was gradually realized, the interesting questions revolved around paternity (the fatherland of which Goldschmidt speaks), filiality, and brotherhood. The national project served to compress the timetable looking backward—women's roles are presented as being circumscribed not by decisions made in ancient Asia Minor but by far more local factors—and looking forward—specifically, women's social position could be improved without outright revolution. But through it all, there was a palpable discomfort with determinism: for where Engels had regarded Lassalle's Hegelianism as overly deterministic, many early German feminists, including socialists, seemed to view Marxism in much the same way.

In a journal entry dated June 30, 1912, Minna Cauer notes that while "the study of Marx has always interested me a great deal," she "cannot jump out of my bourgeois skin, no matter how distant I've grown apart from bourgeois society and its world view."[77] Specifically, she worries about the viewpoint that would "deduce everything and anything from economic foundations," and adds, "I remain convinced that infinite things are inexplicable, and that the inexplicable is often far more important and consequential than that what we deduce by plan or law." At the center of women's position in society, at the center of any efforts to change it, was something ultimately indeterminate, not deducible—something more intimate than probability, iteration, and the law of large numbers would suggest. Something personal in a double sense: something one's own, but also something that is not historically inherited.

5

Wagner, or The Bourgeois Dynasty

The composer Richard Wagner's relationship to bourgeois life-forms was deeply ambivalent. This ambivalence is clear in his treatment of the nuclear family, but it characterizes his art much more broadly. On the one hand, he intended his art as a potent rebuke to the kind of music the bourgeoisie had decided it could live with. In the first half of the nineteenth century, a new economy of composition established itself in Germany: whereas previously, composers had lived at the mercy of sundry courts, now they were entrepreneurs at the mercy of the market. Wagner almost ostentatiously refused to participate in this market. At the same time, his refusal took the shape of a strategy cobbled together from premodern elements and ones that seemed to anticipate the twentieth century. Wagner relied on the patronage of King Ludwig II of Bavaria in a way that far outstripped more traditional composer-patron relationships, such as Haydn's to Count Esterhazy. At the same time, he relied on branding that anticipated modern marketing: a "family business," as Nicholas Vazonyi has put it, that did not begin with the Bavarian town of Bayreuth but simply culminated in the *Festspielhaus* (festival theater).[1]

As Theodor W. Adorno once noted, "The power of the bourgeoisie over Wagner is so absolute that as a bourgeois he finds himself unable to satisfy the requirements of bourgeois respectability."[2] He was, from his beginnings in Magdeburg and in Riga of the Russian Empire, a bit of a confidence man, given to racking up debts and equally given to running away from them. His aesthetic innovations tended to start off visionary and turn out quite expensive. His contemporaries already noticed that his monumental operas might have laid claim to a certain archaic authenticity—for instance, he described *Parsifal* (1882) as a Festival Play for the Consecration of of the Stage (*Bühnenweihfestspiel*) rather than an opera—but behind the scenes they revealed themselves to be the products of the industrial age. As George Bernard Shaw once wrote, "A presentable performance of The Ring is a big undertaking only in the sense in which the construction of a railway is a big undertaking."[3]

Wagner's own family came to play a central part in this strange project. In 1872, Wagner relocated to Bayreuth and began building the villa he christened Wahnfried, "where my yearnings have found peace," according to its prominent inscription. The composer's gloss of the name served to recast his checkered career and sometimes shady business dealings as a mix of heroic quest and self-made advancement. In other words, it was the kind of whitewash typical of industrial dynasties of the day. At the same time, it was a self-citation: in the *Ring*, Wotan similarly glosses to his wife, Fricka, the meaning of Valhalla, the name of their new abode. Mythology and brand management could never be fully disentwined in Wagner's life.

Reinterpretation became something of a family tradition: the Wagners were fond of insisting on the continuity of their project, all the while continuously reinterpreting Richard's legacy to accommodate an ever-changing political environment. After Wagner's death, the composer's friends immediately made sure that his widow, Cosima, and the Wagner clan remained in charge of the annual Bayreuth Festival presenting his works. In the years straddling World War I, Wagner's son Siegfried, though gay, entered a dynastic union of sorts with Winifred Williams (1897–1980) and an unholy alliance with the far-right wing of German politics. After the defeat of Nazism, partly to avoid attempts to wrest Bayreuth from the family, Siegfried's sons Wolfgang and Wieland Wagner sought to ally a "New Bayreuth" with the more left-leaning elite of the postwar Federal Republic. To this day, the fights around the fate of Bayreuth involve fractious wings composed of many combatants who have the composer's nose and the last name Wagner.

Throughout all these realignments, the family remained invested in a heritage they understood in biological terms: propagating Richard's work meant biological procreation. Siegfried sometimes toyed with the idea that his father "belongs not to us, but to the German people"[4]—but characteristically, the statement turned out to be a bit of a confidence game and moreover a maneuver meant to blunt a lawsuit brought by his own sister, Isolde. In truth, Wagner's art was maintained into the present by people who shared his DNA, and the family didn't much distinguish between his physical legacy and his artistic one.

When Cosima Wagner gave birth to Richard's first son, he had to be named Siegfried in honor of the hero at the center of his father's evolving *Ring* cycle.[5] To celebrate the boy's birth, Wagner took his wife's next birthday as the occasion to surprise her with a serenade, the "Siegfried-Idyll," performed by members of the Tonhalle Orchestra Zurich on the steps of their Swiss villa in

Tribschen on the shores of Lake Lucerne. Wagner used the piece to test out much of the thematic material for the opera *Siegfried* (1876), although the theme itself is never sung by Siegfried but by his aunt and lover, Brünnhilde. Wagner's literal progeny and his artistic progeny proliferated in tandem.

As Jonathan Carr has pointed out, when a first Wagner Foundation was set up in 1913, it did not mean that the Wagners had given up their power over Richard's legacy. It was, rather, a dynastic transfer of power from Cosima to Siegfried.[6] And again, the inspiration seems to have come from the entrepreneurial dynasties of the age. While the evolving ecosystem of charitable foundations and government subsidies around the Bayreuth Festival had the look of the grants and divestments undertaken by, say, the Mellons or the Carnegies in the United States, at the core of this complex system remained a family-run company.[7]

Since 1973, Bayreuth has indeed been run by a foundation, governed by a council composed as follows: "Federal Republic of Germany, five votes; Free State of Bavaria, five votes; Wagner family, five votes; City of Bayreuth, two votes; Society of Friends of Bayreuth, one vote; Upper Franconia Foundation, two votes; Region of Upper Franconia, two votes; Bavarian Land Foundation, two votes."[8] The Wagners had once again sensed which way the wind was blowing, integrating the festival into cultural administration and at the same time recognizing postwar Germany's regionalism: note that Bavaria and Franconia have much more of a say than the German federal government. Rather than saying, as Siegfried had done, that Wagner belonged "to the German people," this constitution seems to make the politically far less troubling claim that the composer is part of what makes Upper Franconia attractive to tourists. Even so, as Richard's great-grandson Gottfried Wagner pointed out, the council has only the appearance of democracy. For the same founding charter explains in its second clause that "the Festspielhaus shall in principle be let to a member—if applicable, several members—of the Wagner family."[9]

Siegfried Wagner, despite being a middling composer, worked hard to establish himself as his father's successor, with help of propagandists like the writer Carl Friedrich Glasenapp and the philosopher Houston Stewart Chamberlain.[10] Detractors, like Richard Strauss, instead saw him as "manning [his] daddy's store."[11] It's striking that Glasenapp tries to legitimate Siegfried's inheritance by making it about genetics, and that Strauss makes it about finances. But both were constituent parts of the Bayreuth mythos: artistic aristocracy and nouveau-riche family enterprise, two contradictory nineteenth-century life-forms, found a mirror in the Wagners of Wahnfried.[12]

Gottfried Wagner remembers how his grandmother Winifred would parade him around meetings of the Society of Friends of Bayreuth after grand premieres. While her sons, Wolfgang and Wieland, cross with their mother and with each other in seeking to charm the postwar intelligentsia, including Marxists like Adorno and Ernst Bloch, Winifred's marketing came from a different tradition—"Omi" introduced her grandchildren to various fans as the spitting image of their famous great-grandfather: "When you were in my house as a baby and I had guests, I would always ask them if they wanted to see Richard Wagner as a baby."[13]

These complex familial politics decisively shaped both the creation and the reception of Wagner's works. Listeners have long suspected that his rendering of Wotan, the overextended patriarch of a heavily leveraged divine dynasty, might be a self-portrait.[14] And that while the opera, with its mythic grandeur, its monumental scale and pagan vim, was clearly intended as an antidote to the self-contained and anodyne aesthetics of the bourgeois home, it may have ended up as the portrait of a bourgeois family with fur capes and helmets. When Wotan bids his wife enter their new home, his description of their abode is redolent with the ideology of the *Heim* of Biedermeier aesthetics: the home offers protection, a space of retreat from an inhospitable world.

> The night nears: before its envy
> [the castle] offers its protection.
> So I hail the castle,
> Sheltered from trepidation and fear, follow me, wife:
> Dwell in Valhalla with me!

> Es naht die Nacht: vor ihrem Neid
> bietet sie Bergung nun.
> So grüss' ich die Burg,
> sicher vor Bang' und Grau'n, folge mir, Frau:
> in Walhall wohne mit mir![15]

In his novella *Wälsungenblut* (*Blood of the Valsungs*, 1906), originally conceived in 1906, Thomas Mann tells the story of twins named Siegmund and Sieglinde, overrefined scions of a wealthy bourgeois family, who go to the opera and afterward reenact the first act of *Die Walküre* (*The Valkyrie*, premiered in 1876). The central joke of Mann's pastiche is that Wagner's myths are easily translated into the sphere of bourgeois domesticity, and that they reveal a certain tawdriness once they are so translated. The peculiar magic that the *Ring* cycle performs is that in it, the run-of-the-mill bourgeois can imagine themselves as members of a vaunted line of gods.

Wagner's Valhalla is like the duck-rabbit optical illusion in that it comprises both the nuclear and the dynastic family: it shows its bourgeois audience a familiar world of domestic strife, but convinces it that this struggle is in fact part of a mythic (and dynastic) process. Wotan does not simply step out on his wife, he does so with a grand plan. And she's upset with him, not simply because she feels betrayed, but because she's the guardian of the hearth. Adorno sees in Wotan the erstwhile revolutionary who has given up and now invests his energy in maintaining the status quo[16]—in other words, the life cycle of any good bourgeois. And in her 2013 novel *Rein GOLD*, Elfriede Jelinek has Brünnhilde declare that hers is "like every second family"[17]—wanting a home they cannot afford. Kasper Bech Holten's production of the *Ring* cycle at the Royal Danish Opera House even casts the gods' triumphant (and ultimately short-lived) ascent to Valhalla as the ribbon-cutting ceremony at an office building.

The Racial Family

But Wagner's families were bourgeois in yet another dimension, far less obvious and far more troubling. This other dimension had dogged the Wagners of Bayreuth ever since the publication of Richard's 1850 essay "Das Judentum in der Musik" ("Judaism in Music"), which made his anti-Semitism a matter of public record. That essay, published pseudonymously in the *Neue Zeitschrift für Musik*, largely provoked incomprehension among his contemporaries, if they read it at all. But in 1869, Wagner published an expanded version of the essay. From then on until his death in 1881, "the Jewish Question" was never far from his mind.

In that essay, he had called the Jews "the bad conscience of our modern civilization."[18] His racism would become the bad conscience of the Wagner clan, entwining itself congenitally into the family tree. The family's record in this respect is deeply disturbing, and disturbingly intergenerational. Cosima Wagner made a habit of courting racist thinkers. Her daughter, Eva, was married to Houston Stewart Chamberlain, father of "scientific" anti-Semitism. Her son Siegfried was an early member in the Sturmabteilung (SA) and permitted the complete Nazi takeover of the Bayreuth Festivals even before Hitler seized power. Before the Third Reich came to an end, there were reports of the final chorus of *Die Meistersinger von Nürnberg* (*The Mastersingers of Nuremberg*, first performed in 1868) segueing into the "Horst-Wessel-Lied," adopted anthem of the Nazi Party, during performances of the *Festspiel* largely attended by party grandees.[19] Winifred Wagner maintained a close relationship with Hitler, so close in fact that her children would call him Uncle Wolf, and never bothered to hide it after the war. The family ostracized Siegfried's daughter Friedelind both during and after the Nazi years due to her antifascism. And by the 1970s, after her sons had long been engaged in disentangling the clan's legacy from the Nazis, Winifred sat down for an interview with the filmmaker Hans-Jürgen Syberberg; her holding forth about the "New York Jewish press" and waxing nostalgic over Hitler made her look like a family curse made flesh. She may have intended to be exactly that.[20]

As noted earlier, Wagner's racism has long been a matter of public record. His statements about Meyerbeer and Mendelssohn, his enthusiastic reception of the French ethnologist and social thinker Arthur de Gobineau's *Essay on the Inequality of the Human Races* (1848), testify to an increasing obsession with race in both his aesthetic and his political pronouncements after 1848. Worse, he wrote figures into his operas that seem to reflect de Gobineau's ideas. At the same time, it is important to take Wagner's anti-Semitism seriously as more than an unpleasant personal quirk—the way race functions in at least some of his operas is clearly to solve a set of political and aesthetic problems. As Slavoj Žižek once observed, Wagner's anti-Semitism "does not stand for anti-modernism as such, but at combining modernity with social corporatism."[21] The figure of the Jew allowed Wagner to have his aesthetic cake and eat it too. Racism moved from his everyday discourse, letters, and diaries into his oeuvre because it had work to do there. And that work had to do with the dynasty, with how to square the autonomy of the individual and of art with a renewed sense for the supposed sacrality of dynastic inheritance.

Romanticism had bequeathed to Wagner a theodicy of the nuclear family. In the attraction between lovers, something new and more natural managed to emancipate itself from the strictures of tradition. He likely borrowed these ideas from Young Hegelians like Max Stirner and Ludwig Feuerbach and from Utopian Socialists such as Charles Fourier. The Young Hegelians had been among the first philosophers to link the conditions of the possibility for individual autonomy specifically to economic factors; they and the Romantics had linked them to gender and, in their more self-aware moments, even to race. Nineteenth-century theories of racialized descent tended to dissolve individual autonomy for everyone—white men included—but of course white men miraculously ended up at the top of whatever evolutionary pyramid these theories conjured up. These two ways of resolving embodied contingency are fundamentally incompatible—yet Wagner managed to hold on to both. He never left the Young Hegelian influences entirely behind, but in his later works he combined them with ideas indebted to Arthur Schopenhauer, for whom love was understood as a mere function of the will of the species. As he often did, Wagner picked out of Schopenhauer ideas he liked because he had had similar ideas himself.

An inveterate *bricoleur*, Wagner seemed largely unconcerned that Schopenhauer and de Gobineau intended their picture of the family as a refutation of that of the Romantics; indeed, he held on to his late Romantic and his antihumanist convictions simultaneously. And he probably held them for the same reason: they were profoundly antibourgeois, recuperating a past but reworking it for a modern moment. Wagner encountered de Gobineau and Schopenhauer in the 1850s, and the great tension between their ideas and those of the Young Hegelians animates the monumental tetralogy of operas he began drafting during those years. Some of the most moving parts of *Der Ring des Nibelungen* (*The Ring of the Nibelung*) are moments when his almost anarchistic radical humanism and his curdled veneration of fate are in tension with each other. Some of the most troubling parts of the tetralogy are where he tries to somehow resolve their tension.

Familiarizing the *Ring*

The Ring of the Nibelung tells a story of two families, or of one family spread across two worlds. Initially, Wagner had wanted his opera to portray the tragedy of Siegfried—of his love for Brünnhilde and his conflict with the Giebichungs. As one planned opera expanded first into two, then into the final tetralogy, the character of Siegfried evolved from a solitary hero to being the point of intersection for two dense familial webs, one human, one divine—the place occupied by Hercules and other heroes of Greek antiquity. Through Siegfried, the operas explore the question of how freedom and dependency interact in the family. Siegfried's tragedy in *Götterdämmerung* (*Twilight of the Gods*, premiered alongside the other operas of the tetralogy in 1876) is brought about by the fact that he is never entirely aware of these familial webs, so he always takes himself to be more autonomous than he really is.

This ignorance gives him enormous power: when Wotan confronts him in act 3 of *Siegfried*, he clearly expects some recognition as the father of the gods (and, of course, as Siegfried's grandfather). Yet what Siegfried sees is simply another old person telling him how to live: "As long as I live, / there has always been an old man in my way," he says. Wotan tests his amnesia—but not, or at least not only, with consternation, for Siegfried's ignorance of his dynasty has an important role to play in Wotan's own dynastic plan.

WOTAN:
But who created the strong pieces
From which you made your sword?
SIEGFRIED:
What do I know of all that?
All I know is
That those pieces were useless
Until I forged the sword anew.

WOTAN:
Doch wer schuf die starken Stücke,
Daraus das Schwert du dir geschweißt?
SIEGFRIED:
Was weiß ich davon?
Ich weiß allein,
Daß die Stücke mir nichts nützten,
Schuf ich das Schwert mir nicht neu.[22]

Wagner gives this episode an interesting duality: Wotan clearly expects to be recognized; at the same time, he has a plan that depends on Siegfried's not knowing his interlocutor. It is precisely because Siegfried isn't always aware of how he relates to (and is related to) his family that he can act with an autonomy he wouldn't otherwise possess. But his ignorance of course also undoes him: he recognizes Brünnhilde and is then magically induced to forget who she is, setting in motion the events that lead to his death. He shatters Wotan's spear, destroying the old order, but lacks the sense he would need to put something in its place. If the *Ring* cycle sets up autonomy as an autonomy from family, the family reclaims its right time and again. Divorcing themselves from their family leaves the characters less autonomous, not more.

At the end of the cycle's first opera, *Das Rheingold* (*The Rhinegold*), as the gods are ready to take their first steps into Valhalla, their new home, the Earth Mother, Erda, appears. She warns the gods that the stolen ring by means of which Wotan has secured his home will come to destroy them. But Wotan, guardian of laws and treaties, is prohibited from retrieving the ring, which he has given to the giants Fafner and Fasolt for their services. The opera concludes with Wotan's "great thought,"[23] by which he seeks to resolve this impasse: he will spawn a hero free of Wotan's will, a hero who can retrieve what Wotan is not allowed to retrieve. Wotan's plan involves a suspension of the dynastic principle, albeit a suspension in the service of that same dynastic principle. The Greek word δυνάστης has a component of forced direction—Wotan's decision is to force something by having it happen on its own, or rather, having it happen by its own "natural" inclination.[24] *Natural*, in this case, seems to mean in the absence of Wotan's familial designs.

As Wotan's plan gets under way in the tetralogy's "First Night" (and second opera), *The Valkyrie*, family comes to fulfill an ambiguous function. Whereas Siegfried seems to misunderstand the ramifications of the relationships around him, be they of descent or of love, the characters in *The Valkyrie* differ tragically on what those ramifications are. The work's central relationship, the unprecedented incestuous union between the Valsung twins, Siegmund and Sieglinde, is presented in the conceptual shape the Young Hegelians would have given it: true love breaks with precedent, established convention, and traditional morality; it institutes something altogether new. But of course, the language of descent is never entirely absent: what brings the siblings together is the "blood of the Valsungs."[25] In their union, however, older forms live on and always threaten to reassert themselves. Siegmund and Sieglinde defend their love against the encroachment of commerce, force, commandment, and tradition, against rules for the sake of rules. Meanwhile, Wotan's wife, Fricka, defends those rules, but not simply because they are the rules; she does so in order to prevent marriage from becoming a mere epiphenomenon of the species.

The storm that convulses *The Valkyrie*'s overture ripples through both the opera's worlds—the world of humans and the world of Valhalla. Siegmund staggers into Hunding's house after being tattered by a *Gewitterbrunst* (an agitated storm), while upstairs, Wotan must contend with "der alte Sturm"—namely, the dissatisfactions of his wife. Insofar as the incestuous union brought about by the storm below represents an attack on Fricka herself qua defender of marriage, the storm below may well *represent* the storm above. When the Valsung twins fulfill Wotan's plan by thwarting Fricka's law, they observe nature cheering them on—the storm has cleared. In one of Wagner's most parodied and least translatable lines, "Winterstürme wichen dem Wonnemond,"[26] the winter storms give way to a moon of pleasure.

Family is debated and defended in two locations at the same time, and against two very different threats. One location at first may seem more abstract than the other, in the sense that the guardian or representative of the treaty *as such* and the guardian of the hearth *as such* come into conflict in Valhalla. But given that these two guardians are themselves married, abstract concept and concrete instantiation have a way of collapsing into each other. Where the "true" origin of the family lies remains unclear. Is it something that people first live and experience, only to then find a word for it? Or is it something ordained from some more abstract plane—by divine decree, by the self-binding of custom, or by the fiat of our genes—that directs our life and experience from an Olympian precipice?

Different characters pick up on different philosophical notions Wagner gleaned from his contemporaries or near contemporaries, and it isn't always clear which of the variant justifications they offer we're supposed to side with. For instance, in the course of *The Valkyrie*'s second act, Wotan seems to arrive at a kind of Neo-Hegelian theory that justifies his protection of the Valsung twins. So eloquent is he in his defense that it's hard not to think he has Wagner on his side (and Wagner proffered very similar theories to anyone who would listen). But then again, Wotan's plan turns out to be utterly misbegotten in its consequences. And although shrewish Fricka seems a parody of a moralistic Biedermeier scold, naturally she sees through Wotan's true motivations more clearly than even he himself seems capable of doing.

In *The Valkyrie*, the early Wagner's sexual romanticism squares off against Schopenhauer's curdled view of sex, with hints of the reconceptualization of Schopenhauer that Wagner outlined in his letter draft to the philosopher in the early phase of the *Ring*'s composition. In this letter, which he never sent, he had suggested that the striving of "the Will" can come to rest in another person, that sexual love may prove the "salvation" to the ceaseless striving of the will.[27] Of course, what Wagner proposed in the tone of a minor tweak amounted to a complete reorientation of Schopenhauer's philosophical system—he sought to liberate philosophy's most famous pessimist from his pessimism. What was worse, he sought to "correct" Schopenhauer's view of sexuality in the direction of the very thinkers the philosopher had meant to criticize.

In *Die Welt als Wille und Vorstellung* (*The World as Will and Representation*, 1819/1844), Schopenhauer critiques the traditional metaphysics of sexual love for hypostatizing the individual lovers. For him, what appears to the individual as a potentially salvific self-transcendence is in fact just the senseless churn of the "will of the species." He considers the nuclear, sentimental family to be an illusion by which an endless dynasty tricks us into carrying on. Schopenhauer intended this as a frontal attack on Romantic encomia to love. In his unsent letter, Wagner turned it back into one. But this remained characteristic of his approach to sexuality: for just as Wagner romanticized Schopenhauer's deconstruction of the nuclear family with a view to restoring sentiment to the kind of place it had held in Romanticism, so he rethought the sentimental family in light of philosophical works addressing race, tribe, and species, unconcerned that these were intended by their authors as incompatible options.

The scope of Wagner's views on the family is quite capacious and often contradictory, but it offers an almost seismographic reading of nineteenth-century thinking on a range of topics—autonomy, biology, the stakes of unification. He never entirely abandoned either his valorization of autonomous choice in erotic matters or his conviction that through that choice, something "higher" asserts itself. While Wagner's theoretical writings try to iron out the unbridgeable chasm between Feuerbach and de Gobineau, his operas take no such easy way out. When Fricka dismisses the unprecedented events of *The Valkyrie*'s first act as simply a part of Wotan's design and thus just as rule-bound and heteronomous as her imposition of familial rules on Hunding's household, she turns this theoretical contradiction into the opera's central dramatic conceit.

Act 1 of *The Valkyrie* certainly seems to belong to Young Hegelianism. Only in act 2 does Fricka throw Schopenhauerian cold water on its dizzy raptures. When the twins Siegmund and Sieglinde refer to Hunding as a "salesman"[28] (Schächer), when Wotan disdainfully refers to his marriage as based on an "unholy oath," they all reiterate Wagner's critique of conventional marriage. In so doing, they combine the antireligious animus of Stirner and Feuerbach with a critique of capitalism—Hunding's adherence to rules and his tendency to treat people as objects for barter are one and the same.

The ultimate origins of this line of reasoning lie with Georg Wilhelm Friedrich Hegel's critique of positive religion, but Wagner's direct inspiration is Feuerbach, who defended marriage in *Das Wesen des Christentums* (*The Essence of Christianity*, 1841), insofar as it is "a free commonwealth [*Bund*] of love," which becomes "sacred by the nature of the connection made in it."[29] This "holiness" is something Wotan powerfully discovers in act 2. When he tells Fricka that "I regard as unholy that oath / which unites those that do not love one another,"[30] he seems to be echoing Feuerbach's insistence that what holiness attaches to marriage clings to it "an und für sich selbst" (in and for yourself), not because of divine will, command, or priestly sacrament.[31] Holiness is a *result* of the feelings united in marriage, not their precondition.

By contrast, when Hunding first meets Siegmund he demands that he "treat my house as sacred." It's surely no accident that he imputes dignity to alienated and abstract objects—his house and his line. And yet, as much as Wagner tips his hand that the audience isn't supposed to side with Hunding, it's hard to hear his demand and not think of how unceremoniously Siegmund will treat his house. Successive revisions of the "poem" for *The Valkyrie* suggest that Wagner meant to heighten the sense that, wrong as Hunding may be in his fetishistic preference for dead things over lived freedom, perhaps this does not ultimately justify Siegmund and Sieglinde's betrayal.

Wagner's initial drafts of the opera had spelled out what Wagnerites have happily inferred ever since—that Hunding had a part to play in Sieglinde's abduction (in the final version, he seems to have received her as a gift from her captors), that he forcibly consummated the marriage on their wedding night (why not assume, Herfried Münckler has asked, that Hunding's lack of offspring might well be owed to respect for his unyielding wife?).[32] Bit by bit, Wagner's drafts make Hunding a far more palatable character, and the blitheness with which the Valsung twins violate his trust becomes almost as troubling as in Thomas Mann's version of the same story in *Blood of the Valsungs*. What remains intact is the disdain we as audience members are meant to feel for him, but Wagner troubles the basis for that reaction.

Our disdain has less and less to do with Hunding's actions and eventually boils down simply to the fact that he follows rules that are outdated. Many commenters have noted that he accepts his enemy Siegmund into his house in an act of self-binding (by the law of hospitality) that structurally resembles that of marriage. Wagner's drafts progressively abstract from Hunding's dilemma until the opposition is left standing in its starkest possible guise: Hunding applies rules that preexist their application; Siegmund and Sieglinde generate rules spontaneously from their attraction. Or so Wotan claims. It is worth noting that the Feuerbachian framing of *l'affaire* Hunding is almost entirely Wotan's. And he frames it this way in a dispute with a goddess, who not only guards marriage and the home but in some sense *represents* the institution of marriage as such.

But Fricka's position is deeply ironic. Feuerbach worried about systems of morality in which "God hovers above morality as a being entirely separate from Man."[33] By having the concept of marital fidelity take the stage as a singing goddess, Wagner renders this worry spectacular. The very fact that Fricka hovers above and rules on matters of human contingency of which she knows nothing exemplifies her as what Hegel called bad infinity. And those who flee the concrete existence of marital life for an appeal to Fricka are invariably wrong and pursuing marriage out of *mauvaise foi*—even Siegfried, when he invokes Fricka in *Twilight of the Gods* as he's blundering into bigamy.[34] Fricka represents the abstract rules of marriage, those that people invoke when they've forgotten the feelings that made them want to get married in the first place, or those invoked by people who didn't get married for the right reasons (force, barter, love potions) to begin with.

And yet, however abstract her take on Siegmund and Sieglinde's incest and infidelity may be, Fricka knows full well that their rule-breaking is simply an aftershock of her husband's. The abstractness of her command is moreover a chess move in a highly concrete marital argument. Fricka checks Wotan's argument about freedom of choice by rehearsing an essential point made by Max Stirner against Feuerbach: that declaring "sacred" the autonomy of marriage robs it of that very autonomy. Stirner had argued that whereas Catholic marriage had operated according to the "jesuitische Maxime" that "the ends sanctify the means,"[35] Protestantism declared those means themselves holy. This, according to Stirner, has the result that all things are suddenly candidates for holiness, are shot through with sacrality, a move toward "spiritualization" that culminates in Hegel's panlogism.

Wagner again abstracts toward this point in successive drafts of the libretto: he gradually removes references that would make Wotan's actions vis-à-vis his offspring comprehensible as anything but a long con. Fricka immediately intuits that Wotan's sacralization of marriage as something that happened "by itself" depends on the fact that it didn't really happen "by itself" at all. As Richard Klein has put it, she grasps far more than he does that "free will remains always already absorbed by the absolute will."[36] The Whole is the True, and what appears to the lovers as something that comes about with the logic of myth and dream turns out to be the result of careful dynastic considerations. Wagner likely got this idea from Arthur Schopenhauer, who in his chapter "Metaphysik der Geschlechtsliebe" ("Metaphysics of Sexual Love") in *The World as Will and Representation* posits the marital union as the unconscious realization of the will of the species. In the world of representation, the love of Siegmund and Sieglinde indeed presents itself as presuppositionless; objectively, it presents itself as a mere epiphenomenon of the will—Wotan's will.

Love, Sin, and Family

Wagner's earliest philosophical influences were German Romantic literature and the thought of the Young Hegelians—and it was these Hegelians' theories of the family that shaped his ideas of nuclear family and dynasty. From his very first opera drafts—*Die Hochzeit* (*The Marriage*), *Die Feen* (*The Fairies*), and *Das Liebesverbot* (*The Prohibition on Love*)—onward, he contrasts a love that springs up spontaneously and without dynastic or social buttress with a debased kind of love that is "taught and forced upon us from above." That phrase comes from *Oper und Drama* (*Opera and Drama*, 1851), a text of his Swiss years, and the "above" represents a first evolution of Wagner's thinking on marriage. As would typify his erratic but voracious course of reading throughout his life, Wagner had come across ideas and assimilated them to support and bolster his own preformed ones. In this case, it was the critique of religion among the Young Hegelians.[37]

The image of a detached moral authority that floats "above" concrete existence but to which individuals were supposed to accommodate their lives comes directly from the writings of Ludwig Feuerbach. But it was sufficiently diffused through the zeitgeist of the 1840s that direct influence is harder to pin down.[38] In *Opera and Drama*, Wagner describes love as that "salvation without which force is brutality, and freedom is pure randomness."[39] Throughout his life, he critiqued forms of eros that are pushed onto partners by dynastic concerns, economic concerns, or religious prejudice, and are sustained only by abstract adherence to supposedly divine laws.[40] This emerges most clearly in Wagner's abortive drafts for an opera of the life of Jesus of Nazareth. A project of the revolutionary year of 1848 that consisted of a story treatment along with philosophical commentary by Wagner himself, it was heavily indebted to the thought of Feuerbach as well as to that of Pierre-Joseph Proudhon in its aversion to property and ownership.[41]

Wagner's Jesus is a humanist who seeks to strengthen the individual against supraindividual constraints imposed by law, morality, and property. Humanity's "great error" (großer Irrtum) is to have "secured property through law, but not the essence [*Wesen*] of human nature in its autonomy." The first among these laws that turned relations of freedom into relations of property was marriage: love started out as "perpetual belonging to one another, which eventually ossified into the concept of property":[42]

> Whenever people love one another that love belongs to them and no one else, especially not to any outsiders. The natural right of the individual was thus transferred to those who were in loving relations with that individual: this is how the concept of marriage came about, how it became sacrament, and a matter of right, and this became flesh in the Law. But this right [*Recht*] had to become injustice [*Unrecht*] at that moment when it no longer had its basis in love, and became even more so when the union's supposed sacredness was marshaled against love itself. (11:289)

The sayings of Wagner's Jesus don't sound very different from the heavily Feuerbach-inspired monologue the original *Ring* drafts gave Brünnhilde as she celebrates the passing of the world of laws before riding her horse into Siegfried's funeral barge. As Wagner has Jesus say, "Through my death dies the law, for I show you that love is greater than the law." In Wagner's version, the injunction against adultery becomes something closer to Fichte's indictment of marriage contrary to inclination: "A marriage without love is already adulterous the moment it has been consecrated, and whosoever seeks a wife without love has broken his marriage vows already" (11:290).

But in many respects, Romantic theories of love and marriage inspired by Johann Gottlieb Fichte had understood a loving marriage as the restoration of a prior state of affairs. Just like the circular superbeings in Aristophanes' encomium on love in Plato's *Symposium*, what the Romantics would want most is to return to their anterior existence; but given that this is no longer possible, a loving marriage is a pretty good second place. That's not what Wagner supposes in the drafts for his Jesus opera. He claims that prelapsarian innocence "is the most complete egoism, for it only receives and does not give." Adam's self-alienation into sexual love, his and Eve's Fall from grace, was a first "self-transcendence [*Heraustreten*] of the individual," and thus the first step in humanity's progress toward true "sublation [*Aufhebung*] of egoism" (11:306). The Fall is necessary, he argues, and the transcendence of egoism is of a higher humanity than Adam's blissful unawareness.

Wagner's attachment to these Hegelian (or Young Hegelian) ideas never wavered. For instance, he would revisit this rewriting of the Genesis story in

Siegfried's trajectory in the *Ring* cycle. Siegfried begins the opera that bears his name in a state of perfect egoism, unable to recognize anything outside himself, unable to respect any preexisting rules. If his will and consciousness begin the opera as the undifferentiated night "in which all cows are black," having nothing to attach themselves to, the opera culminates in a moment of recognition of an Other: Brünnhilde, the first woman he has laid eyes on, the first person he recognizes as like him, the first person who causes him to feel fear. Merely facing Brünnhilde's Otherness leads to a moment of joyful annihilation of the self in that Other.

Parsifal's trajectory from self-absorption to compassion (*Mitleid*, literally "suffering-with") is another case in point. He enters the opera an oafish, ignorant young man. He has just slain a swan in the sacred forest, and when the grail knight Gurnemanz asks him,

> Do you understand that you have sinned?
> Tell me, boy, do you understand your guilt?
> How could you commit this?
>
> Wirst deiner Sündentat du inne?
> Sag,' Knabe, erkennst du deine grosse Schuld?
> Wie konntest du sie begehn?[43]

Parsifal simply answers, "I did not know it" (Ich wusste sie nicht). Parsifal is another Wagner hero whose independence from a family background—he does not know where he comes from, who his father is, who sent him this way—makes him a dangerous outsider and a potential savior. But whereas Siegfried's impulsive independence has Wagner's sympathy, *Parsifal* makes clear that the young man sins by remaining willfully obtuse. The grail knights intone that "by sympathy made knowing, the pure fool" (Durch Mitleid wissend, der reine Tor), and indeed: face to face with Kundry and the evil sorcerer Klingsor, the young man understands the suffering of the grail king Amfortas and by extension the suffering of Jesus:

> I saw the wound bleed;
> now it bleeds in me.
>
> Die Wunde sah ich bluten;
> nun blutet sie mir selbst.[44]

Knowing one's provenance in Parsifal means recognizing one's kinship with humanity in general.

Wagner thus stayed loyal to these ideas until his very last performed work. When he gradually fell under the spell of theories entirely opposed to the idea that an autonomous choice in marriage held liberating potential, he did not abandon his earlier ideas but simply grafted the old onto the new. Or, perhaps better, the ideas he received from Schopenhauer and Arthur de Gobineau aligned all too well with ideas he had *also* held alongside his pop Neo-Hegelian ones for decades by the time he could attach someone's proper name to them. Even in the famous passage in Wagner's late essay "Über das Opern-Dichten und Komponiren im Besonderen" (On writing operas and about composition in particular, 1879), in which he likens the *Gesamtkunstwerk* (total work of art) to the "betrothal" ("Vermählung") of music (the woman) and word (the man), he can't help but invoke the mixed marriage between a "Tchandala" and "Brahmin."[45] Those two caste names had become misappropriated and popularized bywords among nineteenth-century racist thinkers.

This famous passage means to argue that the *Gesamtkunstwerk* springs into being spontaneously through the attraction between word and music (as opposed to the composer-father's fiat), but the Tchandala/Brahmin comparison almost immediately suggests that this choice might be misbegotten and actually contrary to nature's will. Wagner, it seems, couldn't conceive one of these ideas without lapsing into its (contradictory) cognate. The way he resolved their contradiction was through Schopenhauer's insistence that sexual attraction wasn't really the lovers' choice but rather a matter of the will of the species. For Schopenhauer, we err when we think of sexual love as in any way involving individual inclinations—in truth, through the funnel of the individual subject pours the will of a potential child to be born, the will of the future, and the will of the species. In his late fragment "Über das Weibliche im Menschlichen" (On the feminine within the human, 1883), Wagner suggests that it is intermixing that has created the "debasement" (Verfall) of human "races."[46]

At first blush, that may seem like a wholesale abandonment of his earlier position that love necessarily involved a self-transcendence, a courageous plunge into difference. But Wagner seems to presuppose that autonomously chosen unions will *never* intermix different races, because through the partners' autonomous choices, the will of nature asserts itself. The only way the races intermix, he suggests, is "through conventional marriages [*Konventions-Ehe*] meant to increase property and ownership."[47] We need not worry about free choice creating "debased" marriages, because free choice could never freely choose such a relationship. Arranged marriage and polygamy debase the human being below the station of animals, that is, below the station nature intends for us. Truly monogamous and autonomous marriage, prime expression of "man's power over nature," is the province of the "most noble white race."[48]

Race and Inheritance

Wotan and Siegfried's meeting at the forest clearing plays a central part in the strange dialectic of autonomy and fatedness that animates Wagner's *Ring*. For on a surface level the struggle between the divine grandfather and his spawn who neither recognizes him nor respects him may distill, to its quintessence, the oedipal struggle of newness against what is foreordained. And yet, as we have seen, Wotan is also testing Siegfried: by not recognizing him in either sense, the young man shows himself a suitable tool for Wotan's grand dynastic plan. Autonomy becomes a tool of the dynasty. And yet, given that it all will turn out perfectly disastrously, it is hard not to credit the surface action with some validity: the audience is witnessing a succession crisis of sorts.

In the moment, Wotan recognizes that he is passing the baton to a new generation, but he does so joyfully:

> What divided against myself in wild pain,
>
> I decided in despair
> I now make reality
> With pleasure and joy.
>
> Was in des Zwiespalts wildem Schmerze
> verzweifelnd einst ich beschloss.
> Froh und freudig
> Führe ich nun aus.[49]

Part of his newfound joy is that he likes his new successors much better: he was close, he says, "to consecrat[ing] this world to the Niblung's avarice" when Sigmund died, but now "I bequeath my inheritance to the wondrous Valsung."[50] Throughout the tetralogy, Wagner suggests that the Valsungs and the Nibelungs constitute two different kinds of dynasties practicing two kinds of dynastic politics: where Wotan and his line are motivated by love and give their offspring autonomy, Alberich begets his offspring through guile and transformation, and begets them as a means to an end. He is motivated, as Wotan makes clear here, by "jealousy" and "avarice"; Alberich himself declares he has sired Hagen as a deliberate "affront" (Hohn) to the gods.[51]

Where Wotan and Fricka's arguments about freedom and determination find Wagner at his most productively ambiguous, moments like this one suggest that to be determined by the right kind of dynasty is just fine. That heredity is liberating so long as it is good heredity. It was certainly how a certain kind of Wagner fan read the tetralogy. Here is one of them providing his interpretation of the meeting between Siegfried and Wotan: "One family

[*Geschlecht*] after the other passes by the 'God'; again and again he is seized by a new hope, each time more noble, more selfless. When Siegmund died, [Wotan] had given up on his dreams of world domination in grim despair, now he joyfully steps back to make way for flowering Siegfried."[52]

The reader in question was Houston Stewart Chamberlain, Wagner's son-in-law and his early biographer. Chamberlain also decisively shaped both the history of racist thought and how the Wagner clan began to think of itself in dynastic terms. Born in England but educated largely on the Continent, the sickly Chamberlain emerged from a grand tour of the spas of Europe a confirmed Germanophile and an avowed antihumanist. He studied geology and botany in Geneva and came under the influence of Wagner and de Gobineau around the same time. In 1892, he attended his first Bayreuth Festival and began a correspondence with Cosima. Like her, Chamberlain was by now a passionate anti-Semite.[53] In 1908, he married Wagner's daughter Eva, and moved to Bayreuth to join the House of Wagner.

In the decades that followed, he established himself as one of the chief intellectuals of the German Far Right. His *Die Grundlagen des Neunzehnten Jahrhunderts* (*The Foundations of the Nineteenth Century*, 1899) was seminal for a new kind of anti-Semitism; among the book's fans was Wilhelm II, who read it all the way through (a rarity for the last kaiser) and who is said to have recited portions of it by heart. A few years later, Chamberlain helped legitimate Adolf Hitler among royalists and nationalists after meeting him for the first time in Bayreuth in 1923. While he could lament in a letter to Kaiser Wilhelm II that "we no longer have a dynasty that expresses a moral force [*eine moralische Macht*],"[54] he was hard at work maintaining the dynasty of Wahnfried.

At the same time, Chamberlain was busy interpreting world history, particularly German history, in explicitly Wagnerian terms. In a 1914 essay to Germany's youth published in a ghoulish little volume intended as a Christmas gift to "academic youth in the field,"[55] he cast Germany as the Siegfried among nations: "The German is young and therefore has the imagination and the naïveté and the drive toward the great and beautiful, without which no achievement is possible. But for the same reason everything in Germany is incomplete [*unfertig*]: state, society, taste."[56] This is why, he argues, all great German artists were also politicians, wanting to intervene in matters of state and society. His example is Richard Wagner. It is this mission that produces among great Germans a "unity" that was "an unknown thing in world history thus far: the great German men—the thinkers, the poets, the researchers, the directors, the creators—constitute one single family."[57]

Two different kinds of inheritance run through Chamberlain's thinking, whether he is contemplating German nationalism, race, or Wagner's operas:

an inheritance that constitutes dead weight, dross made of rules and strictures, or an inheritance that is reactivated, regenerated through iteration. "Since everything new ties itself to something preexisting and older," he notes at the beginning of his magnum opus *The Foundations of the Nineteenth Century*, "the first fundamental question is: which portions of our spiritual capital are inherited? And the second, no less important fundamental question is: who are 'we'?"[58] The nineteenth century, Chamberlain claims, was characterized by twin inheritances—the Aryan and the Jewish.

Not only was Wagner for Chamberlain the paragon of "Aryan" art, the latter made into his central idea Wagner's juxtaposition between the Valsungs and the Nibelungs. One group has an organic history, made up of freely chosen inheritance, while the other has a mechanical one. Each differs with respect to how it constitutes itself and how it transmits itself and by extension how it *makes history*. But where Wagner himself had been interested in the play of the self-contained sentimental family and the larger dynastic family of duty and planning, Chamberlain read the *Ring* cycle as the story of two sorts of dynasties, each with its own mode of transmission and its own legitimacy or illegitimacy.

Chamberlain took Wagner's dramatic juxtaposition of dynastic forms and elaborated them into a complete, if upsetting philosophy of history. Like Wagner, he distinguished between races that inherit certain traits dynastically through blood and those that transmit such knowledge only through guile and commandment—the former were "Aryan," the latter Jews. One heirloom on which Judaism and the German aspects of "our" inheritance differ, according to Chamberlain, is precisely the family. Where the Greek city-state had valorized the *polis* over the *oikos*, the Roman Empire was built on the family and understood itself as a giant family. Unlike Nietzsche and Schopenhauer, Chamberlain thinks that this "inheritance" constitutes the specific difference between "our civilization" and the "Asiatic and Semitic ones" (179). Christianity might have weakened this "sense of family" in favor of a focus on individual salvation, but through the Roman law and through the reliance on imperial structures it never fully went away (180).

Chamberlain insists that the modern Jews aren't identical with the tribes of Israel, but instead constituted themselves "over centuries through the physical excretion from the rest of the Israelite family." Whereas traditional anti-Semitism had charged Jews with being overly familial and thus incapable of integrating into civil society, Chamberlain suggests that Jews are insufficiently tribal, a paradynasty consisting of those who withdrew from "the rest of the Israelite family" (416). He unites two seemingly contradictory anti-Semitic canards: Jews are overly familial and yet not "really" a family.

Inheritance is everywhere in Chamberlain, but how he describes the process makes clear he is not thinking in straightforwardly dynastic terms: "For the nineteenth century is not the child of an earlier century—after all a child starts its life anew—rather it is [the earlier century's] immediate product [*Erzeugnis*]: mathematically expressed it is a sum, physiologically like a particular age of life. We inherited a sum of knowledge, talents, thoughts, etc. and we inherited a certain distribution of economic powers, we inherited errors and truths, representations, ideals, superstitions: some of it . . . had become part of our own flesh and blood" (6).[59] Note how impossibly tight a transmitting relationship Chamberlain envisions here—like Wotan's brood, inheritance passes through channels more intimate than "mere" reproduction. Throughout his introduction and indeed throughout his massive book, Chamberlain vacillates on what exactly this transmission is like. This vacillation isn't owed primarily to his being a poor writer (though he definitely is that). It has to do instead with a central confusion in his portrayal of the nineteenth century's genetic material. For there are central traits of northern European civilization that have traveled almost without any falsification from their Germanic ancestors to the Bayreuth parlor; but there are other, troubling admixtures (above all a "Jewish" Christianity) that somehow *also* have managed to be passed down in this way.

For Chamberlain, those admixtures hail from the Semitic cultures of the ancient Near East, carried into central Europe by the Roman Empire. He is anti-Semitic in a new and more global sense: "In truth, the 'Jewish menace' lies far deeper, the Jew himself bears no responsibility for it; we [i.e., Aryans] have created it ourselves, and we have to overcome it ourselves" (18). Chamberlain's anti-Semitism makes a significant change vis-à-vis the equally virulent anti-Semitism of his famous father-in-law. Richard Wagner had juxtaposed two different types of transmission in two different *types* of families—the good (Germanic) family and the bad (Nibelung) family. Chamberlain posits Jewishness as simply a bad kind of transmission within the good family—an acquired genetic defect that is nevertheless transmitted from quasi generation to quasi generation. The literature of decadence produced around the same time would get interested in the same formation—but saw in it a road past the dominant position of the nuclear and sentimental family.

6

Naturalism, or The Dynastic Romance

When abbot Gregor Mendel died in 1884, his obituary noted his three legacies: a garden with beautiful fuchsia, a single article on plant hybrids, and a progeny of peas—12,980 at one point, though the obituary didn't print that number.[1] Mendel's article had been published in 1866 in the *Verhandlungen des naturforschenden Vereines in Brünn*.[2] But his true heirs were the countless lines of pea plants he had cultivated in his small garden and his greenhouse. He had selected the sires carefully and monitored their progress from generation to generation. His article, largely unread during his lifetime and not fully appreciated for its historical significance until the early twentieth century, had chronicled the distribution of seven isolated characteristics across those generations. What he had discovered would shape late nineteenth-century thinking about the dynasty.

Mendel's experiments relied on something we could call the genetic intuition: Jean-Jacques Rousseau, the Romantics, the revolution that ended the ancien régime, and the counterrevolution against it had relied on pictures of the family that were concerned with the transmission of legitimacy, ideas, and love from one generation to the next. Rousseau's *Émile* had been their model: how do you instill the right values, ideas, and instincts in the *next* generation; or conversely, how do you get people to break with the values, ideas, and instincts of the *previous* generation? Mendel's experiments were part of a shift: it was no longer the next generation one had to worry about— the dismal science of statistics entered the picture in the one after the next, and into every generation thereafter. It wasn't what your parents did to shape you but what was in your far more distant ancestry that determined who you really were.

The space beyond the first filial generation represented not only the chief focus of interest for early genetics, starting with Mendel; it also became the domain of probabilities, of statistics, of distributions. Mendel noted that "those forms [of plants], which take on a recessive character in the first generation, no longer vary in the second generation with respect to their character; they remain constant in their progeny."[3] This meant that traits that *seemed* to have disappeared in the first filial generation had a way of returning into the phenotype in later generations. "It is different with those [plants] which took on the dominant characteristic in the first generation. Of these one third creates progeny in which the traits are found with the distribution of 3:1, while only one third retains the dominant trait consistently."[4]

Just because a trait seemed to have disappeared from the population didn't necessarily mean that it in fact no longer coursed down the dynastic chain: one-third expressed the dominant trait, but two-thirds kept having offspring that had a chance of retaining recessive traits. Mendel's peas weren't a particularly high-stakes example of such heredity; but given that his example used mechanisms familiar from animal breeding (as did many other early pioneering works of genetics),[5] it's no surprise that the dominant and recessive traits soon began being overlaid with evaluative matrices: progressive and retarding, healthy and sick, desirable and undesirable.[6]

Increasingly, a method like Mendel's was interpreted through a moralistic lens. Mendel was anxious to control extraneous variables that might unduly influence hybridization: he placed his peas into pots in order to minimize interference from the soil, then placed a control group in a greenhouse in order to check for "possible disturbance by insects,"[7] above all a particular insect species that interfered with the flowers of the pea plant. The techniques he employed in the spirit of scientific inquiry were drawn yet again from a far less value-neutral field: they were how breeders had kept unwelcome traits out of their populations for millennia.

As the nineteenth century slowly assimilated the discoveries of Mendel and others like him, this methodological borrowing led to a fatal confusion.[8] Mendel, Prosper Lucas, and Charles Darwin had sought to minimize outside interference because it threatened to make invisible the mechanisms of heredity they sought to make visible. Horse breeders had sought to do the same because it threatened the purity of their lines. From the beginning, the nineteenth century had difficulty keeping methodological and moral questions apart—the methodological anxiety that had animated Mendel became a moral one; the purity of descent became not a means to an end but rather an end in itself. To see the consequences, we need to leave Gregor Mendel's garden and enter an imperial hothouse.

The Dynastic Romance

In 1862, Wagner published his set of "Five Songs for Female Voice" (WWV 91) with texts by Mathilde Wesendonck. The third song in the cycle is "Im Treibhaus" ("In the Hothouse"), subtitled "Study to Tristan und Isolde." Motifs from this song would indeed find their way into the final act of *Tristan und Isolde*.[9] Here, they underscore an atmosphere of passionate striving—but one of a decidedly pre-Mendelian persuasion:

> Wide in yearning desire
> You spread out your arms
>
> Weit in sehnendem Verlangen
> Breitet ihr die Arme aus[10]

intones the poetic "I," and soon recognizes a common object of desire:

> Though enveloped in glow and sunlight,
> Our homeland is not here!
>
> Ob umstrahlt von Licht und Glanze,
> Unsre Heimat ist nicht hier![11]

The erotic atmosphere of the hothouse is directed, both among the plants and for the person observing them, at a single telos—even if that telos is ultimately unreachable, unreal, possibly death.

Compare Wesendonck's poem to Ernst Stadler's "Im Treibhaus" (In the hothouse, 1904), where the unidirectional striving has been replaced by a dizzying and directionless fecundity:

> Diseased shoots tongue up and flicker
> From a sea of deeply gashed cups[12]

Stadler writes—his plants are not content to remain plants, so they grow scales and tongues and feathers. Where for Wesendonck the analogy between observer and hothouse was still stable enough to allow for a parallelism, for Stadler the plants trespass by way of metaphor so far into the sphere of the human that the dividing line becomes hard to maintain. The space between Wesendonck's text and Stadler's is the German age of Naturalism—an age belonging to some extent to the Mendelian intuition. But the German conversation was inevitably shaped once again by the French Revolution—or rather, by its faint echoes, in the strange replay of history that was the failure of the French Second Republic and the second Napoleonic Empire.

If, as Lynn Hunt claimed, the French Revolution played out as a "family romance," it did so resolutely within the sphere of the nuclear family.[13] It was certainly viewed that way at the time. Revolutionaries and counterrevolutionaries alike cast the revolution as a revolt of children against their fathers (Edmund Burke), as a fracturing of the nuclear family (Joseph de Maistre), or as a rejection of paternalism (Johann Gottlieb Fichte).

By contrast, the Rougon-Macquart novels of Émile Zola insist on reading the Second Empire as a dynastic romance. From *La Fortune des Rougons* of 1871 to *Le Docteur Pascal*, published in 1893, the novels sketch a grand panorama of the second Napoleonic empire and a study of the reasons for its downfall. This Second Empire, Zola makes clear, was not a new start but a new start that modeled itself on a previous new start—a parental generation separated by a filial one. This was what Karl Marx made clear when he called Napoleon III's seizure of power the "Eighteenth Brumaire" of Louis Bonaparte: the empire was always already a repetition of something that had been genuinely new. Even when it took itself to be striking out into the future, it was in truth simply repeating the past (as "farce," as Marx so memorably put it).[14] To see this truth required the kind of moralized gaze with which discoveries such as Mendel's had furnished the nineteenth-century intelligentsia.

Zola's most potent image for this imperial dynastic romance, with all its rampant growth and complete lack of genuine progress, is a hothouse. As far as emblems of dynastic ambition go, a hothouse is quite perfect. In it we can keep flowers "pure," ensuring that they retain their color, size, or any other relevant features, generation to generation. But perhaps more important, the hothouse is part of an ambition to keep out chance—snow, errant seeds, insects, a sudden frost will do nothing to impede the implacable forward creep of genetic material. Just as in Mendel's experiments using a greenhouse, the hothouse functions like a looking glass, which allows us to take in what in the thick of natural environments may escape our notice.

Mendel had used the relative autarky of his greenhouses as a means of watching alleles, as we call them today, distribute themselves across the generations. He was watching development happen. When Zola presents a hothouse in the second volume of his great analysis of the bourgeois dynasty, he intends for it to suggest something altogether different. It's a buzzing, blooming nimbus of breeding, of activity, of reproduction *without* development: the hothouse manages procreation without permitting the forward thrust Mendel had sought to document. It brings natural history to a standstill, but more important puts in abeyance that other implacable momentum that the nineteenth century was so keen to espy behind the disordered march of generations: progress.

The association between evolution and progress may seem strange to us today—we know evolution isn't meaning to go anywhere in particular, but is rather a constant statistical rearrangement of populations, traits, and probabilities. Darwin knew as much already. But his contemporaries—from social Darwinism, popularizers like Herbert Spencer and comparative anthropologists like Francis Galton—couldn't help themselves and grafted his profoundly fatalistic account of the fate of species onto their unflappable belief in progress.[15] For them, evolution told a story—either of an ascent toward some goal (either previously attained and then lost or yet to be reached) or the fatal slide away from a state of perfection. Evolution is agnostic on progress and decline, but to many nineteenth-century thinkers it seemed to speak of little else.

As for Zola's hothouse, it belongs to Aristide Saccard (born Aristide Rougon). After making a fortune off insider information during the Haussmannization of Paris, Aristide has built an ostentatious estate for himself in the heart of the reconstructed city, a house "hidden under its own sculpture." And just like the house, that "magnificent bastard" pretending to celebrate centuries-old wealth when in fact its stucco hasn't even dried yet, the hothouse is nothing but a riot of activity without a point: "Endless love and voluptuous appetite pervaded this stifling nave in which seethed the ardent sap of the tropics. Renée was wrapped in the powerful bridals of the earth that gave birth to these dark growths, these colossal stamina; and the acrid birth-throes of this hotbed, of this forest growth, of this mass of vegetation aglow with the entrails that nourished it, surrounded her with disturbing odors."[16]

Sex, productivity, reproduction—a stifling, obscene atmosphere of rampant growth pervades the hothouse. But for all the efflorescence, the only thing any of it seems good for is to provide the soil for more reproduction. We have come far from Mendel's garden. The buzz of birthing and propagation is just a prelude to decay, to fertilizing another set of flowers. The hothouse functions as an allegory for the kind of capitalism that has made the Rougons so rich: circulation, speculation, and creative destruction.

But the hothouse properly belongs not to Aristide's ostentation but to Zola's: if it's an allegory for the atmosphere of the Second Empire, it's an incredibly showy one. Zola had toured the *grandes maisons* of the haute bourgeoisie to research *La Curée* (*The Kill*, 1872), but it's unlikely he encountered many hothouses in them. No, the hothouse is there because of its symbolic generativity: like proliferating orchids, it breeds images and meanings; it manages to speak for a world of overheated capitalism in which everything grows rampant, everything is caught in widening gyres of circulation, but nothing progresses. It manages to speak to the stultifying insularity and boredom, the restless ambition without ultimate meaning, that has beset the wealthy branch of the Rougon family tree.

Throughout the Rougon-Macquart cycle of novels, Zola relies on what we might call the dynastic gesture: as though they were plants in a hothouse, he introduces even minor characters by laying out their full family tree, often reaching back well into the mid-eighteenth century, as though this might tell us everything we needed to know about them. Zola's point in doing so is partly political: there's a horrifying sense of claustrophobia when we learn that the coal miners and the mine owners we meet in *Germinal* (1885) have been in their respective positions with no change in their fortunes for five generations. But more important, Zola thinks that finding out about someone's great-grandparents constitutes a crucial bit of characterization: by telling us where someone comes from, Zola means to tell us who they are.

Consider the scene in which Étienne Lantier, distant spawn of the Macquart family, explains his circumstances to Catherine, a coal miner's daughter, granddaughter, and great-granddaughter. When he says that he's had to seek new employment because he hit his boss, Catherine is "dumbfounded, shocked to the depths of her hereditary notions of submission and passive obedience."[17] Étienne himself admits immediately that the character trait that made him rebel was likewise hereditary: he had too much to drink, being "the last child in a long line of alcoholics, who suffered in his very flesh from all this heredity soaked and warped by alcohol."[18]

The scene is overdetermined. This isn't really the story of two people meeting so much as it is of two enormous family trees colliding, two sets of hereditary baggage smashing together. Again and again, Zola's narrator compares the Montsou mine to a giant prehistoric beast that digests human flesh; but the true leviathans the novel is obsessed with are the family lineages that seem to afford the individuals caught in them no more freedom than the dark tunnels the miners burrow into the ground. While the individual novels of the cycle contain trenchant social critique, the cycle itself starts with a family tree rather than a visit to the mines. Zola diagrammed and rediagrammed that family before he ever started telling its story, and long before he ever got to Étienne and Catherine. In designing his family, good plots don't seem to have been his primary interest: most of its members have conflicts and dramatic encounters outside the family—the Rougon-Macquarts aren't the Ewings. No other member of any branch of the family makes an appearance in *Germinal*. And yet their constituent traits are all there. What Zola managed to plan out in astonishing detail are the hereditary features (alcoholism, mental illness, vice) that were to travel from generation to generation.

Reliance on genealogical explanations exploded at the beginning of the nineteenth century. But as Stefani Engelstein has pointed out, that explosion also had a visual component—the family tree became a near-universal heuristic of the age, one that in Zola's case dictated the actual plot of the Rougon-Macquart cycle.[19] At the same time, this rather modern family is shadowed by one of a deeply traditional visual representation of sovereignty. The patricidal moment of revolution, the shock of 1789, far from severing all dynastic connections to the past, simply inaugurated new dynastic lines, the cancellation of hereditary rulership ironically reemphasizing questions of heredity.[20] Behind the rise and fall of the Rougons and the unremitting descent of the Macquarts lies the necessary failure of another family that owes its success to the upheavals of the French Revolution—the Bonapartes, who have managed, just when the Rougons begin their ascent, to place a second *parvenu* at the head of the state, turning the self-made man into a dynastic principle.

The fortunes of the Rougons, petit bourgeois from Provence with more ambition than cash, finally turn the year Napoleon III came to power. The novel whose title is so worded, *La Fortune des Rougons*, appeared in the year he finally had to step down. In Zola's introduction to that novel, he points out that his project "required" "the fall of the Bonapartes," since it "furnished me with the terrible but necessary denouement for my work." The laws of heredity he himself believes he's establishing in and through the Rougon-Macquart family serve as a scientific predictor of the fall of that other, less fictional family, an explanation for why the Bonapartes rose and why they necessarily had to fall.

La Fortune de la Rougons (*The Fortunes of the Rougons*, 1871) is fairly open in making this analogy: at one point, Zola has Monsieur de Carnavant remark that "a new dynasty is never founded excepting upon an affray. Blood is good manure. It will be a fine thing for the Rougons to date from a massacre, like many illustrious families."[21] The Bonapartes and the Rougons are parallel dynasties in that they both arise from the failure of the Republican project, and their fate together will ultimately prove Monsieur de Caravant wrong.

Zola's theory of heredity, such as it was, borrowed heavily from Prosper Lucas, who, unlike Gregor Mendel, unlike Charles Darwin, had sought examples for hereditary traits in the petri dish that is the histories of the great aristocratic dynasties: for pages on pages, Lucas's *Traité philosophique et physiologique de l'hérédité naturelle* (*Philosophical and Physiological Treatise on Natural Heredity*, 1847 and 1850) offers what he calls "illustrations" from Egyptian, Persian, Greek, Roman, and medieval history, well into the eighteenth century. Not surprisingly, he steers clear of the Bonaparte family, but it is unlikely that Zola didn't think of Napoleon III when reading Lucas's accounts of intrafamilial decline—and it is unlikely that Lucas didn't want him to.

Those dwelling in the Second Empire never had to look very hard at their Napoleon to recognize that he did not measure up to the Hegelian "world-soul on horseback" their grandparents had followed into Russia. The very obviousness (which satirists and caricaturists were permitted to explore without fear of censorship) was part of both Zola's method and Lucas's. Lucas opens his "confirmation générale par l'histoire," in which he explores the heredity of history's great dynasties, as follows: "It is an immense book, open for all to read, written in all languages, where the two tableaux unfold all the time, and where the spirit can follow equally, the trace of genealogies, the trace of qualities, of vices, of passions, and of crimes just as great as those once expiated in the prisons or on the gallows."[22]

This passage could equally well describe a biological analysis of French history and the aesthetic Zola envisioned for his own *roman expérimental*. The Rougon-Macquart cycle follows two families, both descended from the same woman—the Napoleon of the family is Adelaïde Fouque, called Tante Dide, an eccentric farmer's wife in the Provençal town of Plassans, whose eccentricity gradually descends into full-blown mental illness by the time she dies at the age of 105. Her marriage to a man named Rougon produces only one child, Pierre, since her husband dies early; Pierre grows up together with two half-siblings: Ursule and Antoine Macquart, whom Adelaïde begets with a small-time crook and alcoholic whom she never marries.

On the Rougon side of the family, the second generation thrives on activity and ambition. Pierre Rougon spends his time in the first novel of the cycle desperately trying to move up in society, but when he does it is largely thanks to the eldest of his five children: Eugène Rougon, who strikes it rich by siding with Napoleon during the coup of 1851. The remaining Rougon children are Aristide, who makes his money as a profiteer during Baron Haussmann's redesign of Paris; Marthe, who takes a quasi-incestuous leap into the Macquart side of the family, with predictably disastrous results; Sidonie, who brims with the same mania for wheeling and dealing as her siblings, but manages to amass no fortune by it; and finally Pascal, the man who will eventually come to share Zola's view of his family and manage to place himself "completely outside of the family" (en dehors complètement de la famille).[23]

On the Macquart side, Ursule Macquart marries a man named Mouret. Her children, lower middle class but not abjectly poor, are François, Hélène, and Silvère Mouret. All these children seek to take charge of their own destiny but fail in their attempts to do so. They (and François's offspring) are failed artists, failed small-time entrepreneurs, failed revolutionaries. If the Mouret branch of the family struggles against the gravitational pull of its heredity, the branch inaugurated by Antoine Macquart, Tante Dide's second child and product of her extramarital liaison, never manages to work its way out from under its defective genes. A line of victims of circumstance buffeted about by alcoholism, a choleric temper, and a tendency toward madness, this branch explores the lowest reaches of the France of the Second Empire. In particular, the children of Gervaise Macquart, an alcoholic we meet in *L'Assomoir* (*The Drinking Den*, 1877), persist in the extreme reaches of the social spectrum: here we find the destitute coal miner and strike leader Étienne Lantier, the prostitute Nana (Anna Coupeau), and the possibly schizophrenic serial killer Jacques Lantier.

Like Mendel, Zola is most interested in the second and third filial generations: it is here that we find most of the protagonists of his single-character books—Nana, Étienne, Jean Macquart, and others. They are also the generation featuring the most interesting characters, for what we might call Mendelian reasons: unlike their parents, who frequently take rather straightforwardly after one parent or the other, the members of the second filial generation are subject to vying inherited impulses—they are mixed forms, much like Mendel's second generation of peas. They are where efforts of will, chance, and statistics can all work their magic. Their parents' ambition, impoverishment, or mediocrity unfolds with the same almost destined energy with which the Second Republic transitioned into the Second Empire.

The third generation, by contrast, lives the reality of the Second Empire. On the Rougon side, they are spoiled, bored, incestuous; on the Macquart side, they are low-down but stagnant, cruelly aware of their vain struggle against biological fate and the economic realities. Only as the Second Empire comes crashing down around them are both sides of the family reunited in fate, as "the hereditary flaw which festered unpredictably somewhere in the depths of . . . youthful vigor" brings them all down, the high as much as the low.[24]

This seems to have been Zola's grand design—a reflection on the laws of heredity intended to analyze the Second Empire as itself a product of heredity gone bad (that tiny but fatal step from Napoleon I to Napoleon III). But what process, exactly, does the family tree chronicle? There are two interesting assumptions with respect to what constitutes the family that are somewhat invisibly embedded in Zola's design. The first is one that Zola drew from his reading of Prosper Lucas: "the constitutions of families begin with one individual." Tante Dide is the key to everything that happens to the bloodline of the Rougons and the Macquarts throughout the five generations Zola portrays. Yet it is her actions, not her ancestry, that seem to influence events in subsequent generations. In this, she differs crucially from her offspring.

Consider the following passage from *Le Docteur Pascal* (*Doctor Pascal*, 1893), in which the title character, for the first time in the cycle, seems to regard the family tree with which Zola started his project in much the same way the author did. As he observes his mother, Félicité, playing with his young grandnephew, the hemophiliac Charles, he realizes it's all because of Tante Dide: "But what struck him above all in that moment was the resemblance to Tante Dide, that had crossed three generations, which jumped from the desiccated visage of the hundred-year-old, with its used features, into the child's delicate figure, how it already defaced that figure, old and used up by the race. Face to face the one and the other, imbecilic child, of a deathly beauty, was like the end of the ancestress, the forgotten one."[25]

Pascal's espying Tante Dide's "visage" behind the family's manifold ailments is, in a sense, a look into a mirror.[26] For what allows Pascal Rougon to see Tante Dide's baleful hereditary stranglehold over the Rougons appears to be a mirror image of her ability to have that kind of a hold in the first place. In his first genealogical tree outlining the different branches of the Rougon-Macquart family, Zola insists on Pascal's *innéité*, which he glosses as "no moral or physical resemblance to his parents." Pascal's moral uprightness comes out of nowhere, as it were. Tante Dide's determining influence over her family, albeit far more negative, seems to be another, far more calamitous case of *innéité*, one that Pascal's goodness (and the death of Charles, the final spawn of Tante Dide's tainted seed) manages finally to reverse.[27] Therefore, the laws of heredity are ironclad, until they're not. Genetic material determines everyone's character and fate, until it doesn't.

In his programmatic exploration of the "experimental novel," Zola had castigated the "idealistic" novels of Romanticism and Realism that at certain strategic moments "cast aside observation and experiment and base their works on the supernatural and the irrational," which at crucial moments "admit . . . the power of mysterious forces outside of the determinism of the phenomena."[28] Now he seemed to invoke exactly this kind of miracle: the determinism of hereditary factors is aligned against Dr. Pascal, but by some higher grace of evolutionary biology he escapes it.

What explains this sudden and seemingly unmotivated relapse into what Zola himself would call Idealism? Why does he claim the novel must abide by certain rules, only to suspend them at certain strategic moments? The answer seems to turn on the term *strategy*. As for narrative strategy, Zola wants to tell the story of a family, and he wants that story to have a beginning, a middle, and an end point. Political strategy is another factor: Zola doesn't intend to instill a biologically tinged fatalism in his audience. His quasi-evolutionary diagnosis of the faulty heredity of the Second Empire is meant to inspire in his readers another *innéité*: like Dr. Pascal, they should want to create a new France without "moral resemblance" to the old.[29]

This leads to the heightened denouements of many of the novels in the Rougon-Macquart cycle, where Zola seems to delight in gestures that belie the measured scientism of his self-professed experimental practice. *La bête humaine* (*The Beast in Man*, 1890) concludes with a train conductor and his fireman in mortal struggle aboard the locomotive of a train bound for the front lines in 1870. Jacques Lantier, true to his Macquart genes, has murdered and raped his way through the novel unmolested, but in taking up with the fireman's wife he has gone too far. As he and the fireman struggle, they fall from the locomotive; and the train, full of soldiers eager to join the fray against the Prussians, hurtles pilotless into the night.

Taken by itself, every part of this scene is already too much: the train resounding with "La Marseillaise," but with a degenerate serial killer at the helm; the bitter irony of an army destined for ignominious defeat extolling an empire with less than a year left in existence; the rottenness at the very head of the French imperial project. All this is before Zola turns to the downright gothic contrivance of having the two men plunge to their deaths, only to leave the train hurtling rudderless toward the abyss with its fresh-faced cargo. We may be reminded of the hothouse of the Saccards: at times Zola can't stop himself, and his supposedly scientific narrative scheme yields climaxes so frankly melodramatic and outré they wouldn't seem out of place in an opera of the time.

Whatever narrative logic licenses such contrivances, it's a clear echo of the *innéité* that sets up the whole cycle. Zola is so ruthless because he's clearing space for a new beginning; he's so shameless in showing his hand because his very heavy-handedness makes a point. His protagonists die because they need to die; the old world, the world of the Rougon-Macquarts, the world of the Second Empire, needs to be cleared away so that something new can have room to begin. In *Doctor Pascal*, Antoine Rougon drinks to excess and accidentally combusts in the process, an event as horrifying as it is funny. Zola doesn't mind tipping his hand when creating a tabula rasa.

His interest in evolutionary science comes with a healthy dose of Aristotle's *Poetics*: his evolution has a beginning, a middle, and an end. The dynasties of the Rougon-Maqart cycle are postrevolutionary. Zola is unable to credit the idea of an Adamic dynastic line à la Sir Robert Filmer, extending, like the Great Chain of Being, from the present moment all the way to the dawn of man. His dynasties have beginnings and they have ends. Even if his theoretical underpinnings pretend to a dispassionate portrait of the uncaring roulette of genetics, he is unwilling to tell stories without an unscientific beginning (with Tante Dide as the *creatio ex nihilo*) and an emotionally satisfying, politically progressive, but equally unscientific end point.

For revolutionaries and reactionaries alike, the French Revolution had constituted a break in the implacable onward flow of what Theodor Adorno called "natural history," that is to say history that behaved as though it were nature.[30] If Edmund Burke and Maximilien Robespierre could agree on one thing, it was that the revolution was an antidynastic rupture. Émile Zola retains this sense: natural history is capable of being interrupted again and again. Each moment of *innéité* offers a possibility of progress.[31]

The first assumption undergirding Zola's dynasties concerns the "emplotment" of evolutionary change: we know that evolution tells no tales, but Zola very much wants it to. His second assumption concerns the kind of story he's telling: he insists that he's chronicling a story of decline, but the reader may not be so sure. In a glossary in each of the novels, Zola's précis for Charles Rougon, member of the fifth generation of the Rougons, provides the following description: "CHARLES ROUGON, alias SACCARD, born in 1857, dies of hemorrhage in 1873. Reverting heredity skipping three generations. Physical and moral resemblance to Adelaïde Fouque. The last outcome of an exhausted stock." This note encapsulates the strange nature of the biological fate Zola wants to trace in his Rougon-Macquart cycle of novels. It manages to offer in its three lines two seemingly contradictory accounts of the origins of Charles Rougon's bad DNA: Does it derive from his "reverting heredity"— namely, the fact that he genetically resembles Adelaïde Fouque (i.e., Tante Dide, the matriarch of the entire clan)? Or does it derive from a process of degeneration *from* Tante Dide, the "exhausted stock" of which the note speaks?

Put bluntly, it isn't as though Tante Dide's stock is brimming with vim and vigor—there wouldn't seem to be all that much in it to exhaust. Of course, given that Zola wanted to trace the interaction between milieu and heredity, the idea might be that material conditions (the extreme concentration of wealth, the immiseration of the masses, the failure of the Republic) brought out the worst in Tante Dide's "stock." But even when in unusually comfortable, stimulating, or sheltering circumstances, Adelaïde Fouque's offspring don't exactly seem to thrive. The problem seems to be that Zola can't help himself—the gaze he casts on his characters is almost obsessively diagnostic and spares no one.

The naturalistic analysts of the bourgeois dynasty often found it difficult to stage decline believably. Their declinism committed them to it; but so unsparing and unadmiring were they in portraying the insufficiencies, the petty pathologies, the hereditary problems of the bourgeoisie, that it was hard to see what exactly these families had declined from. In Germany, many of the naturalistic plays of Gerhart Hauptmann open on a well-to-do family in their suburban home, where they live with servants in relative (though faded) splendor. How this dysfunctional gaggle of alcoholics, wracked with venereal diseases and often violent psychoses, who have emerged from a genetic "swamp,"[32] as more than one character puts it, managed to become this well-off in the first place remains utterly mysterious.

By its very nature, the Rougon-Macquart family tree outlines a particular problem of modern dynasticity. For better or for worse, modernity understands itself as *different* from what came before it—but the dynasty was a difficult figure to turn to when one wanted to account for such difference. Whether it was Descartes speaking in the seventeenth century, Kant in the eighteenth, or Hegel in the nineteenth, being modern meant narrating one's difference from past ages. Declinism was one such narrative on offer. Zola wasn't Schopenhauer—his fascination with biological heredity wasn't supposed to deliver the reader into pessimism or fatalism. But the forces he described, at least when viewed scientifically, seemed to have no beginning, middle, and end, seemed to permit no new beginnings, no *difference* that would allow the kind of narrative that conceptions of modernity traditionally relied on. The very modernity of Zola's narration of the Rougon-Macquart dynasty undercut the claim to modernity of the object he was narrating.

The Poetics of the Dynasty

In his set of notes entitled *Différences entre Balzac et moi* (*Differences between Balzac and Myself*, 1869), Zola sought to outline steps the as yet germinal Rougon-Macquart cycle would take beyond Honoré de Balzac's multivolume collection *La comédie humaine*.[33] In these notes, Zola found the formula for his novelistic experiment: he wanted to ascertain "how the race is modified by the environment."[34] This experimental setup highlights a complication at the heart of his poetics: on the one hand, he seeks to chart heredity diachronically, and on the other he commits himself to fleshing out milieu in almost exhausting levels of detail.

These two aims needn't be contradictory. But what is remarkable is that Zola almost seems to want them to be. In several of the cycle's installments, most noticeably in *The Kill*, he stages a confrontation between rollicking, sweeping narratives and an exhaustive, excessive, and downright punishing level of detailed description. In so doing, he provides a poetics of the dynasty: certain features of the cycle make dynasty visible and narratable, and other features obscure it.

With Walter Benjamin, we could posit the concept of natural history as the concern of the cycle: throughout the novels is a modernity that drives forward, juxtaposed to a natural world that persists in its essences, that remains what it has always been.[35] Consider for instance the opening of *Nana* (1880), the ninth novel of the cycle: it is the time of the Grand Exhibition, which celebrates unprecedented progress, a world illuminated by gaslight but about to be introduced to electric light. At Bordenave's theater, all talk is about the proprietor's "new star," Nana, who will appear in her role as the "blonde Venus." The world's oldest profession and the *dernier cri* of fashion vie with each other in this opening chapter.

The new (fifteen-year-old Nana) appears in the guise of the old (Venus), and the novel seeks to answer the question raised by the fact that either what has always been wears the mask of the unprecedented, or else the utterly new appears dressed up as something perfectly traditional. One of the two is phony, is a mask, but which is it? Is Nana a new kind of woman, or simply another avatar of the world's oldest profession? Zola's answer seems to be the latter: like the spring fashion collection, the latest gadget, or the gossip item, the rejuvenation promised by Nana is illusory. She's simply another iteration, teasing something new but ultimately delivering repetition.

But, following Walter Benjamin's instincts in the Arcades Project, it's worth taking the metaphor of the new star seriously.[36] In the context of a theater that's basically a bordello, the word may sound simply tawdry, but think of the starry heavens that rotate unfalteringly above us each night. How immense an occurrence would a new star be there, how violently would it reshape truths we had hitherto thought eternal, how would it turn on their head the coordinates by which we navigate? The metaphor of Nana as the new star carries both a winking acknowledgment that *new* here doesn't mean truly new and a tremulous fantasy of what *true* newness might look like, the kind of newness promised but not delivered by the World Exhibition.

This is the great theme of Zola's Rougon-Macquart cycle: a world starving for political, social, and intellectual renewal, yet frustrated in this desire at every turn. The first novel of the cycle, *The Fortunes of the Rougons*, opens on marching revolutionary insurrectionists—chanting "La Marseillaise" and waving the *tricolore*, they march on the provincial capital to bring about a new world. *The Kill*, the next novel in the cycle, opens on a traffic jam. The *tricolore* in question is being swung by a virginal girl marching next to her boyfriend, and the traffic jam finds Aristide Saccard's young wife in a state of masturbatory excitement that will eventually lead her to incest. Zola's family tree is the story of hope for renewal and its persistent frustration—every birth is just a continuation of the previous generation's defects. But over it all hangs a sense that it might yet become entirely different, that rebirth might be possible.

Often enough, the gesture of hope Zola presents at the end of each of his novels can seem as contrived as his gesture of closure. And that surely is part of the point. *Doctor Pascal* closes on the birth of the late Pascal Rougon's child—a child of incest, latest spawn of a tainted line. But the novel treats his birth as yet another chance for renewal, hoping against hope that this birth really fulfills the break with the hereditary past envisioned by the boy's father, whom he will never meet. *Germinal* closes on an even stranger, more tantalizing moment of hope: stripped of everything, having barely escaped death in a collapsed mine, a traumatized Étienne Lantier cannot but see signs of rebirth and rejuvenation—of *germinalité*—everywhere. Catherine has her first period as a large swath of the novel's characters are killed in a massacre. As she is about to die in the collapsed mine, she and Étienne sleep together for the first time. Later, he sits near her dead body, and the idea "that she might be pregnant move[s] him."[37]

The suffering that capitalism inflicts on the characters in *Germinal* increasingly comes to seem like an act of fertilization, the fertilization of a coming race, like the one Edward Bulwer-Lytton's narrator encounters after a mine collapse ushers him into the hollow interior of the earth. There he meets the far more advanced Vril, "a people calmly developing . . . powers surpassing our most disciplined modes of force." Étienne offers the reverse of the exhortation with which Bulwer-Lytton closes his novel *The Coming Race* (1871), which ends with a prayer "that ages may yet elapse before there emerge into sunlight our inevitable destroyers."[38] In contrast, Étienne luxuriates in the certainty of their arrival. The novel ends with a vision of the teeming coal pits of northern France as the womb that will breed a revolutionary race; it isn't here yet but will be soon enough.

All around Étienne, dead matter comes alive. If previously the Montsou mine had seemed more like a giant digestive mechanism, the novel now plays up its womblike characteristics. The mine becomes a field, a garden in which a revolutionary harvest grows: "as its belly swelled with a black and avenging army of men, germinating slowly in the furrows, growing upward in readiness for harvests to come, until one day soon their ripening would burst open the earth itself." As Étienne walks away from the mine, we get something of a restaging of Aristide's hothouse—all is growth, newness, youth, "the old world want[ing] to live for another springtime."[39]

But it's growth with a goal, not the rampant, pointless rutting of the orchids in their confined environment: "Was Darwin right, then?" Étienne wonders, and adopts yet again the moralized gaze on heredity Zola was so fond of. But what he sees is not disease, alcoholism, and "warped" heredity—so he adduces evolution as a harbinger of something entirely new and different: "New blood would create a new society. And in his expectation of a barbarian invasion which would regenerate the decadent old nations, there reappeared his absolute faith in a forthcoming revolution, the real one, that of the workers."[40]

Zola renders newness and fatalism throughout the Rougon-Macquart cycle in genetic terms. Even the title *Germinal* refers to efflorescence, to something that isn't fully here yet but will come to be. But this title also points to the fact that we've been here before: it's the neologism the revolutionaries behind the French republican calendar of 1793 coined for the second half of March and early April. And it also points out that we'll be there again: the calendar, which was abolished by Napoleon I, would be reintroduced by the Paris Commune about a decade after the events recounted in *Germinal*, with the month running for eighteen days, from 16 Floréal to 3 Prairial. But distinguishing repetition from genuine renewal seems awfully difficult in the book to which this revolutionary month lends its name: does *Germinal* tell a story of continuity or discontinuity, of continuity masquerading as discontinuity, or vice versa?

Zola's entire scope in the Rougon-Macquart cycle—his scientific pretensions, his family trees, his pop evolutionism—has its one great virtue in not letting us shrug off this question as undecidable. Everything depends on deciding what is progress and evolution and what is just eternal recurrence, and the novels never let us forget it. They drag us along in action-packed set pieces that are breathtaking, only to then drop us in labyrinths of description that are deliberately wearying. The stakes of progress and regress can be felt as bodily effects when reading the Rougon-Macquart novels; they travel straight from the Rougons' nerves to ours.

The Kill in particular is a novel of surfeit and stagnation. The immense wealth surrounding the characters petrifies them; and the description of said wealth constantly threatens to derail the project Zola laid out at the beginning of the Rougon-Macquart cycle. He keeps wanting to describe process (the hereditary process, the advent and fall of the Second Empire), but he constantly ends up describing orchids, balustrades, dinner tables, statues. In his famous essay "Narrate or Describe,"[41] Georg Lukács opposes narration to description and associates the former with Tolstoy, the latter with Zola. He could just have easily juxtaposed Zola to Zola.

The first chapter of the novel deals with one oppressive afternoon spent in a traffic jam and then at an oppressively opulent dinner party. In the second chapter, Zola zips through fifteen years of Rougon-Macquart family history. In addition, this chapter traffics in general nouns—people get rid of "their things," or are discarded "like furniture"; the first, by contrast, suffocates under the amount of detail it amasses. The word *furniture* or *thing* would be utterly out of place. Instead, we're told that a "table, standing in the middle of the wide, dark Persian carpet, which deadened the sound of footsteps, and under the glaring light of the chandelier, surrounded by chairs whose black backs, with fillets of gold, encircled it in a dark frame, seemed like an altar, like a chapel of rest, as the bright reflection of the crystal glass and silver plate sparkled on the dazzling whiteness of the tablecloth."[42] Zola, himself quite poor when he wrote *The Kill*, is said to have toured the great mansions of Paris in order to research his novel—at times it can seem as though every single fruit of his observation has made it onto the page. The details accrue without any view to salience: we need not assume that the tablecloth is white and the crystal sparkles on the mere technicality of seeming perfectly obvious—we'll be told so explicitly.

Nowhere is this clearer than in chapter 1, in Aristide's hothouse. Zola was one to treat description as "an account of the environment which determines and completes man."[43] Important plot developments take place in the hothouse, but the first time we follow a character in, we're treated to page after page of details: of course, the flowers all must be named and their smells described, along with the pools of water in which they stand and the odors that water gives off. At times, Zola's amassing of details can seem like the predicament of the sorcerer's apprentice—the spirits he invokes he can no longer rid himself of. Yet the second chapter reveals his labored massing as a pretense—Zola is, here as ever, very much in control of his literary tricks—though for a moment we can really feel terror at the vision of a narrative buried under the immensity of the detail he has conjured up.

Why does this matter? The second chapter, once released from the burden of excessive description, can finally start narrating its epic story, in many respects making good on the program Zola set out for his cycle. It traces the path of the Rougons from Plassans to Paris; it moves at breakneck speed through marriages and deaths and manages to compress the dizzying ascent of Aristide Rougon into all of forty pages. Furniture is just furniture, a wedding is just a wedding; and if we're treated to pages on pages of description, as when we're introduced to Aristide's sister Sidonie, that description lays out not her home or shop but the pointless gyres of her crooked yet ineffectual business dealings. If the first chapter seems always poised at the brink of petrification, the second liquefies everything into circulation.

It also reconfigures how Zola's text creates meaning. The hothouse is not just an emblem for the Second Empire, it is importantly also a hothouse *of* emblems. Good taste would dictate that writers use their symbols, metaphors, and metonymies with a certain sense of economy and decorum, but whenever his lovers retire to the hothouse, Zola's prose runs riot. Not only is the wealth of details stupefying and not a little bit claustrophobic, so, too, is the wealth of allegories—no opportunity for association, reference, allusion, or parody seems left out: "Under the arches placed here and there between the shrubs hung baskets suspended from wire chains, and filled with orchids, fantastic plants of the air, which pushed in every direction their crooked tendrils, bent and twisted like the limbs of cripples. There were cypripediums, whose flowers resemble a wonderful slipper with a heel adorned by a dragonfly's wings; aerides, so delicately scented; stanhopeas, with pale tiger flowers, which exhale from afar a strong and acrid breath, as from the putrid mouths of convalescent invalids."[44] Some flowers look like women's mouths, we are told, while others smell of putrefaction. The space is alternately described as a church, a factory, a jungle, or a garden. Somewhere in the hothouse, classical statues stand out from the overgrowth. These are metonymies of colonialism, mementos of the Napoleonic Wars, the relationship to Greek antiquity, questions of descent and degeneration; and in the middle of this semiotic thicket rests a "great sphinx in black marble,"[45] asking us a question about the nature of man.

Two of these literary devices would be a bit much. Three feels like overkill. But Zola is not content until he hits double digits. And whenever the characters are in the hothouse, they take on the role of flowers, of pollinating insects, of the statuary or the sphinx. The second chapter, by contrast, will create meaning through behavior—there is much less need for allegory, symbol, or metonymy. Rather than relying on a stock of static, storied, or traditional associations; its sphinx is the teeming compass of human behavior and interaction.

This feels like a confrontation, because Zola works hard to stage it as one. The descriptive rigor of the project threatens at moments to derail the entire enterprise, which is, after all, one of historical narration. The proliferation of details in *The Kill* accomplishes three things: it bogs down the story of the experiment Zola claims to be conducting; it makes the outlines of that story difficult for the reader to espy; and it makes it difficult for even the characters to espy those outlines. Not just the life process of heredity seems to be impacted by the proliferation of stuff around the characters; the all-important *narration* of that process, the "immense book, open to all eyes"[46] of which Lucas speaks, is occluded by the description of that stuff.

This last point matters immensely, because as the last novel in the Rougon-Macquart cycle, *Doctor Pascal*, makes clear, this vantage point is the only one that offers the characters some measure of escape from the biological fate they're caught in. The trickle-down effect of defective heredity, which the reader notices so clearly, is what Dr. Pascal Rougon finally manages to see. It is what dooms all the other members of the family tree to whelm helplessly in the wake of the previous generations' transgressions.

The narrative gestures by which Zola plays off heredity and milieu against each other thus reflect the Manichaean logic of heredity that rules the Rougon-Macquart dynasty. On the one hand, characters are honest with themselves and assess their own modernity or their own atavism with some clarity—this is the viewpoint the titular *Doctor Pascal* finds in the last novel in the cycle. On the other hand, they mistake for progress what was in reality a mired lingering in the cesspools of tradition and heredity—the problem Zola regarded as characterizing the Second Empire in general, which had, as Marx put it, decided to repeat tragedy as farce and call it progress.

But what if the strange generativity Étienne seems to detect at the end of *Germinal* were to bear fruit—a generativity that would not be *hindered* by allegory and symbol but instead would *progress by means* of allegory and symbol? It would no longer be possible to provide a family tree for such a buzzing, blooming profusion, and its genealogy would lack the neatness that Zola imposes on his Rougons and Macquarts. Skipping forward in time, we find another garden and another dynasty—albeit one without a family tree. In the garden of the Guermantes family, Marcel Proust restages the erotic botanism of Aristide Saccard's hothouse but with an entirely different logic of heredity.

Proust's Garden

At the beginning of *Sodome et Gomorrhe* (*Sodom and Gomorra*), the fourth volume in *A la recherche du temps perdu* (*Remembrance of Things Past*, 1913–27), the narrator, Marcel, finds himself in another stately garden. It's the garden of the Paris estate of the Duchesse de Guermantes. While there, Marcel becomes fascinated with a rare orchid the *duchesse* keeps well protected against all contaminants at the center of her garden. He reflects how cosmically improbable it would be that an insect should carry just the right kind of pollen to this exile from more exotic climes, which, with undaunted, unquenchable faith still proffers its flowers to the uncomprehending shores: "Lacking the perspective of the geologist, I at least had that of the botanist, and gazed through the shutters on the stairs at the Duchesse's small shrub and the precious plant exhibited in the courtyard with that insistence with which the marriageable young are thrust forward, and I wondered whether, by some providential chance, the improbable insect would come to visit the tendered and forlorn pistil."[47]

Proust's narrator decides that such a "providential chance" would indeed be a miracle. Zola had insisted that the "experimental" novel was designed precisely not to narrate such moments, even if in moments of *innéité* he seemed to rely on them nonetheless. Instead, in naturalistic genealogy "living beings, in which the vitalists still admitted a mysterious influence, are in their turn brought under and reduced to the general mechanism of matter."[48] No such mechanism should produce the spectacle Marcel is hoping to witness; no statistical distribution in the mode of Gregor Mendel ought to capture it. And yet he lies in wait for it: "I resolved not to be disturbed again for fear of missing, were the miracle to occur, the arrival, almost impossible to hope for (across all the obstacles, the distance, the contrary chances, the dangers), of the insect sent from afar as an ambassador to the virgin whose wait had been so protracted."[49] When the miracle arrives, Marcel is far too distracted, for he's witnessing a different kind of fertilization, another spectacle "almost impossible to hope for." He witnesses the encounter, and the eventual *conjonction*, of the Baron de Charlus and the waistcoat maker Jupien. As he observes their flirt, the baron morphs into an insect and Jupien into a flower, "striking poses with the coquettishness that the orchid might have had for the providential advent of the bumblebee."[50]

It's striking just how far Marcel takes the comparison: for while it's the rarity of the display that draws him into the spectacle of the orchid and the *invertis*, he sustains his analogy far longer than needed. Consider, for instance, his explanation of the dangers of self-fertilization, which sounds an awful lot like Prosper Lucas's or Émile Zola's theories: "If the visit of an insect, that is to say, the bringing of the seed from another flower, is necessary as a rule to fertilize the flower, this is because self-fertilization, the fertilization of the flower by itself, like repeated marriages within the same family, would lead to degeneration and sterility, whereas the crossbreeding effected by insects gives to succeeding generations of the same species a vigor unknown among their elders."[51] The narrator does not return to this bit of pop-evolutionary thought, but the implication is clear: the incredibly rare display of bumblebee and orchid is crucial to the maintenance of the hereditary line, its vim and vigor; what about that other incredibly rare display?[52]

The nineteenth century would have seen in inversion precisely an index of "self-fertilization," of "degeneration," of "sterility."[53] But Proust's image won't permit us that association, because he insists on the uncanny generative power of these unlikely *conjonctions*. What Marcel sees looking on the garden of the Hôtel of the Guermantes is quite different from what Docteur Pascal comes to see in his family tree. It isn't a family tree at all: its branches aren't made solid and universally legible but instead are made of pure evanescence. And yet the narrator insists that they, like the Rougons, constitute *une race*— a *race maudite* (cursed race), a *race des tantes* (literally race of aunts).

Zola's readers are supposed to detect the forces of determinism, of necessity in the distribution of generations, without any intervening "miracle" of free will or divine grace. Marcel looks for something he describes as a miracle, and he sees instead another process he casts in miraculous terms. The *conjonction* of two *invertis*, just as rare, just as improbable, but just as ubiquitous as the fertilization of a precious orchid by a bumblebee, is a biological fluke, but the language of the entire episode brims with awe at that fluke.

At the same time, the productivity seems bound up with the productivity of language. As Emily Eells has pointed out, homosexual signifiers proliferate throughout the *Recherche* precisely where characters (or indeed the narrator) are not fully in control of their discourse, where their word choices, comparisons, or jokes say more than they intend.[54] The generativity of "the multiplicity of these comparisons," by which "the same man seems successively to be a man, a man-bird, or a man-insect, and so on,"[55] gives hereditary, dynastic character to the miraculous, seemingly singular event Marcel witnesses. The very choice of allegory seems to commit the narrator to saying something he probably does not mean to say: that Jupien and the baron, like orchid and bumblebee, procreate, institute a lineage.

The *race des tantes* Marcel describes in exhaustive detail after the episode in the garden is a race constituted entirely through such miracles. It's a lineage that does not follow necessity but rather constitutes itself in and through breaks from what's necessary and probable. This was the mode of dynasty preferred by decadence and early modernism—by Oscar Wilde, Thomas Mann, Frank Wedekind, and others. Such a dynasty has no tree; not a concatenation of nuclear families, each transmitting its heredity to the next, but rather a family without nucleus. An anti-Aristotelian dynasty, it has no beginning, middle, and end. Where Émile Zola and Gerhart Hauptmann once regarded the dynastic space opened up by Mendel and Darwin as a chaotic one in need of harnessing, they came to understand it as one capable of new and unprecedented structuring.

7

Freud, or The Reluctant Patriarch

Her name was Ida Bauer, but the world would come to know her as Dora. Suffering from intermittent loss of voice and a nervous cough, she was brought to the office of Sigmund Freud by her father. In Freud's writeup of her case (as "A Case of Hysteria"), we learn that she had a brother, we hear that she has an aunt. Her mother remains a spectral presence throughout Freud's analysis. "I never made her mother's acquaintance," he notes, but adds that "from the accounts given me by the girl and her father I was led to imagine her as an uncultivated woman, and above all a foolish one."[1] We are introduced to a couple friendly with her parents, Herr and Frau K., who will become important in her analysis. Of her extended family we learn nothing. Freud seems determined to restrict his cast of characters: even when he gets to her mother, his interest dwindles.

This pattern holds in Freud's other case studies. Sergei Pankejeff, immortalized by Freud as "the Wolf Man," had a wide variety of symptoms Freud could trace to a moment of excessive closeness between the infant Pankejeff and his parents: in sharing their bedroom, he had witnessed his father take his mother from behind; Freud deduced that this was the "primal scene" behind his infantile neurosis. In the case of "Little Hans," the patient who furnished Freud with much of his evidence for the Oedipus complex, Freud even deputized the young boy's father to act as his surrogate analyst.

In all these cases, the nuclear family is the cause of, and the solution to, all life's problems. "They fuck you up, your mum and dad,"[2] Philip Larkin wrote, and in Freud's estimation fucking you up appeared to be their exclusive job and prerogative. No one else got to do it. The unhappy families Freud met through his analytic work are self-contained affairs. Grandparents rarely figure into the story, and the kind of *lesions héréditaires* that dominate

Émile Zola's families are entirely absent. Later in life, Pankejeff pointed out how unlikely it was that he, the child of Russian aristocrats, would have slept in his parents' bedroom at all—the kind of intimacy and self-containment presupposed by something like a "primal scene" simply hadn't existed in his household.[3] There was something fantastical, almost phantasmic about the closeness Freud projected onto the families he conjured up during analysis. Even his own familial arrangement didn't adhere to the kind of structure he imputed to those of his analysands.

The families appearing in Freud's writings, both the theoretical texts and the case studies, tend to be nuclear, even if their nucleus is frequently in tatters. They are certainly less complex than the family in which Freud himself grew up, in which his half-brother was his mother's age and seemingly a better match for her too. Whether through an act of repression, canny marketing, or methodological foreshortening, Freud usually presents families as parents and children and little more.

Persons beyond the nucleus factor into the family's dynamics, but usually as triggers and disturbances. In describing Dora's case, Freud settles on a series of culprits for her symptoms—an aunt she adores, a couple friendly with her parents, a governess, a cousin—all of whom hail from outside the girl's nuclear family. But in the end his gaze seems magnetically drawn to Frau K., and above all to Herr K. Compared to the literary texts of Romanticism from which Freud so frequently drew for inspiration, the power of family members outside the nucleus seems considerably weakened.

In later editions of the Dora case, Freud included a footnote about the role of heredity as the main etiological factor in hysteria. Here, he emphasizes that he doesn't want to create the impression that heredity "can be dispensed with." But just as soon as he makes this admission, he circumscribes the sort of heredity he's most interested in—heredity that emerges directly from the parents' actions. For he allows that Dora's mother may well have inherited her hysteria and passed it on to her daughter, but he insists that "there is another factor which is of more significance in the girl's hereditary or, properly speaking, constitutional predisposition." That factor is the syphilis Dora's father had contracted either before marrying Dora's mother or while married to her.[4] Freud seems to regard the transmission of neuroses as proceeding according to a Lamarckian model of evolution, by which acquired traits can be passed down to future generations—but these traits hailed from one's immediate, rather than distant, ancestry.[5]

Freud was more comfortable blaming a two-timing father than a contaminated heredity—and his predisposition agreed with that of many of his contemporaries. Viennese bourgeois of his era tended to think of their politics, their society, their art as profoundly nuclear, in terms Freud would eventually call oedipal—a rebellion of sons against fathers.[6] The people who stepped through Freud's door were often scions of the self-made men who had risen to prominence in the mid-nineteenth century and moved to Vienna only recently. They lived mostly in the ninth district, in grand new constructions not unlike Freud's own building at Berggasse 19. Their Vienna was no longer that of the medieval ramparts but the new Vienna represented by the institutions clustered around the Ringstrasse, which had replaced those ramparts. For them, dynasties were other people; their own lineage was frequently a bit of an embarrassment—whether they were small tradesmen who'd risen to the top of the heap through lucky investments or Eastern Jews shedding the dust and the pogroms of the Bukovina in favor of a *palais* in the fourth district. The Freuds, of course, who hailed from rural Moravia and had moved to Vienna via Leipzig when Sigmund was three, were among them.

More generally, psychoanalysis proceeds from a central assumption that is antidynastic in character, though it may not appear that way at first. There's a simple reason why the people who matter to Freud's picture of sexual development are father, mother, and siblings: sexual development happens in early childhood. This may seem like a trivial point, but Freud's intuition that the etiology of neuroses was to be located inside the nuclear family was a minority opinion among those dedicated to puzzling out the origins of hysteria in the closing decades of the nineteenth century. Jean-Martin Charcot and Josef Breuer both insisted that hysteria was hereditary—that is, they located its origins in the family's past rather than the individual's.[7] Freud entertained this possibility early in his career; but starting with the so-called seduction hypothesis, he increasingly insisted there must be a nonhereditary element to the etiology of hysterical symptoms, and that it's to be sought in that part of the family history the individual was actually present for, even if that individual did not consciously register it.

Freud understood this as his original and revolutionary contribution to the theory of hysteria—and he'd later make it a cornerstone of his picture of the mind. The text in which he did so, the *Drei Abhandlungen zur Sexualtheorie* (*Three Essays on Sexuality*, 1905), makes explicit that its theory of infantile sexuality is meant to replace theories seeking the origins of sexuality in a structure that might be called dynastic—that is to say in the prehistory of the family. Instead, Freud seeks to locate it in the immanence of the nuclear family—in the prehistory of the individual: "It is remarkable that writers who concern themselves with explaining the characteristics and reactions of the adult have devoted much more attention to that prehistory which is given to us by the lifespan of our ancestors, in other words have allotted such outsize importance to heredity, than the other prehistory, which already falls into the individual existence of the person, namely childhood."[8] The concept of infantile sexuality, in other words, is intended as something of a replacement for dynastic modes of explanation. The individual subject is as ignorant about one as the other; but in one depiction the energies threatening the nuclear family are (inherited) factors that transcend that family, while in the other they are native to it.

There is something cheeky in Freud's finding this fact "remarkable," for many of his contemporaries would have seen nothing remarkable in what he describes. As we have seen, the nineteenth century had been obsessed with subsuming individual ends and drives into the dynastic force of the group, the family, the nation. It was commonplace to locate the mysteries of human psychology in the distant past; if anything, it was Freud's claim that their explanation was far closer to hand that stood out. So why "remarkable"? Does Freud think his suggestion better because it locates the etiology of individual psychology closer in time to the adult individual? Is it supposed to be more commonsensical in some way?

Most likely, Freud understood his emphasis on the nuclear family to constitute a kind of residual humanism. Against the anthropologists, the biologists, the craniometers, and the physiognomists, against Zola and his experimental novel and Schopenhauer and the will of the species, he insisted that at long last the key to the mysteries of human experience were to be found . . . in human experience.[9] Of course, the unconscious is no more recoverable, knowable, or domesticated in Freud's account than it was, say, for advocates of evolutionary theory. But at least it came from us as individuals, from our lifetime, from decisions and misapprehensions that we in some way made, albeit before we became properly us. It also made Freud a late scion of Enlightenment thought: a believer in the anthropogenic character of our lifeworld and a believer in our ability to master that lifeworld by understanding our shaping of it more fully.

The paper in which Freud most decisively broke with Charcot, "L'Heredité et l'étiologie des nevroses" ("Heredity and the Etiology of the Neuroses," 1896), makes clear that he also wanted to forestall ethnic or even racial categorization of neuroses—specifically the wide-spread idea of neurosis and neurasthenia as "Jewish" diseases. Against Charcot, he marshaled the fact that people of similar extraction can show very different symptoms, and that people of very different extraction can show strikingly similar ones. His break with dynastic predetermination went along with an emphasis on the universality of hysterical symptoms and the universality of their psychoanalytic remedy.

With the discovery of infantile sexuality, Freud became the Freud we now know. But in abandoning the hereditary theories of Charcot and Breuer, he had initially entertained a different counterproposal and maintained it for quite some time. It was this account of the etiology of neurosis, the so-called seduction hypothesis, that he abandoned in his now-classic treatments of hysteria. The seduction hypothesis proposed that hysteria originated from *actual* experiences during infancy—something happened to us and our infant mind couldn't assimilate the experience. Most frequently, those actual experiences would be some sort of child sexual abuse. In the *Three Essays*, Freud decided that hysteria emerged rather from the fantasy life of the infant, from erotic attentions the infant desired, not from ones it actually experienced.

This move could be seen (and was in fact seen by later feminist critics)[10] as a colossal failure of nerve: Isn't it at least possible that Freud had stumbled on a pattern of victimization of girls by a patriarchal power structure, and had then decided that it was all in the girls' heads? Did Freud declare infants and children perverse in order to not have to accuse his own age of unconscionable perversity? He wasn't usually afraid of upsetting his contemporaries; in fact, he often delighted in doing so. Perhaps, then, the more likely explanation for his rather jarring abandonment of the seduction hypothesis is to be sought in his theoretical premises. That stepping away emancipated the individual unconscious from the last vestiges of dynasticity: everything that roiled the unconscious now originated from the possessor of said unconscious (or, perhaps better, the one possessed *by* said unconscious). What mother and father *did* no longer mattered; what mattered instead was what the child's desire projected onto mother and father.

And yet the decisiveness of these early gestures of bracketing did not effectively banish the troubling possibilities presented by a dynastic unconscious. Kept largely at bay in the classic case studies and in the work on infantile sexuality, it reentered Freud's oeuvre before long. It remained largely absent from his analytic work with patients, but of course he started publishing in fields only distantly tethered to the lavishly draped couch in Berggasse 19. In the years leading up to World War I, Freud started training his analytic acumen on culture at large—the neuroses he sought to investigate in his writings now held entire populations, or even all of humanity, in their grip.

At the same time, the dynasty began to infiltrate his personal life, for Freud started to gain followers. And while most of the designations for the group he gathered around himself were intended to highlight the psychoanalytic movement's horizontal organization (e.g., it was a "society" with elected presidents), in his letters Freud instead cast the movement in emphatically familial terms. He called his younger followers—the first apostate Alfred Adler, the new heir apparent Carl Gustav Jung, and the loyalist Ludwig Binswanger—"dear son,"[11] and wrote to Binswanger that Jung should "inherit it all."[12] His younger colleagues followed his lead. Jung could write to Freud calling him "father," apologizing for "my pranks." And, of course, his unofficial designation as "Freud's crown prince" heightened the dynastic dimensions of the psychoanalytic community in its early years.[13]

As Freud's ambitions grew, and as he began cultivating heirs to carry on his legacy, he began rethinking his opposition to the heredity of neuroses. A late text like *Der Mann Mose und die Monotheistische Religion* (*Moses and Monotheism*, 1939) relies quite heavily on the idea that a repressed memory might travel by way of heredity through the eons, all the way from the murdered Egyptian Moses to modern-day Jewry. Likewise, Freud's insistence that the *Urhorde*'s murder of the primal father was an actual historical event rather than a symbolic process seems intent on going back into the earliest prehistory at the expense of looking for the origins of human aggression in, say, early childhood development.

While the Freud of the *Three Essays* was content to linger within the immanence of the bourgeois nuclear family, the later works often labor under a mania for transcending it, for traveling up and down the dynastic chain. Starting in the 1910s, the term *archaic heritage* began to creep into Freud's writings; by the 1930s it was ubiquitous. In "Analysis Terminable and Interminable," his 1937 essay that can count as something of a sigh of resignation, Freud allows for precisely such a heritage. And in *Moses and Monotheism*, he points out that "the behavior of neurotic children towards their parents in the Oedipus and castration complex abounds in such reactions, which seem unjustified in the individual case and only become intelligible phylogenetically—by their connection with the experience of earlier generations."[14]

A famous passage in *Jenseits des Lustprinzips* (*Beyond the Pleasure Principle*, 1919) suggests that the two—the heredity of neurosis and the dynastic project of psychoanalysis itself—were in fact linked in Freud's mind. When introducing the challenge posed to traditional libidinal theory by the compulsion to repeat, Freud mostly frames his analysis in terms of traumatic neuroses—stark, dramatic pathologies afflicting shell-shocked soldiers and victims of violence. But then he points out that in far less noticeable, far less obtrusive, and far less debilitating ways, the compulsion to repeat asserts itself in the life of "healthy" individuals as well. As so often is the case in such instances, he demonstrates the prevalence of neurotic symptoms even among those who would see no need to seek out a psychoanalyst to alleviate them in their own person. For the portrait he offers is in fact a sly bit of autobiography:

> Thus one knows people with whom every human relationship ends in the same way: benefactors whose protégés, however different they may otherwise have been, invariably after a time desert them in ill-will, so that they are

apparently condemned to drain to the dregs all the bitterness of ingratitude; men with whom every friendship ends in the friend's treachery; others who indefinitely often in their lives invest some other person with authority either in their own eyes or generally, and themselves overthrow such authority after a given time, only to replace it by a new one; lovers whose tender relationships with women each and all run through the same phases and come to the same end, and so on.[15]

The introduction of the death drive, and the repetition compulsion that constitutes its most pervasive symptom, thus coincide with a return of the dynastic family into the etiology of neurosis. Not only does Freud here tell a story of a man frustrated in his dynastic designs; the very experience that occasions his frustrations is no longer to be sought in the prehistory of childhood but rather in the prehistory of the species. By a supreme bit of irony, what frustrates this man's dynastic ambitions is something inherited. He's not acting out an oedipal trauma with these men who are his friends until they disappoint him; he's acting out a drive as old as the species—a ghost from the infancy of mankind, not of the individual.

This was the period when Freud became obsessed with temporal origins, origins lying neither in the individual biography nor in the constitution of the organism. Such events happened once and transmitted themselves in culture. It would be easy to dissolve the doctrine of original sin into a simple operation of the human superego—Freud had done it before and continued to do it. But in *Totem und Tabu* (*Totem and Taboo*, 1913), he found an actual event that had precipitated the idea—an actual guilt, an actual murder, an actual moment of fall. The fourth chapter of this exercise in speculative anthropology draws from Charles Darwin's suggestion that early humans may have been centered on a single alpha male from which male offspring were cast out. As those outcasts rebelled and slew the father, they gave rise in one moment to the Oedipus complex and to the guilt that, Freud believed, lay at the heart of religious feeling. The central structuring engine of the nuclear family, the Oedipus complex, was itself a dynastic inheritance of the oldest provenance, a *lésion héréditaire* on the entire species. *Totem and Taboo* opens the era of the *Urhorde*, of Abraham, of Moses.

Totem and Taboo, the book that roused Jung's oedipal anguish, aims to investigate, as per its subtitle, "correspondences" (einige Übereinstimmungen) "in the mental life of savages and neurotics." The term *correspondence* leaves open what if any causative aspect there is to this link between the analytic patient and the faraway "savage" tribe. In the fourth essay of the book, Freud speaks of the "infantile return" of totemism; in others he is content to speak of "similarities." He is, in other words, leery of just the type of "collective unconscious" that would preexist, and then assert itself in, the mental life of children—an idea that Jung was just then developing.

Freud opens his book by explicitly distinguishing his approach from that of Wilhelm Wundt (the father of *Völkerpsychologie*, the psychology of peoples) and the "Zurich psychoanalytic school," meaning Jung.[16] Whereas they declare the individual unconscious subservient to an unconscious of the *Volk*, Freud argues, the point of *Totem and Taboo* is to assign no such primacy to either the collective or the individual. Notably, Freud does not (as Jung later would) impute to himself the opposite position to the "Zurich school," that is to say making the collective unconscious a function of the individual unconscious—a sign of how far he had moved from the Enlightenment humanism of the *Three Essays*. At the same time, his embrace of the collective isn't total: behind it all, behind eons of human culture and the very origins of guilt looms, yes, another family—not quite nuclear but self-contained, a family not unlike Freud's own.

In the four essays collected in *Totem and Taboo*, Freud seeks to shed light on the psychological origins of totemism, which, thanks to James Frazer and Wilhelm Wundt along with interventions by Émile Durkheim and Edvard Alexander Westermarck, had become a central question in the burgeoning field of anthropology. Freud's intervention in their debate is to reframe the connection between totem (the animal spirit that defines the outlines of a tribe) and the enforcement of exogamy (the "taboo" of the title). Against nominalist theories of the origin of totemism, by which the totem animal behaves rather like a family name, and sociological theories, by which the totem animal is used to police social life, Freud suggests that the totem is actually understood by a tribe as its ancestor. For thinkers like Durkheim, the totem simply "embodies the community, making it the true object of veneration."[17] Yet, as Freud saw it, this took insufficient account of the genealogical dimensions of the totem and the sexual theories that ultimately animated sexual taboos.

The titular link of totem and taboo thus robbed the community of the totem's immanence and inserted it into a dynastic mode of descent: it had little to do with what a tribe took its present situation to be, but rather elaborated a primitive genealogical theory. Totemism can "return" in the mental life of the child, because the original murder of the primal father by the *Urhorde* created the structures (religious guilt and the Oedipus complex) that shape the child's mental life. Thus, "community rests on the common guilt for the communally committed murder, religion on the sense of guilt and regret for the deed, ethical life [*Sittlichkeit*] . . . in part on the deeds of penance demanded by this guilt."[18] Human subjectivity is but a subdeclension of an original sin, Freud argues, and the human psyche the product of an event lost in the distance of time. That this event was in essence a family quarrel, that in other words behind the dynasty looms again the very oedipality it's supposed to explain, is among the rich ironies of Freud's text. But its mode of transmission from generation to generation makes clear that there's nothing spontaneous or self-creating about the subject's mental life: the only humans ever to have had a choice about having an Oedipus complex were the members of the *Urhorde*.

This argument clearly reverses the idea that opens Freud's essay "Infantile Sexuality." Now the etiology of the individual's neuroses is, at least in one important respect, to be found in the history of the family rather than the history of the individual. The feeling of guilt that pervades the family is but a distant reverberation of a millennia-old guilt that has suffused the culture as religious doctrine. In *Moses and Monotheism*, his last published work, Freud famously proposes that Moses was not in fact a Hebrew but rather an Egyptian named Tutmoses, who brought the monotheistic cult of Aton to the slave tribes of Israel, only to be murdered by them. It was a troubling argument, troubling no less to Freud himself, who acknowledges in his preface that 1938 might be a uniquely inappropriate year to be making public a wild theory about the murderous roots of Jewish identity. The thought seems to have forced itself on Freud, but its very unwelcomeness suggests that it might be authentic.

Moses and Monotheism is a story about passing on ideas. Like genetic material, Freud explains, certain suppositions are transmitted unconsciously from generation to generation in families, in tribes, in entire peoples. But *Moses* focuses on two such means of transmission. Freud's historic Moses is one of the last adherents of a religion on the brink of eradication; to save the ideas of Akhenaten's Aton cult, he imparts them to the enslaved Israelites, entrusts these ideas to this tribe for safekeeping. For Freud, the very unlikelihood of this development vouches for its truth content, for this unlikelihood was preserved in memory. The God of Abraham who chooses out of all the nations a small desert tribe to be "his" people is, Freud thinks, a distant echo of the incomprehensible decision leading Tutmoses to entrust his defamed religion to his slaves.

But once Tutmoses is killed, his memory—now as Moses the Hebrew rather than Moses the Egyptian—passes along far less elective lines. As though to atone for the incomprehension with which they repaid the incomprehensibility of his grace, his followers transmit from generation to generation a *lésion héréditaire*—a memory of guilt. Or rather, a memory and a guilt, separately and distinct, like motifs in a dream: this is the hereditary guilt that passes down from Adam as well as the story of their forebear Moses.

Jung, the Crown Prince

In his seminal 1912 essay on transference, Freud raises once again the question of "the amount of etiological effectiveness to be attributed to" constitution and chance, and arrives at a middle-of-the-road answer—namely, that this distribution "can only be arrived at in every individual case separately."[19] Some neuroses may have an etiology that exceeds the confines of the nuclear family, in other words, but those origins can't be generalized. But that more distant etiology lingers over Freud's argument as a threat—and, quite characteristically, he banishes it into a footnote. He closes the footnote by pointing out, "Incidentally, one might venture to regard constitution itself as a precipitate from the accidental effects produced on the endlessly long chain of our ancestors."[20]

Freud leaves it there, the note ends, the overwhelming question raised but not answered. "One might"—would one be right to do so? A good psychoanalyst, confronted with such a conspicuous loose end, would probably follow up. It's no accident that Freud couldn't, or wouldn't, answer at the time, because answering would have led him into the very unconscious of psychoanalysis. And to answer in the affirmative would have brought him into alignment with ideas held by his former favorite son, who by late 1912 was fast in the process of becoming an implacable opponent. For Carl Gustav Jung had ventured to regard our physiology as determinative of an inherited unconscious. He was a declared enemy of nuclearity, in his view on both the etiology of the neuroses and transference.

Where Freud had assumed that in psychoanalyzing Dora, her resistance meant that she had integrated him into her family romance, turning him into a stand-in for her father (since they "both smoked," as he helpfully observed), Jung suggested that in transference analysands turned their analyst into something far less quaint and far more ancient. As he would explain in "On the Psychology of the Unconscious" (1917), transference consists not simply in "making the doctor his father, mother, uncle, guardian and teacher, and all the rest of the parental authorities." Rather, "still other fantasies appear, which represent the doctor as a savior or godlike being."[21]

Jung's essay was, ironically enough, a moment of oedipal resistance against a father figure—cast as a rebellion against the concept of oedipal resistance against father figures. Freud had turned fifty in 1906, when Jung, then thirty, sent Freud a copy of his first book, *Über die Psychologie der Dementia Praecox* (*On the Psychology of Dementia Praecox*), which had been published that year. Their ages matter: a young man looking for a mentor figure found a man at the threshold of old age looking for younger men to carry on his legacy. This was to both make and unmake their friendship.

It's no surprise that Jung's short book on schizophrenia kindled Freud's dynastic hopes. Its preface is an unapologetic love letter to the "ingenious conceptions" of the elder analyst.[22] What led Jung to Freud, he claims there, was the empirical evidence: to come to terms with Freudian claims, one must put in the time to analyze "daily life, hysteria and dreams" from Freud's standpoint—otherwise, one acts "like one of those lauded scientists who refused to look through Galileo's telescope."[23] At the same time, Jung's list of areas to analyze conspicuously downplays the area in which he and Freud most centrally disagreed: "When I recognize the mechanism of the complexes of dreams and hysteria, for instance, that does not mean that I allot exclusive significance to the sexual traumas of youth, as Freud appears to."[24]

This, as almost all historical accounts of their ill-fated friendship point out, was to be the sticking point throughout their friendship: Jung was on board with the hysteria, the dreams, but he had serious misgivings about the libidinal engine of infantile sexuality postulated by Freud in the *Three Essays*. The very fact that even in his rapturous dedication Jung seemingly neglects the fact that "daily life, hysteria and dreams" in Freud's reading are shot through with the residue of infantile sexuality, and moreover speaks of "traumas of youth"—when in fact Freud had moved away from a theory of trauma, and was thinking of *infantile* sexuality, not the sexuality of youth—suggests not so much two thinkers destined to drift apart over time but rather two thinkers destined to realize they fundamentally disagreed.

But for the moment, both Freud and Jung remained almost purposefully blind to those differences. Freud was, as Reuben Fine points out, reenacting an earlier homosocial relationship—just as a young Freud had latched on to Berlin physician Wilhelm Fliess as a kind of father figure, so he now seemed to groom Jung as a kind of son and heir.[25] What exactly inspired him to do so is unclear: Jung's work at the time was capable, but not visionary; the works and ideas that would make him famous still lay in the future. But it was futurity that Jung had in spades, and perhaps that was primarily what Freud wanted. Jung was just the kind of heir Freud wanted for himself: a practicing psychiatrist, an empirical researcher, a Protestant, a Gentile, and, most important, young—"one of those flowering young men who," as Freud wrote to Ludwig Binswanger in 1912, "were supposed to continue my own life."[26] Jung must have appeared to him as the Moses who would lead psychoanalysis out of the various theoretical and cultural ghettos in which he felt it was still confined.

But Jung would reject this role rather dramatically. While most biographers agree that the break between the two men had been a long time coming, it seems both fitting and a bit ironic that Freud's dynastic bid was frustrated by the dynasty. The problem in 1913 was not that Freud and Jung differed on the transmissibility of unconscious content from generation to generation, as they would have differed in 1905, when *Three Essays* was published. What made the difference was Freud's turn to the psychology of religion in *Totem and Taboo* (positing in its subtitle "Resemblances between the Mental Lives of Savages and Neurotics") expanded psychoanalysis into an anthropological realm that Jung seemed to consider his province.

In a letter to Freud, Jung complained that it would be "very oppressive to me, if you too become involved in this area. You are a dangerous competitor, if one wants to speak of competition."[27] His choice of words is deeply revealing: Jung wants to both speak of competition and disavow it, at least for now. The discoverer of the Oedipus complex apparently hadn't noticed that he seemed to inspire a distinctly oedipal energy in his favorite son. Or perhaps he had noticed but thought that Jung would and should work through and master his aggressive impulses. Jung himself seemed to regard his reaction to *Totem and Taboo* that way—his sense of being crowded by Freud, he thought, was part of his own pathology.[28]

The issue that emerged as central in this disagreement was the role of collectivity, and in that collectivity the question of a family larger than the nuclear one emerged with renewed force. It did so in two ways: First, as Jung claimed, if there was a collective (or "interpersonal") unconscious preceding and conditioning the individual unconscious, then infantile psychology and the immediate family that shaped it ceded pride of place to something that came from the more distant past.[29] Second, and correspondingly, unconscious content was transmissible in ways markedly different from the mechanisms Freud had established, at least in his classical formulations.

Those mechanisms, above all the Oedipus complex, had drawn only from the fixed points of the nuclear family, whereas Jung in his 1929 article "Die Bedeutung von Konstitution und Vererbung für die Psychologie" ("The Significance of Constitution and Heredity in Psychology") suggests that the two prehistories of the individual subject, the infantile and the familial, combine to constitute the individual psyche.[30] This constituted a significant shift: the oedipal family in a sense reconstitutes itself in each successive generation; Jung's family reaches deep into the human past. "The psychic process does not start out of nothing with the individual consciousness, but is rather a repetition of functions which have been ages in the making and which are inherited with the brain structure" (1:110).

Jung remained ambivalent about how closely the process he supposed was behind the collective unconscious resembled biological inheritance. His 1929 article linked it rather insistently to physiology. Instead of unconscious contents traveling from generation to generation directly, physiological traits are what make the trip—and the physiological resemblance of each generation to the previous one allows for the structural resemblance of certain ideas, associations, and images. Nevertheless, these physiological traits could be acquired and passed along much further down the dynastic chain than an oedipal infatuation with a mother figure. What's more, Jung often talked as though this continuity went well beyond a function of physiology. In the same essay, he claims that "psychic processes antedate, accompany, and outlive consciousness. Consciousness is an interval in a continuous psychic process" (1:110). This was precisely the view of human inheritance Freud's essay on infantile sexuality had been intended to rebuke: the Schopenhauerian view, whereby the individual is just a blip in the relentless unfolding of the psychic process of the species.

In his final years, Jung arrived at the palatably universalist conviction that mythemes, ideas, and associations had redounded from some common ancestor to all humans. But in decades prior, he hadn't always been so sure. In his 1929 essay, he casts the constituency of the collective unconscious as a family collective, remarking on the "astounding cases of mental similarity [that] can be found in family" (1:111). He wavered between the picture of a familial and racial collective unconscious and a universalist heredity shared by all mankind. His vacillation, often trafficking in rather noxious anti-Semitic tropes, became particularly acute in the years between his break with Freud and the Nazis' rise to power.

In his 1918 article "Über das Unbewusste" ("On the Unconscious"), Jung distinguishes between distinctly Jewish and distinctly German forms of the collective unconscious. Troublingly, his vocabulary in the essay is redolent of later Nazi jargon: he speaks of the Germans as a "host people," implying that Jews are parasites; his Germans are the "blonde beasts" of Nietzsche's later aphorisms, though he does not mean that characterization positively;[31] he assumes a thoroughgoing distinction between Jews and Germans; and he gives the old canard of Jewish double loyalty a psychoanalytic sheen. But behind this objectionable rhetoric lurks a deeper point: Jung seems intent on dealing with the notion that psychoanalysis is a Jewish discourse addressing specifically Jewish problems, and hence is ill-suited to the German psyche. And while his erstwhile friend and mentor turned to the death drive and the Mosaic legacy to comprehend the rise of fascism, Jung located its origins in the German psyche.

In March of 1936, Jung published an article entitled "Wotan" in the *Neue Schweizer Rundschau*. It is in this essay that he describes a specifically German collective unconscious and spells out what it means for his own age, the age of the "rebirth of Wotan."[32] Jung proposes a dynastic unconscious that can go dormant for centuries, only to then reemerge and take hold of Germans in a moment of *Ergriffenheit*, "a state of being seized or possessed" (10:184). But he also claims a different extraction for his own analytic project: he cites the German Youth Movement, he cites Richard Wagner, Friedrich Nietzsche, Stefan George, Ludwig Klages, and Alfred Schuler, but he also cites Nazi rallies. All these individuals and groups, Jung thought, shared an understanding that Wotan helps illuminate a phenomenon "so strange to anybody not a German, that it remains incomprehensible even after the deepest reflection" (10:184). The non-German "anybody" whose "deepest reflection[s]" had to miss Wotan was most likely Freud.

To be sure, Jung in this article evinces no triumph over having understood what Freud could not—if anything, he's quite worried. Wotan "is a fundamental attribute of the German psyche, an irrational psychic factor which acts on the high pressure of civilization like a cyclone and blows it away." But at the same time, he allows that "the Wotan-worshippers seem to have judged things more correctly than the worshippers of reason" (10:186). There lingers in a text like "Wotan" a persistent whiff of self-satisfaction at having been vindicated in his analytic instincts—Jung's fear of having his worries about the German unconscious borne out were largely trumped by his satisfaction at having been right.

More disturbingly, all his obvious misgivings about the rise of Nazism notwithstanding, Jung's texts about the Wotanic extraction of Nazism reverberate with an off-putting awe at the reason-shattering power of the German soul. And the terms in which he frames Freud's incomprehension before the rise of Nazism themselves have troubling racial implications. For on the one hand, it seems Jung had long argued that German Gentiles, rather than Jews, have a more urgent need for psychoanalytic intervention. As he put it in a text from 1918, they are half-domesticated, while their other half roils with "vestiges of the prehistoric age [*Vorzeit*], with the collective unconscious, which is subject to a peculiar and ever-increasing activation." The Jew, by contrast, "already had the culture of the ancient world and on top of that has taken over the culture of the nations amongst whom he dwells. He has two cultures."[33] This can make it sound as though Jung assigned psychoanalysis the role of civilizing the uncivilized Germans. On the other hand, in light of his other writings of the time (above all "Zur Gegenwärtigen Lage der Psychotherapie" ["On the Contemporary Situation of Psychotherapy," 1934]), it becomes clear that Jung means to distinguish between two *forms* of analysis: the rationalist, reductive, erotomanic analysis of the Freudian type can understand only Jews, and cannot understand true Germans—it stirs in "the garbage bin [*Kehrichtkübel*] of unfulfillable childhood wishes and unresolved family resentments," and misses the "hidden depths of the Germanic soul."[34]

By contrast, Jungian analytic techniques, aiming as they do at the collective unconscious, work only when applied to a people that still retains a strong collective unconscious. Freud, for racial reasons, was constitutionally unable to see it, Jung argues. In other words, Freud's problem, as Jung saw it, was his focus on the nuclear family and on infantile sexuality, and more generally his "fanatical one-sidedness" in focusing on "sexuality, on desire,"[35] along with his inability to understand collective (and ancestral) forces at work in the etiology of the neuroses. Rather than fetishizing the childhood of the individual, Jungian analysis harnesses a spirit "not yet fully alienated from youthfulness."[36]

Hitler's rise to power did not serve to nuance this juxtaposition, but Jung began to sound increasingly worried about the semidomesticated state of the German soul. His affirmation of Germanic depth and the cradling certitudes of Wotanic archetypes gave way to an anguished insistence that Germans begin to psychoanalyze the undomesticated depths of their soul.[37] Hitler himself emerged as a direct protuberance of the collective unconscious—in the so-called Knickerbocker interview Jung gave in 1939, he is portrayed as its pure carrier as much as its hapless victim.[38]

After the war, after the end of Nazism, or, as his one essay reflecting on these events puts it, "after the catastrophe," Jung largely abandoned the idea that the collective unconscious was different from one racial group to the other, or that some groups had more of it than others. Instead, he retreated to what may have been his initial instinct anyway—namely, that the family relevant for the collective unconscious is the human family, not some tribal subset of it. He had entertained this universalist opinion throughout. Even in a 1929 essay, four years before "Wotan" and five years before "Present Situation of Psychotherapy," he claims to have merely entertained the idea "that such things could only happen to people belonging to the same race," but to have been convinced otherwise. And in his essay "On the Psychology of the Unconscious," for instance, he claims that this idea has "been stamped on the human brain for aeons. That is why it lies ready to hand in the unconscious of every man."[39]

After the war, this became his exclusive view. Jung's retreat makes it particularly remarkable that the idea of a collective unconscious belonging to a family of descent rather than the species as a whole was developed by a Jewish Holocaust survivor originally from Hungary and living not too far from Jung's Küsnacht, Switzerland, home. The psychiatrist and analyst Léopold (Lipot) Szondi drew from the same sources as Jung—Schopenhauer, neo-Nietzschean thought—but arrived at a very different picture of what he called "the familial unconscious." Jung's Wotan had been "on the one hand the God of rage and fury [*Wut und Raserei*], on the other a reader of runes and a speaker of destiny [*Schicksalskünder*]."[40] Jung was both frightened and excited by the former guise of Wotan; Szondi interrogated the latter valence of the collective unconscious.

The Dynastic Unconscious: Szondi's "Fate Analysis"

Jung had flirted with the idea that families and races could have their own unconscious; the late Freud had seemed to suggest that something like it might well exist. Among the ranks of the rapidly scattering psychoanalytic community, ideas like this were largely greeted with bafflement—they smacked of racism and of nineteenth-century *Völkerpsychologie*, and they bode ill for the portability of psychoanalytic technique beyond its native soil, on which so much depended now for so many. Jung's own insistence on a racially specific familial unconscious in his "Wotan" essay and others served to widely discredit him during and immediately after the war.[41] American ego psychology, for one, doubled down on the antidynastic thrust of Freud's early work; for them, his mistake had not been the elision of the extended family but rather an overemphasis of the family in general, above all the Oedipus complex. Even Freud's own heir Anna admitted to having been "always more attracted to the latency period than the pre-Oedipal phases."[42] Her theory of ego defenses was interested less in the pressures that bear on the ego from without than in the lengths to which the ego goes to do battle with them.

Szondi, however, pursued the opposite instinct: that there exists a familial unconscious, transmitted by uncertain mechanisms well beyond the nucleus. In his view, familial arrangements can influence descendants, even if they have never actually experienced those arrangements. Why, he asked, do individuals seem to seek out marital partners that mirror in their pathologies those of the individuals' ancestors, even if these individuals are unaware of those pathologies or perhaps even those ancestors? Why are people drawn to certain professions or life choices? These inclinations are what Szondi called fate (*Schicksal*), and the appropriate therapy, by means of what would later become known as the Szondi test, was called fate analysis (*Schicksalsanalyse*). Szondi put entire families on the couch—just as Freud had felt quite confident in diagnosing Dora's mother as a neurotic housewife sight unseen, so Szondi cast his analytic net far beyond the actual patient sitting before him.

In the bargain, Szondi also recast the familial extraction of psychoanalysis itself. For what he proposed to analyze as "fate" was really sexual choice—not the *type* of object a drive takes but the specific person one ends up with. It's important to note that this is anything but a new question in the theory of sexuality—if anything, it's the oldest question there is. It was the question of Oedipus, whose problem was after all a very specific object choice. It was the question that Aristophanes' famous story in the *Symposium* was supposed to answer: how come we experience a particular person as our soul mate, our better half? But for just that reason, it was a question that Freud had given little thought to. It was a philosophical question; it seemed basically unanswerable scientifically, and Freud was intent on doing empirical science.

Philosophers were still trying to answer this question in the nineteenth century, up to Freud's own day. Arthur Schopenhauer thought that through sexual choice, a child attempted to will itself into existence—and that it looked for one parent to complement the other parent's traits. The Austrian philosopher Otto Weininger thought that the individual sought out a partner that had the exact converse distribution of male and female traits.[43] Freud read the works of both of these men with some interest, but he was otherwise careful not to place himself in their company. Theirs were grand metaphysical speculations; neither of them intended to furnish medical insight, nor were they especially liable to do so. But by the mid-twentieth century, Schopenhauer and Weininger were basically considered cranks—not the kinds of patron saints you call on for an enterprise as precariously situated between science, art, and voodoo as psychoanalysis.

Szondi's gesture of admitting this banished question back into psychoanalysis turns out to characterize his approach more generally: he seems to have had no problem with uncomfortable ancestors. Freud might relegate Schopenhauer to the deepest footnotes, might confine his fascination with Weininger to letters; Szondi cheerfully adopted them, and their uncomfortable question, as forebears to the analytic project. Problematic ancestors, the prehistory provided by one's forebears rather than one's infancy, were central to his analytic undertaking. Where Freud eclipsed the ancestors in favor of that "other prehistory" of infantile sexuality, Szondi typically began his case studies with an exhaustive rundown of the family tree that produced the person.

Why did Szondi feel the need to be so specific? Unlike Jung's collective unconscious, which is simply passed along from generation to generation, the familial unconscious Szondi identified seemed to be able to skip generations, to become invisible only to reappear. Why did analysands come to Szondi with symptoms, only to discover that their great-grandmother suffered from the same ones? Why did a woman seek out his help for the same neurosis her mother-in-law once saw him for? It was because psychological traits, like physical ones, could be dominant or recessive. Szondi is indeed the rare psychoanalyst to refer to Mendelian inheritance law as much as the works of Freud in discussing his cases. But where the determinists of the nineteenth century had traced how imbecility, moral defects, or addiction traveled directly from one generation to the next, Szondi believed that a family line can carry a certain defect (say, a neurosis or a mania) without ever showing any symptoms.

This idea would seem to invite Hegel's famous objection that someone can have a murderer's brainpan, but unless that person actually murders, he or she is not a murderer. How can we insist someone is mentally ill, despite not showing any symptoms? How can someone be a paranoiac without a fear of surveillance? Szondi's answer to this problem is rather ingenious: the carrier in whom such a defect is latent may not show symptoms, but he or she will seek out sufferers of this very defect. The disease is indeed present in those individuals in whom it fails to assert itself, but it is unconscious—as Szondi puts it, a *repressed* trait. Such a trait predisposes the individual to falling in love with someone in whom the same trait is expressed. The very neurosis that individuals fail to express in their own person they express through their object choice. In our mates, we seek out our ancestral defects—this Szondi called genotropism. Where Freud had insisted that object choice depended centrally on the perversions introduced by the family nucleus, Szondi proposed that "love develops between the healthy, defectless descendants of people suffering from some common hereditary disease."[44]

Szondi reversed how heredity and disease were thought to relate among nineteenth-century determinists. Émile Zola, for instance, had posited that certain compulsions result from hereditary processes—a *lésion* passed down from individual to individual. Fate analysis proposes instead that rather than being the carrier of the unconscious, heredity is an effect of the unconscious. A disease seeks to perpetuate itself in a population and compels the individual to pass it on.

Szondi, like Jung, didn't assign sexuality pride of place. Sexual choice may be the most significant decision to be swayed by the familial unconscious, but so are vocational choices, friendship choices, and even how individuals die. In examining the story of Moses, for instance, Szondi makes none of Freud's adventurous conjectures, but interprets Moses as a palimpsest of the familial relations around him—not only is this Moses not an Egyptian, he is his entire ancestral tree in compacted form.[45] And instead of Oedipus, Szondi insists on a "Cain complex," which derives precisely from the friction between the ego on the one hand and a person's heredity and cultural milieu on the other.[46]

This radical decentering of the subject (which is the result of perversion rather than the site of it) came to ensure the afterlife of Szondi's rather fringe theories. For it shared important features with the poststructuralist account of subjecthood, poststructuralism's own dissatisfaction with the oedipally determined nuclear family. When Gilles Deleuze and Felix Guattari undertook to free psychoanalysis of myth (and thus rethink what it meant to *repeat* the ancestral past), when they sought to "de-oedipalize" and "undo the daddy-mommy spider web,"[47] Szondi became one of their pathways beyond Freud.[48]

At the same time, Szondi retains far more of Freud's humanism than Deleuze and Guattari suppose. He insists that treating genetics as "fate" is not simply to reverse Freud's more humanistic focus on the individual. Szondi distinguishes between an old and a new anancology (fate analysis). The Greek root of this term, *ananke*, has two senses—on the one hand necessity, force, and limitation by outside forces, and on the other hand consanguinity. Traditional anancology, for instance in Schopenhauer, focused entirely on the first sense; Szondi proposes to found his anancology on the second. His dynasties are half fated, half chosen—we end up with the family (and the familial unconscious) we have without having a choice in the matter; but while certain compulsions guide our choice in partner (and though our partner is *genverwandt*, or genetically related), we do choose. It is for that reason that Jens de Vleminck has dubbed Szondi a "tragic humanist":[49] his obsession with genetics does not preclude human action or evacuate our choices of their meaning.

In his book *Freiheit und Zwang im Schicksal des Einzelnen* (Freedom and compulsion in the life of the individual, 1968), Szondi spells out how this shift changes the questions we may pose about fate. Since our genetic material is heterogeneous and different traits and drives vie in us, we do not have *one* fate in the mold of Oedipus. We have a choice and a certain degree of agency in expressing the many frequently contradictory traits seeking to dominate our daily actions. The question for "fate analysis" then becomes how to identify, analyze, and ultimately strengthen that faculty in us that could take on a reflective position vis-à-vis our multiple "fates." The subject thus carves out a kind of freedom, not *from* the dynastic chain but rather *within* it. It is not that everything is possible for us, but we can be led to recognize the range of possibilities that heredity has left open to us. "Fate," Szondi concludes, "is the totality of all inherited and freely choosable modes of existence."[50]

Was this perhaps also a way of addressing the problem of the psychoanalytic project's own vexed heredity? Freud had posited an oedipal family as something liberating and had sensed in the encroachment of the dynastic a threat. From the compulsive neurotics who returned from the war to the political exploiters of the death drive, humanity's familial unconscious seemed to represent those forces that endangered Freud's life and work. It was what made him a refugee, what threatened to demote psychoanalysis to a specifically Jewish cultural practice, a self-analysis of Moses's murderers. Jung, meanwhile, abandoned himself to the reassuring undulations of the collective unconscious with troubling ease. That its stark antihumanism threatened to eclipse the mission of psychoanalysis seemed to matter little to him.

Szondi's way of holding up compulsory fate (*Zwangsschicksal*) against free fate (*Freiheitsschicksal*) offered a third way of addressing the heredity problem. *Schicksal* in German is the thing that is sent to you, the hand you are dealt. But Szondi was insistent that one's double heredity always deals one more than one hand. Psychoanalysis, in its guise as fate analysis, creates the space in which one can take stock and choose which hand to play. As the Nazis scattered the psychoanalytic community throughout the world, sent Szondi and his young children to the concentration camp at Bergen-Belsen in northern Germany, and exterminated his community—what idea could have been more attractive? But for the older Szondi, by then living in safety in Switzerland and not too far from Jung, another idea was perhaps more alluring: that the question of whether psychoanalysis is Jewish, is German, is bourgeois European, might, in each case, be false to begin with. For Szondi, psychoanalysis might have multiple heredities; the trick was to look at them honestly and then choose from among the options they left open. Wotan, Jung had thought, seizes us in a state of *Ergriffenheit* (literally "being grabbed"); we have no say with regard to the past's claim on us. By contrast, Szondi's form of psychoanalysis was premised on the conviction that we could choose what seized us from the past if we understood that past correctly.

Szondi's very designation of his enterprise as *Schicksalsanalyse* reflects that premise. However, no one could hear that term without the thudding associations of what Martin Heidegger would call the *Geschick* (fate), "the history of Being as the *Geschick* of being."[51] *Schicksalsanalyse* could sound like the analysis of that which comes to us without our input—but also the analysis of what opens up for us without any action of our own. This is precisely not what Szondi had in mind: what fate and family bring to us, we can master. In introducing his method to his English-speaking audience, he tips his hand and implies that in fact, his term has a dual extraction. It stands, as all of us do, at the intersection of two family trees. Throughout the English-language article in which he sought to introduce fate analysis to a broader readership, Szondi describes hereditary diseases as "matchmakers." It may strike us as an odd metaphor to use; or at least it's one that has fallen out of fashion in modern genetics—we no longer think of passing on genes in terms as archaic as an extended courtship.

But in using the metaphor, Szondi connects his fate analysis to a longer lineage, one that psychoanalysis had frequently repressed. After all, the matchmaker (*shadchan*) was still a common figure in Jewish culture and literature in the early twentieth century. And the Yiddish term for the magical work performed by the *shadchanim*, somewhere between accident and necessity, between destiny and convenience, was *bashert*—fate. Szondi is thus culling his term for the notion of a dynastic unconscious from specifically Jewish custom. And at the same time, he is suggesting a dynastic unconscious for psychoanalysis: for much of Freud's life, psychoanalysis had avoided the question of how Jewish a practice it was. Szondi was suggesting it was Jewish through and through—but this parentage was not binding or determinative. In fact, *bashert* has also something of the German *Bescherung*: it is a gift we receive without having asked for it. Its multiple parentages weren't its liability but rather the great gift of its past. It was up to psychoanalysis to make its heritage its own.

8

George, or The Queer Dynasty

The early stories and novellas of Thomas Mann teem with young men who are the last in a long family line and who, at the end of the narrative, join another line altogether—the endless row of those disappointed in love. They become part of the long literary history of young men without a future. Mann reproduces the trope obsessively in those early years, the author's homosexuality still a faint thematic rumbling. But the pervasive themes of disappointment and resignation, the lure of the death drive, and a general lack of success in reproductive heterosexuality all conjure a distinctly queer dimension in his early works, one that would remain in the descriptions of the passions of Hanno Buddenbrook and of Gustav Aschenbach in *Die Buddenbrooks* (*Buddenbrooks*, 1903) and *Tod in Venedig* (*Death in Venice*, 1911), respectively. Many of the main characters of these early works—the religious fanatic Hieronymus in *Gladius Dei* (1902), the self-important writer Detlev Spinell in *Tristan* (1903), but above all the incestuous Ahrenthold twins in *Wälsungenblut* (*Blood of the Valsungs*, 1906)—are epigones, modern knockoffs of premodern originals who by their very repetition involuntarily parody what they repeat into the inhospitable light of modernity.

This preoccupation was not Mann's alone. Many writers of literary decadence were interested in alternative modes of inheritance—but most cast them in a far more positive light than Mann did. They actively sought out lines of tradition that lacked the pretensions of naturalness and self-evidence the nuclear family had begun to underwrite. And rather than rebel, through an oedipal anxiety of influence, angels against "the shadow cast by their precursor,"[1] they drew from more distant ancestors, or perhaps one should say cousins. Harold Bloom famously claimed that "influence cannot be willed,"[2] but they were willing to give it a try. And unlike Mann, they willed a future for their dissident lineages as well.

Their willingness to imagine a new past and to imagine a future for that imagined past probably did make them bad children, neurotics that conjure up fevered "family romances," as Freud put it.[3] If writers in the closing years of the nineteenth century resurrected the figure of the dynasty, they resurrected it with a pronounced queer dimension. This wasn't unique to German literature—if anything, French literary figures like Marcel Proust and the comte de Lautréamont or English ones like Algernon Swinburne and Oscar Wilde come to mind as more well-known examples. But it was a German poet and the strange group of like-minded aesthetes he gathered around him that made the dynasty more than a metaphor for influence—that tried to combine it with a politics somewhere between make-believe and perfect seriousness.

As Eve Kosofsky Sedgwick has pointed out in "Tales of the Avunculate," her famous essay on Oscar Wilde's play *The Importance of Being Earnest* (1895), it's hard not to read Wilde's vertiginous family structures as a comment on queer kinship explicitly juxtaposed not just to heterosexuality but to the nuclear family as well. "In married life," as Algernon, one of the play's protagonists, remarks, "three is company and two is none."[4] He doesn't mean that third to be a child but rather Bunbury, an invented friend of his who allows him to get out of social engagements. Whether, then, we sense that Bunburyism may refer to some range of queer activities, such as cruising or nonprocreative sex, it is clear that Bunburyism is all about the impossibility of the kind of self-evidence and transparency that nineteenth-century ideology routinely credited to the nuclear family.

Far from being an outlier, Algie's opinion finds a direct echo in the family structures of the play itself—*The Importance of Being Earnest* presents, as Sedgwick puts it, a tale of the avunculate. "I suggest," she writes, "or I suggest the play suggests: Forget the Name of the Father. Think about your uncles and your aunts."[5] Lady Bracknell, an aunt of Algernon's, upon learning that Ernest (really Jack) Worthing is unaware of his parentage and has been raised by "a handbag," famously remarks that "to lose one parent may be regarded as a misfortune, to lose both looks like carelessness."[6] And indeed, the families Wilde presents are all characterized by some form of such carelessness. To pluck just one characteristically intricate thread from the large and compounding web: Jack is adopted by Thomas Cardew and is guardian to his daughter Cecily, "who addresses me as her uncle," while Jack pretends she's his aunt. The place where all these threads become less gauzy, where they become concrete and less open to interpretation and subterfuge, is precisely in the safe haven of nuclear heterosexuality—the famous "definite proposal" that carries the inherent risk that "one might be accepted."[7]

As we saw in chapter 6, Proust's *race des tantes* makes this link unusually explicit: the narrator, Marcel, marvels at the sheer serendipity, subtlety, and miracle of gay male love. What is true of the family as of explanations in *The Importance of Being Ernest* seems to be true of Proustian homosexuality: "pray make it improbable."[8] But that very improbability did not unmoor the *tantes* from ancestors; it connected them to a *race*, to a different set of secret ancestors.

The poet Algernon Swinburne similarly trains his gaze on hidden, circuitous ancestries—usually at the expense, or in the shadow, of official traditions. For instance, his lifelong preoccupation with Eton College at times celebrated its official continuities and at others focused on its continuities that were deeply hidden, though no less real. In "Eton: An Ode," (1890), he lauds the school's long official history and imagines its future as a straightforward continuation of that official history:

> When four hundred more and fifty years have risen and shone and set,
> Bright with names that men remember, loud with names that men forget.[9]

But in Swinburne's poetry, official Etonian traditions are from the first shadowed by a darker one[10]—namely, the reality of an endless passing-on of rituals of sadism and corporal punishment. The flogging poems he contributed to the anonymously published *Whippingham Papers* exhaustively and repetitiously trace out an alternative lineage of blood: blood drawn by sadistic schoolmasters, blood consecrated in age-old and yet secret rituals. As Swinburne would put it in the exhausting masochistic fantasy "Arthur's Flogging," "Under the birch, and from them every one / The drops of blood as thick as raindrops spun."[11] In lines like these, Swinburne traced another Eton, another tradition: one kept alive through compulsion and violence and transmitted in blood—a secret dynasty of rapturous queer suffering.

And with the blood comes a dynasty of pain. The pure enjoyment of pain, the fetishization of its constituting power, gives a strange institutionalism to Swinburne's ostentatious dissolution. So that even when in "The Triumph of Time" (1866) a poetic "I" ends up in the position of Mann's early narrators—having been rendered infertile, a dead end, by disappointed love—the pain of that disappointment is instead transformed in an enduring structure all its own:

> It will grow not again, this fruit of my heart,
> Smitten with sunbeams, ruined with rain.
> The singing seasons divide and depart,
> Winter and summer depart in twain.
> It will grow not again, it is ruined at root,

> The bloodlike blossom, the dull red fruit;
> Though the heart yet sickens, the lips yet smart,
> With sullen savour of poisonous pain.[12]

All of this would have struck Mann as tawdry and chintzy. As he arduously clambered toward bourgeois respectability, toward a nuclear family, toward heterosexuality, he regarded these alternative lineages with suspicion and offended good taste. In the early short story "Beim Propheten" ("At the Prophet's," 1904), a young "novella writer" who has had some conventional bourgeois success visits a poetic séance, a strange ersatz-religious ceremony that the narrator frames as deeply absurd. The "prophet" of the title (who is out of town and therefore doesn't show up at his own ritual) lives on the top floor of a typical suburban apartment building, and the narrator catalogues the revealing lapses in judgment and taste with almost exhausting élan. A lot of the décor consists of eclectic quasi-religious objects, but the absent prophet has clearly also sought to establish a lineage for himself: "death masks, rose wreaths, a large rusty sword hung on the walls; besides the large painting of Napoleon, various portraits of different styles, of Luther, Nietzsche, Moltke, Alexander VI, Robespierre and Savonarola were distributed throughout the room."[13]

While there is a whiff of dissident sexuality throughout the apartment, the "novella writer" is immune to it, and through him so is the story. He is here for perfectly heterosexual reasons: he wishes to court a young woman whose mother has been coming to these ceremonies. At the center of the makeshift suburban chapel sits a portrait of the prophet himself, an icon that both informs the ritual around it and ensures that even the most obtuse reader knows who the prophet is supposed to be. In the description of "a young man around thirty with a powerfully high forehead that palely recedes, with a beardless, bony face reminiscent of a bird of prey, full of concentrated spirituality,"[14] most readers have been able to espy the face of the German poet Stefan George.

Homoeroticism and the Dynasty

If the dynasty seems like a strange philosophical concern to resurface in the twentieth century, it seems stranger still that it should become important in the work of a poet (rather than, say, a philosopher or a novelist), and a gay poet at that. Mann's "Beim Propheten" casts George's ancestor worship as just an eclectic tic, but in this chapter, I argue that it was quite a bit more than that.

Not only did the lineage he constructed for himself matter greatly to George, it also mattered to the generations of young men he drew to his poetic *Reich*, and who in many respects constituted his dynasty. What has made the legacy of that dynasty so fraught is that it isn't altogether clear whether it was a poetic affair or something political or religious.

As we saw in chapter 7, Freud's theory of infantile sexuality was intended as a replacement of dynastic modes of explanation. The individual subject is as ignorant about one as it is about the other; but in one picture the energies that threaten the nuclear family are (inherited) factors that transcend that family, and in the other they're native to it. Stefan George resisted this immanentist picture of eros: love did not "just" knit together a small nucleus of individuals—through the loved one, it connected the individual to a long line of ancestors, albeit not physical ancestors, and it connected those ancestors to the lover.

This circumstance was particularly important given that George's ancestries were homoerotic, a structure of affect his contemporaries were wont to regard as uniquely antidynastic. When Mann wrote his essay "Die Ehe im Übergang" ("Marriage in Transition," 1925), he combined Freud's thinking about marriage and dynasty with more traditional thinking about homo- and heterosexuality. He presented homoeroticism as "erotic aestheticism," which meant "infertility, lack of perspective, lack of consequence, irresponsibility," a "sterile libertinage."[15] Homosexuality, Mann says, "is non-foundational, does not create families, does not beget dynasties [*geschlechterzeugend*]."[16] It is therefore also profoundly apolitical. Marriage, by contrast, is concerned with "permanence, foundation, continued generativity, a sequence of dynasties [*Geschlechterfolge*], responsibility."[17]

At its most basic, George's dynastic homoeroticism constituted the opposite of a position like Mann's. He was intent on establishing something of a poetic *Geschlechterfolge*, but this would move by way of the writing, recitation, and reception of poetry. He set out to refute the ideology encapsulated by Mann's essay in and through poetic practice, both by thematizing the kinds of modes of transmission Mann had declared impossible, and through a politics that usually lies dormant in poetic form: he imagined not just a dynasty *in* the poem but rather a dynastic scene of reception *for* the poem. In a sense, every poem constitutes an oratory gesture: the poet speaks to a particular addressee with a certain purpose in mind, shares a feeling with an audience, expresses a feeling whether there's anyone to hear it or not. Some of these gestures are more fully imagined than others. With others, the scene implied in the poetic locution is a good deal more ambiguous. But rare is the poem that imagines an entire world beyond its locution or a world created ex nihilo in its locution. And at that point, it would seem, we are on the outer rim of poetry, on the edge of something related but different. If I say something to someone but imagine that someone passing it on to others, and those to yet others, I am not reciting a poem; I am sermonizing, or I am giving a political speech.

George's "dynastic" poems seem to inscribe an unusually complex scene of reception into the poetic locution (Wolfgang Braungart has called them rituals),[18] a scene articulated through metaphors of begetting, inheritance, and legacy. Knowledge, language, feeling, are transmitted from the poet to listeners. Those listeners are envisioned as carrying the message forward. They are compelled to act in certain ways. Other listeners can hear the words but cannot understand them. An entire geography of receptivity unfurls around these poems, and before long we ourselves stand within its compass. Are we among the cognoscenti or the unknowing ones? And once we know, what will we do with what we know? And most important: if we wanted to do something, how would we do it, and within poetry or outside of it?

George not only relied on this imaginary scene in his poems, he also made it a frequent topic of his poetry. The motif of successive disclosure, of knowledge or insight traveling from the audience to another audience, and the idea of poetic locution begetting a dynastic chain both functioned as an allegory of his own poetic technique and his own ambition, an ambition that seemed to fall somewhere between poetry and politics. That's because George's activities from the first seemed to skirt the limits of what constituted poetry. He grouped around himself a gaggle of talented young men and insisted he could impart to them mysterious teachings—a social formation at various times referred to as a covenant (*Bund*), a circle (*Kreis*), and most ominously an empire (*Reich*).[19] The mysteries of his cult had, in the tradition of decadence, a pronounced erotic edge. But what exactly the relationship was between the erotic and the *Bund* he claimed to be setting up was left to his many disciples to puzzle out. As a result, ambiguities in his poetic practice had the side effect (rare for a poet) that his real-life followers could never quite agree on where to locate this world of which his poems were to speak. Was it the *actual* world, the actual *Kreis*, and were his poems no longer poetry but rather quasi-religious or quasi-political locutions? Was it a *hoped-for* world, making his poems poetry *only* until such a time when they could be made real? Or was it a *made-up* world, just another trick in the poet's arsenal to pilfer aesthetic effects from fields outside poetry?

This chapter will explicate the notion of Bund that George deployed in his mature oeuvre. I will draw out how he arrived at his conception of an eroticized Bund and will trace it through forty years of his poetic output.

The temporality of this Bund undergoes various transformations over the decades. The early *Hymnen* (1890) already gives the word an erotic tinge, but conceives of that Bund as temporary, as holy precisely because it's doomed not to last. But gradually, George seems to have grown comfortable with a more stable Bund, and before long his conception of Bund began taking on the kind of quasi-dynastic hues that Thomas Mann had declared impossible. By the time George had begun to refer to his Bund as a *Reich*, the spontaneous and momentary community of the 1890s had given way to something far more stringent.

Two encounters seem to have combined to change George's conception of Bund. He became a reluctant interlocutor to the so-called Cosmic Circle of Neoplatonist mystics in Munich's bohemian Schwabing district (the "suburb" of Mann's short story). And he encountered a young man named Maximilian Kronberger, who would become the George Circle's founding myth under the moniker Maximin.[20] From the Cosmic Circle, George seems to have learned that homoeroticism need not be momentary and doomed but could instead be sustained and institutionalized.[21] Maximin helped him do just that. After the boy passed away shortly after turning sixteen, George turned him into the centerpiece of an ersatz religion. In the process, he reconceived of the Bund as one that could not only endure but was centrally concerned with transmission—a homoerotic dynasty.

Begettings

The poems of *Der Stern des Bundes* (*The Star of the Covenant*), published in 1912, are rife with talk of procreation, of begetting, of inheritance, yet they seem intent on forcing their readers to rethink the mechanisms traditionally designated by those terms. The poem "Ergeben steh ich vor des rätsels macht" ("Resigned I face the riddle that he is"), for instance, constructs a lineage, but this lineage flouts how we usually think of procreation and progeny—and eventually its odd, proleptic mode of procreation comes to envelop even us as the poem's readers:

> Resigned I face the riddle that he is
> My child, and I the child of my own child,
> That Fate commands the great spring from stuff
> Of earth and then, unstained by deed, to fare
> Homeward with smiles and sorrow, that her law
> Decrees that he who sacrificed his blood
> For all and for himself, shall be fulfilled,
> And only through his death beget the deed.

The strongest root feeds on eternal night.
You who surround and question me, let this
Suffice: Through him alone I now am yours.
My life was forfeit, yet I was reborn.
Leave the unfathomed, bow your heads with me,
Calling "O savior!" through the winds of dread.[22]

Ergeben steh ich vor des rätsels macht
Wie er mein kind ich meines kindes kind.
Wie sein gesetz ist dass aus erdenstoff
Der Hohe wird und eh ihn tat versehrt
Mit schmerz und lächeln seinen heimweg nimmt.
Wie sein gesetz ist dass sich der erfüllt
Der sich und allen sich zum opfer gibt
Und dann die tat mit seinem tod gebiert.
Die tiefste wurzel ruht in ewiger nacht.
Die ihr mir folgt und fragend mich umringt
Mehr deutet nicht! ihr habt nur mich durch ihn!
Ich war verfallen als ich neu gedieh.
Lasst was verhüllt ist: senkt das haupt mit mir:
"O Retter" in des dunklen grauens wind.[23]

The emphasis on filiality and procreation in this poem is something rather new in George's work. Phrases that deal with "the child of my own child," "begetting," and "reborn" simply would not have had a place in his early lyric poetry. But if George turns to filiality in this poem (and indeed in others in *The Star of the Covenant*), it is a unique filiality. For one thing, it does not appear to be linear or even unidirectional: the "Retter" is the poet's "child," but the poet is in turn "the child's child." If we think of a dynasty as begetting something that begets, the poet here imagines a dynasty that loops back to its beginning. Further, we are told that "through him alone I now am yours" (ihr habt nur mich durch ihn): the poetic locution itself (or at least the speaker himself) is sired by its own offspring.

The Star of the Covenant, much like *Der Siebente Ring* (*The Seventh Ring*, 1907), the collection that preceded it, presents itself as a pseudoreligious text, and what "Resigned I face the riddle that he is" describes is a filiality of revelation. The poet treats begetting and divine epiphany as connected or even coterminous. This raises the question of what kind of divinity George means to invoke in this poem and specifically, what we could call the temporal, or perhaps even the dynastic, structure of the divine revelation instantiated therein. We might think of the Trinity, for instance, and certainly the poem's first five lines could function as a Christology of sorts—Ernst Morwitz's translation heightens this sense. Another possibility is suggested by the lines "that he who sacrificed his blood / For all and for himself," which call to mind another poem I will be discussing later in this chapter: "Porta Nigra," which appeared in *The Seventh Ring*. There, *sacrifice* refers to sexual submission, as an unnamed Roman emperor (likely George's favorite Algabal/Heliogabalus) prostitutes himself to his legionnaires. A final possibility, at least for George's initiates then as now, would be suggested by the line "My life was forfeit, yet I was reborn." The tone and phrasing here recall the opening of George's epitaph to Maximin in the preface to the *Gedenkbuch* (*Memorial Book*) he put together for Maximilian Kronberger after his death and published privately in 1906—there George describes a crisis from which he was restored by his discovery of "Maximin." The "savior" described here could thus be the ersatz messiah George scouted on a busy Schwabing street.

The godhead described in this poem is internally contradictory: we're invited to identify him with Jesus, with Maximin, with Algabal, perhaps even with Dionysus, and that identification will hold for a verse or two. It is even frequently the same words that perform an identification and dissolve it—in particular how we understand the words *tat* (deed) and *kind* (child). But no single identification can encompass all the predicates with which the poem imbues its savior. Every invocation of him is necessarily partial. If there is a structure that unifies them across their differences, it's not logical or semantic in nature—it's purely poetic. At the same time, poetry does not remain unchanged by that task. The early George would have gestured toward poetry's ability to furnish insights that more quotidian discourses cannot, and stopped there. The late George (and this is on the verge of being a late poem) is more ambivalent about poetry's role in the poem's dynastic project.

For the multiplicity of identifications of disidentifications occurs only so long as we understand *tat* and *kind* to have the same referent in each utterance. Freedom from such semantic compulsion is part of poetry's birthright. The only way to reconstruct who begets whom in this poem is to assume that *tat* and *kind* do not change referents between the lines. In other words, if the poem intends to construct a lineage (an intention it announces in its first line), it cannot avail itself of poetry's full freedom; it must become something less than poetic—must hew to the semantics of the apodictic discourses of theology and philosophy. Of course, the poem doesn't thereby accommodate itself to the semantics of everyday commonsense speech. And the genealogical relationship it wants to set up is anything but commonsense. The strictures to which it submits are not the prose of the world but rather the faith and self-denial of the disciple. They are a poetic order in the monastic sense.

George constructs dynasties by having one figure shade into the other. Are they identical, are they reborn, are they sired? We can't be sure. Procreation happens. And this construction, this shading of one figure into the other (like Maximin into Algabal into Dionysus into Jesus) requires a renunciation, a self-castigation of the poetic. If a reader were to come to the poem assuming that words like "deed" (*tat*) and "child" (*kind*) refer to entirely different entities with each utterance, then the "riddle" (*Rätsel*) of the unity-in-multiplicity of the dynasty unfolded here would remain invisible to that reader.

The poem that follows "Resigned I face the riddle that he is" gives a name to this strange pseudodynasty—it's not a family, it's a Bund. And tellingly, George introduces this word, the German rendition of the Hebrew ברית (*berit*), not to refer to the connection between a *group* of people, but rather to a couple, the poetic "I" and a "Thou"—but it's the very closure of their Bund that connects them to "erlauchte ahnen" (elect ancestors):

> With you I now grow back through generations,
> More close to you in a more secret bond.[24]
>
> Nun wachs ich mit dir rückwärts in die jahre
> Vertrauter dir in heimlicherem bund.[25]

These opening lines point again to the strange temporality George assigns to his Bund. At first glance, it might seem surprising that he would refer to a succession of avatars as a Bund at all. The temporality of a Bund might seem fairly straightforward—unlike a family, it is entered knowingly, sustained by affect, and we can usually tell when it's dissolved. But the Bund George describes here behaves very differently indeed: it grows "back" in time, it somehow manages to precede its own declaration, and it becomes more mysterious to its members with greater intimacy.

In 1922, the sociologist Herman Schmalenbach published his essay "Die Soziologische Kategorie des Bundes" ("The Sociological Category of the Covenant"). In it, he argues that Ferdinand Tönnies's seminal work *Gemeinschaft und Gesellschaft* (*Community and Society*, 1887) had erred in positing two general forms of shared human life. Beyond society (*Gesellschaft*) and beyond the community (*Gemeinschaft*), there existed a third category that governed human sociability—namely, the Bund.[26] Tönnies had understood the family as the nucleus of all community. Not all communities were families, but they all were like the family in important respects: they were fated rather than chosen, compulsory rather than elective, and organically grown rather than spontaneous in structure. But, Schmalenbach argues, there are such agglomerations of people that have all the proximity characteristic of Tönnies's community, all the while being freely chosen, elective in membership, and spontaneous in structure. Those kinds of agglomerations he calls the Bund, which (like society) is not an effect of natural factors (consanguinity or proximity, for instance) but nevertheless manages to create a kind of intimacy otherwise reserved for forms of community.

Schmalenbach's example of a Bund is none other than George's circle. It pulled young men from their families and inserted them into a closely knit but altogether voluntary association. If we compare Schmalenbach's analysis to the opening lines of "Nun wachs ich mit dir rückwärts mit dir in die Jahre," we find that his analysis doesn't entirely coincide with George's own theory of his Bund. Schmalenbach sees the Bund as bringing its members together by uprooting them from their embeddedness in family and community; George suggests that the Bund has in many ways the reverse temporality. Schmalenbach understands the Bund as that community free of all remainders of the family; George sees the Bund as a dynasty, and thus as a kind of family— except one that common sense would barely recognize as such.

Why does George go against Schmalenbach's conception of the Bund and insist that there is something family-like, something dynastic about his Bund? The conception of the Bund Schmalenbach sketches here is clearly indebted to that of the *Jugendbewegung* (youth movement) around the turn of the century, and thus allies George with *the* most important *bündische* form of sociability of the age. Why would he reject it in favor of a model of the Bund that explicitly harks back to the family? Finding an answer to that question requires that we follow the dynasty that, as George describes it, procreates backward "through the generations," traveling back in time, searching for perhaps a more secret Bund.

Under the cover of the Bund, George attempts to contemplate something like a "queer dynasty," queer not simply in the sense of homosexuality but in its dynastic behaviors and its modes of transmission. This places restrictions on poetic form: where the aestheticism of George's early poetry resembles Schmalenbach's Bund in that it detaches words from use and meaning and inserts them into a new poetic context, George's later work increasingly attempts to distill a secondary structure from these unmoored parts—an aestheticist politics. Of course, while the dynasty described in the poems discussed so far is certainly queer in the sense of strange or heterodox, there seems to be no overt acknowledgment of homosexuality. In George's *Hymnen* of 1890, however, we can witness the birth of the Bund from the spirit of homosexuality. To be sure, homosexuality never makes an overt appearance in these poems, either—but it impresses itself on their temporality.

Momentary Queerness

Hymnen (*Hymns*, 1890) was among George's very first volumes of poetry. The poems gathered there explore an exceedingly circumscribed cosmos—"a beloved Thou, a few landscapes, a few paintings and a few foreign situations," as George's disciple Friedrich Gundolf put it.[27] The "beloved Thou" in Gundolf's list is particularly enigmatic. Many poems in the *Hymns* rather insistently suggest through their form or poetic genre that they must be love poetry, but the events they describe give little evidence of that. Again and again, the poems deal with the decomposition of a "we" into an "I" and a "Thou," and whatever erotic charge they contain makes itself felt only in retrospect: they are about a oneness that no longer exists. The gesture of undercutting a moment of togetherness in various ways occurs rather frequently at this stage in George's oeuvre. Occasionally, the poet focuses on moments of ecstatic union, but moments in which that union is undone by memories or anticipations of its dissolution or absence. At other moments, a sense of community seems to undercut itself. In either case, the Bund seems to exist beside itself, seemingly bound up in a paradoxical temporality in which things are over as they begin or fall apart before they ever really are.

This cadence of coming together and falling apart is perhaps most clear in a poem entitled "Auf der Terrasse" ("On the Terrace"). It's obviously structured around an erotic moment, but the eroticism is transitory and requires repeating (often with great effort); and the repetition seems, as so often in these poems, to complicate rather than affirm the nature of the bond. The poem's four stanzas, describing an afternoon on the veranda of a beach house and a contrived chance encounter that (possibly) occurs there, alternate between describing states of *duration*, immobile almost to the point of oppressiveness, and staging moments of *rupture*, in which the lazy existence of the enduring is briefly rent asunder. The third and fourth stanzas run as follows:

> And now the tracks are blotted. I return.
> The goddess casts her shadow on the vase.
> If you were great enough and could discern . . .
> My foolish transport scars me with its blaze.
>
> Oh, triumph! It is you! In sunset flame
> Of glances we exchanged I read my grief.
> A herald of your self you staunchly came,
> And our togetherness was proud and brief.[28]
>
> Ich suche wieder die verwischten gleise.
> Der göttin schatten rastet auf der vase.

> O wärest wirklich du so gross und weise?
> Ich quäle mich in törichter ekstase.
>
> Triumph! du bist es aus dem abendrote
> Getauschter blicke las ich meine trauer
> Doch treu bekennend kamst du selber bote
> Und stolz war unsres bundes kleine dauer.²⁹

The first and third stanzas traffic in tedium: retreating shadows; pointless, foolish searching; unanswerable questions. But the second and fourth stanzas disrupt with moments full of togetherness and meaning. As the first such instance in the poem's second stanza makes clear, those moments are not just concerned with a different temporality, they are also concerned with togetherness: "A flash! For us a chain of runic light." The "we" constitutes itself in a moment, and as a moment is present only in a flash.

But perhaps not surprisingly, George is not content to present one such flash. Togetherness irrupts into the poem twice (in the second and fourth stanzas), and the relationship between these two irruptions is quite complicated. The first irruption is "a flash," natural and spontaneous—and unfortunately with a flash's short duration. Ecstasy happens only momentarily, but it is a messianic moment that arrives independently of our search for it. The second irruption, by contrast, takes effort, search, a pained attempt at re-creating it. And it isn't altogether successful in recapturing the magic of the first iteration. Between the "evening glow" and the melancholy glances heavy with parting, this moment of togetherness is over before it begins. And where the "flash" and the "us" came together and mirrored each other in a momentary conjunction in the second stanza, here "triumph" coincides with "grief," and even the "us" is not identical with itself: the other person, we are told, arrives for this second encounter as "a herald of yourself." The flash-like "us" of the earlier epiphany constitutes a momentary collapse of signifier and signified; in this second epiphany, the "you" arrives as his or her own stand-in ("herald").

The second epiphany is an effort, a wished-for and labored-toward repetition of a miraculous, and perhaps unique, occasion. This effort is the task of poetry: poetry is the name for the effort we need to expend to make lightning strike twice, or, as in "On the Terrace," for there to be an "us" twice. In the very difficulty of the flash-like communion celebrated in that poem, we may recognize the moment of indecision only too familiar to men like Stefan George: this is what Eve Kosofsky Sedgwick called, in her influential book of the same title, "the epistemology of the closet."³⁰ Is this a memory of friendship, of solitude, or of love? Is the "I" in its recollection *with* someone or a confirmed bachelor? The point is not that this is somehow a gay relationship. It's rather that the forms of togetherness this poem knows are momentary, fraught, undecidable, and unrepeatable in ways that taste of the forbidden, the invisible, of that which dare not speak its name. And in "On the Terrace" they're juxtaposed to long, enduring stretches of solitude. This is what the illustrious Schwabing mystagogue Alfred Schuler—who would make George's acquaintance a few years after the publication of the *Hymns*—would call the "closed life,"[31] the life of married heterosexuality. What endures cannot be erotic; genuine eroticism is momentary, paradoxical, imperceptible, teetering on the edge of impossibility.

This is the temporality of homoeroticism Marcel Proust describes in *Sodom and Gomorra*: what George calls the Bund here, Proust terms the *conjonction*— the against-all-odds miracle that is a queer union. In the opening scene, Proust's narrator loiters in the garden of Mme. de Villeparaisis, hoping to witness "the miracle" of an orchid being fertilized by a bumblebee: "the arrival, almost impossible to hope for (across all the obstacles, the distance, the contrary chances, the dangers), of the insect sent from afar as an ambassador to the virgin whose wait had been so protracted."[32] Instead, he witnesses something much rarer and more precious: the tailor Jupien and the Baron de Charlus kissing, an occurrence he explicitly likens to the "miracle" of orchid and bumblebee. The Bund George describes in the *Hymns* is exactly such a miracle.

It is seductive to link this teetering between impossibility and ecstasy to an event that postdated the publication of the *Hymns* by only a few years— George's infatuation with Hugo von Hofmannsthal, who eventually turned him down in a rather dramatic fashion. George had several of these abortive romances, usually rejected once his poetry was clarified into the cold prose of the pickup. But what is more significant is not the attempted liaison with the seventeen-year-old poet but the fact that Hofmannsthal's recruitment was part of George's initial efforts at forming what would later become the "circle" around him. In that respect, the talk of a Bund that closes "On the Terrace" is not to be taken as a euphemism—these were love poems but strange ones, love poems that envisioned homoeroticism as a way not of forging a couple but of sowing the seeds of a community. Around the same period, others pursued a goal of homoerotic community far more explicitly—the Wissenschaftlich-humanitäres Komitee, the first LGBT rights organization, was formed in Berlin 1897, and the first homophile publications emerged around the same time. George's project was not that: his homoerotic community was to be structured around a rejection of the public sphere, a family rather than a society.

This, then, is the position the *Hymns*, and much of George's early poetry, take on the eroticism of the Bund: the poet seems unable to imagine a queer relationship that endures beyond flashes that recede into memory even as they are occurring. Or, perhaps better, he doesn't seem to want to imagine them. The loves described in the *Hymns* are elfin creatures—agile, balletic contortionists. The only thing they seem at once incapable of and uninterested in is enduring. It is hard to say whether George understands this as their great asset or their central tragedy—they steal into view far too shyly for this to become clear. Perhaps George didn't feel like he needed to decide—this is simply what one talked about when one didn't talk of gay love. Tragedy or boon, the momentariness of queer bonds disappears from George's oeuvre, as does the pride the *Hymns* seem to take in it.

If the coiled and tragic temporality of queerness disappears, this leaves poetry in a precarious position, itself in need of reassessment and redefinition. After all, the poems' speakers do not turn to poetry to shroud their love lives in obscurity. The kind of temporality they assign to queerness can be expressed only in poetry and is, it seems, identical to it. How else would one tell of a love that is over before it begins, regretful in the moment of consummation, and proud of its short duration? This question would come to haunt George's own dynasty: If the homoeroticism of the *Hymns* was to some extent an aesthetic/poetic phenomenon, what was the meaning of his move away from that conception of homoeroticism? Was it a retooling of the aesthetic to better capture or instantiate a new conception of Bund, or was it an attempt to leave the aesthetic behind for something else entirely?

The Banishment of Impermanence

The years following the publication of the *Hymns* were the germinal moments of George's *Kreis*, but ironically, poems that celebrate a "wir" in the mode of the *Hymns* become rarer during this period. *Ich* and *du* proliferate. In addition, *Liebe* drops out as a mediating instance. But another term inserts itself in its place, one that would trouble George's reception like few others— when *I*'s and *you*'s relate in *Der Teppich des Lebens* (*The Tapestry of Life*, 1899), they do so through the figure of the leader, the *Meister*. The poem "So komm zur Stätte wo wir uns Verbünden" ("Then come to where we work in unison") does not describe the Bund as a miraculous momentary conjunction but instead traces the poetic labor that goes into making a Bund happen—a Bund may happen in a flash, but *Verbünden* is an effort:

> Then come to where we work in unison,
> Where through my sacred grove a paean rings:

"Though tens of thousands be the form of thing,
You shall give voice to one alone: my own."³³

So komm zur stätte wo wir uns verbünden!
In meinem hain der weihe hallt es brausend:
Sind auch der dinge formen abertausend
Ist dir nur Eine—Meine—sie zu künden.³⁴

The Bund now has a fixed site (*Stätte*). It is no longer transitory, and it is the property of an "I." And that "I," that *Stätte* and poetic locution, become stabilized in tandem. The Bund now has a place, it has a speaker, and it endures; is forced into and kept in reality by the poet-leader's imperative. When the leader concentrates "der dinge formen abertausend" into "nur Eine—Meine" form, what George describes here sounds quite close to what Hermann Schmalenbach described as the operation of the Bund: the leader deracinates his disciples, disconnecting them from their original environment ("No loving friend, nor kisses of a bride / Nor tears can make us faithless to our star"³⁵ [Kein weinen zieht uns ab von unsrem stern / Kein arm des freundes und kein kuss der braut],³⁶ as another poem in the cycle puts it) and bringing them into his own orbit and under his own logic.

This is a formalist poetic gesture transmuted into the realm of the political. Like the one form that can make visible the many identities of the godhead in "Resigned I face the riddle that he is," so *Führung* (leadership) requires a foreshortening of options (into one form and "one alone: my own") and a constitutive renunciation of a measure of autonomy. At the same time, only through such submission to form does the Bund, does the poem, become what it really is. Without it, all we are left with are thousands of possible forms—only *Kündung*, the living voice, the secret meaning, gives form to the bewildering and ultimately empty banquet of possibilities. Poetic form and *Bund* are not just analogous, they constitute the same gesture: in and through receptivity to the leader, we can make sense of the poem and we belong to the Bund.

At the same time, who gets to be part of the Bund and who doesn't emerge as fraught questions during precisely this phase of George's work. In most of the poems of *The Tapestry of Life*, the Bund just comes into existence spontaneously in and through the poetic locution. In one poem, for instance, the collective exists before anything ever constitutes or convokes it, and it seems thunderstruck by its own collectivity: "erstaunt" (Morwitz translates "in awe," but the word also conveys just simple surprise) that it exists as group. But the way the phrase "but undismayed" juts from the syntax seems to suggest that this Bund is just as "erstaunt" that its shock invigorates rather than scares it:

> We are the selfsame children who in awe
> Of your imperial tread, but undismayed,
> Are ready when the battle-trumpets blow
> From open reaches where your flag is spread.[37]
>
> Wir sind dieselben kinder die erstaunt
> Vor deinem herrschertritt doch nicht verzagt
> Uns sammeln wenn ein waffenknecht posaunt
> Dass in dem freien feld dein banner ragt.[38]

The "wir" in the first line and the "uns" in the third come too early: the "us" constitutes itself before the clarion call summons "our" fellowship into existence. And because George places "Uns sammeln" at the opening of its line, neither the squire's call nor the banner calls for "uns." Unlike "ein Blitz" (lightning strike) of the poem "On the Terrace," this call is not, or not just, "für uns" (for us). The call is not addressed to "us" specifically, but "we" constitute ourselves when we answer it. And we constitute ourselves as a "we" as "children," as children surprised to be someone's children. Hearing the call means becoming child to someone (maybe the "herrscher" [ruler], but the poem doesn't say)—it requires entering a filial relationship, requires self-insertion into a line of succession.

The secrecy that characterized the miracle of the Bund in the early poems has been replaced by a public privacy: everyone can hear the call, but only those it speaks to are part of "us."[39] The poem invokes a similar kind of community to the one we encountered in the *Hymns*; but where those earlier communities were caught in a paradoxical temporality to the point that they barely existed at all, the one celebrated here is rendered *stable* by its paradoxical temporality. What the leader calls into existence has always already existed. Where the *Hymns* insisted that "stolz war unsres bundes kleine dauer" (our togetherness was proud and brief), this Bund seems plenty proud without any such short duration. What has survived is the exclusive and exclusionary gesture: the "we" defines itself over and against a world that doesn't understand the community's inner workings or doesn't even understand that there is such a community.

The poem "Wir die als Fürsten wählen und Verschmähn" ("We who as princes choose and cast aside") presents a community of "truest priests of love" (der liebe treuste priester wol) who *are* aristocrats but are being told by the outside world that they are sick, incapable of attaining greatness. Where Thomas Mann and others see homoeroticism as incapable of building anything enduring (a dynasty, a community), this group of "fürsten" know they *can* and *do* just that; the outside world simply doesn't know how to see them. The Bund constitutes itself as an invisible dynasty—it exists thanks to both those who can see it for what it is and those who cannot:

> We who as princes choose and cast aside
> And lift the world from ancient hinges, shall
> We search forever, sick and sorely tried,
> And think we miss the best that can befall?[40]

> Wir die als fürsten wählen und verschmähn
> Und welten heben aus den alten angeln
> Wir sollen siech und todesmüde spähn
> Und denken dass des höchsten wir ermangeln—[41]

When the poem says "Wir sollen," it's hard not to hear contempt and derision as it reels off a list of feelings the "wir" are supposed to have. The "wir" are revolutionaries ("und welten heben aus den alten angeln") and priests of love ("der liebe treuste priester wol"), yet the dictates of the "sollen" would commit them to a life of slavery, regret, and sickness, a life the group contemptuously rejects. More important, these dictates would give their fellowship the temporality that characterized the Bund in the *Hymns*: furtive, momentary loves, long periods of absence and regret, and loss at the moment of fulfillment:

> We who are love's most faithful priests must quest
> For it with hidden grief and hollow eyes[42]

> Dass wir der liebe treuste priester wol
> Sie suchen müssen in verhülltem jammern[43]

This all-too-familiar vision of paradoxical, impossible, momentary fellowship (full of "verhülltem jammern") is revealed as counterfactual in the final five lines. The poem surrenders itself to lament, only to reveal that lament as a ruse. The "wir" rejects a vision of fellowship that would accept, much less take pride in, the disappointment, vanity, and brevity of its *Liebe*. What makes this clear is the sudden midstanza irruption of direct speech, as an "ich" addresses the group ("euch") with a counterfactual of its own: he imagines his brethren not understanding that "Since all the forms you worshipped and forwent" receives its greatness only "through you."

> "I know your heart would break, that you would die
> If I had not the spell that can abate:
> Since all the forms you worshipped and forwent

> Through you are valid and through you are great,
> Do not lament too much what you have lent."[44]
>
> "Ich weiss dass euer herz verblutend stürbe
>
> Wenn ich den spruch nicht kennte der es stillt:
> Da jedes bild vor dem ihr fleht und fliehet
> Durch euch so gross ist und durch euch so gilt . . .
> Beweinet nicht zu sehr was ihr ihm liehet."[45]

But, he suggests, they *do* know this, and thus they do *not* give in to their despair. They know the magic formula by which the "Bild" rules their lives because of the "ich." It's his address, a repeated, ritualized reminder, that keeps their despair at bay and allows them to recognize themselves in their fears and terrors. Significantly, this "ich" does not seem to address group members individually; it addresses the group as a group and suggests that the members as a group are the authors of both the ailments that beset each of them and the only cure for those ailments. The poetic "I," the poet's locution, is the alembic in which despair and futility are somehow transmuted into stability and structure.

In this poem, then, the power of the group, its ability to keep the despair of futility and momentariness at bay, derives from the ever-renewed magic words spoken by a charismatic "ich." The inevitability of the Bund's demise, which the *Hymns* had taken to indicate that it was authentic and poetic, has been transformed into a possibility or a threat. At least in the last poem considered, that very threat of loss in fact constitutes the community: only those who might find themselves mourning in this way, only those whom the leader's *Führung* keeps from despair, can gain admittance to the community. We might say that the community as *The Tapestry of Life* describes it is more stable than that described in *Hymns*—which both is and isn't true: the Bund itself isn't stabilized, just the constituting threat.

This shift has two important consequences going forward. First, the *Hymns* present a kind of bond that is to some extent coextensive with poetry. We the readers of the poem are privy to just the kind of community the poem celebrates. In *The Tapestry of Life*, particularly in "We who as princes choose and cast aside," it is not entirely clear whether we the readers are still included in the "wir." In hearing and understanding the leader's "spruch," we very well may be, but the existential anguish that forms the Bund's constituting threat seems far more exclusive. Poetry and its reception are a necessary condition for access to the Bund, but it's an insufficient condition. The threat is an *Existentiell* in Martin Heidegger's sense, which (1) is required for admission to the poetic community but which (2) decisively exceeds the poetic.

If the Bund described in the poems of *The Tapestry of Life* seems more stable an affair than in the *Hymns*, it also seems altogether static.[46] Other than his poetic "spruch," the leader has nothing to impart to his followers—it is not entirely clear what the followers are to do with the "spruch" once imparted. Other than being ready "to go out into night and death for his glory"[47] ("für seinen ruhm in nacht und tod zu gehn"),[48] they are an audience and nothing beyond that. Within the ten years that followed the publication of *The Tapestry of Life*, George decisively reconceptualized the role of the audience-cum-follower. By doing so, he transcended the static Bund of that poetry collection in favor of (1) a dynastic conception of Bund, which ripples outward from the leader forward and backward in time, and (2) a conception of the dynasty that was no longer "just" poetic. The speaker in these expected something from his listeners (and implicitly from his readers), more than just attention and sentiment—the initiates had become proselytes, the Bund a dynasty.

Stefan George provides the poetic rules for this realignment in *The Seventh Ring*, an uncharacteristically lumbering and baggy collection, with poems that clearly predate the Maximin event and George's falling out with the Cosmic Circle and others that just as clearly postdate them. Nevertheless, the poems' coherence, at least in certain respects, suggests that Dutch poet Albert Verwey was right to claim that George had the founding-myth idea of something like Maximin long before Maximilian Kronberger passed away. This is because *The Seventh Ring*, in its pre-Maximin poems as in its post-Maximin poems, shifts almost obsessively to the question of dynasty, which, as we saw, was still rather marginal in *The Tapestry of Life*. To be sure, George doesn't use the word *dynasty* in this collection, and procreative sexuality is once again absent. But if the *Zeitgedichte* (Poems of the Time) that open the volume obsessively construct ancestors for George's half-poetic, half-political mission, the Maximin sections obsess over how to transmit this mission, how to iterate the Maximin event beyond the sphere of influence of his own charisma—something that George had never worried about in the earlier versions of the Bund he envisioned.

The *Zeitgedichte* are more overtly instruments of cultural critique than George's earlier efforts: they rehearse the critique of civilization common to popular philosophy and to avant-garde poetry around the turn of the century. Each of them describes the present in hues reminiscent of Rainer Maria Rilke's later characterization of the "gedeutete Welt" (interpreted world), of Theodor Adorno's description of the "administered world," or for that matter of Alfred Schuler's conception of "the closed life." Each poem does so by constructing a past vantage before which the present can be shown lacking. For someone like George, steeped in the classicism of Winckelmann, Goethe, and Hegel, the medievalism of the late Friedrich Schlegel or Wilhelm Tieck, or the more recent cultural critiques of Friedrich Nietzsche and Johann Jakob Bachofen, this strategy may not be all too surprising. But the *Zeitgedichte* refuse to settle on one or even several golden ages by means of which to critique the present. Instead, they settle on a *pattern* of interrogation, by which past and present are dynastically connected. George seems to trace a lineage of patron saints, from Roman emperors via Dante to Goethe, Nietzsche, and Pope Leo XIII.

What's more, he seems to suggest that their opposition to the disenchantment of the world was not sporadic. Influenced by Schuler, he understands their lineage as more than intellectual: they transmit their critique through a process of repetition and rebirth, and, as one poem in particular makes clear, they transmit it through "blood." That poem, "Porta Nigra," is explicitly dedicated to Schuler, or rather his spirit ("Ingenio Alf. Scolari"), and picks up his persistent theme of a male-gendered line of succession. In it, a reborn late Roman emperor (the details George provides suggest Heliogabalus) explores the city of Trier (Augusta Treverorum) and bemoans the turn the city has taken since he last laid eyes on it. Old Trier, to hear Heliogabalus describe it, is a far more vibrant (and far sexier) place than its modern incarnation: gladiators, triumphal marches, gods, and gold, now replaced with hovels and markets.[49]

> Why did I have to waken in your era,
> Who knew the stateliness of Treves when she
> Still shared the fame of Rome, her sister city,
> When eyes lit up and widened as they followed
> The trains of clanging legions in the stadium
> The Franks with yellow hair who fought with lions,
> The tubas at the palace and the god
> Augustus, purple in his golden chariot.[50]

> Dass ich zu eurer zeit erwachen musste
> Der ich die pracht der Treverstadt gekannt
> Da sie den ruhm der schwester Roma teilte
> Da auge glühend gross die züge traf
> Der klirrenden legionen in der rennbahn
> Die blonden Franken die mit löwen stritten
> Die tuben vor palästen und den GOTT
> Augustus purpurn auf dem goldnen wagen![51]

Of course, George doesn't mean to construct his imaginary ancestors as blood relations—but when "Porta Nigra" has the boy emperor Heliogabalus charge modern Trier with the loss of "das edelste," that "edelste" turns out to be blood. For a moment, the banal nineteenth-century anxiety of the descent and degeneration of nations seems to rear its head:

Now you have lost what is most priceless: blood!
Though shades, we breathe more deeply. You, the living,
Are only ghosts, laughs Manlius, the boy.
He would refuse to rule you with a scepter[52]

Das edelste ging euch verloren: blut
Wir schauen atmen kräftiger! lebendige
Gespenster! lacht der Knabe Manlius
Er möchte über euch kein zepter schwingen[53]

But if the mention of blood initially calls to mind ideas of race and descent, Schuler's view points in a different direction: his metaphysics of sex centrally revolved around what he called the "Blutleuchten," blood beacons that both signaled the degeneration of occidental society and spoke messianically of the restoration of a pagan past. But for Schuler, his status as "Blutleuchte," the term not withstanding, was not hereditary in any biological sense, though it retroactively inserted him into a kind of dynasty.

While Schuler's cryptic assertions tend to sidestep the mode of transmission that connects the different "Blutleuchten"[54] he identifies, George's poem puts much pressure on that very mode. What transmits the boy emperor's blood? What we moderns have lost, and how we have lost it, seem central to George's *Kulturkritik* in "Porta Nigra." While it isn't procreation, it does appear to be sexual. In fact, the entire poem is constructed around a kind of sex impossible to esotericize and thus de-eroticize in the way that George's more squeamish acolytes tried.[55] To be sure, there *is* an esoteric "spiritual" secret being passed down through the ages in "Porta Nigra" (and getting lost in transit); but that esoteric secret passes through, and is to some extent constituted by, the Porta Nigra—the b(l)ack door. At the center of the poem, like the Porta Nigra, a Roman city gate at the center of Trier, lies a sexual pun so glaring, so obscenely out in the open, that it takes effort to interpret the poem without referring to it.

Just who Manlius is meant to represent here has been the subject of some debate. The poem is uncharacteristically frank in describing Manlius's occupation, but whether he's supposed to represent anything beyond a kind of classical (or perhaps oriental) homoeroticism is less clear. While many readers have posited that he's simply a male prostitute, others, like Georg Dörr, have suggested that he's *also* Alfred Schuler.[56] Another suggestion is that behind Manlius lurks once again the old George favorite, the emperor Heliogabalus, or Algabal.[57] The poem's final lines reference a story told about Heliogabalus, who, Cassius Dio's *Historia Romana* reports, prostituted himself to his own courtiers and took delight in the money he made in this way:

"He set aside a room in the palace and there committed his indecencies, always standing nude at the door of the room, as the harlots do, and shaking the curtain which hung from gold rings, while in a soft and melting voice he solicited the passers-by."[58] And another one of George's favorites is foreshadowed in the poem: the poet borrowed Manlius for his presentation of divine Maximin. George's preface to the Maximin *Gedenkbuch* describes his first encounter with the boy in the terms of "Porta Nigra": young Maximilian Kronberger emerges with "a commander's lordly countenance" (mienen feldherrlicher obergewalt) from a triumphal arch.[59]

As the poem's central metaphor, the Porta Nigra practically constitutes a dare for the reader. Like Manlius sashaying around his arch, like Heliogabalus shaking his gold-ringed curtain, like Maximin peeling himself from the shadowy arch in Munich, the black door at the center of the poem beckons and teases. But it teases knowing full well that however much it flounces and scandalizes, the reader won't follow through the black door. To enter it would be to enter the succession of "Blutleuchten." Manlius/Algabal/Maximin knows as much—and he makes it his primary indictment of modernity. Moderns dare not pass through the Porta Nigra; therefore, Manlius/Algabal/Maximin wouldn't want to be their leader.

The emperor proudly engages in behavior which the modern mind "shrink[s] from naming"[60]—the ability to speak sex, it seems, is another advantage antiquity has over modernity; and the inability to call things by their name is yet another defect Heliogabalus points out in modern Trier. In a strange way, then, the emperor does procreate. It is a homoerotic procreation but given a decidedly carnal hue here. Having gay sex, or rather talking about gay sex, turns out in the poem to be a better, more authentic ways of procreating than begetting biologically (with "women whom even slaves would find too cheap a bargain").[61] The Porta Nigra—the physical object, the metaphor that may not and need not speak its name, and the poem that circles teasingly around it—enables a circular dynasty that, as the poem presents it, passes on far more and far more profound contents than anything biological procreation would be capable of.

"Porta Nigra" gathers around itself a dynasty of avatars, avatars connected by speaking homoeroticism, and it gathers them by means of poetry. But is understanding what the poem is about—knowing about the "Blutleuchten," calling out the pun in the poem's title—still enough for being part of the Bund described in the poem? It would seem not. We may agree with Manlius's indictment of modernity, may stand in disillusionment before the markets and hovels of modern Trier—yet we aren't part of the dynasty of "Blutleuchten."

Poetry is a necessary but no longer sufficient condition for the homoerotic dynasty.

The Seventh Ring follows up these "Zeitgedichte" with poems of mourning for Maximin. These poems are no longer about provenance, about constructing a poetic ancestry of "Blutleuchten": their project is procreation; they seek to construct a dynasty of future "Blutleuchten" instead. It is this double motion that George encapsulates in the opening line of one of the poems in *The Star of the Covenant* mentioned earlier: "With you I now grow back through generations": A Bund moves in two directions at once—as it brings I and Thou closer together, it moves backward and forward in time, claims ancestors for itself, and imagines followers for itself.

The Curse of Permanence: "Secret Germany"

By this point in Stefan George's life, the dynasty had transformed from a mere telos for the Circle into a description of how his influence began to suffuse the German intellectual world. Any legacy inscribed into the form of his poems now had to grapple with the fact of his actual considerable influence, far beyond the confines of the circle. The historian Ulrich Raulff recently subtitled his book about the George adepts *Stefan George's Afterlives*. But what was remarkable about George was that he had an afterlife while he was still alive.[62] The remainder of this chapter deals with George's complicated legacy, as the all-male dynasty he had inaugurated began to grapple with what had been entrusted to it and how that inheritance was to be transmitted.

In the poems gathered in *Das Neue Reich*, paternity and dynasty take center stage, though in the same refracted and rearranged modes we find in *The Seventh Ring* and *The Star of the Covenant*. Every act of procreation is at once an act of reaching back to a tradition of heroes, and only in the act of procreation does the poet manage to insert himself into their lineage. This gesture by now found a clear correspondence in George's own management of the young people organized around his person. Yet *The Star of the Covenant* (published in 1914) and *Das Neue Reich* (published as part of the collected works in 1928) bookend a long period of poetic silence: Before 1914, George had published new volumes of poetry with some regularity, and had contributed poems to the literary magazine *Blätter für die Kunst* in between. There were no new books with George as author during the fourteen years after publication of *The Star of the Covenant*, and the *Blätter* ended its run in 1919. He continued to write poetry, of course, but it was poetry that was accessible to few, and in many cases unknown even to his initiates.

But this didn't mean he was unproductive. For these fourteen years are also the ones in which George's disciples put their intellectual stamp on German thought and culture. These are the years in which Friedrich Gundolf became a literary star, in which young men like Max Kommerell and Ernst Kantorowicz revolutionized their fields. The circle around George no longer consisted of second-rate poets and aestheticist epigones; it was now dominated by literary scholars, classicists, and historians, all with a pronounced missionary zeal. And we only have to glance at some of their most famous works—Kommerell's *Der Dichter als Führer*, Kantorowicz's *Friedrich II*, and Gundolf's *Goethe*, for instance—to realize that they had anointed the peculiar temporality of *The Seventh Ring* and *The Star of the Covenant* as their hermeneutic lodestar: a look back that was at once a look into a future that would restore that past. It was this temporality that, despite all political differences, attracted a young Walter Benjamin to the poet and his disciples. In each case, a historical figure (Goethe, Jean Paul, Friedrich Hölderlin, Friedrich II) became an *Ahnherr* (forefather) who had spawned a secret legacy—a legacy that now lay dormant, awaiting reactivation by the line's last or latest spawn, Stefan George.

George's productivity thus proceeded dynastically, through others, but it did so in the strange mode of dynasticity established in *The Seventh Ring*: at once proleptic and recursive. Not surprisingly, the poems collected in *Das Neue Reich* (written over a twenty-year period, from 1908 to 1928) rely on the same picture of paradoxical dynasticity as the philological works of George's young adepts—but the volume is more explicit in elaborating these mechanics, and more emphatic in eroticizing them.

The centerpiece of the collection is the monumental poem "Der Dichter in Zeiten der Wirren" ("The Poet in Times of Confusion"). The poem casts the roles of "dichter" and "sänger" as procreative, but once again it's a strange kind of procreation, modeled on a metaphor of glowing embers roused anew to new flame:

> He stirs the holy flame that leaps across
> And shapes the flesh in which to burn.[63]
>
> Er schürt die heilige glut die über-springt
> Und sich die leiber formt[64]

He draws "aus büchern" the knowledge that there are embers yet in the ashes, and he renews their promise to reignite in the future, to concretize into the members of a new generation. At the end of this generation stands a male-on-male birth, as the savior ("the only one who can restore") is born from the young "geschlecht":

> A younger generation rises toward him,
> The youths who, steeled by years of galling pressure,
> Again have honest standards for the probe
> Of men and things, who—fair and grave and proud—
> In alien worlds accept themselves for what
> They are, avoid the rocks of brazen boasting
> And the morass of would-be brotherhood
> Spat out the lifeless, stale, and base, and form
> Their consecrated dreams, and deeds, and sorrows
> Begot the only one who can restore.[65]
>
> Ein jung geschlecht das wieder mensch und ding
> Mit echten maassen misst das schön und ernst
> Froh seiner einzigkeit vor Fremdem stolz
> Sich gleich entfernt von klippen dreisten dünkels
> Wie seichtem sumpf erlogner brüderei
> Das von sich spie was mürb und feig und lau
> Das aus geweihtem träumen tun und dulden
> Den einzigen der hilft den Mann gebiert.[66]

The leader gives birth to a young generation (*Geschlecht*) which in turn gives birth to a savior figure. It's lines like these that suggest that George was giving his aestheticist politics one final twist: at the end of poetic transmission stands an unpoetic, unphilosophical birth. The dynasty abandons the circularity of the earlier poems and culminates in a messianic terminus.

Lines like these also came to haunt the George Circle after Hitler ascended to power. As the poet himself lay dying in Switzerland, his followers tried to hold up the kind of community he had envisioned to the one the Nazis claimed to be establishing in Germany—and wondered whether the former had possibly begotten the latter. Much ink and agony have gone into figuring out how similar George's *Reich* was to certain aspects of Nazi ideology, not least on the part of the poet himself. The distaste with which he rejected the Nazis' overtures once again brought out the old aestheticism—but his activities (poetic, editorial, and political) in the previous decade indeed made it clear that he had thought his poetry was moving someplace beyond the playing field of *Lyrik* and thought. What kind of dynasty had he created? And what kind of dynasty had he meant to create?

In evaluating the relationship between George and the Third Reich, his followers were forced to articulate how they understood the nature of the poet's "Secret Germany," and how they envisioned its mode of transmission—and it was in this articulation that the different conceptions of the Bund that I traced in this chapter reasserted themselves one last time. Whether they rushed to declare the Nazis' new Germany the realization of George's *Reich* or rejected any such comparison out of hand, they drew from different stages of his poetic thinking about the Bund and (its) legacy.

Soon after the Nazi ascendancy, far too early for the comfort of even those George disciples who harbored no ill will toward the new rulers, Woldemar von Üxküll-Gyllenband gave a lecture entitled "Das revolutionäre Ethos bei Stefan George" ("The Revolutionary Ethos of Stefan George") at the University of Tübingen. For Üxküll-Gyllenband, a professor of ancient history, the young generation and the Nazis were essentially George's *children*, the political realization of his aestheticist Bund. That Bund, Üxküll-Gyllenband thought, had always been political but had to camouflage its position as an aestheticist "secret."

Even more explicitly, the Cologne literary scholar Ernst Bertram (himself only a peripheral figure in the Circle)[67] claimed George for the new rulers and insisted that the poet's vision and theirs were identical. His infamous lecture "Deutscher Aufbruch" ("German Awakening"), delivered at a book burning in early 1933, had opened with martial language straight from the anti-Semitic weekly tabloid *Der Stürmer*, but it ended by quoting George.[68] In a lecture he gave on the occasion of George's birthday in July of that year, Bertram posited the Third Reich as the "powerful reality" that George's poetic speech had "called forth."[69] Like Üxküll-Gyllenband, he insisted that the transition from the poetry of *Das Neue Reich* to the actual Third Reich had been a process of concretization. What had previously been diffuse and confined to the realm of poetic language had been at last rendered real, just as George had intended.

Also like Üxküll-Gyllenband, Bertram cast George's aestheticism as a sort of exile. Both men understood the process I have been tracing in this chapter as a gradual concretion and a gradual de-poeticization of the idea of the Bund. They emphasized its forward thrust along with the idea of George as a shaper of the "younger generation" spoken about in "The Poet in Times of Confusion." Yet Bertram's lecture wasn't intended merely as a recognition of these supposed facts. It was also supposed to insist on the rights of poetry— just as George's poetic vision was "realized" into the Third Reich, Bertram thought, so the new powers in Germany needed to be educated in the ways of the poetic, the not-quite-actual. The reason was that they needed to be cured of their own myopia that had them fixate on their *Reich*'s Germanic roots at the expense of the dynasty of forebears George identifies—a dynasty that includes Germans but is certainly not limited to them.

Üxküll-Gyllenband's lecture was immediately printed as a small pamphlet, and in an act of supreme cluelessness, he sent a copy to Ernst Kantorowicz. Kantorowicz, like the professor, had been among the George Circle's most conservative members; unlike the professor, he was Jewish, and had decided to resign from his academic post at the University of Frankfurt almost immediately after the *Machtergreifung*. He was briefly reinstated in late 1933 and began lecturing again in the winter semester of that year.[70] Kantorowicz appears to have received Üxküll-Gyllenband's pamphlet during his period of forced unemployment. Incensed and repelled by the readiness with which his former friend aligned George's poetic vision with the Nazis' project, he used his first lecture of the new term to present a very different reading of George's vision of the Bund and its relationship to Nazism. The title of his lecture picked up on one of the most suggestive and controversial poem titles from George's *Das Neue Reich*: it was called "Das Geheime Deutschland" ("Secret Germany").[71]

Kantorowicz gave the lecture on November 14, 1933—George would be dead within two weeks. The fulcrum of his rebuttal to Üxküll-Gyllenband's speech is that the very notion of declaring something the realization or manifestation of the Secret Germany is bound to miss the point. "The rulers of the 'Secret Germany' are immune [*gefeit*] against weaponization [*Gewaffen*]," he declares, "and you will not get a hold of them by dragging their image into the street, making them resemble the marketplace and then celebrate them as one's own flesh and blood."[72] Kantorowicz thus holds on to the most bedeviling feature of George's authoritarian streak: he celebrates "domination" (the exponents of the Secret Germany are *Herrscher* [rulers]), but insists that this *Herrschaft* cannot be turned into political authority—it is the very opposite of "flesh and blood." In fact, his turn of phrase follows George's repeated suggestion that this *Herrschaft* is something incredibly fragile and vulnerable, something to be piously protected rather than wantonly projected.

Where other George disciples thought the Nazi ascendancy meant that George's vision had moved beyond being an aestheticist secret, Kantorowicz insists on the intrinsic necessity of both.[73] He reads George's poem "Das Geheime Deutschland" as a rebuke to those who jumped to tether the concept to "goals of the day, special wishes, small grouplets and little covenants [Tageszielen und Sonderbelangen, Grüppchen und Bündchen]"[74] and thus "watered down" the concept. While the Secret Germany resembles a family and has a "genealogy" (Genealogie dieses Reiches [82]), its temporality eschews the propulsive and the procreative. As Hegel suggested, in the process of begetting, the creators come face to face at some point with a new thing they have created. The generative creativity of their Bund has concretized into a thing (a *Bündchen* perhaps), and the boundless potential of the moment of creativity has ossified into a creation that exists in one mode rather than another.

Kantorowicz proposes a different temporality for the Secret Germany, one indeed quite close to George's concept of Bund. The Secret Germany is not dynastic in that one determinate link in the chain begets another determinate link, which in turn forges another. While this Secret Germany has a kaiser and an aristocracy, neither group is constituted or legitimated by "rules of procreation" (Zeugungsregeln) but rather "by the procreation of most secret powers" (durch die Zeugung geheimster Mächte). He quotes from "Neuer adel den ihr suchet" ("The New Nobility That You Seek") another poem from George's *The Star of the Covenant*: "Stammlos wachsen im gewühle / Seltne sprossen eignen ranges" (81). George's lines suggest a tree without trunk, a thicket of branches each with its own rank (eignen rang)—this is the kind of dynasty the Secret Germany tries to set up, according to Kantorowicz.

Unlike a traditional "genealogy," which traces back to what has been, Kantorowicz claims that "this has never come to pass [*zugetragen*], but it exists enduringly and forever [*immerwährend und ewig*]" (80). For he calls the "emperors or aristocracy" of the Secret Germany "elect" (erkoren); they are "carriers" (Träger). The metaphor of carriers again suggests nonlinear modes of transmission, beyond paternity, beyond primogeniture, beyond heredity. As such, the Secret Germany is the very opposite of the triumphalist narrative preferred by Nazis like Üxküll-Gyllenband and Bertram, in which somehow the Germanic tribes of Tacitus have passed on some kind of aristocracy to modern-day Germans, and have done so through the figure of Stefan George as one generation along that line. Instead, the Secret Germany constitutes itself as the history of outsiders, the unpopular ones, the invisible ones, the ones that seem "most foreign" (84).

Kantorowicz's account of George's conception is far from revisionist, of course. While it doesn't reach the chauvinistic fever pitch of, say, Bertram's addresses, his text is nonetheless strident in its nationalism. He insists that the Secret Germany is German and superior to other nations, and he even claims that one day it will become politically realized. The main point of difference indeed concerns the temporality and mode of transmission implied by the concept. Kantorowicz emphasizes the retroactive temporality of the "Geheimes Deutschland." He is not content to dispute the equation of the Nazis with the Secret Germany, so he denies that anything can be identified with that Secret Germany at all. Just like the Bund described in George's late poetry, the Secret Germany moves toward both the past and the future. As a result, it can only be prophesied or reflected on—it can be said that it will be or that it has been. We can't say that or what it *is*. Nevertheless, the Nazi student groups got the message of Kantorowicz's lecture: they declared a boycott of his lectures, and he soon decided to discontinue them.[75]

Kantorowicz used his lecture to insist on the persistence of George's aestheticism. To him, the Secret Germany is necessarily autonomous in ways that resemble the autonomy of the aesthetic, even if they are not identical to it. The Bund can never be straightforwardly political, nor can any group be George's "children." Whereas Üxküll-Gyllenband presupposes that George's gradual commingling of poetry and politics was in fact an attempt to segue from poetry to politics, Kantorowicz retains the poetic as a central feature of George's politics. In so doing, Üxküll-Gyllenband returns the Bund to more traditional forms of dynasty, whereas Kantorowicz insists on the bizarre temporality the poet had suggested for his Bund.

These three texts, then, differ precisely on how they understand the trajectory of George's idea of a Bund. Üxküll-Gyllenband and Bertram essentially understand the process I have been tracing as a gradual concretion and a gradual de-poeticization of the idea of the Bund. At the same time, they emphasize its forward thrust, the idea of George as a shaper of the "junge Geschlecht" of which "The Poet in Times of Confusion" speaks—they "unqueer" the Bund's mode of dynastic procreation. Kantorowicz by contrast emphasizes the retroactive temporality of the "Geheimes Deutschland." He isn't content to dispute Üxküll-Gyllenband's equation of the Nazis with the Secret Germany, so he denies that anything can be identified with that Secret Germany at all: just like the Bund described in George's late poetry, the Secret Germany moves toward both the past and the future. As a result, it can only be prophesied or reflected upon—it can be said that it will be or that it has been. We can't say that or what it *is*. Rather than suggest that George's gradual commingling of poetry and politics constitutes a straightforward trajectory, moving naturally from poetry to politics, Kantorowicz retains the strange, proleptic temporality of the Bund, and maintains that only through it can the poetic be retained as the central feature of George's politics.

Inheriting Secret Germany

The phrase "Secret Germany" remained contentious well after Kantorowicz, Bertram, and Üxküll-Gyllenband fought over its meaning during the early years of the Third Reich. If anything, it began to present itself with renewed force once the dictatorship had ended. When Claus Graf Schenk von Stauffenberg was led before the firing squad in Berlin on July 21, 1944, one day after the unsuccessful coup attempt, he supposedly called out something as the shots rang out. It's impossible to ascertain whether he said "long live sacred Germany" (lang lebe das geheiligte Deutschland) or "long live secret Germany" (lang lebe das geheime Deutschland), or indeed whether he said anything at all. But it's worth reflecting on why it matters what he called out. As Thomas Karlauf has noted, "The concept of a Secret Germany was as vague and enigmatic in the context of 20 July 1944 as it was in the middle of the 1920s."[76] But the legend that he invoked the national mysticism of the George Circle in his final moment (1) continues a line of tradition, (2) retrospectively reinterprets a line of tradition, and (3) reinterprets it forward into the post-Nazi future.

While it's certainly plausible that Stauffenberg, a great admirer of Stefan George and deeply immersed in the cosmology of the Circle, used the phrase, it's perhaps more interesting to consider the line of inheritance and tradition instituted by those insisting he used it. Hearing Stauffenberg call out "Secret Germany" while being executed for his role in the attempt to end the Nazi dictatorship placed the George Circle more on the side of the resistance than on that of the Nazi state. It made the group palatable as a conservative but nonfascist alternative in the postwar era. Whether Stauffenberg's final words are real or imagined, then, they're an act of a dynastic imagination, either on the condemned man's part or on the part of those seeking to interpret his words.

And in a way, the invocation—or the invocation of the invocation—makes an argument for dynasticity itself, for not abandoning the past, for accepting certain inheritances. Insisting that the words *Secret Germany* were uttered near the Bendlerblock on July 21, 1944, is an act of "the temporary destruction of forgetfulness" of which Nietzsche claims life also has need. In the middle of a situation that, more than anything, "deserved its destruction,"[77] it raises questions of continuity in spite of everything. In imagining Claus von Stauffenberg invoking George on that July morning, postwar Germans got to imagine him imagining a post-Nazi Germany, and they got to raise an old question of continuity—of how to inherit properly.

EPILOGUE

Black Sheep

"It appears that I am fated to take care that the chain of black sheep will not be interrupted in my generation."[1] In Heinrich Böll's story "Die schwarzen Schafe" (Black sheep, 1951), a man who seems half vexed, half proud of his outsider status both within his larger family and within society more broadly seeks a successor. In its bare outlines, this is a situation that wouldn't be altogether out of place in a text by Adalbert Stifter or Gottfried Keller, that could have animated the young Thomas Mann and the late Stefan George—but the political and social premises of such a story had of course shifted significantly by 1951. The narrator describes the rest of his family as exemplary exponents of Rhenish capitalist bourgeoisie—the engines of the postwar economic miracle, busy repressing the Nazi years and getting on with their lives. Of this, the narrator insists, he is incapable, a fact for which he blames (or rather credits) an uncle, the "black sheep" of the previous generation. Being a black sheep thus consists of a strange relationship to dynasticity: it means standing outside the family but inaugurating a dynastic line of transmission all one's own. If a single black sheep is the prototypical outsider, then what are we to make of a whole mob of them? How does a group of black sheep self-organize?

Here is the point at which what the George Circle had propagated on the Right before the war reemerged afterward as a tool of social critique on the Left. From the first, Böll's tale of outsiders was intended for self-organized outsiders. Böll initially read the story at a meeting of the famous Gruppe 47, a group of young writers seeking a literary renewal after the Nazi years, in this case in 1951 in Bad Dürkheim.[2] As so often in this book, this interrogation of family dynamics, of the relationship between generations, offered something of a philosophy of history. Specifically, it seemed to ask about the possibility of a new start. And of course, the "zero hour" of 1945 stood in the background of Böll's story—the return to the family took place in the context of the complete moral and legal collapse of the state.

At the same time, Böll's story noticeably treats the status of black sheep as a matter of family economics rather than family politics. The narrator and his uncle cement their outsider status largely by being unable to function economically within the family. Uncle Otto starts one failed business venture after another and keeps hitting up relatives for money until "the phrase 'by the way, would you mind . . .' became a word of sheer terror in our family, there were women—aunts, great-aunts, nieces even—who were close to fainting at the word 'short-term.'"[3] The short-lived nature of his projects stands in contrast to the solidity and extensiveness of the family tree: on the one hand, we have "aunts, great-aunts, nieces even"; on the other, Uncle Otto and his requests for "short-term" loans. The narrator meanwhile finds himself horrified by work life, where "once again a day of my life had passed which had netted me only exhaustion, some anger, and about as much money as was necessary to keep going to work" (5:163).[4] Money constitutes the arena in which an individual's outsider status becomes clearly visible—but money also becomes the way in which the lineage of outsiders constitutes and maintains itself. The narrator insists that it was an inheritance from Uncle Otto that first made his life jump its tracks; and as he contemplates his successor black sheep in the next generation, he decides to set aside some money to be bequeathed to whoever winds up being the new generation's family outcast. "The main thing," he reflects, "is that he doesn't owe them anything" (5:163).[5]

Böll's story closes with the narrator wondering "who will follow me in the generation growing up now; which one of these flowering, playing pretty children, which my brothers and sisters have put out into the world, will be the black sheep of the next generation" (5:163).[6] He never explains just how he would transmit his status as black sheep to the next generation of black sheep, nor does he seem clear about how he came to follow in his uncle's footsteps. There is throughout the story a pronounced ambivalence about what kind of fact being a black sheep ultimately is supposed to be. The narrator's status as one is "offenbar" to him—a word that both registers a certain amused surprise and invokes the language of revelation (*Offenbarung*). But at other times, there seems to be a logic of fate at work: "someone had to be it, and I happen to be it" (5:160). When the phrase recurs about Uncle Otto, it is presented as a truth universally acknowledged, moreover one that is transhistorically true—someone *has* to be "it," but Otto *was* "it."

Böll plays with pronouns throughout the narrative: even though the narrator thinks any of the "flowering, playing pretty children" sired by his brothers and sisters could be the next black sheep, in closing the story he clearly imagines his successor as a "he." Being a black sheep is described as being "it"; and having "it" upsets "aunts, great-aunts, nieces even" who represent the solid, successful, business-as-usual aspect of the extended family. In other words, the story seems to conceive of the black-sheep status as another all-male lineage, with the traditional, functioning family implicitly feminized. It wouldn't have been difficult for readers or listeners in 1951 to make the connection to their lived reality, in which men were returning from the war late, broken, or barely functioning, while women had to hold families together and reap the benefits of the incipient economic miracle (*Wirtschaftswunder*). In many stories and plays of the era—from Wolfgang Borchert's *Draußen vor der Tür* (*The Man Outside*, 1947) to Arno Schmidt's *Brand's Haide* (1951)—men are doomed to wander a landscape in which women represent stability, continuity, and a sense of purpose.

At the same time, Böll's story must be understood in a context in which family-as-usual was profoundly delegitimated. Transmitting *past* the traditional family, as Böll's black sheep do, became morally important. In *Draußen vor der Tür*, for instance, the returning soldier Beckmann tries to come home, but we learn that the home itself no longer exists, since "your old man exhausted himself a bit for the Nazis."[7] Alternative modes of kinship carried a disruptive and potentially utopian charge—Borchert's famous poem "Dann gibt es nur eins" imagines a mother who is asked to bear a future soldier or nurse and who simply says no.[8] In "Die schwarzen Schafe," this parafamilial mode of transmission shades into queerness. Eve Kosofsky Sedgwick once pointed out how the avunculate can function as "a bad fit" to how both descent and the nuclear family are imagined to work in heteronormative ideology. Uncles and aunts represent a zigzag of influence, a mix of biology and choice. "The badness of their fit with each other," but above all "with the streamlined modern models of 'family' and of same-sex attachment," helps the avuncular figure disrupt the modern binary of heteropatriarchal family and its homosexual Other.[9]

When Uncle Otto recruits the narrator in Böll's story, the process isn't erotic, but the way the narrator in turn seeks to groom a youngster seems tinged with homosociality. The uncle figure, Sedgwick wrote, relies "on a pederastic/pedagogical model of male filiation"[10]—the uncle has the power to divert, to subvert, but it's unclear what gives him this power. What's true for the modern familial imaginary in general was doubly true for postwar Germany—where missing fathers, incomplete nuclear families, and interrupted lineages were becoming an obsession, the uncle (real or metaphorical) served as a decentering presence.[11] There is a way in which men are meant to function in families, a way in which they relate to the future, that both Uncle Otto and the narrator seem perfectly incapable of. "It may be the case," Jack Halberstam proposes, that one must "adopt forgetting as a strategy for the disruption of the regularity of Oedipal transmission."[12] The lineage of black sheep as described by Böll is one that reconstitutes itself with every generation, one in which each generation stands without memory and without comprehension before its predecessor. And yet we're told that "a family without black sheep isn't a characteristic family"[13]—there's no heteronormative family without its queer shadow.

While "Die schwarzen Schafe" explicitly thematizes and subtly satirizes the world of the family in the age of the postwar economic miracle, it doesn't make overt reference to another dimension of family politics circa 1951—the aftereffects of Nazism. War and displacement had made the family an important source of continuity, but at the same time that very continuity made it suspect for those who distrusted the attempts of the postwar German state's readiness to move on and be done with the past.[14] The mode of transmission from black sheep to black sheep that Böll describes, opaque even to itself, constituted something of a moral demand in much postwar German fiction. For many postwar writers, the nuclear family was discredited as the ideological handmaiden of the Nazi state or its ex post facto repression, and they searched with some urgency for modes of passing on stories, morals, and resistance *outside* the family.

The Nazis' accession to power accelerated a modernization of German family structures and how they were understood. For all its traditional gender politics, the Nazi state was hostile to traditional authorities—be they churches, the workingmen's movement, or private households. And however much the regime promised a return to the past, it socialized families to an extent that had been previously unthinkable. In other words, the "dissolution of the family" that Hegel had described theoretically all the way back in 1817 was made something of a lived reality by the Nazis.[15] The family was at once strengthened and weakened: strengthened ideologically as the "germ cell of the *Volk*";[16] weakened insofar as it was supposed to serve as little more than that. The family unit was the biological handmaiden, the transmitter of ideology—but no longer a moral institution in its own right. The far dynastic future no longer belonged to the family but to the *Volk*. "Whoever is not healthy or worthy in mind and body, must not be allowed to eternalize his infirmity in the body of a child," Hitler had written in *Mein Kampf*.[17]

But if the Nazi years had weakened the nuclear family, the period also brought the return of concepts and questions that seemed to invoke the dynastic family. Concepts like *Sippe* (clan) and *Geschlecht* (house or family) re-emerged with a vengeance, and the conception of race as an ultimate distant family requiring protection of its hereditary material became official raison d'état. At the same time, while the racial system of the Nazi state had its pseudoscientific basis, how the Nazis actually treated the family testified to the fuzziness of their family concepts. The way racial pseudoscience was codified into law, or simply applied without bothering with the law, created paradoxical and contradictory situations. There was no clear sense, in other words, of what constituted a *Rasse* (race), a *Sippe*, or a *Geschlecht*, just that these extended much further back than the more immediate horizon of the bourgeois family.

The system by which persons applying for certain jobs within the Nazi state had to prove their "Aryan" roots expanded the conception of the relevant family quite far into the distant past. Any candidate had to provide a notarized *Ahnentafel* or *Ahnenpass*, an "ancestral tree" or "ancestral passport." The so-called Lesser Aryan certificate (Kleiner Ariernachweis), required of a broad swath of administrators, educators, lawyers, students, and the like, encompassed seven birth or baptismal certificates as well as three marriage certificates. The Greater Aryan certificate (Großer Ariernachweis), meanwhile, required for joining the Nationalsozialistische Deutsche Arbeiterpartei (NSDAP) and the SS paramilitary organization, called for documentation of the family all the way back to 1800, and even to 1750 in the case of the SS. The family that German citizens carried with them was thus massively expanded during the Nazi years. As Eric Ehrenreich has pointed out, as unrealistic as these requirements seem to us today, it is striking that a great many Germans could indeed provide this sort of information. Not the least reason for this was the growing interest in genealogical research during the German Empire and the Weimar years.[18] While sometimes mixed with eugenic questions, much of this interest had been comparatively innocent, owed in fact to the subterranean appeal of dynastic family conceptions I have traced in this book. In the Nazi state, that phantasmic family suddenly became a matter with terrifying real-life consequences.

Another place where the family did matter in Nazi Germany was for purposes of punishment—and here again, it was something of a fiction made brutally true by the institutions of the Nazi state. The practice of *Sippenhaft* involved taking dissidents' families hostage in concentration camps. It drew its name from yet another ambiguous figuration of family, namely the *Sippe*. Even in the years in which this study opened, the concept was largely considered obsolete. The imagination behind it seems to have been something like a clan—although there are clear antecedents in Roman law, which refers to the stirps or gens.[19] Robert Loeffel has illuminated the practice of *Sippenhaft*, but points out that the legal justification for it was exceedingly thin and its application largely haphazard.[20] The sheer number of individuals arrested in connection with, for instance, Claus Graf Schenk von Stauffenberg, gives us a sense of whom the Nazis considered as belonging to a *Sippe*—it appears to have been something more than the nuclear family, but in practice not far beyond. The Nazis, it seemed, wanted to operate with a more expansive sense of family, but their imagination remained resolutely nuclear.

Nevertheless, the fetish the Nazis made of concepts like *Sippe* probably bolstered the moral cachet the nuclear family would enjoy in postwar Germany on both sides of the Iron Curtain as well as in Austria. In fact, the language of the dynasty was often used to describe those aspects of German history one sought to distance oneself from—as though the nuclear family could enable a new start within the dangerous inheritances handed down dynastically. In 1946, the Austrian writer Ilse Aichinger formulated an "Aufruf zum Mißtrauen" (Appeal for mistrust) as a moral imperative after the war. In the nineteenth century, she wrote, "one came up with a thousand guardrails, to guard against the dirty, the tattered, the starving. But no one guarded against himself. This is how the beast was able to grow, unguarded and unobserved, through generations." In World War II and the Holocaust, Aichinger said, "we experienced [the beast]! We suffered it!"[21]

Just how unnatural the concept of the dynastic family had come to seem can be seen in Carl Zuckmayer's 1946 play *Des Teufels General* (The devil's general), where the title character seeks to propose a dynastic family tree that would function as the exact opposite of the Nazis' ideology of *Sippe* and *Rasse*. One officer, Hartmann, worries that he can't trace his Rhenish family far back enough to get an Ariernachweis. With some irritation his commanding officer, the general of the title, points out that there's no such thing as a pure bloodline along the Rhine, "the great mill of peoples [*Völkermühle*]."[22] The Rhine has created "the best in the world," because "the peoples all got mixed up here." And it is this mixing rather than the purity valued by the Nazis that, according to General Harras, vouched for the excellence of Hartmann's line. "Imagine your row of ancestors since the birth of Christ," the general tells his subordinate. "There was a Roman major, a black fellow, brown like a ripe olive, who taught Latin to a blond girl. Then a Jewish spice merchant came into the family," the general says, and launches into a long list of other imaginary forefathers from many nations, "all of whom lived by the Rhine and fought by it, and got drunk by it and sang by it and begat children." This," he declares in closing his soliloquy, "is natural aristocracy. This is race. Be proud of it, Hartmann!"[23] It's not a passage that has aged well, and it was critiqued even at the time—no matter what someone looked for in the distant familial past, the very act of looking was deeply suspect.

Perhaps as a result of this shift in the cultural climate, the nuclear family underwent something of a renaissance in both East and West Germany after the war. It remained a focus of intense anxiety immediately after the war, but it also promised a sense of renewal and stability amid an otherwise completely delegitimated and defunct social landscape.[24] The Grundgesetz (Basic Law) the Federal Republic adopted in 1949 explicitly hands over "marriage and the family" to "the particular protection of the state." As the phrase "marriage and the family" already suggests, the rest of article 6 is about the nuclear family: paragraph 2 explains that "care and education of the children is the natural right of the parents and their primary duty," with the state reduced to "supervising [*wacht*] their conduct." As occurs so often in the Basic Law, article 6 tells a clear story of which aspects of the Nazi state these provisions are meant to forestall: the family has no function vis-à-vis the state; it is its own end. And the family here is resolutely nuclear: banished are legal entities like the *Sippe* and the kinds of influence they may have on the individual. The family is about parents educating their children. And while the German Democratic Republic, in both its constitution of 1949 and its Protection of Mothers and Children law of 1950, summarily removed all aspects of family law that hitherto had kept wives subservient to their husbands, they did so by once again emphasizing the importance of the nuclear family at its most compact—albeit as an engine of change rather than one of continuity.[25]

By the same token, however, when the family later came under attack as an engine of repression and social and political conservatism, it was once again the nuclear family. When Alexander and Margarete Mitscherlich wrote their best seller *Die Unfähigkeit zu Trauern* (The inability to mourn, 1967) in postwar (West) Germany, their diagnosis not only relied on an analogy between identification with a state and the dynamics of a family, it also problematized the nuclear family as a central cause of repression. The Mitscherlichs traced in their analysands strategies the patients had learned in their family (repression, displacement, and projection) that they then used to fend off consciousness of their actions during the Nazi years—in order to "receive and retain recognition and a sense of belonging in the great 'family *Bundesrepublik*.'"[26] The Mitscherlichs' conceptual arsenal was largely Freudian, so their "family" tended toward the nuclear—it was defined by oedipal energy and the relationship between two generations. But this family, they argued, rearranged the state to fit its particular pathologies.

In fact, the coauthors open their first chapter with a quote from Erich Kahler's *Verantwortung des Geistes* (The responsibility of the spirit, 1952), which specifically discounts a genealogical etiology of Nazism: "The Germans have attributed to their Germanic or 'nordic' hereditary line [*Erbstrang*] their supposed 'heroic,' 'Faustian,' infinitely seeking nature," but "they share this hereditary line with most of the peoples of Europe. The unique character of the Germans," Kahler concludes, referring to the crimes of Nazi Germany, "does not stem from their origins [*Herkunft*], but from their development."[27] Kahler, a careful reader of Freud, probably intended for his assessment of Germany's murderous neuroses to echo Freud's assessment at the beginning of the *Three Essays on Sexuality*. There, Freud expresses surprise that psychologists "have devoted much more attention to that prehistory which is given to us by the lifespan of our ancestors" over and above "the other prehistory, which already falls into the individual existence of the person."[28] Jung had warned about the "Wotan" element "seizing" Germans from within; Kahler implies that the entire thrust of that question seems designed to let Germans off the hook.

Alexander and Margarete Mitscherlich's books tended to position the German family at an intersection between general historical trends (namely, a modernization of social structures) and historical events unique to Germany (the transference of pubescent energy onto group and *Führer* during the Nazi years). Part of the problem, Alexander Mitscherlich claims in *Auf dem Weg in die Vaterlose Gesellschaft* (Society without the father, 1963), was the lack of the kind of "Ego-Ideal" furnished by ancestors.[29] The advice Goethe's Faust gives in his famous soliloquy, that

> What you received but as your fathers' heir,
> Make it your own to gain possession of it[30]
>
> Was du ererbt von deinen Vätern hast,
> Erwirb es, um es zu besitzen[31]

as Mitscherlich proposed, had become increasingly impossible due to processes of modernization. But that impossibility itself interacted in several ways with the Nazi past: modernization (the fracturing of an intergenerational compact, but also the fraying of the nuclear family) had given rise to the fascination with Hitler. And the aftereffects of that fascination, the ability to let go of it entirely, had damaged and overdetermined the German nuclear family in the Bundesrepublik.[32]

This psychoanalytic entwinement of family and memorial culture anticipated a long-brewing intergenerational conflict that would ultimately come to a head in the late 1960s. In 1962, as the Eichmann trial was nearing its conclusion in Jerusalem, Dieter Bielenstein of the Association of German Student Organizations remarked that it was the historical responsibility of a young generation untarnished by associations with Nazism to "demand answers from the older generation," those who had been active in the Third Reich. "Today," he remarked, "the students of those years are our professors, lawyers, teachers, journalists and administrators. They are the old gentlemen in our fraternities, and they are our parents."[33] Or, as Ulrike Meinhof would put it, "This generation was not involved in the crimes of the Third Reich or in determining the direction that was taken in the postwar period; it has grown up with and into the arguments of the present, entangled in the blame for something it is not responsible for." However, this did not "free this young generation from facing the responsibilities of the present."[34]

The famous slogan of the 1968 student rebels, first voiced at the *Rektoratsfeier* at the University of Hamburg in 1967, that "under the [professors'] frocks" was "the must of a thousand years," in its own way reopened the broad, intergenerational perspective of the nineteenth century that I have traced in this book. For on its face, the slogan referred to a metaphorical thousand years: the supposedly thousand-year Reich that had ended up lasting just about twelve. But behind those metaphorical "thousand years" stood very real ones, as the Nazi years came to stand in for academic tradition as such, for a long tradition of political and familial repression.[35] At the same time, this extensive past was noticeably telescoped into the personages of the nuclear family. In the Oberhausen Manifesto (1962) that inaugurated New German Cinema, it was "daddy's cinema" that was declared dead.[36] The way the student rebels knew to undo "a thousand years" of anything was through oedipal struggle. The dynastic dimension had given way to a historic myopia two hundred years in the making.

Acknowledgments

This book has been seven years in the making. During that time, I had to beat several paths through the material before I arrived at the one I present now. I couldn't have undertaken these repeated expeditions into the branching thickets of dynastic thinking without the guidance, support, and help of friends and colleagues. I want to thank my colleagues at Stanford University, so many of whom, in large ways and small, have shaped the manuscript immeasurably.

I thank Sepp Gumbrecht for his wisdom; Robert Harrison, whose work on age as an existential category first opened my eyes to a workable definition of the dynastic imagination; and Denise Gigante, who as a writer, reader, and co-instructor has shaped my sense for the stakes of the Romantic project across traditions. Estelle Freedman, Karen Otten, and all the faculty fellows at the Clayman Institute (2016–17) were instrumental in getting me to think about how early feminist thought drew from older traditions. Tom Grey sharpens my thinking about Wagner every time we talk. Claire Jarvis helped me clarify my thoughts about sentiment and the family, and she made sure there was enough Hardy and Swinburne in the book. Samuel Clowes Hunecke provided invaluable insights on how to frame the introduction.

The faculty colleagues and doctoral students at Stanford's Department of German Studies helped shape my ideas over the last few years. The members of my George Seminar in the 2012 winter quarter put up with hermetic texts and my even more hermetic readings. The Stanford Humanities Center class of 2013, including Héctor Hoyos and Marisa Galvez, helped energize the project at its very inception. The amazing postdoctoral fellows of the Mellon Program, including Colleen Anderson, Luca Scholz, and Jamele Watkins, helped me bring it home.

The individual chapters owe so much to individuals who supported, guided, and challenged my ideas. Russell Berman helped me refine the ideas that would become chapter 1. Liliane Weisberg's brilliant advice gave shape to chapter 7. David Wellbery, David Levin, and Eric Santner helped me think through the difficult status of the work of Stefan George in this book. Milinda Bannerjee, Ilya Afanasyev, and all the participants at "The Modern Dynasty," the altogether brilliant conference at BRIC Birmingham (2017), allowed me to try out my ideas on feminism and the dynasty. The amazing group gathered for the Wagnerjahr at the University of Luxemburg (2013), including Georg Mein, Elisabeth Strowick, and Stefan Börnchen, helped me hone my thoughts in chapter 5. Sepp Gumbrecht and the students of his seminar on Zola allowed me to try out my ideas about the dynastic romance of the Rougon-Macquart clan. The phenomenal faculty of the German Department at the University of Colorado at Boulder, above all Lauren Shizuko Stone and Helmut Müller-Sievers, helped me think through the queerness of the dynasty. I owe an immense and peculiar debt to Arne Höcker, who asked me a brilliant question that stumped me. The answer eventually became chapter 4 of this book.

Many colleagues have invigorated the research, framing, and organization of this book with important suggestions. Stefani Engelstein, whose own magisterial *Sibling Action* took shape over the same period, was an invaluable interlocutor on the page and off. Peter Sloterdijk asked all the right questions while I began work on this book and while he was at work on *Die Schrecklichen Kinder der Neuzeit*. David Wellbery read drafts and made invaluable suggestions. Dora Zhang's brilliant mind and unparalleled knowledge of modernist literature are constant inspirations. John Lyon's brilliant report for the University of Chicago Press was absolutely essential to finally wrangling this book into a definitive state. I also want to thank the press's readers at earlier stages of this book who preferred to remain anonymous—thank you for your interventions and suggestions; you are the spectral guides in the margins of these pages. Alan Thomas and Randy Petilos took over shepherding the manuscript late in the game, and I am so deeply grateful I got to work with them. I want to thank Ashe Huang and Christina Nikitin, who were of invaluable help to me as my research assistants.

A book about the extended family is always also an excursion into one's own. I lost my grandfather early in the writing process and my grandmother while finishing the manuscript, and I believe that my realizations about what I knew and didn't know about their world shaped my thinking about how family is available to us. I want to thank my parents for their love and support, and my husband for putting up with my late-night typing.

ACKNOWLEDGMENTS

My greatest debt is owed to Doug Mitchell, who first expressed an interest in the book back in 2013 and signed the manuscript to the University of Chicago Press in 2017. Unfortunately, Doug did not live to see our collaboration in print. We produced two books together, and I would have gladly collaborated on twenty more. *The Dynastic Imagination* is also about the great spectral dynasty of the dead that clusters around the small, precious nucleus of the living. Doug is part of that dynasty for me—so I dedicate this book to him.

~

Portions of chapter 2 appeared as "The State as a Family" in *Republics of Letters*, vol. 2, no. 2 (2009), courtesy of the editors. A few select passages previously appeared in "All Evil Is the Cancellation of Unity" in *Joseph de Maistre and His European Readers*, edited by Carolina Armenteros and Richard Lebrun (2011). Portions of chapter 5 appeared in Stefan Börnchen, Georg Mein, and Elisabeth Strowick, eds., *Jenseits von Bayreuth: Richard Wagner heute; Neue kulturwissenschaftliche Perspektiven*, © 2014 Wilhelm Fink Verlag, an imprint of Brill Gruppe (Koninklijke Brill NV, Leiden, The Netherlands; Brill USA Inc., Boston, USA; Brill Asia Pte Ltd, Singapore; Brill Deutschland GmbH, Paderborn, Germany). And portions of chapter 8 were previously published as "Ein Blitz: Für Uns—Stefan George's Queer Dynasties," in *Deutsche Vierteljahresschrift für Literaturwissenschaft und Geistesgeschichte* 90 (2016), published by J. B. Metzler.

Notes

Introduction

Translations from German and French (and from English into German) are my own, unless otherwise indicated. I have not provided the original German for quoted material if doing so would be irrelevant to the discussion.

1. Giuseppe Tomasi di Lampedusa, *Il gattopardo* (Milan: Feltrinelli, 2002), 59: "Potremo magari preoccuparci per i nostri figli, forse per i nipotini; ma al di là di quanto possiamo sperare di accarezzare con queste mani, no abbiamo abblighi." Translation in the text is from Lampedusa, *The Leopard*, trans. Archibald Colquhoun (New York: Knopf Doubleday, 2013), 34.
2. Friedrich Nietzsche, "Vom Nutzen und Nachteil der Historie für das Leben," in *Werke in Drei Bänden*, ed. Karl Schlechta (Munich: Hanser, 1954), 1:229: "Es ist nicht die Gerechtigkeit, die hier zu Gericht sitzt; es ist noch weniger die Gnade, die hier das Urteil verkündet: sondern das Leben allein, jene dunkle, treibende, unersättlich sich selbst begehrende Macht."
3. Nietzsche, 1:229: "Es gehört sehr viel Kraft dazu, leben zu können und zu vergessen, inwiefern leben und ungerecht sein eins ist."
4. Nietzsche, 1:229: "Mitunter aber verlangt eben dasselbe Leben, das die Vergessenheit braucht, die zeitweilige Vernichtung dieser Vergessenheit; dann soll es eben gerade klarwerden, wie ungerecht die Existenz irgendeines Dinges, eines Privilegiums, einer Kaste, einer Dynastie zum Beispiel, ist, wie sehr dieses Ding den Untergang verdient."
5. Johann Wolfgang von Goethe, *Faust*, trans. Walter Arndt, ed. Cyrus Hamlin, Norton Critical Edition (New York: W. W. Norton, 2001), 37.
6. Nietzsche, "Vom Nutzen und Nachteil der Historie für das Leben," 1:229–30: "Denn da wir nun einmal die Resultate früherer Geschlechter sind, sind wir auch die Resultate ihrer Verirrungen, Leidenschaften und Irrtümer, ja Verbrechen; es ist nicht möglich, sich ganz von dieser Kette zu lösen."
7. Oswald Spengler, *Der Untergang des Abendlandes: Umrisse einer Morphologie der Weltgeschichte* (Munich: Beck, 1963), 46: "Zur Weltstadt gehört nicht ein Volk, sondern eine Masse. Ihr Unverständnis für alles Überlieferte, in dem man die *Kultur* bekämpft (den Adel, die Kirche, die Privilegien, die Dynastie, in der Kunst die Konventionen, in der Wissenschaft die Grenzen der Erkenntnismöglichkeit) . . . alles das bezeichnet der endgültig abgeschlossenen Kultur, der Provinz gegenüber eine ganz neue, späte und zukunftslose, aber unvermeidliche Form menschlicher Existenz."

8. *Damen-Conversations Lexikon* (Leipzig: Volckmar, 1835), 3:246.

9. Johann Christoph Adelung, *Grammatisch-kritisches Wörterbuch der Hochdeutschen Mundart* (Leipzig: Breitkopf, 1796), 2:610. Subsequent references are given in the text.

10. David Warren Sabean, "Kinship and Class Dynamics in Nineteenth Century Europe," in *Kinship in Europe: Approaches to Long-Term Development (1300–1900)* (New York: Berghahn, 2007).

11. Niklas Luhmann, *Love as Passion: The Codification of Intimacy* (Cambridge: Polity, 1986).

12. Stefani Engelstein, *Sibling Action—the Genealogical Structure of Modernity* (New York: Columbia University Press, 2017).

13. Auguste Comte, *Positive Philosophy*, trans. Harriet Martineau (New York: Blanchard, 1856), 588.

14. Karl Ludwig von Haller, *Restauration der Staats-Wissenschaft; oder, Theorie des natürlich-geselligen Zustandes, der Chimäre des künstlich-bürgerlichen Entgegengesetzt: Makrobiotik der Patrimonial-Staaten* (Winterthur, Switzerland: Steiner, 1821), 3:457.

15. Friedrich von Gentz, "Konnten die verbündeten Mächte 1815 Italien in ein Reich verschmelzen," in *Friedrich von Gentz: Ein Denkmal*, ed. Gustav Schlesier (Mannheim: Hoff, 1840), 84.

16. Gentz, 85.

17. Adam Heinrich Müller to Friedrich von Gentz, August 7, 1819, in *Briefwechsel zwischen Friedrich Gentz und Adam Heinrich Müller, 1800–1829*, by Friedrich von Gentz and Adam Heinrich Müller (Stuttgart: Cotta, 1857), 269: "Die Erhaltung der regierenden Dynastien und der an ihre Existenz geknüpften Ordnung."

18. Johann Wolfgang von Goethe, *Epimenides Erwachen*, in *Goethes Werke*, critically reviewed and annotated by Erich Trunz, Hamburg ed. (Hamburg: Christian Wegner, 1948), act 2, scene 6, 5:389.

19. Goethe, act 2, scene 6, 5:390: "Noch weiter? Nein, ihr Guten, nein, ach nein!"

20. Goethe, act 2, scene 6, 5:390.

21. The author is indebted to Millinda Banerjee for this formula.

22. Georg Wilhelm Friedrich Hegel, *Elements of the Philosophy of Right*, ed. Allen Wood, trans. H. B. Nisbet (Cambridge: Cambridge University Press, 1991), 218 (§180).

23. Karl Marx, *Critique of Hegel's "Philosophy of Right,"* in *Early Writings*, trans. Rodney Livingstone and Gregor Benton (London: Penguin, 1992), 246.

24. Thomas Hardy, "The Family Face," in *The Collected Poems of Thomas Hardy* (London: Macmillan, 1923), 407.

25. Friedrich der Große, *Denkwürdigkeiten zur Geschichte des Hauses Brandenburg*, in *Die Werke Friedrichs der Großen in Deutscher Übersetzung*, ed. Gustav Berthold Volz and Friedrich von Oppeln-Bronikowski (Berlin: Hobbing, 1913), 17.

26. Thucydides, *Thucydides: The War of the Peloponnesians and the Athenians*, ed. and trans. Jeremy Mynott (Cambridge: Cambridge University Press, 2013), 282.

27. Michel Foucault, *The Government of Self and Others: Lectures at the Collège de France, 1982–83*, ed. Arnold Davidson and trans. Graham Burchell (New York: Picador, 2011).

28. Jean-Jacques Rousseau, *The Government of Poland*, trans. Willmoore Kendall (Indianapolis: Hackett, 1985), 51.

29. Michel Foucault, *The History of Sexuality: An Introduction*, trans. Robert Hurley (New York: Vintage, 1990), 124.

30. Foucault, 124.

31. Prosper Lucas, *Traité philosophique et physiologique de l'hérédité naturelle dans les états de santé et de maladie du système nerveux* (Paris: Baillière, 1847), 1:543–45.

32. Daniel Pick, *Faces of Degeneration: A European Disorder, 1848–1918* (Cambridge: Cambridge University Press, 1993).

33. Devin Griffiths, "The Fertile Darwins: Epigenesis, Organicism, and the Problem of Inheritance," *Romanticism and Victorianism on the Net*, no. 66/67 (2016), https://ronjournal.org/s/3450.

34. Émile Zola, *The Fortune of the Rougons*, trans. Brian Nelson (Oxford: Oxford University Press, 2012), 3.

35. Lee Edelman, *No Future: Queer Theory and the Death Drive* (Durham, NC: Duke University Press, 2004), 4.

Chapter One

1. Lynn Hunt, *The Family Romance of the French Revolution* (Berkeley: University of California Press; Ann Arbor: MPublishing, University of Michigan Library, 1992), 10. Downloadable archival material.

2. Ludwig Uhland, "Die Vätergruft," in *Werke*, ed. Hartmut Fröschle and Walter Scheffler (Munich: Winkler, 1980), 114.

3. Johann Wolfgang von Goethe, *Iphigenie auf Tauris*, in *Goethes Werke*, critically reviewed and annotated by Erich Trunz, Hamburg ed. (Hamburg: Christian Wegner, 1948), act 3, scene 2, 5:41: "Von euerm Stamme der letzte Mann."

4. Goethe, act 3, scene 2, 5:41: "Was ihre gesät, hat er geerntet."

5. Friedrich Engels, letter to diplomats written between the end of December 1887 and March 1888, in *Marx-Engels-Werke* (Berlin: Dietz, 1962), 21:407: "Die kleinste Dynastie galt mehr als das größte Volk."

6. Franz Grillparzer, *Die Ahnfrau*, in *Sämtliche Werke*, ed. Peter Frank and Karl Pörnbacher (Munich: Hanser, 1960), act 3, 1:664.

7. Grillparzer, act 5, 1:706.

8. Grillparzer, act 4, 1:680.

9. Johann Wolfgang von Goethe, *Unterhaltungen deutscher Ausgewanderten*, in *Goethes Werke*, ed. Siegfried Seidel (Berlin: Aufbau, 1960), 12:280: "Um den Bedrängnissen zu entgehen, womit alle ausgezeichnete Personen bedroht waren, denen man zum Verbrechen machte, daß sie sich ihrer Väter mit Freuden und Ehren erinnerten, und mancher Vortheile genossen, die ein wohldenkender Vater seinen Kindern und Nachkommen so gern zu verschaffen wünschte."

10. Peter Fritzsche, *Stranded in the Present* (Cambridge, MA: Harvard University Press, 2004), 12.

11. Suzanne Desan, *The Family on Trial in Revolutionary France* (Berkeley: University of California Press, 2004), 61.

12. Peter Sloterdijk, *Die Schrecklichen Kinder der Neuzeit* (Frankfurt: Suhrkamp, 2014), 23–24.

13. Johann Gottlieb Fichte, *Addresses to the German Nation*, ed. Gregory Moore (Cambridge: Cambridge University Press, 2008), 15.

14. Heinrich Heine, *Deutschland, ein Wintermärchen*, in *Werke und Briefe in Zehn Bänden*, ed. Hans Kaufmann (Berlin: Aufbau, 1972), 1:435.

15. Johann Wolfgang von Goethe, *Faust*, trans. Walter Arndt, ed. Cyrus Hamlin, Norton Critical Edition (New York: W. W. Norton, 2001), lines 1970–77, p. 52. Subsequent page references are to the Norton edition.

16. Goethe, *Faust*, line 1980, p. 47. Johann Wolfgang von Goethe, *Faust: Der Tragödie Erster Teil*, in *Goethes Werke*, critically reviewed and annotated by Erich Trunz, Hamburg ed. (Hamburg: Christian Wegner, 1948), 3:63: "Vom Rechte, das mit uns geboren ist, von dem ist leider nie die Frage."

17. Johann Wolfgang von Goethe to Georg Sartorius, in *Goethes Werke (Weimarer Ausgabe)*, 4. *Abtheilung, Briefe* (Weimar: Hermann Böhlau, 1912), 36:174.

18. Cited in Dagmar von Gersdorff, *Goethes Enkel: Walther, Wolfgang und Alma* (Munich: Insel, 20080, 13.

19. Friedrich Wilhelm Joseph Schelling, *Clara, or On Nature's Connection to the Spirit World*, ed. and trans. Fiona Steinkamp (Albany: SUNY Press, 2002), 10.

20. Annette von Droste-Hülshoff, "Vorgeschichte," in *Sämtliche Werke in 2 Bänden*, ed. Bodo Plachta (Munich: Deutscher Klassiker Verlag, 1973), 1:211. Subsequent references are given in the text.

21. Theodor Fontane, *Wanderungen durch die Mark Brandenburg*, in *Sämtliche Werke*, vol. 9, ed. Edgar Gross (Munich: Nymphenburger Verlagshandlung, 1960), 440: "Von da ab gehen die Zieten auf Wustrau und die Jürgaß zu Ganzer in Leid und Freud mit- und nebeneinander, um schließlich auch, wie ein altes Paar, gemeinschaftlich in den Tod zu gehen."

22. Adalbert Stifter, *Der Hochwald*, in *Studien* (Leipzig: Amelang, 1882), 142: "Wenn sich der Wanderer von der alten Stadt und dem Schlosse Krumau, dieser grauen Wittwe der verblichenen Rosenberger, westwärts wendet."

23. Stifter, 144: "Oft und gern verweilte ich dort, selbst als ich das Schicksal Derer noch nicht kannte, die zuletzt diese wehmüthige Stätte bewohnten."

24. Stifter, 145: "Und nun, lieber Wanderer, wenn du dich satt gesehen hast, so gehe jetzt mit mir zwei Jahrhunderte zurück."

25. Adalbert Stifter, *Witiko* (Leipzig: Amelang, 1864), i: "Als Jüngling ging ich diesen Spuren nach, und habe manchen Tag in den Trümmern der Stammburg dieses Geschlechtes zugebracht."

26. Fontane, *Wanderungen durch die Mark Brandenburg*, 9:7.

27. Theodor Fontane, "Gustav Freytags Die Ahnen," in *Sämtliche Werke*, vol. 21.1, ed. Kurt Schreinert (Munich: Nymphenburger Verlagshandlung, 1963), 231: "An dessen Grenze wir selbst noch standen oder von dem uns die Eltern noch erzählten."

28. Theodor Fontane, *Vor dem Sturm*, in *Romane und Erzählungen in Acht Bänden*, ed. Peter Goldammer, Gotthard Erler, Anita Golz, and Jürgen Jahn (Berlin: Aufbau, 1973), 2:437. Subsequent references are given in the text.

29. Theodor Fontane to Gustav Karpeles, March 14, 1880, quoted in Edda Ziegler, "Fremd auf dieser Welt: Das Aparte an Fontanes literarischen Heldinnen," in *Fontane und die Fremde, Fontane und Europa*, ed. Konrad Ehrlich (Würzburg: Königshausen and Neumann, 2002), 25.

30. Fontane, *Vor dem Sturm*, 3:66.

31. Theodor Fontane, *Die Poggenpuhls*, in *Romane und Erzählungen in Acht Bänden*, ed. Peter Goldammer, Gotthard Erler, Anita Golz, and Jürgen Jahn (Berlin: Aufbau, 1973), 7:320.

32. Gottfried Keller, *Die Leute von Seldwyla*, in *Sämtliche Werke* (Berlin: Aufbau, 1958), 252: "Ich bin der Erste des meinigen, will soviel heißen als Ich habe mich entschlossen, ein solch großes und rühmliches Geschlecht zu gründen, wie Sie hier an den Wänden dieses Saales gemalt

sehen! Dieses sind nämlich nicht meine Ahnen, sondern die Glieder eines ausgestorbenen Patriziergeschlechtes dieser Stadt.... Denn ich besaß ein großes Vermögen, aber keinen Namen, keine Vorfahren, und ich kenne nicht einmal den Taufnamen meines Großvaters."

33. Ida Boy-Ed, "Königliche Hoheit," in *Ida Boy-Ed: Eine Auswahl*, ed. Peter de Mendelssohn (Lübeck: Weiland, 1975), 141: "Gesundes Bürgerblut vereinigt sich mit dem Blut einer uralten Dynastie, ihre neue Blüte verheißend."

34. Daniel Pick, *Faces of Degeneration: A European Disorder, 1848–1918* (Cambridge: Cambridge University Press, 1993).

35. Philipp Sarasin, *Darwin und Foucault: Genealogie und Geschichte im Zeitalter der Biologie* (Frankfurt am Main: Suhrkamp Verlag, 2009).

36. Friedrich Nietzsche, *Human, All Too Human*, trans. R. J. Hollingdale (Cambridge: Cambridge University Press, 1996), 167. "Auf eine ununterbrochene Reihe *guter* Ahnen bis zum Vater herauf darf man mit Recht stolz sein—nicht aber auf die Reihe; denn diese hat jeder."

37. Nietzsche, 167. "Eine einzige Unterbrechung in jener Kette, *ein* böser Vorfahr also, hebt den Geburtsadel auf."

38. Adalbert Stifter, *Werke und Briefe: Historisch-Kritische Gesamtausgabe*, ed. Alfred Doppler and Wolfgang Frühwald (Stuttgart: Kohlhammer, 1978), 377.

39. Adalbert Stifter, "Die Narrenburg," in *Studien (Gesammelte Werke in Sechs Bänden)*, ed. Max Stefl (Wiesbaden: Insel, 1959), 394.

40. Adalbert Stifter, *Prokopus*, in *Erzählungen*, ed. Johannes Aprent (Pest, Hungary: Heckenast, 1869), 1:23: "Wir richten nur unsere Sachen in Ordnung und schauen mit Sorgfalt in die Zukunft."

41. Sigrid Weigel, "Zur Dialektik von Geschlecht und Generation um 1800: Stifters Narrenburg als Schauplatz von Umbrüchen im genealogischen Denken," in *Generation: Zur Genealogie des Konzepts-Konzepte der Genealogie*, ed. Sigrid Weigel, Ohad Parenes, Ulrike Vedder, and Stefan Willer (Munich: Wilhelm Fink Verlag, 2005), 109–24.

42. Sloterdijk, *Die Schrecklichen Kinder der Neuzeit*, 23.

43. Gustav Freytag, *Die Ahnen* (Munich: Droemer, 1953), 1380: "Ich will dir, du Verehrer aller Familienerinnerungen, sogar etwas anderes und Größeres zugeben. Vielleicht wirken die Taten und Leiden der Vorfahren noch in ganz anderer Weise auf unsere Gedanken und Werke ein, als wir Lebenden begreifen. Aber es ist eine weise Fügung der Weltordnung, daß wir nicht wissen, wie weit wir selbst das Leben vergangener Menschen fortsetzen, und daß wir nur zuweilen erstaunt merken, wie wir in unsern Kindern weiterleben."

44. Ulrike Vedder, "Erbe und Literatur: Testamentarisches Schreiben im 19. Jahrundert," in *Erbe: Übertragungskonzepte zwischen Natur und Kultur*, ed. Stefan Willer, Sigrid Weigel, and Bernhard Jussen (Frankfurt: Suhrkamp, 2013), 142.

45. Jens Beckert, *Unverdientes Vermögen: Soziologie des Erbrechts* (Frankfurt: Campus, 2004), 36.

46. Clemens August von Droste-Hülshoff, *Lehrbuch des Naturrechtes oder der Rechtsphilosophie* (Bonn: Marcus, 1831), 105§55: "Der Wille des Verstorbenen ist ein Grund, welchen ... niemand zu achten hat."

Chapter Two

1. Wilhelm Heinrich Riehl, *Die Familie* (Stuttgart: Cotta, 1861), 247.

2. Adrian Daub, *Uncivil Unions: The Metaphysics of Marriage in German Idealism and Romanticism* (Chicago: University of Chicago Press, 2012), 269.

3. Adam Müller, *Vermischte Schriften über Staat, Philosophie und Kunst*, pt. 1 (Vienna: Camesina, 1812), 1:4: "Der Wille, die Manier der Herrschaft, die Familienzüge der Ahnherren treten, jugendlich wieder erweckt, an den hellsten Tag."

4. Cited in Paul Bailleu, *Königin Luise* (Berlin: Giesecke and Devrient, 1908), 49: "Und ein Werfen mit Sträußen dass wir ordentlich in Blumen badeten."

5. Cited in Bailleu, 48: "Es war eine feierliche Stunde für mich, da ich Berlins Einwohnerin ward."

6. Catriona MacLeod, *Fugitive Objects: Sculpture and Literature in the German Nineteenth Century* (Evanston, IL: Northwestern University Press, 2014).

7. Theodor Körner, "An Die Königin Luise," in *Werke*, ed. Hans Zimmer (Leipzig/Vienna: Bibliographisches Institut, 1893), 1:90–91.

8. Christopher Clark, *Iron Kingdom* (Cambridge, MA: Harvard University Press, 2006), 316.

9. Müller, *Vermischte Schriften über Staat, Philosophie und Kunst*, 1:8: "Dass bey einander bleibt, was zusammen gehört, Monarch und Volk und Hauptstadt und der Provinzenstamm des alten Reiches und die Gräber der Könige."

10. Müller, 1:21: "Es hieße sich eindrängen wollen in den heiligen Schmerz unsers Königs, wenn man zu sagen wagte, was er als Gemahl verloren."

11. Müller, 1:24: "Die Sitte, der von Gott die Kraft gegeben ist, die Gesetze zu verklären, aber auch sie zu zermalmen, hat keine Statthalterin, keine Beschützerin mehr in diesem Reiche."

12. Novalis [Friedrich von Hardenberg], "Glaube und Liebe," in *Novalis, Schriften: Historisch Kritische Ausgabe*, ed. Paul Kluckhohn and Richard Samuel (Stuttgart: Kohlhammer, 1960), 2:494–95.

13. Novalis, 2:292.

14. Joseph de Maistre, "On the Sovereignty of the People," in *Against Rousseau: On the State of Nature and On the Sovereignty of the People*, trans. Richard A. Lebrun (Montreal: McGill-Queen's University Press, 1996), 46.

15. Louis de Bonald, *On Divorce*, trans. Nicholas Davidson (New Brunswick, NJ: Transaction, 1992), 21.

16. Maistre, "On the Sovereignty of the People," 53.

17. Bonald, *On Divorce*, 22.

18. Johann August Freiherr von Starck, *Der Triumph der Philosophie im Achtzehnten Jahrhunderte*, pt. 1 (Germantown: Rosenblatt, 1804), 232.

19. Starck, 215.

20. Starck, 234.

21. Karl Ludwig von Haller, *Restauration der Staats-Wissenschaft; oder, Theorie des natürlich-geselligen Zustandes, der Chimäre des künstlich-bürgerlichen Entgegengesetzt* (Winterthur, Switzerland: Steiner, 1820).

22. Charles Philippe Dijon de Monteton, *Die Entzauberung des Gesellschaftsvertrags* (Frankfurt: Peter Lang, 2006).

23. Haller, *Restauration der Staats-Wissenschaft*, 338. Subsequent references are given in the text.

24. Franz von Baader, "Socialphilosophische Aphorismen," in *Sämmtliche Werke*, ed. Emil August von Schaden (Leipzig: Hermann Bethmann, 1852), 5:267: "So wie die Liebe Gottes zum Menschen sich herablässt (amor descendit), . . . so breitet sich diese Liebe horizontal als Liebe

der Gleichen (Bruder- oder Menschenliebe) aus, und steigt abwärts als die unter dem Menschen seiende (nichtintelligente) Natur und Creatur zu sich erhebend."

25. Baader, 5:267: "Und es ist dahin gekommen, dass die Menschen mit derselben Gleichgültigkeit ihr altes Stamm-Erbe verlassen oder sich von ihm verlassen sehen, mit welcher wir in den Zeiten der Revolution sie ihre alten Dynastien verlassen sahen."

26. Riehl, *Die Familie*, iv: "Die Familie ist der Urgrund aller organischen Gebilde in der Volkspersönlichkeit."

27. Adalbert Stifter, *Der Nachsommer*, in *Studien (Gesammelte Werke in Sechs Bänden)*, ed. Max Stefl (Wiesbaden: Insel, 1959), 4:840: "Die Familie ist es, die unsern Zeiten Noth thut, sie thut mehr Noth, als Kunst und Wissenschaft, als Verkehr, Handel, Aufschwung, Fortschritt, oder wie Alles heißt, was begehrungswerth erscheint. Auf der Familie ruht die Kunst, die Wissenschaft, der menschliche Fortschritt, der Staat."

28. Riehl, *Die Familie*, vii.

29. Riehl, 247.

30. Christian von Zimmermann, "'Aber komme, reiche mir die Hand, ich werde dich führen . . .': Enkel-Erziehung in Adalbert Stifter's 'Granit' (1853)," *Zeitschrift für Germanistik* 18, no. 3 (2008): 559.

31. Martin Swales, *Adalbert Stifter: A Critical Study* (Cambridge: Cambridge University Press, 1984), 37.

32. Helena Ragg-Kirkby, *Adalbert Stifter's Late Prose: The Mania for Moderation* (Rochester, NY: Camden House, 2000), 67.

33. Adalbert Stifter, *Der Hagestolz*, in *Studien (Gesammelte Werke in Sechs Bänden)*, ed. Max Stefl (Wiesbaden: Insel, 1959), 2:257: "Die lächerlichen Bande eines Weibes tragen und wie der Vogel auf den Stangen eines Käfiches sitzen?"

34. Stifter, 2:390: "Dann scheint immer und immer die Sonne wieder, der blaue Himmel lächelt aus einem Jahrtausend in das andere, die Erde kleidet sich in ihr altes Grün, und die Geschlechter steigen an der langen Kette bis zu dem jüngsten Kinde nieder: aber er ist aus allen denselben ausgetilgt, weil sein Dasein kein Bild geprägt hat, seine Sprossen nicht mit hinunter gehen in dem Strome der Zeit.—Wenn er aber auch noch andere Spuren gegründet hat, so erlöschen diese, wie jedes Irdische erlischt—und wenn in dem Ocean der Tage endlich alles, alles untergeht, selbst das Größte und das Freudigste, so geht er eher unter, weil an ihm schon alles im Sinken begriffen ist, während er noch athmet, und während er noch lebt."

35. On Stifter's "gentle law" and the telescoping of the violence of cosmic forces, see Eric Downing, *Double Exposures: Repetition and Realism in Nineteenth-Century German Fiction* (Stanford, CA: Stanford University Press, 2000), 28–29.

36. Stifter, *Der Nachsommer*, 4:841: "Wenn Ehen nicht beglücktes Familienleben werden, so brings Du vergeblich das Höchste in der Wissenschaft und Kunst hervor, Du reichst es einem Geschlechte, das sittlich verkommt, dem Deine Gabe endlich nichts mehr nützt, und das zuletzt unterläßt, solche Güter hervor zu bringen."

37. Stifter, 4:841: "Die Familie ist es, die unsern Zeiten nottut."

38. Riehl, *Die Familie*, 145: "Auflösung des Familienbewußtseyns." Subsequent references are given in the text.

39. "Die einzelnen Genossen des 'Hauses' in Gruppen absondern: Mann und Frau, die Kinder, das Gesinde, die Geschäftsgehülfen."

40. "Das Haus als Inbegriff einer socialen Gesammtpersönlichkeit . . . hat der Vereinzelung der Familie weichen müssen."

41. "Eine mögliche Vetterschaft, deren Enthüllung späteren Forschungen der Genealogen vorbehalten bleibt."

42. "Hallt er hier nicht einmal für den Einzelnen durch's ganze Leben wider."

43. Adalbert Stifter, *Nachkommenschaften*, in *Erzählungen* ed. Johannes Aprent (Pest, Hungary: Heckenast, 1869), 1:172.

44. Stifter, 1:178.

45. Stifter, 1:215.

46. Georg Wilhelm Friedrich Hegel, *Elements of the Philosophy of Right* (Cambridge: Cambridge University Press, 1991), 261 (§235).

47. Stifter, *Nachkommenschaften*, 1:183.

48. Stifter, 1:249.

Chapter Three

1. Friedrich Schlegel, *Athenäum*, in *Kritische Friedrich Schlegel Ausgabe*, ed. Ernst Behler (Paderborn: Schöningh, 1958), 2:198.

2. On the concept of tendency, see Ives Radrizzani, "Zur Geschichte der Romantischen Ästhetik: Von Fichtes Transzendentalphilosophie zu Schlegels Transzendentalpoesie," in *Fichte und die Romantik*, ed. Wolfgang H. Schrader, Fichte Studien 12 (Amsterdam: Rodopi, 1997), 181–202.

3. Friedrich Schlegel, "Über die Unverständlichkeit," in *Kritische Friedrich Schlegel Ausgabe*, ed. Ernst Behler (Paderborn: Schöningh, 1958), 2:367.

4. Schlegel, 2:367.

5. Barbara Johnson, "The Last Man," in *The Other Mary Shelley: Beyond Frankenstein*, ed. Audrey Fisch, Anne K. Mellor, and Esther H. Schor (New York: Oxford University Press, 1993), 263.

6. Constance Walker, "Kindertotenlieder: Mary Shelley and the Art of Losing," in *Mary Shelley in Her Times*, ed. Betty Bennett and Stuart Curran (Baltimore: Johns Hopkins University Press, 2000), 134.

7. Denise Gigante, *Life: Organic Form and Romanticism* (New Haven, CT: Yale University Press, 2009), 160.

8. Nicholas Boyle, *Goethe: Der Dichter in seiner Zeit*, vol. 2, *1791–1803* (Munich: Beck, 1999), 327.

9. Johann Wolfgang von Goethe to Friedrich Schiller, cited in Boyle, 2:327.

10. Johann Wolfgang von Goethe to Friedrich von Schiller, in *Goethes Werke, Abtheilung 4: Goethes Briefe* (Weimar: Hermann Böhlau, 1910), 10:354, cited in Franz Schwarzbauer, *Studien zur Vorgeschichte der Weimarer Klassik* (Stuttgart: Metzler, 1993), 137: "Daß die Rezensionen des poetischen Theils der Horen in die Hände eines Mannes aus der neuen Generation gefallen ist, mit der alten werden wir wohl niemals einig warden."

11. Inge Hoffman-Axthelm, *"Geisterfamilie": Studien zur Geselligkeit der Frühromantik* (Frankfurt: Akademische Verlagsanstalt, 1973).

12. Friedrich Wilhelm Joseph Schelling to Louise Gotter, September 24, 1809, in *Schelling als Persönlichkeit: Briefe, Reden, Aufsätze*, ed. Otto Braun (Leipzig: Eckardt, 1908), 135.

13. Friedrich Wilhelm Joseph Schelling, *Erster Entwurf eines Systems der Naturphilosophie* (Leipzig: Gabler, 1799), 92.

14. David Farrell Krell, *Contagion: Sexuality Disease and Death in German Idealism and Romanticism* (Bloomington: Indiana University Press, 1998), 96.

15. Friedrich Wilhelm Joseph Schelling, *Clara, or On Nature's Connection to the Spirit World*, trans. Fiona Steinkamp (Albany: SUNY Press, 2002). Subsequent references are given in the text.

16. Gigante, *Life*, 21.

17. Mary Shelley, *The Last Man* (Oxford: Oxford University Press, 2006), 165.

18. Shelley, 451.

19. Shelley, 456.

20. Shelley, 449.

21. Shelley, 458.

22. Georg Wilhelm Friedrich Hegel, *The Science of Logic* (Cambridge: Cambridge University Press, 2010), 677.

23. Friedrich Wilhelm Joseph Schelling, *Clara, oder Über den Zusammenhang der Natur- mit der Geisterwelt* (Stuttgart: Cotta, 1865), 8.

24. Shelley, *The Last Man*, 63.

25. Shelley, 48.

26. Eva Horn, "*The Last Man*: The Birth of Modern Apocalypse in Jean Paul, John Martin and Lord Byron," in *Catastrophes: A History and Theory of an Operative Concept*, ed. Nitzan Lebovic and Andreas Killen (Berlin: De Gruyter, 2014), 56.

27. Fiona J. Stafford, *The Last of the Race: The Growth of a Myth from Milton to Darwin* (Oxford: Clarendon, 1994), 221.

28. Morton Paley, "Envisioning Lastness: Byron's 'Darkness,' Campbell's 'The Last Man' and the Critical Aftermath," *Romanticism* 1 (1995): 1–14.

29. Shelley, *The Last Man*, 55.

30. Shelley, 56.

31. Shelley, 72.

32. Johnson, "The Last Man," 264.

33. Steven Goldsmith, *Unbuilding Jerusalem: Apocalypse and Romantic Representation* (Ithaca, NY: Cornell University Press, 1993), 267.

34. Shelley, *The Last Man*, 217.

35. Shelley, 289.

36. Shelley, 290.

37. Anne K. Mellor, *Mary Shelley: Her Life, Her Fiction, Her Monsters* (London: Routledge, 2012), 189.

38. Mary Wollstonecraft Shelley, *Frankenstein; Or, the Modern Prometheus*, ed. D. L. Macdonald and Kathleen Scherf (Peterborough, ON: Broadview, 1999), 190.

39. Mellor, *Mary Shelley*, 119.

40. Shelley, *Frankenstein*, 190.

41. Edmund Burke, *Reflections on the Revolutions in France*, in *Revolutionary Writings*, ed. Iain Hampsher-Monk (Cambridge: Cambridge University Press, 2014), 32.

42. Shelley, *The Last Man*, 462.

43. Shelley, 466.

44. Johann Wolfgang von Goethe, *Faust*, ed. Cyrus Hamlin, trans. Walter Arndt, Norton Critical Edition (New York: Norton, 1976), p. 171. Subsequent page references are to the Norton edition.

45. Johann Wolfgang von Goethe, *Faust: Der Tragödie Zweiter Teil*, in *Goethes Werke*, critically reviewed and annotated by Erich Trunz, Hamburg ed. (Hamburg: Christian Wegner, 1948), 3:208, lines 6815–18. Subsequent references are to this edition.

46. Johann Wolfgang von Goethe, "Einleitung in die Propyläen," in *Schriften zur Bildenden Kunst I* (Berlin: Aufbau, 1965), 19:178: "Er wünscht sein Verhältnis zu den ältesten Freunden dadurch wieder anzuknüpfen, mit neuen es fortzusetzen und in der letzten Generation sich wieder andere für seine übrige Lebenszeit zu gewinnen. Er wünscht der Jugend die Umwege zu ersparen, auf denen er sich selbst verirrte, und, indem er die Vorteile der gegenwärtigen Zeit bemerkt und nützt, das Andenken verdienstlicher früherer Bemühungen zu erhalten."

47. Robert J. Richards, *The Romantic Conception of Life* (Chicago: University of Chicago Press, 2002), 200.

48. Johann Wolfgang von Goethe, *Wilhelm Meisters Wanderjahre*, in *Goethes Werke*, critically reviewed and annotated by Erich Trunz, Hamburg ed. (Hamburg: Christian Wegner, 1994), 8:464: "Eine geistige Form wird aber keineswegs verkürzt, wenn sie in der Erscheinung hervortritt, vorausgesetzt daß ihr Hervortreten eine wahre Zeugung, eine wahre Fortpflanzung sei. Das Gezeugte ist nicht geringer als das Zeugende, ja es ist der Vorteil lebendiger Zeugung, daß das Gezeugte vortrefflicher sein kann als das Zeugende."

49. Johann Wolfgang von Goethe, *Goethes Gespräche*, ed. Flodoard von Biedermann (Leipzig: Biedermann, 1910), 3:291.

50. Goethe, 4:227.

51. Goethe, 6:182.

52. Johann Wolfgang von Goethe to Georg Sartorius, September 26, 1822, in *Goethes Werke, Abtheilung 4: Goethes Briefe* (Weimar: Hermann Böhlau, 1912), 36:174.

53. Wendy C. Nielsen, "Goethe, *Faust*, and Motherless Creations," *Goethe Yearbook* 26 (2016): 60.

54. Goethe, *Faust*, p. 93.

55. Goethe, *Faust: Der Tragödie Zweiter Teil*, 3:208, lines 6813–14.

56. Jane K. Brown, *Goethe's "Faust": The German Tragedy* (Ithaca, NY: Cornell University Press, 1986), 175.

57. Gigante, *Life*, 158.

58. Gail K. Hart, *Tragedy in Paradise: Family and Gender Politics in German Bourgeois Tragedy, 1750–1850* (Rochester, NY: Camden House, 1996), 73.

59. Nielsen, "Goethe, *Faust*, and Motherless Creations," 60.

60. Gernot Böhme, *Goethes "Faust" als philosophischer Text* (Zug, Switzerland: Graue Edition, 2005), 112.

61. Søren Kierkegaard, *Kierkegaard's Writings, I*, vol. 1, *Early Polemical Writings*, ed. and trans. Julia Watkin (Princeton, NJ: Princeton University Press, 2009), 107.

62. Jon Stewart, *Kierkegaard's Relations to Hegel Reconsidered* (Cambridge: Cambridge University Press, 2003), 105.

63. Friedrich Nietzsche, in *Gesammelte Werke*, ed. Richard Oeler (Munich: Musarion, 1920), 3:172.

64. Karl Rosenkranz, "Zur Literatur der Faustdichtung," in *Zur Geschichte der deutschen Literatur* (Königsberg: Bornträger, 1836), 118: "Verstand, das negative Bestimmen"; "um nicht in der unendlichen Allgemeinheit des Denkens unterzugehen"; "wohl kaum etwas Anderes als die Welt der reinen Gedanken."

65. Goethe, *Faust*, p. 191. Goethe, *Faust: Der Tragödie Zweiter Teil*, 3:206, line 6759: "Mit dem Geist nicht ebenbürtig."

66. Goethe, *Faust*, p. 192. Goethe, *Faust: Der Tragödie Zweiter Teil*, 3:207, line 6794: "Die Welt war nicht, eh' ich sie erschuf."

67. Goethe, *Faust*, p. 192. Goethe, *Faust: Der Tragödie Zweiter Teil*, 3:207, line 6791: "Wenn ich nicht will, so darf kein Teufel sein."

68. Goethe, *Faust*, p. 173. Goethe, *Faust: Der Tragödie Zweiter Teil*, 3:209, line 6870: "Künftig auch ein Denker machen."

69. Goethe, *Faust: Der Tragödie Zweiter Teil*, 3:209, line 6844.

70. Goethe, *Faust: Der Tragödie Zweiter Teil*, 3:209, line 6850; Goethe, *Faust*, p. 172.

71. Goethe, *Faust*, p. 195. Goethe, *Faust: Der Tragödie Zweiter Teil*, 3:209, lines 6857–58.

72. Goethe, *Faust*, p. 194.

73. Goethe, *Faust: Der Tragödie Zweiter Teil*, 3:209, lines 6838–39.

74. Goethe, *Faust*, p. 194.

75. Goethe, *Faust: Der Tragödie Zweiter Teil*, 3:209, lines 6847–50.

76. Tanja Nusser, *"Wie sonst das Zeugen Mode war": Reproduktionstechnologien in Literatur und Film* (Freiburg: Rombach, 2011).

77. Franz von Baader, "Die Liebe selber ist ein Kind der in Liebe sich Verbindenden," in *Sämtliche Werke* (Leipzig: Hermann Bethmann, 1852), 6:343–46.

78. Baader, 6:344: "Dass die Liebe selber in ihrem Urstande nur ein Kind ist, aber ein Kind, das die liebenden Eltern in sich empfangen und in sich, nicht wie das durch Fortpflanzung gewordene Kind von und aus sich gebären."

79. Goethe, *Faust: Der Tragödie Zweiter Teil*, 3:251, line 8322.

80. Astrida Orle Tantillo, *The Will to Create: Goethe's Philosophy of Nature* (Pittsburgh: University of Pittsburgh Press, 2002), 10.

81. Schelling, *Erster Entwurf eines Systems der Naturphilosophie*, 42.

82. Schelling, 41.

83. Schelling, 50.

84. Goethe, *Faust*, p. 176.

85. Goethe, *Faust: Der Tragödie Zweiter Teil*, 3:213, lines 6999–7000.

86. Goethe, *Faust: Der Tragödie Zweiter Teil*, 3:209, line 6862.

87. Jocelyn Holland, *German Romanticism and Science: The Procreative Poetics of Goethe, Novalis, and Ritter* (New York: Routledge, 2009), 6.

88. Johann Friedrich Blumenbach, *Über den Bildungstrieb* (Göttingen: Dieterich, 1789), 6, quoted in Holland, 5: "Oder man verwirft alle Zeugung in der Welt."

89. Joseph D. O'Neill, *Figures of Natality: Reading the Political in the Age of Goethe* (New York: Bloomsbury, 2017), 29.

90. Angela C. Borchert, "Goethe and the Grotesque: The 'Classical Walpurgis Night,'" in *Goethe's "Faust": Theatre of Modernity*, ed. Hans Schulte, John Noyes, and Pia Kleber (Cambridge: Cambridge University Press, 2011), 142.

91. Hannah Arendt, *The Human Condition* (Chicago: University of Chicago Press, 1998), 247.

92. Goethe, *Faust: Der Tragödie Zweiter Teil*, 3:244, lines 8096–97: "Gebilde, strebsam, Götter zu erreichen, / Und doch verdammt, sich immer selbst zu gleichen."

93. Goethe, *Faust*, p. 198.

94. Goethe, *Faust: Der Tragödie Zweiter Teil*, 3:213, lines 7005–6.

95. Goethe, *Faust*, p. 193.

96. Goethe, *Faust: Der Tragödie Zweiter Teil*, 3:208, lines 6809–10.

97. Goethe, *Faust: Der Tragödie Zweiter Teil*, 3:249, line 8248.

98. Hartmut Fröschle, *Goethes Verhältnis zur Romantik* (Würzburg: Königshausen and Neumann, 2002), 191.

99. Goethe, *Faust: Der Tragödie Zweiter Teil*, after line 8076var, cited in *Die Enstehung von Goethes Werken in Dokumenten*, ed. Momme Mommsen and Katharina Mommsen (Berlin: De Gruyter, 2017), 5:774.

100. Borchert, "Goethe and the Grotesque," 142.

101. Johann Wolfgang von Goethe, *Versuch, die Metapmorphose der Pflanzen zu erklären* (Gotha: Ettinger, 1790), 4.

102. Goethe, 3: "Gleichsam auf einer geistigen Leiter."

103. Albert Dietrich, *Botanik für Gärtner und Gartenfreunde* (Berlin: Herbig, 1837), 409.

104. Augustin Pyramus Candolle and Kurt Sprengel, *Grundzüge der wissenschaftlichen Pflanzenkunde* (Leipzig: Knobloch, 1820), 362.

105. Goethe, *Goethes Gespräche*, 524.

106. Karl Leberecht Immermann, *Die Epigonen: Familien-Memoiren in Neun Büchern* (Berlin: Ehle, 1854), 273: "Sie duldet kein langsames, unmittelbar zur Frucht führendes Reifen, sondern wilde, unnütze Schößlinge werden anfangs von der Treibhaushitze, welche jetzt herrscht, hervorgedrängt, und diese müssen erst wieder verdorrt sein, um einem zweiten gesünderen Nachwuchse aus Wurzel und Schaft Platz zu machen."

Chapter Four

1. Louise Dittmar, *Das Wesen der Ehe: Nebst einigen Aufsätzen über soziale Reform* (Leipzig: Wigand, 1849), 27: "Die rächende Nemesis folgt dem Verbrecher durch Jahrhunderte, bis sie ihn ereilt; aber sie trifft den Schuldigen nicht immer in der Person, sondern in der Idee. Der schuldlose Ludwig XVI. büßte auf dem Schaffot, was seine Vorgänger auf den Dünger warfen."

2. Georg Wilhelm Friedrich Hegel, *Phenomenology of Spirit*, trans. A. V. Miller (Oxford: Oxford University Press, 1977), 7.

3. Rebecca Comay, *Mourning Sickness* (Stanford, CA: Stanford University Press, 2011), 82.

4. Louise Dittmar, *Skizzen und Briefe aus der Gegenwart* (Darmstadt: Leske, 1845), 53.

5. Holly Case, *The Age of Questions* (Princeton, NJ: Princeton University Press, 2018), 73.

6. August Wilhelm Schlegel, "Wechsel der Dynastie in den Philosophen-Schulen," in *August Wilhelm Schlegel's Sämmtliche Werke*, ed. Eduard Böcking (Leipzig: Weidmann, 1846), 6:231.

7. Schlegel, 6:231.

8. Schlegel, 6:231: "Nachdem es lang von sich gesprochen / Ward ihm zuletzt der Hals gebrochen."

9. Karl Marx, "Theses on Feuerbach," in *Selected Writings*, ed. Lawrence Simon, trans. Loyd D. Easton and Kurt H. Guddat (Indianapolis: Hackett, 1994), 101.

10. Georg Wilhelm Friedrich Hegel, *Elements of the Philosophy of Right*, ed. Allen Wood, trans. H. B. Nisbett (Cambridge: Cambridge University Press, 1991), 219 (§181).

11. Eduard Gans, "Necrolog von G. W. F. Hegel," in *Vermischte Schriften* (Berlin: Duncker, 1836), 2:251: "Kant sah Fichte in seinem Alter, Fichte erlebte die jugendliche Schärfe Schellings, Schelling fand Hegel neben ihm heranwachsen und überlebt ihn jetzt . . . Hegel hinterläßt eine Meinge geistreicher Schüler, aber keinen Nachfolger."

12. Dale E. Snow, *Schelling and the Ends of Idealism* (Albany: SUNY Press, 1996).

13. Walter Jaeschke and Christoph Bauer, "Georg Wilhelm Friedrich Hegel: Das Editionsprojekt der *Gesammelten Werke*," *Deutsche Zeitschrift für Philosophie* 62, no. 1 (2014): 41–63.

14. John Toews, "Transformations of Hegelianism, 1805–1846," in *The Cambridge Companion to Hegel*, ed. Frederick C. Beiser (Cambridge: Cambridge University Press, 1993), 389.

15. Toews, 390.

16. Bettina von Arnim to Heinrich Bernhard Oppenheim, December 28, 1841, in Bettina von Arnim, *Werke und Briefe in Vier Bänden*, ed. Walter Schmitz and Sibylle von Steinsdorff (Frankfurt: Deutscher Klassiker Verlag, 1986), 4:459: "Gesundheit der Hegelschule."

17. Bettina von Arnim to Heinrich Bernhard Oppenheim, December 28, 1841, in von Arnim, 4:458: "Er sei von Hegel abgesprungen während er doch wie Pech an ihm klebt."

18. Bettina von Arnim to Heinrich Bernhard Oppenheim, December 28, 1841, in von Arnim, 4:460: "Nun, da die christliche Religion die Bastille geworden des gesunden Menschenverstandes."

19. Bettina von Arnim to Heinrich Bernhard Oppenheim, December 28, 1841, in von Arnim, 4:460: "Eine wahre Revolution kann nur ie sein wo die Wahrheit gegen die Lüge kämpft."

20. Bettina von Arnim to Heinrich Bernhard Oppenheim, December 28, 1841, in von Arnim, 4:461: "Es ist die konzentrierte Kraft jener Generation, die in ihm zu Fleisch geworden, um die Lüge zu überwinden."

21. Louise Aston, *Meine Emancipation, Ausweisung und Rechtfertigung* (Brüssel: Vogler, 1846), 12: "Ich weiß es, welcher Entwürdigung eine Frau unter dem heiligen Schutze des *Gesetzes und der Sitte ausgesetzt ist*; wie sich diese hülfreichen Penaten des Hauses in nutzlose Vogelscheuchen verwandeln, und das Recht zum Adjudanten brutaler Gewalt wird!"

22. Aston, 50.

23. Aston, 50.

24. Ludwig Feuerbach, *Abälard und Heloise, oder Der Schriftsteller und der Mensch* (Ansbach: Brügel, 1834), 56: "Die, selbst mit Widerwillen, nur in Folge eines physischen, moralischen oder pekuniären Bankerotts geschloßen warden."

25. Feuerbach, 56: "Um dadurch die Zahl unglücksseeliger Körper- und Geisteskrüppel bis ins Unendliche zu vermehren."

26. Feuerbach, 56: "Denn die Kinder der Liebe, seien sie nun außer- oder innereheliche, machen der Welt gar viel zu schaffen, weil ihr Blut nicht in dem lauen Wasser eines bloßen pflicht- und schulgerechten ehelichen Amtseifers überschlagen, sondern aus dem Brunnen der Natur Frisch herausgeschöpft worden ist, weil sie nur selten in ihrem Temperamente und Charakter die Beschaffenheit ihres Vaterlandes, die Glut des südlichen Himmels verleugnen."

27. Shawn Jarvis, "Trivial Pursuit? Women Deconstructing the Grimmian Model in the Kaffeterkreis," in *The Reception of Grimm's Fairy Tales* (Detroit: Wayne State University Press, 1993), 103; see also p. 207 of Jarvis's afterword.

28. See Karl August Varnhagen von Ense, *Tagebücher* (Leipzig: Brockhaus, 1862), 159.

29. Gustav Konrad, ed., *Märchen der Bettine, Armgart und Gisela von Arnim* (Frechen: Bartmann, 1965), 18: "Er hatte nämlich einen Urururgroßvater, der, weil er viermal Ur war, das Uhr- und Maschinenwerk von Grund aus verstand; er wurde wegen einer Maschine, mit welcher er Peter dem Vorersten einen Leibschaden heilte, zum Grafen zu Rattenweg ernannt."

30. Konrad, 20: "So viel Reiser werden doch wohl am hochgräflichen Rutenstammbaum draußen wachsen, um einer kleinen mutlosen Dirne das Blut etwas schneller zum Hasenherzen zu treiben."

31. Konrad, 21: "In meinem und meiner Brüder Namen."

32. Ernst Kantorowicz, *The King's Two Bodies: A Study in Medieval Political Theology* (Princeton, NJ: Princeton University Press, 1997), 296.

33. Jon Cowans, *To Speak for the People* (London: Routledge, 2001), 94.

34. Eric L. Santner, *The Royal Remains: The People's Two Bodies and the Endgames of Sovereignty* (Chicago: University of Chicago Press, 2011), 81.

35. Ludwig Feuerbach, *Kritik des "Anti-Hegel's": Zur Einleitung in das Studium der Philosophie* (Ansbach: Brügel, 1835), 14: "Sollen verkrüppelte Bastarde oder nicht vielmehr die genuinen Erzeugungen die Modelle des Philosophen sein?"

36. Malwida von Meysenbug, *Memoiren einer Idealistin*, vol. 1 (Berlin: DVA, 1927), 185.

37. "Familie der freien Wahl," in Meysenbug, vol. 2 (Berlin: Schuster and Löffler, 1905), 183.

38. Theodor Althaus, *Die Zukunft des Christenthums* (Darmstadt: Leske, 1847), 90: "Wenn die Väter sich einen König gewählt haben zum erblichen Monarchen, so sind sie frei unter dem Herrn ihrer Wahl, die Söhne, über die der geborne Herr herrscht, sind nicht mehr frei."

39. Althaus, 90: "Alles Gesetz ist zuerst freie That, aber alle freie That einer Gemeinschaft wird nothwendig zum Gesetz."

40. Ludwig Feuerbach, *Das Wesen des Christentums* (Leipzig: Wiegand, 1849), 362.

41. Albrecht Koschorke, *The Holy Family and Its Legacy* (New York: Columbia University Press, 2003), 152.

42. Feuerbach, *Das Wesen des Christentums*, 116: "Gott entspringt aus dem Gefühl eines Mangels."

43. Feuerbach, 112: "Daß jener der Erzeuger, dieser der Erzeugte ist."

44. Max Stirner, *Der Einzige und Sein Eigentum* (Leipzig: Reclam, 1845), 60: "Ein Wesen über Mir . . . ein Übermeiniges."

45. Bettina von Arnim and Heinrich Bernhard Oppenheim, *Und mehr als einmal nachts im Thiergarten: Briefe*, ed. Ursula Püschel (Berlin: Bettina von Arnim-Gesellschaft, 1990), 111: "Jeder geschichtlichen Weihe Hohn sprechen."

46. Fanny Lewald, *Erinnerungen aus dem Jahre 1848* (Braunschweig: Vieweg, 1850), 44–45: "Mag man die geistige Berechtigung der Frauen noch so sehr anerkennen, ihr persönliches Auftreten in der Volksmasse liegt außerhalb des deutschen Charakters."

47. Von Arnim and Oppenheim, *Und mehr als einmal nachts im Thiergarten*, 128: "Absolut sei der König, sagten die Minister der damaligen Zeit und *sie* waren es doch, die mit dem Teufel einen Bund machten aus seiner Absolutheit wider ihn."

48. Manuela Köppe, "Die Freiheit des Geistes," in *Vom Salon zur Barrikade: Frauen der Heinezeit*, ed. Irina Hundt (Berlin: Metzler, 2002), 287.

49. Peter C. Caldwell, *Love, Death and Revolution in Central Europe* (London: Palgrave, 2009), 69.

50. Quoted in Manuela Köppe, "Louise Dittmar (1807–1884): 'Die Freiheit des Geistes,'" in *Vom Salon zur Barrikade: Frauen der Heinezeit*, ed. Irina Hundt (Stuttgart: Metzler, 2002), 286.

51. Dittmar, *Das Wesen der Ehe*, 15: "Der Mann ist der Fürst des Weibes, ihr absoluter Monarch."

52. Gordon J. Schochet, *Patriarchalism in Political Thought* (New York: Basic Books, 1975), 194.

53. Stirner, *Der Einzige und Sein Eigentum*, 227: "Denn der Staat ist . . . die erweiterte *Familie* ('Landesvater—Landesmutter—Landeskinder')."

54. Dittmar, *Das Wesen der Ehe*, 15: "Dann ist der Vertreter Vormund und nicht Organ." Subsequent references are given in the text.

55. "In der absoluten Monarchie ist Alles absolut: Der Staat, Recht, Gesetz, Ordnung, der liebe Gott, die Religion, das Christenthum, der Geistliche oder Kirchen- und Religionsmeister, der Schulmonarch, die Eltern, der Ehemann, die Dienerschaft."

56. "Macht jede Verbindung nur von der Freiheit der Neigung abhängig."

57. "Dann wäre der Fürst der sicherste Bürge und Vertreter seines Volkes und diese dürfte sich sorglos und vertrauensvoll in die väterlichen Arme legen."

58. Christine Nagel, *"In der Seele das Ringen nach Freiheit": Louise Dittmar, Emanzipation und Sittlichkeit im Vormärz und in der Revolution 1848/49* (Königsstein im Taunus: Helmer, 2005).

59. Dittmar, "Charlotte Corday," in *Das Wesen der Ehe*, 28–29: "Wie Johanna d'Arc unter'm Zauberbaum den Ruf ihrer Mutter Gottes empfing, so mag auch Charlotte in dieser Einsamkeit manche ermuthigende Aufforderung von ihren himmlischen Vorgängern erhalten haben."

60. Dittmar, 28: "Solche Bilder waren geeignet, ihren Geist zu stählen und jene Seelenruhe in ihr zu begründen, die sie mitten in den Stürmen entfesselter Leidenschaften ihren scharf gezeichneten Weg verfolgen ließ."

61. Dittmar, 31: "Heroismus die Antriebe der Alltäglichkeit unterzubreiten."

62. Dittmar, 31: "Nur durch völlige Verkennung der Person und des Gegenstandes kann ihre That in Verbindung mit diesem Gefühl gebracht warden."

63. Peter Davies, *Myth, Matriarchy and Modernity: Johann Jakob Bachofen in German Culture* (Berlin: De Gruyter, 2010).

64. Lionel Gossman, *Basel in the Age of Burckhardt: A Study in Unseasonable Ideas* (Chicago: University of Chicago Press, 2000), 143.

65. Carl Pletsch, *Young Nietzsche: Becoming a Genius* (London: Free Press, 1991), 113.

66. Hedwig Dohm, *Der Jesuitismus im Hausstande: Ein Beitrag zur Frauenfrage* (Berlin: Wedekind and Schwieger, 1873), 1: "Es gilt einen Kreuzzug gegen den Jesuitismus! (nicht gegen die Jesuiten). Kein heilig Grab ist dabei zu erobern, im Gegentheil die Seele soll von einem Alp, einem Leben heuchelnden Alp befreit werden. An diesem Kampf der Ritter gegen den modernen Lindwurm 'Heuchelei' als einer der bescheidensten Knappen oder Schildträger theilzunehmen, ist all mein Ehrgeiz."

67. Dohm, 2.

68. Cynthia Eller, *Gentlemen and Amazons: The Myth of Matriarchal Prehistory, 1861–1900* (Berkeley: University of California Press, 2011), 122.

69. Henriette Goldschmidt, *Vortrag, gehalten im Frauenbildungs-Verein zu Leipzig am 15. Juli 1868* (Leipzig: Matthes, 1868), 4: "Wenn wir Spätgeborene also noch im Zusammenhang mit jenen Völkern stehen, die nicht nur durch die Jahrtausende, sondern durch eine Menge anderer unnennbarer Unterschiede von uns getrennt sind, umwievielmehr steht jeder Einzelne im Zusammenhang mit dem Volke und der Zeit, zu denen er gehört."

70. Goldschmidt, 4: "In der kühnen Hoffnung, daß das, was als vernünftig erkannt wird, auch wirklich werden müsse, geht sie getrost vorwärts und beachtet die bestehenden Verhältnisse kaum, geschweige, daß sie sie achtet."

71. Hegel, *Elements of the Philosophy of Right*, 218 (§180).

72. Hegel, 219 (§178).

73. Johann Jakob Bachofen, *Das Mutterrecht* (Stuttgart: Krais and Hoffmann, 1861), 1.

74. Friedrich Engels, *Der Ursprung der Familie, des Privateigenthums und des Staats* (Stuttgart: Dietz, 1892), 186: "Als gläubiger Althegelianer, leitet die römischen Rechtsbestimmungen ab, nicht aus den gesellschaftlichen Verhältnissen der Römer, sondern aus dem 'spekulativen Begriff' des Willens."

75. Goldschmidt, *Vortrag, gehalten im Frauenbildungs-Verein zu Leipzig am 15. Juli 1868*, 4.

76. Goldschmidt, 6: "Das Vaterland, in das jeder Mensch hineingeboren wird wie in seine Familie, diese erste Bedingung unsere Seins, die man vorfindet, wie man Vater und Mutter vorfindet, wir Deutsche mußten es erst geistig in uns erzeugen und erschaffen."

77. Else Lüders, ed., *Minna Cauer: Leben und Werk* (Gotha: Klotz, 1925), 160.

Chapter Five

1. Nicholas Vaszonyi, *Richard Wagner: Self-Promotion and the Making of a Brand* (New York: Cambridge University Press, 2010), 172.

2. Theodor W. Adorno, *In Search of Wagner*, trans. Rodney Livingstone, with a foreword by Slavoj Žižek, new ed., Verso Modern Classics (London: Verso, 2005), 7.

3. George Bernard Shaw, *The Perfect Wagnerite* (London: Richards, 1898), 139.

4. Jonathan Carr, *The Wagner Clan: The Saga of Germany's Most Illustrious and Infamous Family* (London: Faber and Faber, 2007), 129.

5. On the evolution and changing structure of the *Ring* cycle, see Adrian Daub and Patrick McCreeless, "The Ring of the Nibelungs," in *The Cambridge Wagner Encyclopedia*, ed. Nicholas Vaszonyi (Cambridge: Cambridge University Press, 2019), 494–95.

6. Carr, *The Wagner Clan*, 129.

7. Nike Wagner, *The Wagners: The Dramas of a Musical Dynasty* (Princeton, NJ: Princeton University Press, 1998).

8. Gottfried Wagner, *Twilight of the Wagners: The Unveiling of a Family's Legacy* (New York: Picador, 1997), 86.

9. G. Wagner, 86.

10. Adrian Daub, *Tristan's Shadow: Sexuality and the Total Work of Art after Wagner* (Chicago: University of Chicago Press, 2014), 154–55.

11. Richard Strauss and Clemens Krauss, *Briefwechsel*, ed. Günther Brosche (Munich: Beck, 1964), 236.

12. Friedlind Wagner, *Heritage of Fire*, trans. Page Cooper (New York: Harper and Brothers, 1945).

13. G. Wagner, *Twilight of the Wagners*, 21.

14. John Deathridge, "Wagner Lives: Issues in Autobiography," in *The Cambridge Companion to Richard Wagner*, ed. Thomas S. Grey (Cambridge: Cambridge University Press, 2008).

15. Richard Wagner, *Das Rheingold*, in *Sämtliche Schriften und Dichtungen* (Leipzig: Breitkopf and Härtel, 1911), 5:267.

16. Adorno, *In Search of Wagner*, 122.

17. Elfriede Jelinek, *Rein GOLD: Ein Bühnenessay* (Reinbek bei Hamburg: Rowohlt, 2013), 7.

18. Richard Wagner, "Das Judentum in der Musik," in *Sämtliche Schriften und Dichtungen* (Leipzig: Breitkopf and Härtel, 1911), 5:85.

19. Brigitte Hamann, *Winifred Wagner: A Life at the Heart of Hitler's Bayreuth* (London: Granta, 2005), 204.

20. See Adrian Daub, "The Politics of Longevity: Hans-Jürgen Syberberg's Essayism and the Art of Outliving Oneself," *New German Critique* 40, no. 3 (2013): 137–70.

21. Slavoj Žižek, "Why Is Wagner Worth Saving?," foreword in Adorno, *In Search of Wagner*, xi.

22. Richard Wagner, *Siegfried*, in *Sämtliche Schriften und Dichtungen* (Leipzig: Breitkopf and Härtel, 1911), 6:159.

23. Max Kalbeck, *Das Bühnenfestspiel zu Bayreuth: Eine Kritische Studie* (Breslau: Schletter, 1877), 36.

24. Thomas Koch, *Recht, Macht und Liebe in Richard Wagners "Der Ring des Nibelungen"* (Baden Baden: Nomos, 1996), 34.

25. On the question of incest and *Blutschande*, see Claudia Jazebowski, *Inzest: Verwandtschaft und Sexualität im 18. Jahrhundert* (Cologne: Böhlau, 2005).

26. Richard Wagner, *Die Walküre*, in *Sämtliche Schriften und Dichtungen* (Leipzig: Breitkopf and Härtel, 1911), 6:15.

27. Richard Wagner, "Metaphysik der Geschlechtsliebe," in *Sämtliche Schriften und Dichtungen* (Leipzig: Breitkopf and Härtel, 1911), 12:289.

28. Wagner, *Die Walküre*, 6:14.

29. Ludwig Feuerbach, *Das Wesen des Christentums* (Leipzig: Wiegand, 1849), 371: "durch sich selbst, durch die Natur der Verbindung, die hier geschlossen wird, heilig."

30. Wagner, *Die Walküre*, 6:26: "Unheilig acht ich den Eid, / Der Unliebende eint."

31. Feuerbach, *Das Wesen des Christentums*, 371.

32. Herfried Münckler, "Hunding und Hagen: Gegenspieler der Wotanshelden," in *"Alles Ist Nach Seiner Art": Figuren in Richard Wagners "Der Ring des Nibelungen,"* ed. Udo Bermbach (Stuttgart: Metzler, 2001), 144.

33. Feuerbach, *Das Wesen des Christenthums*, 371: "Über der Moral schwebt Gott als ein vom Menschen unterschiedenes Wesen."

34. Richard Wagner, *Götterdämmerung*, in *Sämtliche Schriften und Dichtungen* (Leipzig: Breitkopf and Härtel, 1911), 2:194: "Freija, die Holde, heiß ich dich: / Fricka laß uns nun rufen, / Wotans heilige Gattin, / Sie gönne uns gute Ehe!"

35. Max Stirner, *Der Einzige und sein Eigentum* (Leipzig: Reclam, 1845), 89.

36. Richard Klein, *Solidarität mit Metaphysik? Ein Versuch über die musikphilosophische Problematik der Wagner-Kritik Theodor W. Adornos* (Würzburg: Königshausen and Neumann, 1991), 167: "Der freie Willen bleibt von vornherein in den absoluten Willen einbehalten."

37. See also Adrian Daub, "The State as a Family: The Fate of Familial Sovereignty in German Romanticism," *Republics of Letters* 2, no. 2 (2011): 35.

38. David Leopold, *The Young Karl Marx* (Cambridge: Cambridge University Press, 2007).

39. Richard Wagner, *Oper und Drama*, in *Sämtliche Schriften und Dichtungen* (Leipzig: Breitkopf and Härtel, 1911), 4:152.

40. For a more in-depth discussion of this streak in Wagner's thinking, see Daub, *Tristan's Shadow*, 7–10.

41. Barry Millington, *The Sorcerer of Bayreuth: Richard Wagner, His Work and His World* (New York: Oxford University Press, 2012).

42. Richard Wagner, "Metaphysik der Geschlechtsliebe," 11:288. Subsequent references are given in the text.

43. Richard Wagner, *Parsifal*, in *Sämtliche Schriften und Dichtungen* (Leipzig: Breitkopf and Härtel, 1911), 10:335.

44. Wagner, 10:358.

45. Richard Wagner, "Über das Opern-Dichten und Komponiren im Besonderen," in *Sämtliche Schriften und Dichtungen* (Leipzig: Breitkopf and Härtel, 1911), 10:167.

46. Richard Wagner, "Über das Weibliche im Menschlichen," in *Sämtliche Schriften und Dichtungen* (Leipzig: Breitkopf and Härtel, 1911), 12:342.

47. R. Wagner, 12:342.

48. R. Wagner, 12:343.

49. Richard Wagner, *Siegfried*, in *Sämtliche Schriften und Dichtungen* (Leipzig: Breitkopf and Härtel, 1911), 6:156.

50. R. Wagner, 6:156: "Dem herrlichen Walsung weis' ich mein Erbe nun an."

51. See Daub, *Tristan's Shadow*, 37.

52. Houston Stewart Chamberlain, *Richard Wagner* (Munich: Bruckmann, 1907), 1:406.

53. Geoffrey G. Field, *The Evangelist of Race* (New York: Columbia University Press, 1981), 153.

54. Houston Stewart Chamberlain to Wilhelm II, February 4, 1903, in *Briefe, 1882–1924: Und Briefwechsel mit Kaiser Wilhelm II* (Munich: Bruckmann, 1928), 174.

55. Houston Stewart Chamberlain, *Deutsche Weihnacht: Eine Liebesgabe deutscher Hochschüler* (Kassel: Furche, 1914), 33.

56. Houston Stewart Chamberlain, "Gipfel der Menschheit," in *Deutsches Wesen: Ausgewählte Aufsätze* (Munich: Bruckmann, 1916), 181.

57. Chamberlain, 182.

58. Houston Stewart Chamberlain, *Die Grundlagen des Neunzehnten Jahrhunderts* (Munich: Bruckmann, 1907), 16. Subsequent references are given in the text.

59. "Das neunzehnte Jahrhundert ist nämlich nicht das Kind der früheren—denn ein Kind fängt das Leben von Neuem an—vielmehr ist es ihr unmittelbares Erzeugnis: mathematisch betrachtet eine Summe, physiologisch eine Altersstufe. Wir erbten eine Summe von Kenntnissen, Fertigkeiten, Gedanken, usw., wir erbten eine bestimmte Verteilung der wirtschaftlichen Kräfte, wir erbten Irrtümer und Wahrheiten, Vorstellungen, Ideale, Aberglauben: manches . . . in Fleisch und Blut übergegangen."

Chapter Six

1. Edward Edelson, *Gregor Mendel and the Roots of Genetics* (Oxford: Oxford University Press, 1999), 9.

2. Gregor Mendel, "Versuche über Pflanzen-Hybriden," *Verhandlungen des naturforschenden Vereines in Brünn* 4 (1866): 3–47.

3. Mendel, 16.

4. Mendel, 12.

5. Roger J. Wood and Vitezslav Orel, *Genetic Prehistory in Selective Breeding: A Prelude to Mendel* (Oxford: Oxford University Press, 2001), 123.

6. Nicholas Saul, "Darwin in German Literary Culture 1890–1914," in *The Literary and Cultural Reception of Charles Darwin in Europe*, ed. Thomas Flick and Elinor Shaffer (London: Bloomsbury, 2014), 3:63.

7. Mendel, "Versuche über Pflanzen-Hybriden," 16.

8. Peter Bowler, *The Mendelian Revolution* (London: Athlone, 1989), 11.

9. Eric Chafe, *The Tragic and the Ecstatic—the Musical Revolution of Wagner's "Tristan and Isolde"* (Oxford: Oxford University Press, 2005), 241.

10. Mathilde Wesendonck, text to Richard Wagner, "Im Treibhaus," reproduced in Gustav Lange, *Musikgeschichtliches* (Berlin: Gaertner, 1900), 22.

11. Wesendonck, 22.

12. Ernst Stadler, "Im Treibhaus," in *Dichtungen* (Hamburg: Ellermann, 1954), 2:207.

13. Lynn Hunt, *The Family Romance of the French Revolution* (Berkeley: University of California Press 1992), 67.

14. Karl Marx, *The Eighteenth Brumaire of Louis Bonaparte*, trans. Daniel de Leon (Chicago: Kerr, 1913), 9.

15. Jean-Marc Bernardini, *Le darwinisme social en France (1859–1918): Fascination et rejet d'une idéologie* (Paris: Edition CNRS, 1997).

16. Émile Zola, *The Kill*, trans. Brian Nelson (Oxford: Oxford University Press, 2004), 39.

17. Émile Zola, *Germinal*, trans. Peter Collier (Oxford: Oxford University Press, 2008), 46.

18. Zola, 46.

19. Stefani Engelstein, *Sibling Action—the Genealogical Structure of Modernity* (New York: Columbia University Press, 2017), 150.

20. Daniel Pick, *Faces of Degeneration: A European Disorder, 1848–1918* (Cambridge: Cambridge University Press, 1993), 78.

21. Émile Zola, *The Fortune of the Rougons*, trans. Brian Nelson (Oxford: Oxford University Press, 2012), 91.

22. Prosper Lucas, *Traité philosophique et physiologique de l'hérédité naturelle dans les états de santé et de maladie du système nerveux* (Paris: Baillière, 1847), 1:532: "Il est un livre immense, ouvert à tous les yeux, écrit dans toutes les langues, où ces deux tableaux s'exécutent de tout temps, et où l'ésprit peut suivre également, à la trace des généalogies, la trace de qualités, de vices, de passions, et de crimes aussi grands que ceux qui s'expient aux bagnes ou sur les échafauds."

23. Émile Zola, *Les Rougon-Macquart: Histoire naturelle et sociale d'une famille sous le Seconde Empire; "L'argent," "La debacle," "Le Docteur Pascal"* (Paris: Gallimard, 1967), 1568.

24. Zola, *Germinal*, 46.

25. Émile Zola, *Le Docteur Pascal* (Paris: Charpentier, 1902), 75: "Mais ce qui frappait surtout, en ce moment, c'était sa ressemblance avec Tante Dide, cette ressemblance qui avait franchi trois générations, qui sautait de ce visage desséché de centenaire, de ces traits usés, à cette délicate figure d'enfant, comme effacée déjà elle aussi, très vieille et finie par l'usure de la race. En face l'un de l'autre, l'enfant imbécile, d'une beauté de mort, était comme la fin de l'ancêtre, l'oubliée."

26. Laura Otis, *Organic Memory—History and the Body in the Late Nineteenth and the Early Twentieth Century* (Lincoln: University of Nebraska Press, 1994), 74.

27. David Baguley, "Darwin, Zola, and Dr. Prosper Lucas's Treatise on Natural Heredity," in *The Literary and Cultural Reception of Charles Darwin in Europe*, ed. Thomas F. Glick and Elinor Shaffer (London: Bloomsbury, 2014), 428.

28. Émile Zola, "The Experimental Novel," in *The Experimental Novel, and Other Essays*, trans. Belle M. Sherman (New York: Cassell, 1893), 26.

29. Zola, 26.

30. Theodor W. Adorno, "On the Concept of Natural History," *Telos*, no. 60 (1984): 112.

31. Nicholas White, "Zola's Family Planning," in *The Cambridge Companion to Zola*, ed. Brian Nelson (Cambridge: Cambridge University Press, 2007), 22.

32. Gerhart Hauptmann, *Das Friedensfest: Eine Familienkatastrophe* (Berlin: S. Fischer, 1907), 35.

33. Scott Lee, "Balzac's Legacy," in *The Cambridge Companion to Balzac*, ed. Owen Heathcote and Andrew Watts (Cambridge: Cambridge University Press, 2017), 180.

34. "En montrant le jeu de la race modifiée par les milieu": cited in Pierre Martino, *Le naturalisme français (1870–1895)* (Paris: Colin, 1923), 38.

35. See Susan Buck-Morss, *The Dialectics of Seeing: Walter Benjamin and the Arcades Project* (Cambridge: MIT Press, 1991), 159–60.

36. Walter Benjamin, *The Arcades Project*, trans. Howard Eiland and Kevin McLaughlin (Cambridge, MA: Harvard University Press, 1999), 179–80.

37. Zola, *Germinal*, 511.

38. Edward Bulwer Lytton, *The Coming Race* (Leipzig: Tauchnitz, 1873), 296.

39. Zola, *Germinal*, 520.

40. Zola, 520.

41. Georg Lukács, *Writer and Critic, and Other Essays* (London: Merlin, 1970), 131.

42. Zola, *The Kill*, 22.

43. Émile Zola, "Description," in *The Experimental Novel, and Other Essays*, trans. Belle M. Sherman (New York: Cassell, 1893), 233.

44. Zola, *The Kill*, 38.

45. Zola, 38.

46. Lucas, *Traité philosophique et physiologique de l'hérédité naturelle dans les états de santé et de maladie du système nerveux*, 1:532: "il est un livre immense, ouvert à tous les yeux, écrit dans toutes les langues."

47. Marcel Proust, *Sodom and Gomorrah*, trans. Christopher Prendergast (New York: Penguin, 2005), 6.

48. Zola, "The Experimental Novel," 16.

49. Proust, *Sodom and Gomorrah*, 4.

50. Proust, 6.

51. Proust, 7.

52. See also Lisa Guenther, "Other Fecundities: Proust and Irigaray on Sexual Difference," *differences* 21, no. 2 (2010): 28.

53. Simon Porzak, "Inverts and Invertebrates: Darwin, Proust, and Nature's Queer Heterosexuality," *Diacritics* 41, no. 4 (2013): 10.

54. Emily Eells, *Proust's Cup of Tea: Homoeroticism and Victorian Culture* (Aldershot, UK: Ashgate, 2002), 114.

55. Proust, *Sodom and Gomorrah*, 7.

Chapter Seven

1. Sigmund Freud, "A Case of Hysteria," in *The Standard Edition of the Complete Psychological Works of Sigmund Freud*, ed. James Strachey (London: Vintage, 2001), 7:20.

2. Philip Larkin, "This Be the Verse," in *Collected Poems*, ed. Anthony Thwaite (New York: Farrar, Straus and Giroux, 1988), 142.

3. Karin Oberholzer, *The Wolf-Man: Conversations with Freud's Patient Sixty Years Later* (New York: Continuum, 1982).

4. Freud, "A Case of Hysteria," 14.

5. Sander L. Gilman, *Freud, Race and Gender* (Princeton, NJ: Princeton University Press, 1993), 90.

6. Carl E. Schorske, *Fin de siècle Vienna: Politics and Culture* (New York: Vintage, 1981), xxvi.

7. Gilman, *Freud, Race and Gender*, 87.

8. Sigmund Freud, "Infantile Sexuality," from *Three Essays on Sexuality*; in *The Standard Edition of the Complete Psychological Works of Sigmund Freud*, ed. James Strachey (London: Hogarth, 1953–74), 7:173. Translation modified for emphasis and accuracy.

NOTES TO PAGES 158–169   241

9. Andrew Zimmerman, *Anthropology and Antihumanism in Imperial Germany* (Chicago: University of Chicago Press, 2001), 52.

10. See Susan Brownmiller, *Against Our Will: Men, Women, and Rape* (New York: Simon and Schuster, 1975); Florence Rush, *The Best Kept Secret: The Sexual Abuse of Children* (Upper Saddle River, NJ: Prentice Hall, 1980); Jeffrey Moussaieff Masson, *The Assault on Truth* (New York: Farrar, Straus and Giroux, 1984).

11. Sigmund Freud and Carl Gustav Jung, *The Freud-Jung Letters*, ed. William McGuire, trans. Ralph Manheim and R. F. C. Hull (Princeton, NJ: Princeton University Press, 1994), 105.

12. Ronald Hayman, *A Life of Jung* (New York: Norton, 2002), 130.

13. Peter Gay, *Freud: A Life for Our Time* (New York: Norton, 2006), 219–20.

14. Sigmund Freud, *Moses and Monotheism*, in *The Standard Edition of the Complete Psychological Works of Sigmund Freud*, ed. James Strachey (London: Hogarth, 1958), 23:99.

15. Sigmund Freud, *Beyond the Pleasure Principle*, trans. C. J. H. Hubback (London: International Psycho-Analytical Press, 1922), 22.

16. Sigmund Freud, *Totem und Tabu* (Vienna: Internationaler Psychoanalytischer Verlag, 1920), iii.

17. Freud, 151.

18. Freud, 196.

19. Sigmund Freud, "The Dynamics of Transference," in *The Standard Edition of the Complete Psychological Works of Sigmund Freud*, ed. James Strachey (London: Hogarth, 1958), 12:99n.

20. Freud, 12:99n.

21. Carl Gustav Jung, "On the Psychology of the Unconscious," in *The Collected Works of C. G. Jung*, vol. 7, trans. R. F. C. Hull (Princeton, NJ: Princeton University Press, 1953), 64.

22. Carl Gustav Jung, *Über die Psychologie der Dementia Praecox* (Halle: Marhold, 1907), iii.

23. Jung, iv.

24. Jung, iv.

25. Reuben Fine, *A History of Psychoanalysis* (New York: Columbia University Press), 83.

26. Sigmund Freud to Ludwig Binswanger, April 14, 1912; cited in Gay, *Freud*, 229.

27. Cited in Gay, 223.

28. Gay, 235.

29. Carl Gustav Jung, "The Structure of the Unconscious" (1916), in *The Collected Works of C. G. Jung*, vol. 7, trans. R. F. C. Hull (Princeton, NJ: Princeton University Press, 1953), 263–92.

30. Carl Gustav Jung, "The Significance of Constitution and Heredity in Psychology" (1929), in *The Collected Works of C. G. Jung*, vol. 1, trans. Gerhard Adler and R. F. C. Hull (Princeton, NJ: Princeton University Press, 1960), 112. Subsequent references are given in the text.

31. Carrie B. Dohe, *Jung's Wandering Archetype: Race and Religion in Analytical Psychology* (London: Routledge, 2016), 136.

32. Carl Gustav Jung, "Wotan," in *The Collected Works of C. G. Jung*, vol. 10, ed. Sir Herbert Read, trans. R. F. C. Hull (Princeton, NJ: Princeton University Press, 1964), 180. Subsequent references are given in the text.

33. Carl Gustav Jung, *Civilization in Transition* (New York: Bollingen, 1964), 13.

34. Carl Gustav Jung, "Zur gegenwärtigen Lage der Psychotherapie (1934)," in *Zivilisation im Übergang* (Olten: Walter, 1986), 191.

35. Jung, 184.

36. Jung, 191.

37. Barbara Hannah, *C. G. Jung: Sein Leben und Wirken* (Küsnacht, Switzerland: Stiftung für Jung'sche Psychologie, Küsnacht 2006), 273.
38. Robert Ellwood, *The Politics of Myth: A Study of C. G. Jung, Mircea Eliade, and Joseph Campbell* (New York: SUNY Press, 1999), 37.
39. Jung, "On the Psychology of the Unconscious," 7:69.
40. Carl Gustav Jung, "Wotan," in *Gesammelte Werke* (Olten: Walter, 1991), 10:213.
41. Deirdre Bair, *Jung: A Biography* (Boston: Little, Brown, 2003), 510.
42. Cited in Elizabeth Young-Bruehl, *Anna Freud: A Biography* (New York: Summit, 1988), 455.
43. See Chandak Sengoopta, *Otto Weininger: Sex, Science and Self in Imperial Vienna* (Chicago: University of Chicago Press, 2000).
44. Leopold Szondi, "Contributions to Fate Analysis," *Acta Psychologica* 3 (1937): 26.
45. Leopold Szondi, *Moses, Antwort auf Kain* (Bern: Huber, 1973), 105.
46. Leopold Szondi, *Kain, Gestalten des Bösen* (Bern: Huber, 1969), 115.
47. Gilles Deleuze and Felix Guattari, *Anti-Oedipus: Capitalism and Schizophrenia*, trans. Robert Hurley, Mark Seem, and Helen R. Lane (London: Continuum, 2004), 123.
48. Deleuze and Guattari, 319.
49. Jens de Vleminck, "Tragic Choices: Fate, Oedipus, and Beyond," in *The Locus of Tragedy*, ed. Arthur N. Cools and Thomas K. M. Crombez (Boston: Brill, 2008), 198.
50. Leopold Szondi, *Freiheit und Zwang im Schicksal des Einzelnen* (Bern: Huber, 1968), 21.
51. Martin Heidegger, *The Principle of Reason*, trans. Reginald Lilly (Bloomington: Indiana University Press, 1996), 110.

Chapter Eight

1. Harold Bloom, *The Anxiety of Influence* (New York: Oxford University Press, 1993), 11.
2. Bloom, 11.
3. Sigmund Freud, "Family Romances," in *The Freud Reader*, ed. Peter Gay (New York: Norton, 1989), 298.
4. Oscar Wilde, *The Importance of Being Ernest* (London: Broadview, 2009), act 1, p. 79.
5. Eve Kosofsky Sedgwick, "Tales of the Avunculate," in *Tendencies* (Durham, NC: Duke University Press, 1993), 59.
6. Wilde, *The Importance of Being Ernest*, act 1, p. 88n.
7. Wilde, act 1, p. 72.
8. Wilde, act 1, p. 76.
9. Algernon Charles Swinburne, "Eton: An Ode," in *Poems* (London: McKay, 1910), 613.
10. Jennifer Ingleheart, *Masculine Plural: Queer Classics, Sex, and Education* (Oxford: Oxford University Press, 2018), 143.
11. Algernon Charles Swinburne, "Arthur's Flogging," in *Major Poems and Collected Prose*, ed. Jerome McGann and Charles Sligh (New Haven, CT: Yale University Press, 2004), 420.
12. Algernon Charles Swinburne, "The Triumph of Time," in *Poems* (London: McKay, 1910), 22.
13. Thomas Mann, "Beim Propheten," in *Gesammelte Werke*, ed. Hans Mayer (Berlin: Aufbau, 1956), 300.
14. Mann, 299: "Etwa dreißigjährigen jungen Mann mit gewaltig hoher, bleich zurückspringender Stirn und einem bartlosen, knochigen, raubvogelähnlichen Gesicht von konzentrierter Geistigkeit."

15. Thomas Mann, "Die Ehe im Übergang," in *Gesammelte Werke*, ed. Hans Mayer (Frankfurt: S. Fischer, 1960), 10:199: "Unfruchtbarkeit, Aussichtslosigkeit, Konsequenz- und Verantwortungslosigkeit."

16. Mann, 10:199: "Ist nicht gründend, nicht familienbildend, und geschlechterzeugend."

17. Mann, 10:199: "Dauer, Gründung, Fortzeugung, Geschlechterfolge, Verantwortung."

18. Wolfgang Braungart, *Ästhetischer Katholizismus: Stefan Georges Rituale der Literatur* (Tübingen: Niemeyer, 1997).

19. Melissa S. Lane, "The Platonic Politics of the George Circle: A Reconsideration," in *A Poet's Reich: Politics and Culture in the George Circle*, ed. Melissa S. Lane and Martin Ruehl (Rochester, NY: Camden House, 2011), 133–64.

20. Robert E. Norton, *Secret Germany: Stefan George and His Circle* (Ithaca, NY: Cornell University Press, 2002), 338–39.

21. Thomas Karlauf, *Stefan George: Die Entdeckung des Charisma* (Munich: Blessing, 2009), 333.

22. Stefan George, "Resigned I face the riddle that he is," in *The Works of Stefan George*, trans. Olga Marx and Ernst Morwitz (Chapel Hill: University of North Carolina Press, 1974), 318.

23. Stefan George, "Ergeben steh ich vor des rätsels macht," in *Der Stern des Bundes*, vol. 8 of *Gesamtausgabe* (Berlin: Bondi, 1931), 13.

24. Stefan George, "With you I now grow back through generations," in *The Works of Stefan George*, trans. Olga Marx and Ernst Morwitz (Chapel Hill: University of North Carolina Press, 1974), 318.

25. Stefan George, "Nun wachs ich mit dir rückwärts in die jahre," in *Der Stern des Bundes*, vol. 8 of *Gesamtausgabe* (Berlin: Bondi, 1931), 14–15.

26. Herbert Schmalenbach, "Die Soziologische Kategorie des Bundes," *Dioskuren: Jahrbuch für Geisteswissenschaften* (1922): 35–105.

27. Friedrich Gundolf, *George* (Berlin: Bondi, 1921), 72.

28. Stefan George, "On the Terrace," in *The Works of Stefan George*, trans. Olga Marx and Ernst Morwitz (Chapel Hill: University of North Carolina Press, 1974), 19.

29. Stefan George, "Auf der Terrasse," in *Hymnen, Pilgerfahrten, Algabal*, vol. 2 of *Gesamtausgabe* (Berlin: Bondi, 1928), 40.

30. Eve Kosofsky Sedgwick, *Epistemology of the Closet* (Berkeley: University of California Press, 1990), 219.

31. Peter J. Davies, *Myth, Matriarchy and Modernity: Johann Jakob Bachofen in German Culture, 1860–1945* (Berlin: De Gruyter, 2010), 187.

32. Marcel Proust, *Sodom and Gomorrah*, trans. Christopher Prendergast (New York: Penguin, 2002), 4.

33. Stefan George, "Then come to where we work in unison," in *The Works of Stefan George*, trans. Olga Marx and Ernst Morwitz (Chapel Hill: University of North Carolina Press, 1974), 174.

34. Stefan George, "So komm zur Stätte wo wir uns Verbünden," in *Der Teppich des Lebens und die Lieder von Traum und Tod*, vol. 5 of *Gesamtausgabe* (Berlin: Bondi, 1932), 20.

35. Stefan George, "We are the selfsame children who in awe," in *The Works of Stefan George*, trans. Olga Marx and Ernst Morwitz (Chapel Hill: University of North Carolina Press, 1974), 181.

36. Stefan George, "Wir sind dieselben kinder die erstaunt," in *Der Teppich des Lebens und die Lieder von Traum und Tod*, vol. 5 of *Gesamtausgabe* (Berlin: Bondi, 1932), 33–34.

37. George, "We are the selfsame children who in awe," 181.

38. George, "Wir sind dieselben kinder die erstaunt," 33–34.

39. Jan Steinhausen, *"Aristokraten aus Not" und ihre "Philosophie der zu hoch hängenden Trauben"* (Würzburg: Königshausen and Neumann, 2001), 471.

40. Stefan George, "We who as princes choose and cast aside," in *The Works of Stefan George*, trans. Olga Marx and Ernst Morwitz (Chapel Hill: University of North Carolina Press, 1974), 175.

41. Stefan George, "Wir die als Fürsten wählen und Verschmähn," in *Der Teppich des Lebens und die Lieder von Traum und Tod*, vol. 5 of *Gesamtausgabe* (Berlin: Bondi, 1932), 22–23.

42. George, "We who as princes choose and cast aside," 175.

43. George, "Wir die als Fürsten wählen und Verschmähn," 23.

44. George, "We who as princes choose and cast aside," 175.

45. George, "Wir die als Fürsten wählen und Verschmähn," 22.

46. Norton, *Secret Germany*, 235.

47. George, "We who as princes choose and cast aside," 123.

48. George, "Wir die als Fürsten wählen und Verschmähn," 23.

49. Jens Malte Fischer, "Alfred Schuler—Antike als Kostümfest," in *"Mehr Dionysos als Apoll": Antiklassizistische Antike-Rezeption um 1900*, ed. Achim Aurnhammer and Thomas Pittroff (Frankfurt: Klostermann, 2002), 428.

50. Stefan George, "Porta Nigra," in *The Works of Stefan George*, trans. Olga Marx and Ernst Morwitz (Chapel Hill: University of North Carolina Press, 1974), 161.

51. Stefan George, "Porta Nigra," in *Der siebente Ring*, vol. 6 of *Gesamtausgabe* (Berlin: Bondi, 1931), 15–17.

52. George, "Porta Nigra," in *The Works of Stefan George*, 161.

53. George, "Porta Nigra," in *Der siebente Ring*, 15–17.

54. Raymond Furness, *Zarathustra's Children: A Study of a Lost Generation of German Writers* (Rochester, NY: Camden House, 2000), 87.

55. Horst Rüdiger, "Stefan Georges 'Porta Nigra,'" in *Wissen aus Erfahrungen: Werkbegriff und Interpretation heute*, ed. Alexander von Bormann and Anthonius H. Touber (Tübingen: Niemeyer, 1976), 592–606.

56. Georg Dörr, *Muttermythos und Herrschaftsmythos: Zur Dialektik der Aufklärung um die Jahrhundertwende bei den Kosmikern, Stefan George und in der Frankfurter Schule* (Würzburg: Königshausen and Neumann, 2007), 79.

57. Eckhard Heftrich, Paul Gerhard Klussmann, and Hans Joachim Schrimpf, eds., *Stefan George Kolloquium* (Köln: Wienand, 1971), 19.

58. Dio Cassius, *Roman History*, trans. Earnest Crary (Cambridge, MA: Harvard University Press, 2000), 463.

59. Stefan George, "Vorrede zu Maximin," in *Tage und Taten: Aufzeichnungen und Skizzen*, vol. 17 of *Gesamtausgabe* (Berlin: Bondi, 1933), 74.

60. George, "Porta Nigra," in *The Works of Stefan George*, 221.

61. George, "Porta Nigra," 221.

62. See Ulrich Raulff, *Kreis ohne Meister: Stefan Georges Nachleben* (Munich: Beck, 2010).

63. Stefan George, "The Poet in Times of Confusion," in *The Works of Stefan George*, trans. Olga Marx and Ernst Morwitz (Chapel Hill: University of North Carolina Press, 1974), 365.

64. Stefan George, "Der Dichter in Zeiten der Wirren," in *Das Neue Reich*, vol. 9 of *Gesamtausgabe* (Berlin: Bondi, 1928), 38.

65. George, "The Poet in Times of Confusion," 365.

66. George, "Der Dichter in Zeiten der Wirren," 9:41.

67. Michael Petrow, *Der Dichter als Führer? Zur Wirkung Stefan Georges im "Dritten Reich"* (Marburg: Tectum, 1995), 49–58.

68. Ernst Bertram, "Deutscher Aufbruch: Eine Rede vor studentischer Jugend," *Deutsche Zeitschrift* 10 (1932/33): 609–19.

69. Ernst Bertram, "Möglichkeiten Deutscher Klassik: Rede zu Georges Letztem Geburtstag," in *Deutsche Gestalten: Fest und Gedenkreden* (Leipzig: Insel, 1934), 291–324; quotation is from p. 291.

70. Eckart Grünewald, "'Übt an uns mord und reicher blüht was blüht'—Ernst Kantorowicz spricht am 14. November 1933 über das 'Geheime Deutschland,'" in *Ernst Kantorowicz*, ed. Robert L. Benson and Johannes Fried (Stuttgart: Steiner, 1997), 60.

71. Ernst Kantorowicz, "Das Geheime Deutschland," in Benson and Fried, *Ernst Kantorowicz*, 77.

72. Kantorowicz, 80: "Gegen alles Gewaffen sind die Herrscher des 'geheimen Deutschland' gefeit, und man wird ihrer nicht habhaft, indem man ihr Bild auf die Strasse zerrt, sie dem Markt anähnelt und dann als eigen Fleisch und Blut feiert."

73. On Kantorowicz's reading of George's aestheticist (and "symbolist") politics, see Kantorowicz's *Briefwechsel* with Maurice Bowra: Robert E. Lerner, "Letters by Ernst Kantorowicz concerning Woldemar Uxkull and Stefan George," *George Jahrbuch* 8 (2010): 170.

74. Kantorowicz, "Das Geheime Deutschland," 79. Subsequent references are given in the text.

75. Grünewald, "'Übt an uns mord und reicher blüht was blüht,'" 73.

76. Thomas Karlauf, "Stauffenberg: The Search for a Motive," in *A Poet's Reich: Politics and Culture in the George Circle*, ed. Melissa S. Lane and Martin Ruehl (Rochester, NY: Camden House, 2011), 327.

77. Friedrich Nietzsche, *Werke in Drei Bänden*, ed. Karl Schlechta (Munich: Hanser, 1954), 1:229.

Epilogue

1. Heinrich Böll, "Die Schwarzen Schafe," in *Werke (Kölner Ausgabe)*, ed. Bernd Balzer (Cologne: Kiepenheuer and Witsch, 2004), 5:160.

2. Ralf Schnell, *Heinrich Böll und die Deutschen* (Cologne: Kiepenheuer und Witsch, 2017).

3. Böll, "Die Schwarzen Schafe," 5:161: "Die Phrase 'Übrigens, kannst du mir . . .' wurde zu einem Schreckenswort in unserer Familie, es gab Frauen, Tanten, Großtanten, Nichten sogar, die bei dem Wort 'kurzfristig' einer Ohnmacht nahe waren." Subsequent references are given in the text.

4. "Ärgerte ich mich, daß wieder ein Tag meines Lebens vergangen war, der mir nur Müdigkeit eintrug, Wut und ebensoviel Geld, wie nötig war, um weiterarbeiten zu können."

5. "Hauptsache, daß er ihnen nichts schuldig bleibt."

6. "Wer mir folgen wird in dieser Generation, die dort heranwächst; wer von diesen blühenden, spielenden, hübschen Kindern, die meine Brüder und Schwestern in die Welt gesetzt haben, wird das schwarze Schaf der nächsten Generation sein?"

7. Wolfgang Borchert, *Draußen vor der Tür, und ausgewählte Erzählungen* (Reinbek: Rowohlt, 1986), 48.

8. Borchert, 162.

9. Eve Kosofsky Sedgwick, "Tales of the Avunculate," in *Tendencies* (Durham, NC: Duke University Press, 1993), 60.

10. Sedgwick, 60.

11. Elizabeth D. Heineman, *What Difference Does a Husband Make? Women and Marital Status in Nazi and Postwar Germany* (Berkeley: University of California Press, 1993), 108.

12. Jack Halberstam, *The Queer Art of Failure* (Durham, NC: Duke University Press, 2010), 71.

13. Böll, "Die Schwarzen Schafe," 5:167.

14. Harald Welzer, Sabine Moller, and Karoline Tschuggnall, *"Opa war kein Nazi": Nationalsozialismus und Holocaust im Familiengedächtnis* (Frankfurt: Fischer, 2002).

15. Winfried Speitkamp, *Jugend in der Neuzeit: Deutschland vom 16. bis zum 20. Jahrhundert* (Göttingen: Vandenhoek and Ruprecht, 1998).

16. Cornelia Schmitz-Berning, *Das Vokabular des Nationalsozialismus* (Berlin: De Gruyter, 2007), 195.

17. Cited in Barbara Zehnpfennig, *Adolf Hitler: "Mein Kampf"—Weltanschauung und Programm* (Munich: Fink, 2018), 195.

18. Eric Ehrenreich, *The Nazi Ancestral Proof: Genealogy, Race Science and the Final Solution* (Bloomington: Indiana University Press, 2007), 18.

19. Ekkehart Kaufmann, "Sippe," in *Handwörterbuch der deutschen Rechtsgeschichte*, ed. Adalbert Erler and Ekkhart Kaufmann (Berlin: Schmidt, 1990), 4:1668–72.

20. Robert Loeffel, *Family Punishment in Nazi Germany: Sippenhaft, Terror and Myth* (London: Palgrave Macmillan, 2012), 32.

21. Ilse Aichinger, "Aufruf zum Mißtrauen," *Plan* 1, no. 7 (1946): 588: "Und man bot tausend Sicherungen auf, um sich gegen die Schmutzigen, Zerrissenen und Verhungerten zu schützen. Aber keiner sicherte sich gegen sich selbst. So wuchs die Bestie unbewacht und unbeobachtet durch die Generationen. Wir haben sie erfahren! Wir haben sie erlitten."

22. Carl Zuckmayer, *Des Teufels General: Drama in Drei Akten* (Frankfurt: Bermann-Fischer, 1946), 70.

23. Zuckmayer, 70.

24. Robert G. Moeller, *Protecting Motherhood: Women and the Family in the Politics of Postwar West Germany* (Berkeley: University of California Press, 1993), 33.

25. See Jutta Limbach and Siegfried Willutzki, "Die Entwicklung des Familienrechts seit 1949," in *Kontinuität und Wandel der Familie in Deutschland*, ed. Rosemarie Nave-Herz (Oldenburg: Lucius and Lucius, 2002), 8.

26. Alexander Mitscherlich and Margarete Mitscherlich, *Die Unfähigkeit zu Trauern* (Munich: Piper, 1967), 49.

27. Erich Kahler, *Verantwortung des Geistes: Gesammelte Aufsätze* (Frankfurt am Main: Fischer, 1952), 95, quoted in Mitscherlich and Mitscherlich, 13.

28. Sigmund Freud, "Three Essays on Sexuality," in *The Standard Edition of the Complete Psychological Works of Sigmund Freud*, ed. James Strachey and Anna Freud (London: Vintage, 2001), 7:173 [translation modified for emphasis and accuracy].

29. Alexander Mitscherlich, *Auf dem Weg zur Vaterlosen Gesellschaft* (Berlin: Beltz, 2003), 145.

30. Johann Wolfgang von Goethe, *Faust*, ed. Cyrus Hamlin, trans. Walter Arndt, Norton Critical Edition (New York: Norton, 1976), p. 20, line 684.

31. Johann Wolfgang von Goethe, *Faust: Der Tragödie Zweiter Teil*, in *Goethes Werke*, critically reviewed and annotated by Erich Trunz, Hamburg ed. (Hamburg: Christian Wegner, 1948), 3:28, line 684.

32. Hanna Schissler, ed., *The Miracle Years: A Cultural History of West Germany, 1949-1968* (Princeton, NJ: Princeton University Press, 2001), 123.

33. Quoted in Ulrike Meinhof, "Hitler within You," in *Everybody Talks about the Weather... We Don't: The Writings of Ulrike Meinhof*, ed. Karin Bauer (New York: Seven Stories Press, 2011), 138–43; quotation is from p. 140.

34. Meinhof, 138.

35. Wolfgang Kraushaar, "Symbolzertrümmerung: Der Angriff der Studentenbewegung auf die Insignien universitärer Macht," in *Akademische Rituale*, ed. Falk Bretschneider and Peer Pasternack (Leipzig: Arbeitskreis Hochschulpolitische Öffentlichkeit, 1999), 47–57.

36. Eric Rentschler, ed., *West German Filmmakers on Film: Visions and Voices* (New York: Holmes and Meier, 1988).

Index

Adelung, Johann Christoph, 3–4
Adler, Alfred, 159
Adorno, Theodor, 114, 117–18, 145, 195
affection, familial, 47–48, 50–52. *See also* love
aging, 66–67, 72–73, 75, 78–80
Aichinger, Ilse, 212
Althaus, Theodor, 102
America, psychology in, 170
ancestors, inhumanity of, 11
androgyny, 84–85
antihumanism, 111
antimodernism in Germany, 48
anti-Semitism, 118, 132–33, 167, 169; in mental health, 158
architecture, 37. *See also* castles; galleries, family portrait
Arendt, Hannah, 86
aristocracy, 4–5, 8, 13–14, 17, 24–25, 29, 35–41, 43–44, 54–55, 61, 99–101, 140, 192, 204. *See also* castles; galleries, family portrait
Aristophanes, 171
Aristotle, 12–13, 144
Arnim, Bettina (Brentano) von, 18, 96, 103–4
art, 62
Aston, Louise, 18, 97–98, 107
Augspurg, Anita, 108
August, Clemens, 45
authority, familial, decline of, 47
avunculate, 177, 209

Baader, Franz von, 17, 47, 57–58, 84
Bachmann, Carl Friedrich, 101
Bachofen, Johann Jakob, 19, 107–9, 111, 196
Balzac, Honoré de, 146
Bataille, Georges, 101
Bauer, Bruno, 96–97, 104

Bayreuth, 20, 114–16, 118, 131
Bebel, August, 108
Benjamin, Walter, 146–47, 200
Bertram, Ernst, 202, 204–5
Bielenstein, Dieter, 214
Binswanger, Ludwig, 159, 165
Bloch, Ernst, 109, 117
Blumenbach, Johann Friedrich, 86
Böhme, Jakob, 84
Böhmer-Schlegel-Schelling, Caroline, 68–69
Böll, Heinrich, 207–10
Bonald, Louis de, 46, 51–57
bourgeoisie, 14, 17, 37, 41, 61, 157
bourgeoisification, 35
bourgeois respectability, 179
Boy-Ed, Ida, 41
Breuer, Josef, 157–58
Bulwer-Lytton, Edward, 148
Burke, Edmund, 29, 72–73, 77, 137, 145
Byron, Lord George Gordon, 66, 74–75

capitalism, 124–25, 138, 148
Carlsbad Decrees, 9
Case, Holly, 93
caste, 14
castles, 24, 28, 32, 36–38, 42–43, 99–10, 117
Catholicism, 125. *See also* religion
Cauer, Minna, 108, 113
Chamberlain, Eva (Wagner), 131
Chamberlain, Houston Stewart, 116, 118, 131–33
Charcot, Jean-Martin, 157–58
children, 183, 213, 215. *See also* generations; transmission, alternative
citizenship, 4
collectivity, 166
communities, private, 189–92, 194–95

Comte, Auguste, 6
constitution, 51
Conversations of German Refugees (Goethe), 29
Corday, Charlotte, 106
Cosmic Circle, 182, 195, 199
Cousin, Victor, 79
creativity, 40, 43

Darwin, Charles, 14, 41, 109, 111, 135, 138, 140, 148, 161
Darwinian imagination, 15
death, 17–18, 33, 44, 50, 66, 68–76, 80, 148
decline, 145–46, 153–54. *See also* dynasty: end of
de Gobineau, Arthur, 119–20, 123, 129, 131
Deleuze, Gilles, 173
democratization, 35
Descartes, René, 86, 146
description, 149–51
de Staël, Germaine, 47
Diderot, Denis, 12, 46, 86
disease, 30, 74–75
Dittmar, Louise, 18, 91–92, 103–5, 107–8
divine right of kings, 5
Dohm, Hedwig, 108–10
Dora (Freud patient), 155–56, 164
Droste-Hülshoff, Annette von, 32–34, 36, 40, 43–45
Durkheim, Émile, 162
dynasty, 2–3; alternative, 21; biological, 14; chosen, 180; distinct from family, 5, 26; end of, 26–29, 31, 33–40, 91, 99–100, 144–46, 176; fantastic, 42; as fantasy of perpetuity, 6, 8; freedom from, 107, 110–11; in Germany, 7; intellectual, 93–98, 199–206; invented, 40–41; legitimation of, 92–93; monstrous, 76; obligations of, 5; of oppression, 106; origins of, 27–29, 100, 180, 207–9; political, 8–9, 11–13, 16, 25, 40, 91–92; as refuge from emotionalism, 12; as relic, 7, 12–13, 15; religious, 32; self-creating, 183–87, 192–93, 195–201, 204–6; as source of epistemic order, 10–11; as source of trauma, 160–61; spiritual, 67–68, 70–72; as state of dependence, 56–57; succession of, 94–95, 98, 140; suspension of, 121; unwanted, 6

Edelman, Lee, 15–16
egalitarianism, 54
1848 revolutions, 92–93, 102–7
emotion, 12; royal, 49
Engels, Friedrich, 19, 27, 82, 107–8, 112
Engelstein, Stefani, 5, 140
Enlightenment, 13–14, 16–17, 46, 53–56, 56
Epimenides' Awakening (Goethe), 7, 9–10
equality, 58
eroticism, 84, 187, 189
Eton, 178
evolution, 14

fairy tales, 99, 104
family, 2–3; decline of, 54–55, 61, 64; dissolution of, 94, 104–6; distinct from dynasty, 4–5; extended, 58–64; freedom from, 121; ideal and actual, 101–3; at intersection of politics and religion, 97; and love, 98; as model for community, 185; as model for politics, 16; as model for state, 46–48, 50–57, 102–6, 107–11, 132–33; nuclear, 8–10, 58–59, 76–77, 110–13, 119, 122–23, 157, 210–14; as site of oppression, 102–3; as site of politics and culture, 9; as transmitter of ideology, 210–11
family resemblance, 12, 28, 117, 143
family trees, 32–34, 211. *See also* galleries, family portrait
fate, 170–75. *See also* Szondi, Léopold (Lipot)
feminism, 18, 92, 103–4, 107–8; and criticism of Freud, 159
Feuerbach, Ludwig Andreas von, 81, 94, 96–98, 101–4, 119, 123–27
Fichte, Johann Gottlieb, 30, 65, 67–68, 81, 83, 92, 95, 127, 137
Filmer, Sir Robert, 46, 51, 53, 105, 144
Fliess, Wilhelm, 118–19, 165
Fontane, Theodor, 35, 37–39
Forster, Georg, 68
Forster, Therese, 68
Foucault, Michel, 13–14
Fourier, Charles, 119
Frazer, James, 162
Frederick the Great, 12, 49
freedom, 111
French Revolution, 7–8, 14, 16–17, 20, 24–25, 29, 54–55, 57, 65, 75, 91, 98, 101, 104–6, 134, 136–37, 140, 145; critiques of, 46
Freud, Sigmund, 21–22, 43, 170, 177, 214; and dynasty, 160–63, 170; as founder of dynasty, 159–62, 164–66; humanism of, 158, 173; ideas of family of, 155–59, 164, 169–70; scientific approach of, 171
Freundesverein, 95, 97
Freytag, Gustav, 43
Friederike, Princess of Prussia, 49
Friedrich Wilhelm I (the Great Elector), 49
Friedrich Wilhelm III, 47–52, 96
Friedrich Wilhelm IV, 96, 99, 104
future, 59

Gage, Matilda Joslyn, 19, 108–9
galleries, family portrait, 24–25, 32, 39, 42; bourgeois, 40; bourgeois views of, 37; grotesque, 43; legitimation function of, 24; of living people, 40; as site of connection with the dead, 70; spiritualism of, 38
Galton, Francis, 138
Gamble, Eliza Burt, 108
Gans, Eduard, 95, 98–99, 107

gender, 33–34, 53–55, 209
genealogy, 211–12
generations, 78–80, 88–90, 142; biological, 13–15, 20
Gentz, Friedrich von, 8–9, 47–48
George, Stefan, 21–23, 108, 168, 179–83, 185–92, 194–207
Germany, 7; distinctiveness of, 11; nationalism in, 8–9; Secret, 202–6. *See also* identity, German
German Youth Movement, 168
ghosts, 39
Gilman, Charlotte Perkins, 108–9
Glasenapp, Carl Friedrich, 116
God, 53, 56–57. *See also* religion
Goethe, August von, 80
Goethe, Johann Wolfgang von, 1, 7, 9–11, 18, 26, 29–31, 67, 77–79, 81, 84–90
Goethe, Johann Wolfgang von, works of: *Faust*, 30–31, 67, 214; *Faust II*, 67, 77–83, 85–86, 88; "Lullaby for a Young Mineralogist," 31; *Wilhelm Meister's Apprenticeship*, 31, 65, 89–90; *Wilhelm Meister's Journeyman Years*, 78
Goethe, Walther Wolfgang, 31
Goldschmidt, Henriette, 110, 112–13
Greece, ancient, 7, 12–13, 132, 195
grief, 50
Grillparzer, Franz, 26–29
Grün, Karl Theodor, 81
Gundolf, Friedrich, 187, 200
Gutzkow, Karl, 82

Haeckel, Ernst, 41
Haller, Karl Ludwig von, 7–9, 17, 20, 47, 55–57
Hardy, Thomas, 11–12
Hauptmann, Gerhart, 145
Hegel, Georg Wilhelm Friedrich, 11, 18, 44, 63, 73, 81–82, 92, 95–96, 102, 107, 110–11, 124, 146, 203, 210; concept of the family, 101–3
Hegelianism, 20, 82, 90, 93–94; Young, 97–98, 102–3, 119–21, 123, 126–27
Heidegger, Martin, 174, 194
Heine, Heinrich, 30
heredity, 15, 41; of hysteria, 156–57, 160. *See also* inheritance; Mendel, Gregor
hetaerism, 107
heterosexuality, 177, 179. *See also* sexuality
hierarchy, 54; naturalness of, 56–57
hiking, 35–37. *See also* tourism
historical change, 86
history, 1–2; philosophy of, 131–33, 137–38, 140
Hitler, Adolf, 118, 131, 169, 201, 210. *See also* Nazis
Hofmannsthal, Hugo von 189
Holten, Kasper Bech, 118
Holy Family, 102–3
homoeroticism, 22, 180, 190, 192, 197; institutionalized, 182

homosexuality, 21. *See also* sexuality
hope, 148
hothouse, 135–38, 150–52
Hunt, Lynn, 20, 25, 137

Idealism, 18, 77–82, 87, 93, 97
identity, German, 58, 169–70, 174, 202–6, 213–15
identity, Jewish, 4, 163, 169, 174–75
Immermann, Karl Leberecht, 90
inequality, 6, 58
inheritance: of behavior, 139–43, 145–46, 148; cultural, 132–34; of ideas, 134; law of, 10, 44–45, 99, 107, 111–12; of social position, 139–43. *See also* heredity
insanity, 42
Iphigenia in Tauris (Euripides), 26

Jelinek, Elfriede, 118
Jens de Vleminck, 173
Jesus, as figure in Wagner, 126–27. *See also* religion
Judaism. *See* anti-Semitism; identity, Jewish; Moses; religion
Jung, Carl Gustav, 22, 159, 161–62, 164–70, 174, 214

Kahler, Erich, 213–14
Kant, Immanuel, 68, 74, 95, 146
Kantorowicz, Ernst, 200, 203–5
Kautsky, Karl, 108
Keller, Gottfried, 37, 40, 207
Kierkegaard, Søren, 81–82
Klages, Ludwig, 108, 168
Kleist, Heinrich von, 50
Kommerell, Max, 200
Kotzebue, August von, 9
Kronberger, Maximilian. *See* Maximin

Lafargue, Paul, 108
land, 57
Larkin, Philip, 155
Lassalle, Ferdinand, 112
law, 44–45, 107; natural, 55. *See also under* inheritance
legitimacy, 6, 8–9, 101; intellectual, 93–95, 98, 103–4; political, 105–6; of women, 103–4
Lenin, Vladimir, 108
Lewald, Fanny, 103–4
LGBT rights, 189
Louis (brother of Friedrich Wilhelm III), 49
love, 12, 84, 98, 101, 119, 122, 126–28, 180; as will of the species, 123, 129. *See also* affection, familial
Lucas, Prosper, 14–15, 20, 135, 140–42, 153
Luise, Crown Princess of Prussia, 49–50, 52
Lukács, Georg, 149

Maistre, Joseph de, 20, 29, 46–47, 51–58, 137
Mann, Thomas, 41, 117, 124, 176, 179–80, 192, 207

marriage, 11. *See also* family: nuclear
Marx, Karl, 11, 81, 94, 97, 107, 113, 137
matriarchy, 107–12
Maximin, 22, 182, 184, 195, 198–99
Meinhof, Ulrike, 215
Mendel, Gregor, 20, 134–35, 137, 140, 142, 172
Mendelssohn, Felix, 119
Meysenbug, Malwida von, 102–3
Mime and Alberich, 19
Mitscherlich, Alexander, 213–14
Mitscherlich, Margarete, 213–14
modernity, 2, 6–7, 15–17, 31, 49–50, 60–61, 146, 198
modernization, 35
Mommsen, Katharina, 87
monarchy, 16. *See also* dynasty: political
money, 208
morality, 125–26
Morwitz, Ernst, 183
Moses, 172
mothers, 33. *See also* family
Müller, Adam Heinrich, 9, 47–48, 50–51

names, 61, 63–64
narrator, as literary figure 35, 37–39
nationalism, 112–13, 131–33. *See also* identity, German; Germany
Naturalism, 136
nature, 54–56
Nazis, 118, 168–69, 174, 201–4, 206, 210–12, 214
Nietzsche, Friedrich, 1–2, 6, 41, 82, 107–8, 132, 168, 196
nobility of birth, 41. *See also* aristocracy
Novalis, 47–48, 51–52, 57, 90
novelty, 137, 147
nuclear family, 33; as source of affective legitimacy, 45. *See also* dynasty: biological; Freud, Sigmund; Hegel, Georg Wilhelm Friedrich: concept of the family

Oppenheim, Heinrich Bernhard, 96, 103
organicism, 74
original sin, 5

pain, 178
Pankejeff, Sergei, 155–56
past, 59; rejection of, 215
patriarchy, 92
physiological traits, 41
Plato, 84, 127
poetry, as oratory, 180–81, 184–85, 191, 194–97, 205
politics, 8–9
posterity, 43
procreation, 81–82, 98; of plants, 137–38, 152–53; sexual, 83–89, 101
progress, 138, 149, 152
property, 126–27. *See also* inheritance; land

Protestantism, 125. *See also* religion
Proudhon, Pierre-Joseph, 126
Proust, 21, 152–53, 177–78, 189
psychoanalysis, 21–22
purity, 135, 137

queerness, 15–16, 176–80, 186–90
queer theory, 15

race, 4, 76, certification of, 211
racism, 15, 118–19, 132–33
Realism, 143
Reinhold, Carl Leonhard, 79
religion, 96–98, 102–3, 109, 124, 126, 161–63, 166; invented, 183–85
repetition, 137, 147, 160–61
repression, 172
resemblance, 32, 42; family, 167; psychological, 167. *See also* inheritance, of behavior
revenge, 91, 106
revolution, 28. *See also* French Revolution; 1848 revolutions
Riehl, Heinrich, 46–47, 58, 60–61, 63
Rilke, Rainer Maria, 195
Ring cycle (Wagner), as critique of family, 124; as family portrait, 120–23; inheritance in, 130–33; morality in, 125, 128; as portrait of bourgeois family, 117–18
risk, 19–20
Robespierre, Maximilien, 145
Romantic, 48
Romanticism, 12, 16–18, 47, 52, 65–67, 78–82, 88–89, 92, 110, 119, 126–27, 134, 143, 156
Rosenkranz, Karl, 82
Rousseau, Jean-Jacques, 13, 46, 51, 53–56, 134

Sabean, David Warren, 5
Sartorius, Georg, 31, 79
Savigny, Friedrich Carl von, 45
Schadow, Johann Gottfried, 49
Schelling, Friedrich Wilhelm Joseph, 18, 31–32, 48, 57, 66–73, 81, 84–85, 88, 95
Schiller, Friedrich von, 67, 89–90
Schlegel, August Wilhelm, 47, 52, 65–68, 70, 72, 87, 93–94
Schlegel, Friedrich 47–48, 90, 195
Schmalenbach, Herman, 185–86, 191
Schopenhauer, Arthur, 11–12, 111, 119–20, 123, 126, 129, 132, 146, 158, 167, 170–71, 173
Schuler, Alfred, 168, 189, 195–97
sculpture, 49
Second Empire, 137–38, 140–44, 150
seduction hypothesis, 159
Sedgwick, Eve Kosofsky, 21, 177, 188, 209
self-making, 37
sex, 14

sexuality, 84–85
Shaw, George Bernard, 115
Shelley, Mary, 18, 66, 72–76, 78, 88
Shelley, Percy Bysshe, 18, 66, 75
Sloterdijk, Peter, 30, 43
social Darwinism, 14, 138
sovereignty, 54
species, as dynasty, 123
Spencer, Herbert, 138
Spengler, Oswald, 2, 6, 31
spiritualism, 71–72; bourgeois views of, 39
Stadler, Ernst, 136
Stanton, Elizabeth Cady, 108
Starck, Johann August Freiherr von, 47–48, 54–55, 57
Stauffenberg, Claus Graf Schenk von, 205–6, 212
Stifter, Adalbert, 17, 35–36, 42–43, 57–64, 207
Stirner, Max, 103–5, 119, 124–25
Storm, Theodor, 37
Strauss, Richard, 116
surprise, 43
Swinburne, Algernon, 178
symbolism, 150–54
Szondi, Léopold (Lipot), 22, 170–74

temporality, 187–90, 193–95, 200
Tieck, Wilhelm, 195
Tönnies, Ferdinand, 185–86
tourism, 35–39, 116. *See also* aristocracy
tradition, 50
traits, 12
transference, 164
transmission, alternative, 21; of cruelty, 178; homoerotic, 198–201; of ideas, 163, 181–83; of misfortune, 208–10; of neuroses, 171–74; outside dynastic framework, 101; of unconscious content, 166–67. *See also* inheritance

Uhland, Ludwig, 25–26, 35
unconscious, 21–22, 166–67; familial, 170. *See also* Freud, Sigmund; Jung, Carl Gustav
universalism, in psychoanalysis, 169

Utopian Socialists, 119
Üxküll-Gyllenband, Woldemar von, 202–3, 205

Verwey, Albert, 195
Voltaire, 55
von Arnim, Bettina, 97, 99, 106–7

Wagner, Cosima, 115–16, 118, 131
Wagner, Friedelind, 118
Wagner, Gottfried, 116
Wagner, Isolde, 115
Wagner, Richard, 19–21, 168; anti-Semitism of, 118–19, 133; as Aryan ideal, 132; as founder of family business, 114–16; humanism of, 120, 127–28; ideas of love, 126, 129–31; interplay of art and family, 115–17; racism of, 119, 129–31; reinterpretation of, 115; romanticism of, 123. *See also Ring* cycle (Wagner); Wotan (character)
Wagner, Siegfried, 20, 115–16, 118
Wagner, Winifred, 116, 118
Wagner, Wieland, 115, 117
Wagner, Wolfgang, 115, 117
Weber, Max, 44
Weininger, Otto, 108, 171
Wesendonck, Mathilde, 136
Westermarck, Edvard Alexander, 162
Wieland, Christoph Martin, 90
Wilde, Oscar, 21, 154, 177
Wilhelm Heinrich Riehl, 17, 46, 57
Wilhelm II, 131
Wolf Man (Freud patient), 155–56
Wotan (character), 19, 115, 117–18, 120–26, 130–31
"Wotan" (Jung essay), 168–70, 174, 214
Wundt, Wilhelm, 162

youth, 88. *See also* children, generations

Zetkin, Clara, 108
Žižek, Slavoj, 119
Zola, Émile, 15, 20, 137–50, 153, 158, 172
Zuckmayer, Carl, 212

www.ingramcontent.com/pod-product-compliance
Lightning Source LLC
Chambersburg PA
CBHW051354290426
44108CB00015B/2003